D0463724

A Changing Wind

A Changing Wind

—

Commerce and Conflict in Civil War Atlanta

Wendy Hamand Venet

Yale

UNIVERSITY PRESS

NEW HAVEN AND LONDON

Map of central Atlanta, 1864, on pages xii–xiii is courtesy of the Geospatial Laboratories, Georgia State University.

Copyright © 2014 by Wendy Hamand Venet.
All rights reserved.
This book may not be reproduced, in whole or in part, including illustrations, in any form (beyond that copying permitted by Sections 107 and 108 of the U.S. Copyright Law and except by reviewers for the public press), without written permission from the publishers.

Yale University Press books may be purchased in quantity for educational, business, or promotional use. For information, please e-mail sales.press@yale.edu (U.S. office) or sales@yaleup.co.uk (U.K. office).

Set in Fournier type by IDS Infotech Ltd., Chandigarh, India.
Printed in the United States of America.

Library of Congress Cataloging-in-Publication Data

Venet, Wendy Hamand.
A changing wind : commerce and conflict in Civil War Atlanta / Wendy Hamand Venet.
    pages   cm
Includes bibliographical references and index.
ISBN 978-0-300-19216-2 (hardback)
1. Atlanta (Ga.)—History, Military—19th century. 2. Civilians in war—Georgia—Atlanta—History—19th century. 3. Atlanta (Ga.)—Social conditions—19th century. 4. Atlanta (Ga.)—Race relations—History—19th century. 5. Social change—Georgia—Atlanta—History—19th century. 6. Atlanta (Ga.)—Commerce—History—19th century. 7. Georgia—History—Civil War, 1861–1865—Social aspects. 8. United States—History—Civil War, 1861–1865—Social aspects. 9. Reconstruction (U.S. history, 1865–1877)—Georgia—Atlanta. 10. United States—History—Civil War, 1861–1865—Influence. I. Title.
F294.A857V46 2014
975.8'03—dc23
2013041255

A catalogue record for this book is available from the British Library.

This paper meets the requirements of ANSI/NISO Z39.48-1992 (Permanence of Paper).

10 9 8 7 6 5 4 3 2 1

For Allen

Contents

Acknowledgments

As a faculty member at Georgia State University, I revisit Civil War Atlanta every day of my working life, for our campus lies squarely in the middle of what was once the Civil War city. My office on Peachtree Street is half a block from the site of Atlanta's Confederate Arsenal storehouse, half a block in another direction from the city's principal theater, and a short distance farther from its major hotel. Over time, I have led hundreds of students in my Civil War classes on tours of central Atlanta, pointing out the location of important buildings and describing significant events that occurred in the city during a pivotal time in its history. The idea for this book came from those tours.

My list of individuals to thank must begin with the archivists and librarians of the Atlanta History Center, which houses the largest and best manuscript collections pertaining to the Civil War in the city. Sue VerHoef has assisted me on literally dozens of occasions. Her knowledge of the collections and her understanding of Atlanta history helped me immeasurably. Helen Matthews and Paul Crater have also lent their expertise and help, and Paige Adair assisted with photographs. Although librarians and archivists at many repositories helped me, I owe special thanks to Matthew Turi at the Southern Historical Collection of the University of North Carolina's Wilson Library, Chuck Barber at the Hargrett Rare Book and Manuscript Library of the University of Georgia Libraries, and Bruce Kirby at the Library of Congress. I also want to extend my thanks to the librarians and staff of

Georgia State University Library, including those in the Circulation, Reference, and Interlibrary Loan Departments; history librarian Jill Anderson helped me in particular.

I am grateful to Dean William Long and Associate Dean William Downs of Georgia State University's College of Arts and Sciences, and History Department Chair Michelle Brattain, for a reprieve from teaching in the fall semester of 2012 that allowed me to finish writing the book. Jack Reed from Georgia State's Geospatial Laboratories demonstrated both skill and patience in creating the map of central Atlanta in 1864.

Colleagues and friends have offered advice and read and commented on parts of the manuscript. I am indebted to the late Thomas Dyer, whose scholarship about wartime Atlanta has been especially helpful, and Anne Boylan, with whom I share an interest in women's history. David Moore and Larry Upthegrove shared their expertise about Oakland Cemetery. Tim Crimmins read sections of the manuscript and offered helpful comments. Stephen Davis, Ken Denney, Glenn Eskew, Kent Hackmann, Brian Ingrassia, Cliff Kuhn, Cynthia Schwenk, David Sehat, and Diane Willen also offered valuable advice. My sister Carol Stephens read and commented on sections of the manuscript at an early stage, and my work benefited from her keen editorial sensibility. Bill Link read the manuscript and offered many helpful comments as part of the review process for Yale University Press.

My agent Lisa Adams has been a supporter of the project from the beginning. Her efforts strengthened my proposal and also my resolve to finish the book.

At Yale University Press, I would like to thank my editor, Chris Rogers, for commissioning the work and navigating it through the review and production process, and assistant editor Christina Tucker, who faithfully answered every email query. My special thanks go to senior manuscript editor Dan Heaton for his skillful editing and for the reassuring manner and sense of humor he displayed in all of his interactions with me.

Finally, I thank my family, including sons Jason and Andrew, and my husband, Allen, who through twenty-five years of marriage never tires of hearing stories of my latest archival "find" and never objects to conversations around the dinner table about my latest effort to make sense of events that occurred 150 years ago. I dedicate this book to him.

A Changing Wind

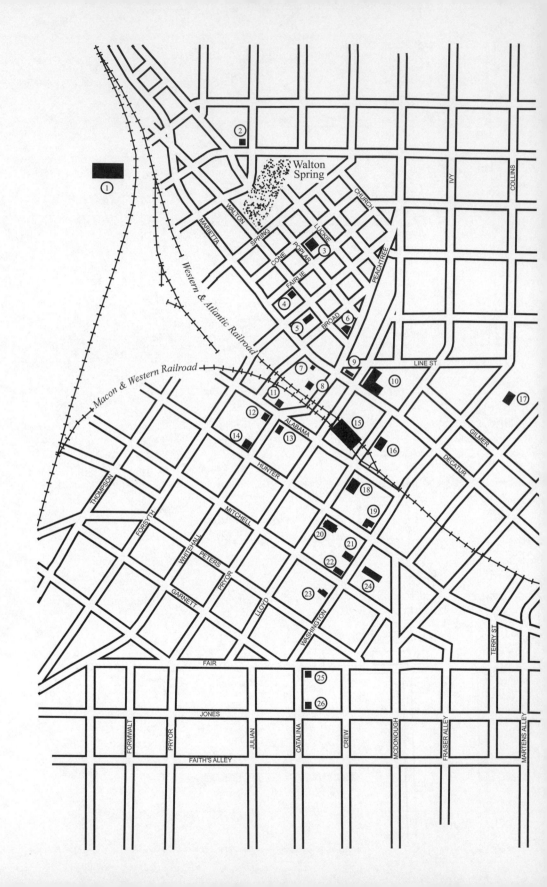

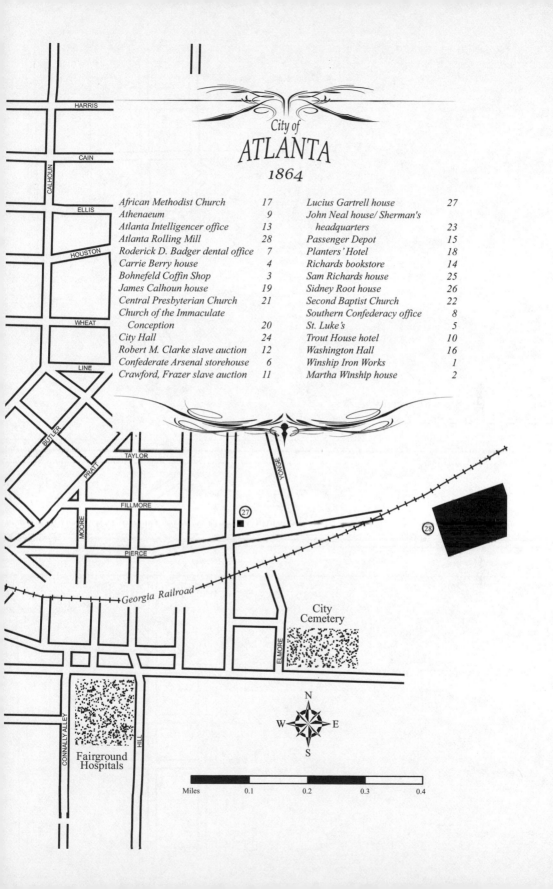

City of

ATLANTA

1864

African Methodist Church	17	Lucius Gartrell house	27
Athenaeum	9	John Neal house/ Sherman's	
Atlanta Intelligencer office	13	headquarters	23
Atlanta Rolling Mill	28	Passenger Depot	15
Roderick D. Badger dental office	7	Planters' Hotel	18
Carrie Berry house	4	Richards bookstore	14
Bohnefeld Coffin Shop	3	Sam Richards house	25
James Calhoun house	19	Sidney Root house	26
Central Presbyterian Church	21	Second Baptist Church	22
Church of the Immaculate		Southern Confederacy office	8
Conception	20	St. Luke's	5
City Hall	24	Trout House hotel	10
Robert M. Clarke slave auction	12	Washington Hall	16
Confederate Arsenal storehouse	6	Winship Iron Works	1
Crawford, Frazer slave auction	11	Martha Winship house	2

HARRIS

CAIN

CALHOUN

ELLIS

HOUSTON

WHEAT

LINE

BUTLER

PRATT

TAYLOR

YONGE

MOORE

FILLMORE

27

28

PIERCE

Georgia Railroad

City
Cemetery

ELMORE

N
W E
S

CONNALLY ALLEY

HILL

Fairground
Hospitals

Miles   0.1   0.2   0.3   0.4

Prologue: City of the Dead

Oakland Cemetery is the resting place for sixty-nine hundred Confederate soldiers, thousands of Atlanta's nineteenth-century citizens, and *Gone with the Wind* author Margaret Mitchell, whose novel has dominated our historical memory of Civil War Atlanta. Nineteenth-century Americans often used the term "cities of the dead" to describe cemeteries, and Oakland Cemetery is Atlanta's city of the dead. Founded in 1850 and originally called City Cemetery, Oakland is located a short distance east of downtown. Today, mounds of pink and red azaleas add splashes of color under a canopy of oaks and magnolias. The cemetery's gardens, together with tombstones, mausoleums, and monuments, create a space of beauty, sadness, and reflection.[1]

Historians estimate that 40 percent of Atlanta burned in the Civil War, with most of the rest of its mid-nineteenth-century buildings destroyed in the next hundred years, razed or paved over to build newer structures in the name of "progress."[2] Today, other than formal historical markers erected long after the events themselves, there are few physical reminders of the Civil War in the area that once encompassed the city's central district. But reminders of the Civil War are everywhere at Oakland, and the tombstones of Oakland provide our first glimpse of the stories of Atlanta's Civil War civilians.

Congressman Lucius Gartrell is buried here, between the graves of his first and second wives, with only his name and his birth and death dates engraved on his stone. Gartrell's grave presents the image of a dedicated husband equally devoted to both of his wives. A marker put up sometime later references his brief role as brigade commander in the final months of the war.[3] The cemetery provides no clues, but newspaper accounts and published speeches uncover a different side of Gartrell, the story of a militant secessionist who played a leading role in Atlanta's support for disunion.

Sam Richards is buried next to his wife of fifty-two years, with several of their children and grandchildren nearby. A prewar Unionist who moved to Atlanta to run a bookstore, Richards became an enthusiastic Confederate who benefited from an expanding wartime economy and earned profits he would have found unimaginable before the war. Richards then watched it all start to unravel. He kept a diary that uncovers Atlanta's story of economic gain and decline, of citizens' anger toward an increasingly intrusive wartime government, of family joys and family sorrows.[4]

Amanda Lin, a widow struggling to support four children, survived the war but died just two years later at age fifty-four. She is buried next to her three daughters, none of whom married. It was not easy for young women of the wartime generation to find husbands, since so many young men died in the war. Lin and her daughters left a small collection of letters that tell of their struggles to survive in times of scarcity, inflation, and disease, and chronicle one family's determination to keep its only son from being conscripted.[5]

A slave named Bill is also buried at Oakland, but no one knows exactly where. Cemetery records tell us that he was owned by S. S. Thrasher, that he died the age of forty-one on June 19, 1864, and that he was buried the same day at Slave Square. After the war, by order of the Atlanta City Council, Bill's bones and those of hundreds of other African Americans were dug up and moved to a new area designated "colored pauper grounds" so that the old Slave Square could be replotted for white burials. Bill lived and died in bondage, his bones moved for the convenience of white people, a forgotten figure in an unmarked grave. Bill's legacy carries with it one memorable coda: his is the last recorded slave burial at City Cemetery. A few weeks after his death, federal soldiers of General William T. Sherman entered Atlanta, and hundreds, perhaps thousands, of slaves who had not already liberated themselves took the opportunity to do so.[6]

Margaret Mitchell's grave is located in the western part of the cemetery, just south of Lucius Gartrell's and a few plots away from Sam Richards's. A surprisingly modest family tombstone marks her grave and that of her husband and parents, surrounded by bushes of pink roses that Mitchell loved during her life. In some ways, Mitchell and her legacy cast a symbolic shadow over the cemetery and the nation's memory of the Civil War. Since the publication of *Gone with the Wind* in 1936 and the release of the film version in 1939, its story of love and loss, victory and defeat have dominated the landscape of Civil War memory and especially the memory of Atlanta. The book sold one million copies in its first six months and has never gone out of print.[7] A compelling narrative and a vivid love story, *Gone with the Wind* taps into something essential about Atlanta during and after the war: the desire of its people to move forward, to compete, to endure, and to rebuild. Margaret Mitchell called it "gumption." Others have called it the "Atlanta spirit." The fictional character of Scarlett O'Hara had it, and so did the real figures of Lucius Gartrell, Sam Richards, and many others. It was and is a real phenomenon in the city.

As an interpreter of the Civil War, Mitchell was ahead of her time in several ways. Though a writer of fiction, she researched the historical background, reading manuscripts and newspapers in addition to relying on her family's history in Atlanta and rural Jonesboro south of the city. At a time when many writers extolled the Confederacy's virtues uncritically, Mitchell wrote a story about protagonists who question the idea of a Confederate war for independence. Scarlett complains loudly and often about being asked to make personal sacrifices for the war effort. Before the war even starts, Rhett suggests that the South cannot win.[8]

If Mitchell's fictional world captures the energy and drama of wartime Atlanta, it misses other elements. In Mitchell's fictional city, there are no Unionists, no slaves who run away from bondage, no destitute women who cannot support their children on government wages, and no children who work in factories to keep their families afloat. Historical Atlanta included all of these citizens. In Mitchell's story of Reconstruction, Republicans are ostentatious and vulgar, while Democrats are virtuous and righteous. African Americans are duped by Carpetbaggers and Scalawags who do not have their best interests at heart. In historical Atlanta, the story of Reconstruction is much more complex and multifaceted, a place where some African Americans struggled and succeeded financially, while many others struggled and did not, a place where prewar politicians and businessmen representing both parties emerged after the war to launch the city's economic revival.

In *A Changing Wind* I seek to find the stories behind the graves of Oakland Cemetery and the reality behind the fictional story told by Margaret

Mitchell. One central theme I consider is the evolution of the wartime city. Already a rising transportation hub in the 1850s, Atlanta grew in importance as the Confederacy's Second City during the war, a center for railroads, supply, industry, commerce, hospitals, and news gathering. With the exception of Richmond, no other southern city faced the same level of wartime change and wartime trauma. Bombarded for five weeks in 1864, the city suffered extensive artillery damage and further damage by the firing and destruction ordered by General William T. Sherman. But Atlanta's wartime importance brought national attention that helped Atlanta to become a New South city after the war.

Atlanta's businessmen were the city's economic, social, and political leaders, and many of them opposed or resisted secession before 1860. Although loyalty remained a contested issue during the war, most of Atlanta's men of commerce eventually cast their lot with the Confederacy, and their gamble paid off in profits during the first two years of the war. After the war, they gambled on Atlanta's economic recovery and helped the city both to prosper and to gain recognition as the state capital and as an economic center in the Southeast.

Over the course of the war, as an increasing number of men served in the military, Atlanta became a city of women. The war forced Atlanta's white women into independent roles. Some women supported the Confederacy as benevolent volunteers; others questioned the war and challenged authority in ways that undermined civic unity in the city. The war did not lead to dramatic changes for white women in the postwar period. Middle- and upper-class women had limited life choices, while impoverished white women and their children struggled.

Atlanta's African Americans took advantage of the war to stretch the boundaries of slavery both economically and personally. Some slaves ran away, while others attempted to improve their circumstances in a variety of ways. Sherman's army emancipated slaves from bondage, but the postwar period offered only limited economic and political opportunity.

The Civil War led to extraordinary challenges, great upheaval, and both triumph and tragedy for the people of Atlanta. It brought a "changing wind" to the city.

1. Gate City to the South

Nothing in Atlanta's early history suggested that it would amount to much. Founded in the late 1830s as the terminus for the Western and Atlantic Railroad, Atlanta showed so little promise as an urban center that one railroad engineer predicted that it would make "a good location for one tavern, a blacksmith-shop, a grocery-store, and nothing else." During its early years, this prediction appeared prophetic. In 1845, Atlanta contained only twelve to fourteen families and three general stores. However, the town grew in fits and starts during the late 1840s as the Georgia Railroad and the Macon and Western added connecting lines. The Atlanta and West Point added a fourth railroad to Atlanta the following decade. By the time the Civil War began in 1861, Atlanta had begun to call itself Gate City to the South, and its rail lines connected Atlanta eastward to Augusta, southward to Savannah and the coast, westward to Montgomery, Alabama, and northward to Chattanooga, Tennessee.¹ Railroads put Atlanta on the map and railroads kept it there.

Economic growth spurred by the railroads led to commercial growth. In 1846, two hotels opened near the railroad tracks: Washington Hall and the Atlanta Hotel. The latter, constructed and owned by the Georgia Railroad, was two stories tall and the city's first brick structure. Atlanta's first bank was opened in 1847 by an agent of the Georgia Railroad, and a second was opened the following year by financiers based in Macon, Georgia. A newspaper editor named Cornelius Hanleiter moved his *Southern Miscellany* from Madison, Georgia, to Atlanta in 1847. Billing itself as a "weekly family newspaper," the *Miscellany* supported the Whig political party in national affairs, endorsing its leader, Henry Clay, and the party's platform of business development. The *Miscellany* carried advertisements for retail establishments including a dry goods store, a butcher, and a bookseller. In 1849, the Macon and Western Branch Telegraph Company offered Atlantans telegraphic connection to other cities, and Hanleiter was the city's first telegraph operator. By the end of the decade, Atlanta had a population of just over two thousand people.[2]

During the 1850s, Atlanta's population grew dramatically, and so did the number of area businesses, most of them located on Alabama and Decatur Streets, which ran parallel to the tracks of the Macon and Western Railroad, or on Whitehall Street, which bisected the tracks to the southwest, while the more residential Peachtree Street ran to the north. A newspaper called the *Weekly Intelligencer* acted as a booster for local development. Growing ad revenue and circulation rewarded its efforts. By 1860, the *Intelligencer* issued daily as well as weekly editions and its circulation expanded from seven hundred to three thousand. Religious, cultural, and educational institutions also flourished during this decade. Starting in the late 1840s, the Episcopal, Baptist, Methodist, Presbyterian, and Catholic denominations constructed houses of worship, usually frame buildings of modest size that satisfied the immediate needs of their small congregations but would quickly prove inadequate to the population of the growing city. A variety of private schools catered to the interests of Atlanta's more affluent residents, although efforts to reach a wider audience through proposals for tax-supported "free schools" stalled.[3]

Railroads, industry, and commerce drove Atlanta's economy in the 1850s. The four railroads were major employers, and Atlanta's industrialists profited from contracts with them. Some railroads ran their own machine shops, but privately run foundries also employed a significant number of men. The Atlanta Rolling Mill of William Markham and Lewis Scofield employed 150 men and made eighteen thousand tons of iron rails annually. Next to Richmond's Tredegar Iron Works, the factory of Markham and Scofield had the largest capacity of any iron-producing factory in the South. Joseph and Isaac Winship opened the Winship Iron Works in Atlanta and the Bartow Iron Works in Cartersville. Initially they built railroad cars, but later they began manufacturing boilers, engines, and iron railings. Atlanta's manufacturing interests also included the Peters Flour Mill owned by Richard Peters and a variety of small manufacturing operations that produced buggies and wagons, harnesses, tinware, furniture, candy, copper stills, hats, barrels, cotton gins, cigars, brooms, whiskey, and beer.[4]

By the 1850s, more than one in five Atlantans held commercial jobs, and seventy-seven stores in Atlanta sold dry goods, clothing, shoes and boots, and furniture, with most of the products imported from manufacturing establishments in the North. The firm of Bartley M. Smith and William E. Ezzard ran advertisements in the newspapers claiming it could sell consumers anything from "window-glass to dental and surgical instruments." Some of the merchants who made money from commercial ventures began to build warehouses along Whitehall and Alabama Streets, with rental space in these structures adding to their profit margins. Because most Atlanta merchants sold goods on a "cash only" basis, avoiding credit-based sales, the city's businessmen avoided bankruptcy during the national depression of 1857.[5]

The wagon trade also powered Atlanta's economy. Twice every week, wagons pulled by mules or oxen filled the city streets carrying wheat, fruits and vegetables, meat, and eggs for sale at Atlanta's public market. Farmers also sold modest amounts of cotton, though the fluffy fiber was not a major crop in the piedmont surrounding Atlanta. Open from before sunrise to 7:00 P.M., the market was an economic and social gathering place. The city charged a tax on farmers who sold their goods there, a major source of revenue for the city. Lucy Hull Baldwin grew up in Atlanta in a house on Peachtree Street, and many years later she recalled seeing the biweekly procession of wagons pass her home headed for the market. Lucy and other children stood near their gates to watch their mothers purchase meat and produce from women in shabby calico dresses and sunbonnets.[6]

By the mid-1850s, Atlanta's population was 80 percent white and 20 percent enslaved African American, a relatively low percentage of African Americans when compared with other Georgia cities. Savannah's prewar population of twenty-two thousand was 36 percent black. Of Augusta's twelve thousand citizens, 33 percent were African Americans. Columbus's population was slightly higher than Atlanta's at ninety-six hundred but was 37 percent black. These Georgia cities had a large interest in plantation agriculture and a correspondingly higher stake in slavery. Atlanta's smaller dependence on slavery can be attributed to its business-based economy and a population that included entrepreneurs, mechanics, and merchants. In 1850, Atlanta had 139 slaveholders, most of them owning small numbers of slaves.

Only two Atlantans owned twenty or more slaves, the number that federal census enumerators used to define a "planter." In this case, both men owned hotels, not farms. Ten years later, Atlanta's slaveowning residents had grown to 373, with 44 of these men owning twenty or more slaves. Atlanta bondspeople worked for railroads, hotels, factories, and private homes.[7]

Like other urban slaves, Atlanta's African Americans had many opportunities to elude their masters' direct supervision. They attended church, ran errands, visited friends. Typically, cities subjected urban slaves to a curfew of 9:00 P.M., and Atlanta was no exception. The ringing of bells signified the nightly curfew, but enterprising slaves sometimes found opportunities to dodge this restriction. Patrick Calhoun, son of Atlanta's future mayor and a boy during the 1850s, recalled many years later that he forged his father's name on passes for "lovesick negroes" so they could visit their girlfriends and evade the city's curfew. Occasionally he wrote love letters on their behalf.[8]

In some extraordinary cases, Atlanta slaves lived in quasi-freedom. The slaves of Ephraim and Ellen Ponder provide the notable example. A wealthy investor and slave trader, Ephraim retired to Atlanta in the 1850s, bringing with him his wife, Ellen, and sixty-five bondspeople. He owned twenty-five acres on Marietta Road, on which he built a fine mansion and gardens, along with outbuildings used as housing and working places for the slaves, many of whom were mechanics.[9]

With the exception of members of their immediate household staff, the rest of the Ponder bondspeople "were permitted to hire their own time," according to Henry Flipper, a child owned by the Ponders who would later achieve renown as the first black graduate of West Point. Hiring out was a common practice in the South, for even though it was unlawful, it was socially tolerated. Evidently the Ponder slaves kept at least some of the money they made, with permission, for Flipper wrote that these bondspeople were "virtually free" and "acquired and accumulated wealth." However, self-hired slaves were still slaves, whose lives depended on the circumstances of their owners, as the Ponder slaves soon learned. In 1861, Ephraim Ponder filed for divorce, citing his wife's infidelities dating back to 1854. He moved to Thomasville, while Ellen remained in their Atlanta home on Marietta Road, engaging in what Henry Flipper called "illegitimate pleasures." With a legal guardian now in charge of the slaves, they continued to work outside the Ponder home, although Ellen evidently collected their wages.[10]

Most Atlanta slaves did not enjoy privileges given to the Ponder bonds-people. Instead, like the vast majority of slaves in the antebellum South, legally they were chattel and treated as such. The 1859 city directory lists three slave dealers: William K. Bagby, Henry C. Holcomb, and the firm of William W. Watkins and Z. A. Rice. Many consignment merchants also sold slaves, along with other products. S. J. Shackleford opened an office contig-uous to the railroad tracks, advertising frequently in the *Daily Intelligencer* that "he is prepared to receive Consignments of all kinds of MERCHANDISE and PRODUCE. . . . He will also give strict attention to the sale of NEGROES, REAL ESTATE, HORSES &c." by auction or on commission.[11]

The city of Atlanta placed restrictions on what slaves could do and when they could do it, and slaveowners were expected to control their bonds-people. The City Council fined owners who allowed their slaves to live outside of their households. Moreover, slaves found with alcohol or caught swearing or being "impudent" to white people faced arrest, jail, and whip-ping of up to thirty-nine lashes, their court expenses charged to their owners. Fear of slave uprising led whites to suspect the intentions of every action slaves took. In September 1854, two slaves identified only as Ned and Nathan applied to the Atlanta City Council for permission to "form themselves into a moral society" along with other bondspeople. After deliberating the matter, the Council granted their request with the understanding that a city marshal must attend every meeting. In making this ruling, the Council illustrated white people's fear that any gathering of slaves could be a front for incen-diary activities.[12]

Slaves who tried to test the limits of servitude often encountered resist-ance even if their owners were sympathetic. Roderick D. Badger practiced dentistry with the permission of his father, a white man named Joshua Badger, who was also his owner. Joshua Badger, a farmer and also a dentist in rural DeKalb County, taught dentistry skills to Roderick, then allowed him to establish his own practice in Atlanta. Badger's skills and success angered white dentists, who protested to the City Council in 1859. The Council chose to ignore the protests, and Badger is listed as a dentist in Atlanta's first city directory, which was published that year.[13]

Atlanta's free black community officially consisted of only seven people in the mid-1850s (though others may not have been counted), and white people viewed them with suspicion. A city ordinance required each to have a white sponsor. Another ordinance passed in 1859 required each free African

American to pay $1,000 for the privilege of living in the city, though it is unclear whether the city made efforts to enforce this ordinance. Free blacks had to request permission even to entertain visitors. On September 1, 1854, a free woman named Laura Kelly applied for permission to allow her mother and niece to travel from Augusta and to remain with her for five to six weeks. Evidently, the Council found Kelly's story acceptable, for it deliberated and approved her request at its next meeting. However, in 1856, the City Council sent a petition from an African American seeking to "vend ice cream" on to the ordinance committee, where no further action appears to have been taken.[14]

In spite of its economic dynamism, 1850s Atlanta was still rough around the edges, especially when compared with the older, more established southern cities. Atlanta lacked a riverfront since the Chattahoochee was six miles to the north. Because it began as a railroad terminus instead of a planned community, Atlanta lacked a coherent set of streets, and the hilly landscape further complicated matters. Sarah Massey moved to Atlanta as a young matron in the 1850s and lived in a house on Washington Street. Many years later she recalled the lack of paved and graded streets in the Gate City: "We had to walk up hill and down hill and through the mud or stay at home." In wintertime, Atlanta's unpaved streets were so muddy that they remained impassable to carriages for weeks at a time. In addition to its issues with streets, the city did not address problems involving sanitation, including garbage dumped everywhere, stray hogs on the loose, and a water supply that was inadequate to Atlanta's needs.[15]

The city also had troubles with poverty and crime. Many of Atlanta's poorest citizens lived in a shantytown at Decatur and Pratt Streets called Slabtown because the flimsy houses were constructed of the excess wood donated by a local citizen who owned a sawmill. Lawlessness characterized sections of the city, including the area known as Murrel's Row, a stretch of Decatur Street bordered by Pryor and Peachtree Streets. Blood sports, especially cockfighting, drew large crowds, and drunken melees were common. Prostitution also flourished. Another area, even more notorious, was Snake Nation, located south of the city center.[16]

Fed up with disorder, businessmen began to exercise increasing control over social, economic, and political matters in their city. In 1851, a group of entrepreneurs, embarrassed by the town's rougher element and the eyesore that was Decatur Street, raided Snake Nation and dispersed the gamblers and lawbreakers. They tore down the shanties and warned rowdies not to return. These measures did not end lawlessness altogether. Groups of young boys continued to wander on city streets since there were no public schools to keep them occupied. In taverns, including the famous Alhambra drinking saloon on Whitehall Street, workingmen imbibed, sometimes to excess. But progress was being made. In 1854, the City Council passed measures to improve governance by dividing the city into wards. The following year, gas lighting came to Atlanta when the city constructed a gas plant at a cost of $50,000 and ordered fifty streetlamps to illuminate the town. The city contracted to have Whitehall Street paved from Marietta Street to Mitchell.[17]

By the mid-1850s, businessmen in Atlanta established a pattern of taking turns running for and being elected to the City Council and mayoralty. They were willing to share responsibility for governance because they held a common vision for economic development, one that emphasized business growth, infrastructure improvements, control of lawlessness, and increasing Atlanta's visibility within the state of Georgia. One important step called for Atlanta to separate from DeKalb County and make itself the centerpiece of an entirely new county. Atlanta's men of commerce now regarded the county seat of Decatur, an older and more settled community to the east of Atlanta, as a competitor. In keeping with its status as a growing and affluent metropolis, Atlanta became the capital for a new county, Fulton, which split off from DeKalb County in December 1853. The City Council appropriated money in 1854, eventually totaling $30,000, for the construction of a new building to house both City Hall and the Fulton County Court House. The handsome two-story structure was located on Washington Street and surrounded by fine homes and churches, including Central Presbyterian Church and Second Baptist Church, constructed the same year after Baptists concluded that they needed a second church to accommodate growing numbers. Methodists ran out of space at Wesley Chapel and built a second church, Trinity Methodist, on a nearby lot, dedicated with great fanfare in September by Bishop James O. Andrew. A growing number of Atlantans began to talk about mounting a campaign to move the state capital from Milledgeville to Atlanta.[18]

With railroads as its principal economic engine, Atlanta needed a new depot to replace the existing wooden structure that locals called the "car shed." In 1852 work began on a new passenger depot, completed and opened in 1854. Described by William Wadley of the Western and Atlantic Railroad as a "commodious Passenger Depot," it was a fine modern brick building, one hundred by three hundred feet, with ticket offices, baggage rooms, separate "saloons" for men and women, and a "Refreshment Saloon." The *Daily Intelligencer* described this station as "one of the most admirable structures in the United States used as a depot for the reception of passengers arriving by our several trains." Atlanta proudly began to call itself the Gate City to the South.[19]

To further showcase Atlanta, the local business elite competed with Macon, Savannah, and Athens to host the Southern Central Agricultural Society's annual fair. The Society's purpose was to provide a vehicle through which to demonstrate the state's economic potential beyond the cotton belt. After the Atlanta City Council appropriated a modest sum for a building to feature exhibits, Atlanta held its first fair on a ten-acre tract of land donated by railroad construction engineer and real estate investor Lemuel P. Grant. The event attracted more than ten thousand people. Atlanta became the fair's permanent home in 1857.[20]

Lemuel Grant's civic-mindedness was matched by that of other Atlantans, especially those who could turn a profit at the same time. James E. Williams constructed a building on land that once was part of the notorious Murrel's Row. On the first floor he sold bacon, lard, corn, and oats as a commission merchant. On the second he opened an eight hundred–seat theater that quickly eclipsed the existing smaller entertainment venues. During the first week of December 1854, the Athenaeum presented J. B. Roberts as Richard III, and the *Daily Intelligencer*'s review called the tragedian "an actor of the very highest order," on par with the best actors in "any theatre in America." The Athenaeum would be Atlanta's principal theater before and during the Civil War.[21]

In 1854–55, Atlanta opened its first institution of higher learning, the Atlanta Medical College. The brainchild of Dr. John G. Westmoreland, a graduate of the Medical College of Georgia who moved to Atlanta in 1853, the medical college included Westmoreland's brother Willis on its faculty, as well as seven additional physicians. John Westmoreland ran for a seat in the Georgia legislature in order to lobby for state appropriations to help the fledgling institution. In 1854, the Medical College held a lecture series in City Hall, and the following year it began constructing its own building at Butler and Jenkins Streets. During the 1857–58 session, the Georgia legislature appropriated $15,000 to the school in exchange for its promise to train, free of charge, one doctor from each congressional district in Georgia. While the Atlanta Medical College lacked the cachet of older and more established educational institutions, including the University of Georgia (founded 1785) in Athens and even Emory College (founded 1836) in nearby Covington, nonetheless it gave Atlanta a certain claim to respectability. The Westmoreland brothers also began a journal called the *Atlanta Medical and Surgical Journal*.[22]

Atlanta gained its first luxury hotel at the end of 1854. The Trout House on Decatur Street, named for its owner Jeremiah F. Trout, became Atlanta's largest and grandest hotel. Four stories high and across the street from the picturesque City Park, the hotel contributed to the further gentrification of Decatur Street. It contained "furniture entirely new, Rooms well ventilated, large and airy Halls." The *Daily Intelligencer*, in reporting its opening on November 11, 1854, gushed, "We take pleasure" in announcing the opening of the Trout House and printed names of guests arriving at the grand hotel. Newspaper-reading Atlantans were thereby given a sense of their city's importance, as the Trout House registered guests not only from New Orleans and Charleston but from such faraway cities as Philadelphia, New York, and Washington, D.C. In the coming years, the Trout House added a restaurant that boasted three varieties of oysters, wild game in season, and a well-stocked bar featuring "the Choicest" liquors and cigars. By 1860 there were six hotels in Atlanta, all of them located near the passenger depot.[23]

Ten years after Atlanta's remarkable building boom, in the midst of a war that few had anticipated and with a level of destruction that no one could have foreseen, the Gate City lay in shambles. In 1861, by a vote of its faculty, the Medical College suspended operations as a school and reopened as a hospital.[24] Dr. Willis Westmoreland's wife, Maria, created a new organization of volunteers called the Ladies' Soldiers' Relief Society. Isaac Winship's wife, Martha, led the rival Atlanta Hospital Association. The Atlanta fairgrounds were used to build a vast hospital complex that treated thousands of soldiers during the war. It was evacuated and abandoned shortly before the arrival of federal soldiers of General William T. Sherman.

The Athenaeum entertained thousands of Atlantans during the war. From secession speeches to fund-raisers for soldiers, from local amateur productions to traveling professional shows, the Athenaeum served as Atlanta's wartime cultural center. When federal soldiers arrived in Atlanta during September 1864, they organized a fund-raiser for a widow who wished to go to the North. A few weeks later, they set fires in the city that destroyed the theater.

The elegant mansion of Ephraim and Ellen Ponder sustained extensive damage from federal artillery shells, rendering it uninhabitable. Today, photographs of the mansion are iconic symbols of the city's destruction.

The Trout House welcomed high-ranking Confederate political and military leaders during the war, including President Jefferson Davis and General John Hunt Morgan. By 1864, it had become a symbol for Atlanta's decline in the face of war, its collapsing economy, and crime. In September, Yankee soldiers claimed it as a prize, as they were later to claim City Hall. They held a party at the Trout House in mid-September 1864. Two months later, they burned it to the ground.

The passenger depot likewise became a symbol, of Atlanta's economic rise and its importance to the Confederate economy on the one hand, of its decline and destruction on the other. By 1864, the passenger depot had become a forlorn place, a residence for homeless people and refugees living in tents and abandoned boxcars. Union soldiers marching into Atlanta commented on the large and impressive edifice. One soldier from Illinois called it a "magnificent structure."[25] Its destruction by General Sherman's departing army was to be a symbol of Atlanta's defeat. But in 1861, no one could imagine what was to come.

2. Unionism and Secessionism in the Gate City

In the years leading up to the Civil War, Americans debated the meaning of liberty, the future of slavery, and the role of the national government in curtailing slavery's spread into the western territories. By 1860, southern radicals, known as fire-eaters, convinced that slavery could not be protected in the American Union, advocated secession from the United States and the formation of a new nation of slave states. "No one knew what the world outside the United States would be like," one scholar has written, "though the fire-eaters promised a political and economic Garden of Eden."[1] In Atlanta, they would not have an easy time making their case, for Atlanta's domination by profit-minded businessmen, not rural planters, made Unionism a formidable force in the Gate City.

By 1860, Atlanta was a thriving and relatively prosperous community of ninety-five hundred people that had replaced Macon as Georgia's fourth-largest city. In the previous decade, all of Georgia's cities had grown, but Atlanta's population had increased by a remarkable 286 percent. The railroads continued to be the engine driving Atlanta's economy, with four lines using Atlanta as a major hub and forty-four trains leaving and entering the city every day. The city's central business district included two hundred retail and business offices.[2] Atlanta's political leadership continued to be closely tied to its business community. This political-business community showed a marked degree of Unionism before the Civil War. Happy to earn money in the American Union, Atlanta's men of commerce did not believe that sectional tensions warranted drastic action.

Over the course of the 1850s, debate over the status and future of slavery in America resulted in an increasingly vocal group of fire-eaters winning support for the cause of secession; in Atlanta their leader was Congressman Lucius Jeremiah Gartrell. Born in Wilkes County in 1821, he had attended the University of Georgia before studying law in the office of Robert Toombs, the brilliant, articulate state legislator who became Gartrell's law coach and political mentor. Gartrell joined the bar and began "an extensive and lucrative practice." He and Toombs supported the Whig Party, a national-minded, business-oriented party that competed with states' rights Democrats in the South and nationally. Gartrell's political career began with his election to the Georgia legislature in the 1840s. By the 1850s, national debate over slavery had led to the Whig Party's collapse. Gartrell joined the Democratic Party, and in 1856 he was elected to Congress representing Atlanta, which had become his home two years earlier. A handsome, charismatic man with a full head of brown wavy hair and a full beard, Gartrell established a successful legal practice in Atlanta, and his home east of the city became the site of large social gatherings when the congressman was in residence.[3]

Gartrell had a personal as well as a political stake in the national debate over slavery, for he became a litigant in a highly visible Georgia Supreme Court case involving the will of his late father-in-law, Francis Gideon. The will bequeathed Gideon's slaves to the American Colonization Society, with funds left in trust for their manumission and transportation to Liberia, the African nation founded as a place for the colonization of former American slaves. Gartrell broke the will by calling upon legal and political contacts in the state who sympathized with his position and by finding a technicality on which to hinge his case. First, he persuaded the executors named in the document to decline the job, acting as executor himself. Next, he fought the case in Fulton County Superior Court and later in the Georgia Supreme Court. He was represented by Robert Toombs, who had become a United States senator with a national reputation. Gartrell's position was that the American Colonization Society's charter allowed only for *freed slaves* to come under its purview.[4]

The courts sided with Gartrell. Writing for the majority, Chief Justice Joseph Lumpkin concluded, "For the Society to carry them to Africa, the slaves must be free and give their consent as a condition precedent." Lumpkin, who shared the proslavery views of Gartrell and Toombs, then used the case as a vehicle through which to condemn the American Colonization Society in the same year the U.S. Supreme Court, via the *Dred Scott* case, invalidated attempts to limit the spread of slavery in the territories. At one time, Justice Lumpkin wrote, "I was . . . in common with the great body of my fellow citizens of the South, the friend and patron of this enterprise." However, Lumpkin judged the experiment in manumission a failure. He wrote that the African nation of Liberia consisted of "a few thousand thriftless, lazy semi-savages, dying of famine, because they will not work!" The chief justice concluded: "Be disabused of the false and unfounded notion that slavery is sinful." Lucius Gartrell profited directly from the Court's decision when his wife inherited her father's slaves, instead of the American Colonization Society. Because married women lacked property rights in Georgia, Lucius Gartrell now owned the Gideon slaves.[5]

As a relative latecomer to national politics, Gartrell is less well known today than Georgia's trio of celebrated politicians, Robert Toombs, Howell Cobb, and Alexander Stephens, but he played a major role in the Georgia secession debate, and no one could match him when it came to brashness and oratorical grandstanding. Gartrell's maiden speech to the House of Representatives on January 25, 1858, referenced the need to protect the South's slave interests and ended with the declaration "*equality in this Union or independence out of it.*" On January 10, 1860, the year in which the Union was threatened with collapse, Gartrell gave another speech to the U.S. House of Representatives that highlighted his personal support for the institution of slavery, his belief that the Union was in peril, and his deftness as a debater. Most of the speech emphasized the notion of the South as victim of an unsympathetic North and an aggressive Republican Party, the national party that replaced the Whigs in the mid-1850s. Because the constitution protected slavery in the South, its possible containment in the western territories had become a major political issue during the 1850s and the centerpiece of the Republican platform. Gartrell condemned the Republican Party for threatening the right of southerners to take their slaves into the territories; indeed, he denied the right of anyone in the territories to "deprive me of my slave property" through taxation or "unfriendly legislation." The latter statement was an obvious stab at Illinois Senator Stephen A. Douglas, the leading national figure in the Democratic Party, and a likely presidential candidate. Douglas had told audiences they might limit slavery's spread in the territories if the majority wished to do so. For Gartrell, an attorney and an apologist for slavery, human property was the same as any other type, and the U.S. Constitution sustained him. In this instance, he claimed, "All the rights and laws of property attach to my negro as much as to your horse."[6]

Interrupted several times by congressmen who pressed him on one point or another and addressing each argument presented to him, Gartrell also elicited laughter from the audience when he veered away from the slavery topic momentarily in order to complain that the national government earned twice as much tax money from the South as from the North. "We give you, in other words, a bonus of $20,000,000 to sing songs to the Union. It costs too much: I can buy songs cheaper than that at home—original poetry at that." Attempting to find something positive to report in the present political circumstances, Gartrell placed his confidence in northern Democrats. He hoped they would have the "moral courage" to support the interests of southerners in the coming election. But he also threatened secession. "I pray God that the result at the ballot-box may not be such as to force upon my people the necessity of appealing to the cartridge-box." Gartrell's speech was printed and distributed under the title "The Dangers of Black-Republicanism, and the Duty of the South."[7]

In February 1860, the House of Representatives debated the choice of a new speaker, and Congressman Gartrell used this platform to explore Georgia's options within and outside of the Union. Atlanta's newspaper-reading public enjoyed verbatim reports of these debates reprinted in the *Daily Intelligencer*. In one exchange, Gartrell tangled with Congressman Edwin M. Stanton of Ohio, alleging that a northern visitor to the South would find no impoverished slaves, while a southern visitor to the North would see "a thousand emaciated hands stretched out for alms." Gartrell told Stanton, "Attend to your own poor and your own affairs." In another exchange, Congressman John Hickman of Pennsylvania attempted to deflect Gartrell's argument about the viability of secession. Hickman contended that the United States government could easily crush a southern rebellion since the North had more than twice the population of the South and "we can make more arms and ammunition in ninety days than the South can buy." Gartrell would not let the charge go unanswered. He responded confidently that "one cotton crop of Georgia would buy all the arms in Pennsylvania."[8]

Despite Gartrell's efforts, Unionists held a prominent place on the public platform in Atlanta until the national Democratic convention met in April

1860. James M. Calhoun, a native South Carolinian, local attorney, and onetime state legislator, later recalled that throughout the spring, summer, and fall of 1860 he was a "Union man . . . in favor of peace all the time."[9]

Calhoun was part of a Unionist circle in Atlanta that included an estimated one hundred families in 1860, and they represented individuals of northern and southern birth, former Whigs and current Democrats. A heartfelt sense of loyalty to nation defined their position, although Unionists also worried about their business investments. William Markham is a good example. Born in Connecticut, Markham moved to Atlanta in 1853, quickly built a successful business career, and became a pillar of the First Presbyterian Church where he served as a deacon. Markham's investments included construction, real estate, and banking. He also ran a rolling mill with another Yankee named Lewis Scofield. Markham became a central figure in the Unionist circle. He confided to his son Marcellus that if the Union dissolved, "The South will be overrun, our property will be confiscated, and we will be ruined." The elder Markham had "no confidence in the success of the South, in case of war."[10]

The *Daily Intelligencer* ran a series of articles by an anonymous writer calling himself "Plebian," whose columns represent the fullest expression of Unionism in Atlanta's public press. Plebian may have been James A. Stewart, the prosperous owner of a flour mill and until recently a resident of Unionist-dominated east Tennessee. Neither Plebian nor any of Atlanta's Unionists raised questions in a major public venue about the morality of slavery or its continued existence; indeed, a number of them owned slaves. Plebian defended the institution of slavery but insisted that slavery could be protected within the American Union. "If Georgia desires either to perpetuate or abolish slavery, no other State has the right to interfere," Plebian wrote in a column published on January 16, 1860. "If the people of a Territorial Government wish either to establish or abolish slavery it is their privilege to do so, at their own time and in their own way." Plebian regarded secessionist threats as "internal treason." On February 6, he condemned the extremism of secessionists by calling their rhetoric the "language of deluded men." Stewart hoped that the Democratic Party would nominate Stephen A. Douglas or Andrew Johnson, either of whom would protect slavery and ensure that "our Union is safe."[11]

The *Daily Intelligencer*'s willingness to publish multiple pro-Union letters from Plebian indicates that Georgia's future in the American Union was a subject of public debate in Atlanta up to the spring of 1860. The *Intelligencer* did not agree with Plebian, but did regard him as "honest and patriotic," and also believed that the public deserved to hear both sides of the debate. James J. Diamond represented the other side of the debate, one that openly advocated unseating Douglas, the putative front-runner for the Democratic presidential nomination. Diamond believed that Douglas could not be trusted as an unequivocal defender of slavery. In a letter published in the *Daily Intelligencer,* Diamond predicted that Southern men might bolt the convention to nominate their own candidate. The *Intelligencer* did not endorse Diamond's position, instead counseling reason and the "harmonious action of the party."[12]

There would be no harmony at the Democratic convention. As Diamond had predicted, the April meeting held at Charleston, South Carolina, dissolved into chaos as delegates representing the cotton states of the deep South left the convention, eventually meeting in Richmond and nominating John Breckinridge of Kentucky, who stood for slave interests and southern unity. Mainstream Democrats nominated Douglas at a separate meeting in Baltimore. Border-state voters chose yet another candidate, John Bell, a Tennessee Unionist. The once-cautious *Daily Intelligencer* criticized mainstream Democrats for nominating Douglas despite the impossibility of his winning southern votes.[13]

After the Democratic convention, vituperative language became more common in Atlanta's political discourse. When the Fulton County Democratic Party met on May 19, it issued a call for unity in order to forestall the election of a "Black Republican" to the presidential chair. A succession of speakers condemned the candidacy of Stephen A. Douglas and applauded those who had walked out of the Charleston convention. The Reverend P. L. J. May declared that "the slavery question is paramount to every question that now agitates the country," and that the South must stand firm: "*No more compromises* of Constitutional rights." In a three-sentence article appearing alongside reports of the Fulton Democratic meeting, the *Intelligencer* noted that Abraham Lincoln had been nominated by the Republican convention in Chicago.[14]

Congressman Gartrell also weighed in. He delivered a lengthy speech at City Hall on July 14, 1860, reprinted in its entirety in the *Daily Intelligencer.* Using the same type of passionate language that had earned him attention in the national Congress, Gartrell condemned Douglas for failing to uphold the

Dred Scott decision and indeed for suggesting ways that territorial residents could keep slavery out via taxation or legislation. As he often did, Gartrell made no distinction between human property and other types, telling listeners, "You have as much right under the Constitution to go into the territory with your slaves, as the Northern man has to go there with his sheep or his mules." Next, he suggested that John Bell, though a southern man, was "far from being an acceptable candidate." Gartrell reminded listeners that Bell voted against the Kansas-Nebraska Act of 1854, legislation that opened these territories to the possibility of becoming slave states. For Gartrell, Bell's vote made him untenable as a presidential candidate, and he told the audience that only by supporting John Breckinridge for president and Joseph Lane for vice president could the people of Atlanta maintain "the rights of every section and the constitutional equality of the States as handed down to us by our ancestors." To "immense applause," he concluded: "The position of our candidates is based on the rock of truth, and cannot be shaken!"[15]

While Congressman Gartrell beat the drum of secession, other proslavery interests in Atlanta published articles and pamphlets purporting to show slavery's regional importance, economic benefits, and benign qualities. In May 1860, the *Daily Intelligencer* ran a story that even claimed slaves expressed pride in their monetary worth. In "The Proud Darkey," a Virginia slave allegedly bragged to another about being worth $1,500. Pointing at a poor white man in the vicinity, the slave compared himself favorably to the white vagrant and claimed to have "dignity" in comparison with the poor white man.[16]

White people often congratulated themselves on their benevolent paternalism by retelling stories about allegedly happy slaves who led productive, Christian lives. One such story appeared in the *Daily Intelligencer* in the spring of 1860. Titled "A Remarkable Man" and reprinted from the *Southern Christian Advocate*, the article told of the death of a slave named Charles, alleged to have been 106 years old. Born in South Carolina, owned by a Tory family during and after the Revolutionary War, Charles became part of Isaac Winship's household in 1835. An exemplary worker, he was also an exemplary man, never "out of temper or inconsistent as a Christian," according to Winship, one of the brothers who owned iron foundries in Atlanta and Cartersville. Charles served as preacher to African Americans in the Methodist Episcopal Church and kept the Sabbath so strictly that he fasted from noon on Saturdays until sunset on Sundays. As a reminder of slavery's allegedly benign qualities, Charles was reported to be "cheerful and happy" on his deathbed, for he had had a long life and was secure in the knowledge that he would soon be "at home with Jesus." White and black admirers mourned for Charles, following the hearse bearing his coffin to church and City Cemetery. Charles was so beloved by Isaac and Martha Winship that "his owners feel as if one of the family is gone."[17]

Many white people chose to believe that slaves preferred their condition to that of northern industrial workers, or at least that they should. Early in 1861 the Atlanta publishing house Franklin Printing produced a remarkable pamphlet called *Slavery and Abolition, as Viewed by a Georgia Slave*. Attributed to a local slave named Harrison Berry and selling for twenty-five cents, the forty-one-page document told the story of Berry, originally owned by David Berry of Butts County and given to his daughter upon her marriage to S. W. Price of Covington, Georgia. In 1861, Harrison Berry was working as a shoemaker in Atlanta. A literate man despite his enslavement, Berry had access to Georgia newspapers.[18]

Berry felt compelled to defend slavery because of concern about the "Abolition party" whose activism increased after John Brown's raid in 1859. If Brown's plan to liberate slaves in Virginia had succeeded, reprisals against blacks would have been extreme: "I can imagine that I see gibbets all over the Slave-holding States, with negroes stretched upon them like slaughtered hogs." He noted that blacks in the North were badly treated, for "the colored man is a colored man any where. He is but the tool North, and the servant South." According to this account, Southern slaves received better treatment than "four-fifths of the laboring population of the country."[19]

Harrison Berry probably wrote the pamphlet, for it contains a testimonial from Henry Hornady, minister of First Baptist Church of Atlanta, who emphasized Berry's motivation to write "from a firm conviction that Abolitionist agitators are the worst enemies of the Slave, and from settled opinion that Slavery is according to Divine Law." Like most clergy in Atlanta and throughout the South, Hornady supported slavery because his reading of scripture convinced him that the Bible authorized it. Another testimonial came from the Atlanta shoemaker A. M. Eddleman, who wanted readers to know that Berry, while writing a tract, nonetheless knew his "proper place" as a slave.[20]

Why would a black man write a pamphlet that appeared to defend slavery? Berry favored the colonization of American blacks in Africa, a political position at odds with northern Republicans who appear to be Berry's intended targets. Based on his reading of Georgia newspapers, Berry probably believed that Republicans were too radical and that their policies carried the possibility of creating sectional divisions that could lead to violence against African Americans. As a slave, Berry was obliged to do his master's bidding and may have been encouraged to write the pamphlet by Hornady and others. Clearly, *Slavery and Abolition, as Viewed by a Georgia Slave* would never have been published by an Atlanta company if it had not contained arguments with which white southerners concurred. One of the few extant copies of the pamphlet bears a postmark and is addressed to John Maclean, Jr., president of Princeton College. No doubt, slavery's sympathizers wished to use Berry's work to convince important national leaders of the purported benefits of slavery. However, the *Daily Intelligencer* doubted Berry's authorship of the pamphlet, writing that such a polemic "never proceeded from the pen of a *full-blooded* negro since the world began."[21]

While slavery's apologists continued to fight a propaganda war locally, the election of 1860 entered its final weeks. The *Daily Intelligencer* predicted that Breckinridge would carry the state of Georgia. In October, the newspaper concluded that secession was inevitable. "The ties which have for so long a time bound this Union together, have been well nigh sundered," one article suggested. "All fraternal feeling seems to have been lost" between the sections.[22]

Atlanta Unionists did not regard the election's outcome as inevitable, and they turned for leadership to Alexander Stephens. A lawyer, former Whig congressman, and brilliant debater, Stephens had been a leader in the convention that produced the Georgia Platform, a response to congressional passage of the Compromise of 1850. The Compromise angered some southerners because it allowed the admission of California as a free state, ended the slave trade in the District of Columbia, and permitted settlers in Utah and New Mexico to decide for themselves whether they wanted slavery. Slavery's staunchest defenders wanted no limits on where and when slavery could spread. The Georgia Platform affirmed the state's commitment to Union but also to the preservation of slavery and threatened "resistance" if slavery came under attack. During the 1850s, many of Stephens's colleagues and friends, including Robert Toombs, left the Unionist ranks to embrace secessionism. Stephens, along with Georgians Hershel Johnson and Benjamin Hill, remained committed to Union. In 1858, the man popularly known as

"Little Aleck" retired from Congress and returned to his beloved home, Liberty Hall, in Crawfordsville. Political events soon forced him back into the public maelstrom.[23]

Alexander Stephens supported Stephen A. Douglas in the presidential contest and believed that the Democratic nominee's popularity was growing in Georgia. Douglas's choice of Hershel Johnson as his running mate would surely attract votes in the state. Stephens also believed that there was a reasonable prospect that no candidate would win a majority at the national level; the lame-duck House of Representatives would decide the election in Douglas's favor. Stephens gave pro-Union speeches in Atlanta and half a dozen other locations in September and early October. "Our cause is gaining daily and rapidly," he wrote to a friend, but he also complained about unsympathetic newspapers offering unflattering and in some cases erroneous coverage. Moreover, Stephens's optimism fluctuated from one week to the next. A slight, frail man, Stephens struggled to keep up a grueling campaign schedule. He told a reporter for the *New York Herald* on September 29 that he feared the election's outcome. "I hold revolution and civil war to be inevitable," he wrote. "The demagogues have raised a whirlwind they cannot control."[24]

On October 30, Stephen A. Douglas appeared in Atlanta, part of a campaign tour that also included Memphis and Nashville, Tennessee, Macon and Columbus, Georgia, and Huntsville and Mobile, Alabama. Alexander Stephens accompanied and introduced him to the crowd in Atlanta. Because presidential candidates traditionally did not campaign openly, instead having surrogates represent them on the stump, Douglas's decision to campaign in person generated a great deal of popular interest, even drawing spectators who took the train from surrounding areas. In an era before microphone amplification, only the closest spectators could actually hear the speech, but it was considered special just to be in the presence of this famous Senate leader known as the Little Giant. He spoke for three hours. The *Daily Intelligencer* acknowledged the importance of Douglas's appearance, calling it "an important event in our history . . . the first time that a candidate for the Presidency has so honored us." However, the newspaper did not treat Douglas's speech so kindly, for Douglas regarded the Union as inviolable and would support any president in squelching treason. Calling the speech "a rehash of what he has previously said on many occasions," the newspaper estimated the crowd at only two thousand to four thousand and dismissed

Douglas as "no greater orator than hundreds we have in our own State . . . barely third rate."[25]

On election day, despite the support of the *Daily Intelligencer*, the local congressman, and many important citizens, Breckinridge failed to carry the Gate City. John Bell won a plurality (1,070 votes), Breckinridge came in second (835), and Douglas third (335). Still, the votes of the two Unionist candidates, Bell and Douglas, totaled 63 percent of the vote. In Fulton County, the contest was slightly closer: 1,195 for Bell, 1,018 for Breckinridge, 347 for Douglas. Abraham Lincoln, the "Black Republican" so feared by Atlantans, prevailed nationally. He was not on the ballot in ten southern states, including Georgia.[26]

Businessmen almost certainly influenced the outcome in Atlanta. Despite the pronouncements of Congressman Gartrell and others, men of commerce in Atlanta and elsewhere in the South feared the economic disruption that secession and even the threat of war might bring. As a transportation hub and home to merchants who profited directly or indirectly from slavery, Atlanta certainly had a stake in protecting the institution, but Unionism still prevailed before Lincoln's election. Bell also did well in several other southern cities, winning pluralities in Richmond and New Orleans. Elsewhere, Breckinridge prevailed, including in Baltimore and in Savannah, where Chatham County cast two-thirds of its votes for Breckinridge. South Georgia, with its direct ties to the cotton economy, lacked the support for Union that was evident in Atlanta. Breckinridge carried the state of Georgia by 49 percent to Bell's 40 percent and Douglas's 11 percent, an indication of how closely divided the state continued to be on the decision to secede.[27]

When Abraham Lincoln's election became a reality, Unionism began to collapse in Atlanta. Some Unionists now embraced Confederate nationalism, even if they did so reluctantly. Others kept their Unionist views to themselves. An estimated thirty-five to forty unconditional Unionists remained in Atlanta, many of them prominent citizens, and a dozen of them began holding secret meetings at the office of Nedom L. Angier, a local physician who had moved to Atlanta from New Hampshire. In private, these men discussed the best ways to thwart Georgia's move toward secession. However, most Atlantans focused on what the *Daily Intelligencer* called the "Doleful News" of Lincoln's election. The election's outcome confirmed "our worst apprehensions" and meant "peace and harmony in the Union is at an end." The newspaper then issued an immediate call to arms: "Lincoln is elected and we are destined to wear the yoke of Black Republican rule, unless we rise up in our defence."[28]

The election had a galvanizing effect on citizens who hoped for a different outcome and who equated Lincoln with radical abolitionism. Although Lincoln took the position that the Constitution protected slavery in the South, his opposition to its spread into the territories made him an abolitionist in the minds of many southerners, including schoolteacher Jennie Lines. Lines resided in Atlanta's First Ward with her husband Sylvanus, a printer. The newlywed couple struggled to get by, boarding with a Mrs. Gardner and hoping to save enough money that they might set up a household of their own. Jennie kept a diary in which she recorded the common view that northerners failed to understand what southerners had to contend with. "Mrs. G. has been in my room this morning recounting her trials with [her slave] Caroline," Jennie wrote on November 27, 1860. "Negroes seem to be a *necessary* evil. If abolitionists *knew them* surely they would not wish to abolish slavery." Jennie Lines wrote of Lincoln's election: "The report is that Lincoln is elected. Wo[e] to the union if he is! It does not seem possible that there are abolitionists enough in the United States to elect a president." She noted with apprehension that northern Wide Awakes—Republican political clubs that held torchlight parades at night—and southern militia groups called Minute Men were preparing for war. Hoping to find an escape from news of national turmoil, Jennie and Sylvanus attended a concert at the Athenaeum where the entertainment featured four small children who sang on stage. Jennie enjoyed the performance until cries of "fire" led the crowd of six hundred to head for the doors in great confusion. The fire, it turned out, was not at the Athenaeum but at another venue on nearby Whitehall Street. Nonetheless, Jennie seemed to find in this episode a symbol for what was happening in the country. "The political world is in great commotion," she wrote after describing the evening.[29]

In Atlanta, as elsewhere in the South, white citizens feared slave uprisings, all the more so in the highly charged atmosphere of late fall 1860. During November 1860, the *Daily Intelligencer* reported news of an alleged "insurrectionary plot" unearthed on a plantation south of Atlanta in Crawford County. The newspaper attributed the plot to two white men, one of them a Yankee schoolteacher, and reported their arrest and the jailing of forty slaves. Jennie Lines heard rumors of a slave uprising during the Christmas holidays in 1860. "There are some fears of an insurrection among the negroes," she confided to her diary on December 27, "but we have seen no manifestation of it as yet, and I trust we shall not."[30]

In addition to slavery, economic uncertainty in Atlanta exacerbated political tensions during 1860 and led some to search for scapegoats. Jennie Lines wrote about Lincoln's election causing "a great amount of trouble and anxiety. Business of nearly all kinds is nearly defunct. Hundreds are thrown out of employment." She blamed abolitionists in the North. Jennie's economic assessment matched that of William Ezzard, Atlanta's mayor, whose state-of-the-city report included an economic analysis. "Owing to the shortness of the crop and the very sudden change in pecuniary affairs on account of our political convulsions," Ezzard wrote, "many of the laboring class of our citizens have been thrown out of employment. Some have found it difficult to procure even the [necessities] of life." He went on to emphasize the city's efforts to help the needy and to provide employment to members of the most destitute families. On January 23, Jared I. Whitaker was sworn in as Ezzard's replacement. Owner and editor of the *Daily Intelligencer*, Whitaker supported secession unequivocally.[31]

Secessionists in Atlanta, including Congressman Gartrell, sought ways to further their goal of disunion in the aftermath of Lincoln's election. Specifically, secessionists needed a way to encourage disunion among those who were satisfied making money under the current governmental system. Their answer: convince businessmen that the South's salvation lay in freeing itself from economic dependence on the North and establishing direct ties to Europe.[32]

Lucius Gartrell complained of the South's economic dependence on the North when he addressed Congress in January. On November 1, the *Daily Intelligencer* printed an article containing statistics showing the South supporting the North financially in a variety of ways, including the collection of customs revenue, fees for agents and brokers, even salaries of teachers sent from the North. Several days before the national election, the *Daily Intelligencer* issued an editorial that focused solely on the argument that "European nations stand ready to open *free trade*" with the South. The newspaper drew the conclusion that the South must "stop the flow of Southern wealth to the North and keep it at home and enrich the South." On the day that it reported Lincoln's election, the *Intelligencer* again hammered this theme: "Any Southern merchant who has credit in New York, can get credit in Liverpool."[33]

In its inaugural issue under new editors, Atlanta's daily newspaper, the *Gate City Guardian*, addressed the economic issue. Coeditors Thomas C. Howard and R. A. Crawford touted their birth and education in Georgia and assured readers that they had no interest in "ties outside their own State and Section." Their newspaper would be "Independent in all things, neutral in nothing." The *Guardian* analyzed the issue of European dependence on southern cotton by reviewing an article by Thomas Prentice Kettell called "Southern Wealth and Northern Profits." Accusing England of hypocrisy for criticizing southern slavery while carrying on the slave trade for 274 years, Kettell concluded that while England might be able to find sources for raw cotton from elsewhere in the world, this cotton would not be "the peculiar kind they so much need." By arguing that the South stood to profit from leaving the Union, secessionists found an argument that resonated with those for whom defending slavery's morality held less sway.[34]

The actions of businessman Sidney Root reveal the business community's shift toward secessionism. Like many Atlantans, Root had moved to the Gate City from a northern upbringing, in his case in western Massachusetts. After first moving to Lumpkin, Georgia, to seek employment through a brother-in-law and marrying a local woman whose father gave the couple three slaves, Root relocated to Atlanta in the 1850s. Years later, he recalled being attracted to Atlanta's "rugged, hopeful people" and being "fascinated with the idea of building a town." He formed a dry goods business with another Yankee expatriate named John N. Beach. A prewar Whig and a strong supporter of the Compromise of 1850, Root nonetheless came to regard southern nationalism as an unfortunate necessity.[35]

While there is no reason to doubt Root's sincerity, it *is* possible to suggest that he might have had a financial interest in secession. Root took to heart the calls to consider direct trade with Liverpool, and he saw opportunities for profit in cultivating an emerging leadership in the secession movement. He was to prove successful at both. Throughout the Civil War, Root suspected that his partner John Beach was a secret Unionist, but that did not stop Beach from welcoming the opportunity to earn money during the national calamity. Within a matter of months, Sidney Root and John Beach reached an agreement whereby Beach would represent their partnership in Liverpool. As the world's leading port of entry for American cotton, Liverpool had many merchants ready to solidify economic ties with southern businessmen.[36]

Richard Peters provides another good example. A native of Germantown, Pennsylvania, Peters moved to Georgia in the 1830s to work in railroad construction and to Atlanta in the 1840s as superintendent of the Georgia Railroad. In Atlanta, his investments included the largest flour mill in the

South and four hundred acres of prime real estate on Peachtree Street. He also owned a plantation in Gordon County staffed by slaves. By the 1850s Peters was one of Atlanta's wealthiest residents, married to the daughter of a prominent hotelier, and the father of several children. He opposed secession because he feared that economic upheaval would culminate in the demise of slavery; however, he soon jumped on the secession bandwagon when he realized that he could make money in the new Confederate nation. Peters sold the engine that powered his flour mill to the government "for their powder-mills at Augusta," and by insisting on payment in gold, he turned a significant profit. He then sold the land on which the flour mill once stood to the Georgia Railroad for $20,000, thus increasing his profits even more. Like Root, he soon invested in a blockade-running company.[37]

Sidney Root and Richard Peters had assets that placed them in the top tier of Atlanta businessmen, but profit-based secessionism also attracted the attention of middling businessmen. Samuel P. Richards moved to Atlanta from Macon in 1861 at the urging of his brother Jabez, who had established a branch of the brothers' bookstore in the Gate City. An admirer of Alexander Stephens, Sam Richards referred to secessionists as "*professional* men and young *squirts* who have but little or nothing to lose in any event, or *politicians* who aspire to office in a Southern Confederacy." With memories of the slow recovery from the Panic of 1857 and uneasiness about the possible impact of war on business, Richards wanted nothing to do with political extremism. In the space of a few months, he changed his mind. Caught up in the political momentum of secession, Richards also began to see that it might be possible to earn money in an independent South. For a time, he was to be astounded by the profits he earned.[38]

While politicians and businessmen honed their constitutional and economic arguments favoring secession, the Minute Men—mentioned by an apprehensive Jennie Lines—began making military preparations. Part of a network of militia groups springing up around the South, Minute Men held drills and parades that helped publicize the prosecession cause. Atlanta Minute Men won the endorsements of more than one hundred Atlantans whose names the *Daily Intelligencer* printed in its November 6 edition. Congressman Lucius Gartrell's name led the list, which also contained those of prominent professionals including Dr. John F. Alexander and businessmen such as Jeremiah Trout. At their inaugural meeting at the local armory, the Minute Men heard speeches and voted to correspond with similar units in other states. The Minute Men held a second meeting after news of Lincoln's election reached Atlanta. Sidney Root gave an "eloquent speech" reviewing the outrages of the "abolition power" upon the South's constitutional rights, whereupon the group passed resolutions insisting that "the time has come for us to assert our rights, and we now stand ready to second any action that the sovereign State of Georgia may take in asserting her independence."[39]

In the coming weeks, support for secession gained momentum. A citizens meeting numbering four hundred to five hundred convened at the court house at noon on November 13. Led by Jared Whitaker and others, the group called for *"peaceable secession"* as the only remedy to the election of "a sectional Abolition majority." At the end of November, Atlantans observed a day of fasting, humiliation, and prayer. Even the solemnity of this occasion failed to stop the prosecession juggernaut. While the *Daily Intelligencer* noted the closing of businesses and the religious observance of citizens, it also noted the sermon of the Reverend William Crumley of Trinity Methodist Church, who emphasized the "moral, social and political good" of slavery and the fanaticism of the North.[40]

Atlanta's secessionist women demonstrated their interest in the political showdown playing out around them. In an era in which women did not speak at the lectern, they were nonetheless believed to exert moral influence over men, and secessionists solicited and publicized their activism. On November 3, the *Daily Intelligencer* included a story under the headline "The Ladies for Secession," reprinted from the *Columbus Times,* that focused on secessionist women in attendance at a speech of Robert Toombs in Montgomery. The women wore the blue cockade, a symbol of secession, and reportedly felt disdain for those who would cooperate with Unionist sentiments.[41]

On November 19, the *Daily Intelligencer* reprinted the letter of "A Georgia Woman" written expressly for the newspaper. By concealing her identity, the Georgia Woman presented the appearance of modesty. Indeed, she made clear that she would gladly defer to "the better judgment of noble men." Nonetheless, she wanted readers to know that Georgia needed women to speak to their men. "It has heretofore been thought unlady-like for women to interest themselves in political affairs," she wrote. Yet the national crisis called upon women to use their "influence" in "encouraging our husbands and brothers" to choose between "independence" or "submission to a Black Republican President." The *Daily Intelligencer* added a brief commentary applauding the author, suggesting that there were no Tory women during the

American Revolution, and comparing the current crisis to that glorious one. Lucius Gartrell had played a gender card in his congressional speech when he suggested that "every matron and every fair daughter of the South" would join in the struggle for southern independence.[42]

Atlanta's Minute Men issued a call to women to stitch blue cockades. Women in Charleston, Savannah, Macon, Columbus, and Augusta were believed to be involved in similar efforts, according to a report in the *Daily Intelligencer* on December 3, 1860. Atlanta women did not disappoint. Three days later, the newspaper reported that Mrs. John W. Leonard had made a formal presentation of women's hand-stitched cockades to the Minute Men of Fulton County. Another presentation of cockades was made four days later by a Mrs. Judge Lyons.[43]

Despite the widespread activism of Atlanta secessionists, Unionism remained a powerful force locally and statewide, as legislative debate in the state capital of Milledgeville during November and December revealed. While Robert Toombs and T. R. R. Cobb thundered from the platform about abolitionist outrages and Black Republican rule, Alexander Stephens, Benjamin Hill, and Hershel Johnson answered with persuasive rhetoric of their own. Stephens, who had served in Congress with Lincoln in the 1840s, denied that the president-elect would "do anything to jeopard[ize] our safety or security . . . for he is bound by the constitutional checks which are thrown around him."[44]

After their strong showing at Milledgeville, Unionists immediately began to lose ground, as secessionists aggressively courted public opinion. They had a valuable ally in Governor Joseph E. Brown, who issued a public letter on December 7, 1860. A self-made man who had worked a variety of jobs to finance his education at Yale Law School, Brown won election to the state senate and then to the governorship in 1857. His public letter argued for secession based on the direct threat Republican rule posed to Georgia's "honor, and the rights of her people." Brown envisioned a state and region free of northern middlemen and one where slaveowner and nonslaveowner stood united in the preservation of southern values. The governor called for a convention in which elected delegates would decide the issue.[45]

Secessionists built upon their momentum by staging several spectacular public demonstrations. On December 10, proponents of separation from the North held a Grand Secession Demonstration at the Athenaeum that included speeches condemning compromise and culminating in a torchlight procession. One thousand men, including six hundred torchbearers, marched along

Decatur, Marietta, Whitehall, Hunter, and Peachtree Streets accompanied by two brass bands and encouraged by an audience including hundreds of "the fair daughters of Atlanta," who showed their support with "their approving smiles." The procession culminated at the Atlanta Hotel for another round of speeches. The *Daily Intelligencer* called the gathering "one of the greatest demonstrations ever witnessed in the city of Atlanta."[46]

On December 22, secessionists in Atlanta held a mass rally to celebrate South Carolina's historic action in becoming the first state to secede from the Union. To an audience assembled at the Athenaeum, the Reverend J. L. Rogers of First Presbyterian Church asked God's protection from "the assaults of our adversaries." Howell Cobb, a former congressman, governor, and U.S. secretary of the treasury, then spoke. Cobb pronounced the Union "gone forever" and emphasized economic arguments, building the case as others had done previously based on the South's disproportionate contribution to U.S. exports and the federal government's alleged pattern of discrimination against the region. His speech was followed by others and then by a torchlight procession that stretched a full mile in length. Fireworks and Roman candles ended the festivities, along with the burning of Abraham Lincoln's effigy at the Planters' Hotel. In the coming days, Congressman Gartrell and Senator Toombs sent letters and telegrams supporting secession. The outgoing mayor, William Ezzard, added his own benediction to disunion and paid homage to the end of the year by endorsing secession in a public letter on December 31.[47]

When Georgians went to the polls to elect delegates to the state secession convention on January 2, 1861, it became clear that advocates for southern independence had done their job effectively. Atlanta Unionists warned Stephen A. Douglas in December that momentum was shifting toward secession in the Gate City, and Douglas telegraphed in response, "Don't give up the ship. Don't despair of the Republic." Unionists, now known as cooperationists, fielded a slate of candidates. The cooperationists included diehard Unionists and those who questioned whether political differences over slavery made sectional division inevitable. In Atlanta, their slate of candidates included the respected attorney James Calhoun. But there was no stopping the secession movement in Atlanta. Statewide, the vote between secessionists and cooperationists was extremely close, but in Atlanta candidates John Alexander, Joseph P. Logan, and Luther J. Glenn defeated their opponents handily, winning a combined total of 2,859 (66 percent) to their opponents' 1,461

(34 percent). Everyone was to remember the election for the torrential rains that did not discourage local voters from braving the elements. The *Daily Intelligencer* interpreted the storm as symbolic—"The stream of Secession rolled in"—and saw more symbolism several days later when a mild earthquake rattled the city. The *Intelligencer* suggested that the ten-second quake represented the nation's political convulsions, and the beautiful, clear sky that followed it revealed Georgia's bright future outside of the Union.[48]

On January 16, 1861, delegates from around the state gathered in the capital of Milledgeville to debate and vote on the issue of secession. Slaveowners literally dominated the proceedings, for the number of delegates per county was based on the legislative-congressional formula that granted seats based on the white population plus three-fifths of the slave population. While only one in three Georgians owned slaves, more than four-fifths of convention delegates did.[49]

As they had on previous occasions, secessionists outmaneuvered their opponents through a combination of political skill and popular momentum. They chose a former Whig and Unionist Eugenius Nisbet to introduce the secession resolution, knowing that Nisbet's standing with moderates would be persuasive. Hershel Johnson then countered with a proposal that called for an alternative to secession: a meeting of slave state representatives in Atlanta to focus on ways to guarantee rights for slaveowners. Johnson's resolution went nowhere, in part because cooperationists had no neighbors left with whom to cooperate: Alabama, Mississippi, and Florida had followed South Carolina by seceding from the Union. Moreover, following the lead of Governor Brown, who on January 3, 1861, had seized Fort Pulaski on the Georgia coast, other southern governors launched efforts to rid federal forts of U.S. Army troops. In the lower South, momentum clearly lay with those favoring secession. When Alexander Stephens seemed unable or unwilling to mount an effective response to the secessionists, support for Union among the delegates began to collapse. The first vote on secession was close, 166 to 130, but changing loyalties led to a second vote of 208 to 89. With this vote, Georgia became the fifth state to leave the Union.[50]

When news of the Milledgeville convention's prosecession vote reached Atlanta, the city responded with a demonstration that lacked the intensity of December's spectacles but nonetheless involved the firing of rockets, the noise from which could be heard in surrounding rural areas. Secessionists illuminated hotels, houses, the passenger depot, and the offices of the *Atlanta Intelligencer*. In the event of war, the *Intelligencer* predicted that the U.S.

Army of barely twelve thousand would be no match for the two hundred thousand "brave volunteers" the South could easily muster.[51]

After the secession celebrations ended, Atlanta faced a more sobering reality, for Georgia's decision to leave the Union ended the consensus among Atlanta's political-business elite about the path forward for themselves and their city. Unionists led by William Markham and Nedom Angier continued to believe that future prosperity could be achieved only in the American Union. Secessionists including Sidney Root and Richard Peters now endorsed separation and independence. Although the election of a prosecession mayor, Jared Whitaker, provided another powerful voice for the independence movement, many Atlantans wondered whether a majority of citizens would support independence if it meant military service and potential loss of life. Alexander Wallace commanded the Atlanta Grays, one of several military units recruiting and training men locally. Wallace felt "humiliated" by the need to quell rumors that members of his unit had failed to show a proper level of enthusiasm for defending the state in the event of war. Calling his men a "gallant band of volunteer forces," Wallace assured Atlantans that he and they stood ready to fight the Yankees "in the event of a collision with the Northern States." Nonetheless, not every Atlantan stood ready to defend his state and region. Warren Campbell was a young professional who had moved to Atlanta from Hall County in north Georgia, seeking to make his fortune as had so many others during the previous decade. In letters home, Campbell made clear that he had no taste for war and did not wish to fight in the event that war came to the South. Declining to participate in secession-related public displays, he wrote to his father, "I hope we will not have war for I am certain I do not want to go."[52]

Moreover, economic travails continued to press Atlantans, a topic for worry as winter set in. Warren Campbell marveled at the high prices for basic goods in Atlanta's shops, complaining that shoes cost as much as $11.00 a pair and asking his father to send him cheaper shoes if he could find them in north Georgia. Campbell complained as well about paying $19.00 per month for room, board, and laundry at a local boardinghouse. Atlanta's underclass, already squeezed by a weak harvest and correspondingly high grain prices, faced even bleaker prospects in winter. In response to a call for local actors to organize a benefit for the poor, the *Daily Intelligencer* argued instead that wealthy Atlantans should be taxed so that "the *parsimonious* rich . . . will be compelled to contribute his quota, as well as the *liberal* man in moderate circumstances."[53]

Having cast their lot for secession, Atlanta's mayor and City Council moved quickly to establish the Gate City's place in the emerging southern nation. On January 11, 1861, more than a week before the secession vote in Milledgeville, the City Council passed a resolution. Whereas "it is now manifest that the Cotton State[s] will secede from the Union," and understanding that delegates would soon meet to form a government, the Council suggested there was "no place possessing more advantages or more appropriate for such a meeting than the City of Atlanta," given its central location, rail access, and abundant hotel rooms. The governor of each southern state received a copy of this resolution. When Confederate states rejected their suggestion, meeting instead in Montgomery, Alabama, the Council voted to send a delegation to the convention with the aim of selling Atlanta as an ideal location to become the permanent "Capital of the Southern Republic." The *Gate City Guardian* took up the cause and published a lengthy article extolling Atlanta's virtues while denigrating Montgomery's. Atlanta's railroads provided unparalleled access for people and markets. Its abundant iron ore, coal, and timber made it ideal for government building purposes. Its access to fresh produce, chickens, and eggs could not be matched by Montgomery. Complaining about Montgomery's hot summers, the *Guardian* insinuated that yellow fever and cholera were more prevalent there.[54]

Jennie Lines followed events in the secession winter of 1860–61 by considering the speeches of its principal partisans. Her husband Sylvanus read aloud to her a pro-Union speech of Alexander Stephens. She admired Stephens's reasoned and dispassionate approach, but the passionate oratory of Howell Cobb, the fiery secessionist who had anchored the December demonstration, impressed her deeply. Sylvanus and Jennie Lines struggled to get ahead in Atlanta's tough economy, with what they thought were unreasonably high living costs. Ultimately, Sylvanus Lines decided the couple should move to Greenville, Georgia, in order to seek a business opportunity in the printing business. Jennie disagreed with her husband's decision, for she was eager to make Atlanta her permanent home, and because she had just taken a first step toward domestic stability by joining a local church. But nineteenth-century social mores dictated that Jennie's duty was to defer to her husband's wishes, and she did so, albeit reluctantly. Ultimately, the couple did not thrive in Greenville, and returned to Atlanta. When they came back, they found the Gate City transformed by war, and Jennie wrote in her diary about the myriad challenges of daily living in the wartime city.[55]

3. The Rise of a Confederate City

During the winter and spring of 1861, public sentiment favoring Confederate nationalism solidified in Atlanta. Diehard Unionists remained a small though important presence, but many Atlantans, caught up in a wave of patriotic sentiment that swept the city, cast their lot with the new Confederacy. Political speeches, departure ceremonies for military units, newspaper editorials, and public theatricals all played roles in this process, which played out in communities across the South. "Most Southern whites seemed willing, if not eager, to turn their back on the Union in favor of the new nation," one historian has written, "and to do so with nary a backward glance."[1]

On February 4 representatives of seven seceded states met in Montgomery, Alabama, to form a new nation, the Confederate States of America. After drafting a constitution, delegates elected Jefferson Davis of Mississippi as provisional president and Georgia's Alexander Stephens as vice president. Both leaders visited Atlanta, with Davis arriving first. A West Point graduate and Mexican War veteran, Davis served during the 1850s in the U.S. Senate, where he established a reputation as a national spokesman for southern rights but not a secessionist. His election to the presidency signaled that moderate voices, not radical ones, would dominate the new government. Notified of his election, Davis traveled to Montgomery accompanied by a delegation that included Atlanta businessman Sidney Root. The Atlantan described Davis as "the finest and most magnetic speaker I ever heard."[2]

Davis appeared in Atlanta on the morning of Saturday, February 16, 1861, and spoke from the balcony of the Trout House Hotel, flanked by Mayor Jared Whitaker and former Congressman Lucius Gartrell. He told a crowd estimated at five thousand that nationhood and especially economic independence were the South's destiny, for southern cotton "clothed the world." Davis believed the Confederacy might expand its borders to include islands in the Caribbean, even sections of northern Mexico. Listeners knew that Davis's rhetoric about new territories included slavery's possible spread into these areas. He concluded by trumpeting the "Free Trade" theme, insisting that the South had much to gain by trading directly with the rest of the world instead of with the Yankees in Boston.[3]

Alexander Stephens visited Atlanta in March. Chosen by the Montgomery convention to be the Confederacy's provisional vice president in part because he had been a reluctant secessionist, Stephens made an appearance in Atlanta after first traveling to Savannah, where on March 7 he joined other Georgia delegates in ratifying the Confederate Constitution. His "cornerstone of the Confederacy" speech at Savannah revealed how completely he now allied himself with secessionists he had once opposed. He drew a stark contrast between North and South. Northerners claimed that "all men are created equal," Stephens said, but southerners had founded a government whose "cornerstone rests upon the great truth, that the negro is not equal to the white man; that slavery—subordination to the superior race—is his natural and normal condition." In Atlanta a few days later, Stephens gave a speech that emphasized the "unselfish patriotism" of those dedicated to Confederate nationalism, the virtues of the new constitution, including a two-thirds vote needed for appropriations from the treasury, and the possibility for the Confederacy to expand westward in the absence of northern opposition. Stephens told Atlantans that peaceable separation from the North could be achieved. Privately, after listening to telegraphic reports of Abraham Lincoln's inaugural address, he told Sidney Root that he believed war was likely.[4]

The formation and recruitment of military units provided Atlanta men with opportunities to show their support for Confederate nationalism, and the elaborate farewell ceremonies that accompanied their departure for military service solidified civilian support for the Confederate cause. A dozen new units formed by the end of 1861, with bounties offered as inducements. Some of these units lacked weapons, horses, and other equipment.

Soldiers were expected to provide their own uniforms, though local women came forward to stitch uniforms in the early months of the war.[5]

The departure festivities for the Gate City Guard served as a model for other such ceremonies, though few would match this one in drama, spectacle, and citizen turnout. Founded in 1857 as a militia company, the Gate City Guard included representatives of Atlanta's "best element," according to its 1915 official history. Partly for this reason, the Guard was "a favorite Company with our citizens," as the *Daily Intelligencer* put it. After months of training, the Guard left Atlanta on April 2, 1861, destined for Pensacola, Florida, where an assault was planned against Fort Pickens, still in federal hands.[6]

Members of the Guard impressed all who saw them. They wore dark blue uniforms embellished with epaulettes and gold trim. Their distinctive black hats modeled the French shako, including a white plume cascading from the high crown. One year earlier, in April 1860, a group of Atlanta women had presented the Guard with an enormous silk flag measuring six by four and a half feet. Josephine Hanleiter was chosen to present the flag because her father, Cornelius Hanleiter, was an important businessman, owner of Franklin Printing, and onetime member of the Gate City Guard and the City Council. On behalf of the women, Josephine Hanleiter gave an address in which she declared: "May the day never, never arrive when either of the stripes, representing the glorious 'Old Thirteen' shall be sundered from their blood-cemented companionship." In 1861, the blood-cemented companionship of states had been sundered.[7]

In April 1861, Josephine Hanleiter again presented the Gate City Guard with a flag, reworking the original flag by replacing the stars and stripes with seven stars to represent the Confederacy and adding the Latin phrase "In Hoc Signo Vinces" (by this sign you shall conquer). With war looming, Atlantans held to traditional notions about women being removed from military confrontation, protected by menfolk, and relegated to the periphery of the political sphere. The sendoff ceremonies for the Gate City Guard reinforced these notions. Josephine Hanleiter presented Captain William L. Ezzard with the newly reconfigured flag, but this time she did not make a speech. In keeping with social norms decreeing that on momentous occasions, men gave speeches and women presented flags, a military officer spoke "on the part of the ladies." He emphasized traditional themes: the North tried to force racial equality on the South; the South rightly believed that "the Black Race are, and should be, our Slaves"; the North forced Georgia to "resume our sovereignty"; and "the Union was dissolved by them." The Gate City Guard then presented a gold watch to Miss Hanleiter, one that carried a symbolic message. On one side, the watch had thirteen jewels to represent the American colonies that had declared their independence from British tyranny; on the other were seven jewels to represent the original southern states that declared independence from the "Irrepressible-Conflict-Rail-Splitter," a reference to the newly inaugurated president, Abraham Lincoln.[8]

The 104 members of the Guard left Atlanta, after girls from a local private school presented each of them with a miniature flag made by the presenter. Sallie Clayton, a teenager from a prominent local family, recalled the "very large crowd" gathered at the passenger depot to wish the Guard Godspeed. Crowds gathered in many other places as well. With cannons booming in the background, an estimated that seven thousand citizens waved and cheered from the Trout House, the Atlanta Hotel, and every other public venue in Atlanta as the Guard and several other military companies boarded a special thirteen-car train.[9]

Less than two weeks later, the Civil War began when Confederates led by General P. G. T. Beauregard began firing at Fort Sumter, the U.S. Army's military installation in the harbor at Charleston, South Carolina. The Union presence in this and other federal installations located in seceded states was a thorn in the side of southerners, and the Davis administration decided to take military action against the garrison. Shelling of Fort Sumter began on the morning of April 12, after its commander refused to surrender. The following day he did so after more than a day of shelling. Under the headline "War at Last," the *Southern Confederacy* (né the *Gate City Guardian*) provided a series of reports, touting its ability to showcase telegraphic technology in battlefield reporting.[10]

Sarah Massey, the wife of a local doctor and an active congregant at Atlanta's Second Baptist Church, heard the news while attending a political meeting at which Francis Bartow was the featured speaker. A former state legislator from Savannah and currently a member of the Confederate Provisional Congress, Bartow advocated for military preparedness in the face of probable war. In the middle of his remarks, a gentleman interrupted the speech by whispering a few words to Bartow and with his permission proceeded to read a telegraph he had just received to the audience. "The war had commenced," Massey recalled. "The house went wild; there was tossing of hats and waving of handkerchiefs." William Barnes, who directed a group of local thespians called the Atlanta Amateurs, ended the program with a song that he improvised to the tune of "Jordan Is a Hard Road to Travel." It ended with: "Pull off your coat and roll up your sleeves / For secession is a hard road to travel, I believe." Francis Bartow immediately resigned from the Confederate Congress, entered the military, and raised a Confederate regiment, the 8th Georgia, serving as its colonel.[11]

Sarah Huff, a child who was to turn five years old a month after the event, remembered vividly her family's reaction to Fort Sumter when she wrote a memoir in the 1930s. The Huff family lived a few miles north of the Atlanta city limits, on Marietta Road. Sarah's mother, Elizabeth, first heard news of war and summoned her husband, Jerry, in from the fields by blowing a trumpet. A neighbor then joined the family to discuss the military events late into the evening. Sarah also recalled her father's decision to join the military, and her mother's hard work stitching uniforms, the dining table covered in gray wool cloth. Mrs. Huff sewed the uniforms by hand because "sewing machines were unknown" in her household. Sarah's father had a photograph made of his wife and children and carried it with him to war.[12]

In 1860, Atlanta's newspapers had played a vital role in building support for secession; in 1861 they played an equally important role in preparing civilians for war. They continued to print stories emphasizing the South as victim of an overreaching North, and also emphasized slavery's alleged benefits to the state and region. The *Gate City Guardian*, which soon changed its name to the *Southern Confederacy*, boldly proclaimed "A Slave Republic" in an editorial on February 23, 1861. "The institution of African Slavery produced the Secession of the Cotton States," the *Guardian* declared. "If it had never existed, the Union of the States would, to-day, be complete. But, by the existence of African Slavery in the Southern States, civilization has arrived at a degree of perfection equal to that of any age in the history of the world."[13]

The *Daily Intelligencer* pressured men to enlist in the Confederate Army. The *Intelligencer* was especially scathing toward "men of wealth in Atlanta," accusing those who had prospered during good times of wanting to "lie down on soft couches, live on the fat of the land, and enjoy perfect security during this grand Revolution which is upon us." Vice President Alexander Stephens stopped in Atlanta en route to Montgomery shortly after Fort Sumter's fall and gave an impromptu speech at the passenger depot. Stephens told the assembled crowd that the South would not be subdued, even in light of Lincoln's post-Sumter call for volunteer troops. Stephens, who once publicly claimed there would be no war at all, now predicted it would be over quickly.[14]

Both newspapers drew parallels between the Confederate States and the patriots of 1776. New nations need patriotic narratives around which to explain their origins, create an identity, and win foreign recognition. Confederates looked to the American Revolution, believing themselves heirs of the Revolutionary generation, true keepers of the republican ideals that had inspired the Founding Fathers. According to this reasoning, what the Founders began in the 1770s, the Confederacy would perfect. A sendoff ceremony honoring the Atlanta Grays reveals the way this process played out in the Gate City during May 1861. Sponsored by the Atlanta Amateurs and held at the Athenaeum, the festivities began with a dramatic "battle" between the character of Yankee Doodle and the character of Dixie in which the badly defeated Doodle "hustled off the stage in disgrace." As told by the *Southern Confederacy*, an enthusiastic audience of Atlantans packed the hall and cheered as the Confederate flag was waved in salute to the triumphant Dixie. Following the presentation of a flag stitched by local women, Captain Thomas Cooper spoke for the men in his company. "We go to defend the same rights, principles and laws that were consecrated and made sacred by the blood of the Revolution," he said. The Grays would journey to Virginia, home of George Washington, "a land in which Liberty must forever live and flourish, and where tyranny must sicken and die." Atlantans who did not attend this event had opportunities to read about it in the local newspapers.[15]

Later that month, the *Atlanta Daily Intelligencer* reported on the progress of military recruitment in Atlanta. In addition to the Gate City Guard and the Atlanta Grays, another thousand men from Fulton County organized into companies and prepared for war. One company was called the Free Trade Rifles, an indication of the city's interest in the European trade issue. The newspaper suggested that Fulton's success made it a model for the rest of Georgia and concluded by invoking a familiar theme: "Let us look to the fathers and mothers of the American Revolution, and from them gather an example worthy of imitation." They fought "for the cause of freedom."[16]

After the shooting war began at Fort Sumter, Atlanta's business community stepped up its efforts to establish direct trading partnerships with European nations, notably Britain and France. Their efforts followed the official policy of the Confederate government, which actively encouraged

economic ties with Europe. As chairman of the Committee on Foreign
Affairs for the Confederate Congress, Robert Barnwell Rhett of South
Carolina, a leading prewar fire-eater, argued that Britain should be encouraged to recognize Confederate independence by receiving most-favored-
nation status and the promise of import duties no higher than 15–20 percent
for twenty years. Rhett knew that Britain needed southern cotton to sustain
its textile industries, which led him to conclude that Britain's opposition to
slavery was superficial. But Rhett's ability to influence diplomatic policy
proved to be limited, for he failed to win appointment as secretary of state,
which Jefferson Davis gave to Georgia's Robert Toombs.[17]

In March, Davis sent to England a diplomatic team consisting of William
Lowndes Yancey, Pierre Rost, and Ambrose D. Mann and charged them
with winning British recognition of the Confederacy, then moving on to
France, Belgium, and Russia to achieve the same outcome. Yancey, an
Alabaman whose reputation as a radical secessionist made him an unlikely
candidate to be a successful diplomat, headed the mission and held the title
Commissioner to Europe. The *Daily Intelligencer* called the diplomatic team
"The European Embassy." Davis did not empower the diplomats to solicit
foreign aid or negotiate treaties, since no one anticipated that the Confederate
independence movement would be a protracted one. On May 13, Britain's
Queen Victoria announced her nation's official policy of neutrality, which
the Lincoln administration feared would allow the Confederacy to borrow
money and to purchase military hardware from Britain. Privately, William
Lowndes Yancey wrote to his brother Ben, an Atlanta resident, assuring him
that the British public favored the Confederacy.[18]

Atlanta's political leaders moved quickly to secure the city's place in the
new international order. During the Montgomery convention, the Atlanta
City Council directed Sidney Root, S. B. Robson, and Francis Shackleford to
represent the city in requesting that Atlanta become a port of delivery for
foreign goods. The Provisional Confederate Congress granted this request
in March, and Shackleford became collector of customs for the city of
Atlanta. The Gate City was port of entry and delivery for an area that encompassed north Georgia.[19]

The Confederate Congress approved a tariff in March that did not create
free trade but was nonetheless considerably lower than the Morrill Tariff
passed by the United States Congress. The *Daily Intelligencer* compared the
Confederacy's tariff to the "model" tariff of 1857, in contrast to the

protectionist "blundering and pernicious enactment" passed by the North. The newspaper forecast European recognition of the Confederacy on this basis, for Europe needed southern cotton, and the Morrill Tariff was "the surest means of grinding down and subjugating the poor, laboring classes."[20]

Having cast their lot in favor of secession, Atlanta's business community moved forward to build manufacturing in the Gate City. One area of interest was textile manufacturing. In February 1861, a group calling itself the Direct Trade and Cotton Spinners' Convention met in Atlanta. Its goal was to encourage the manufacture of textiles for export to France, Germany, Belgium, Switzerland, and Russia. Britain was not mentioned, perhaps because businessmen feared competition from or alienation of a country the Confederacy needed to have on its side. Delegates heard an address from C. G. Baylor of Texas, a former U.S. consul in Manchester, who emphasized that "separate political existence, unaccompanied by financial and commercial independence, was but the shadow without the substance of liberty."[21]

The Cotton Spinners met again in March. They organized formally as the Manufacturing and Direct Trade Association of the Confederate States, electing William Gregg of South Carolina as president and making plans to move forward by securing a loan from "Foreign Bankers" to allow "a cash advance on all shipments of cotton yarns, with guarantee of proceeds or balances of sales." The Cotton Spinners hoped to hire an agent to help jump-start European sales. A delegate named A. V. Brumby noted that unless Cotton Spinners could import the necessary machinery from Europe, it would be futile to expect a textile industry to develop in the Confederacy. Subsequently, the delegates voted to request that Congress allow the duty-free importation of such equipment.[22]

Governor Joseph E. Brown, a vigorous spokesman for secessionism long before the war started, moved quickly to help the state's economic situation by attempting to enforce the Sequestration Act, legislation passed by the Confederate Congress that prohibited southerners from paying debts owed to northern creditors. This law made the Confederate government the recipient of debts owed by southerners to citizens of the United States. However, Brown issued a proclamation on April 26 whereby he attempted to redirect such money to the state treasury. The text of the Sequestration Act appeared on the front page of the *Daily Intelligencer* for weeks. It stated that creditors would be paid in full at the end of the war when the Confederacy had established its independence free of military hostilities.[23]

Atlanta's business community remained hopeful that the Gate City might become the Confederacy's permanent capital, so it came as a great disappointment when the Confederate Congress announced in May its decision to abandon Montgomery, Alabama, but to relocate to Richmond, Virginia, not to Atlanta. Richmond's economic advantages included its larger population, correspondingly higher numbers of hotels and boardinghouses, and its importance as an iron manufacturing center. The *Daily Intelligencer* called the choice of Richmond "a good move" because of the need for the seat of government to be near the likely military front, in Virginia. The newspaper held out the hope that the move might be temporary. Nonetheless, the *Daily Intelligencer* urged Atlantans to press their case for free trade when Congress reconvened in July and to insist on a separate department to handle foreign trade.[24]

Sidney Root and John Beach took leadership roles in Atlanta's direct trade movement. In Atlanta, Root became head of a group calling itself the Chamber of Commerce of Atlanta, Georgia, Confederate States of America, and undertook to correspond with similar groups in European countries. In a letter he planned to circulate internationally, Root explained the "impracticality and hopelessness of any future union" between the North and South, and also explained the need to achieve "commercial, while asserting . . . political independence." By necessity, the southern states previously had traded through the port of New York. However, the independent South would now use southern ports. He claimed that Confederate tariffs would not exceed 15 percent, while United States tariffs averaged 59 percent. Moreover, Root wanted foreign capitalists to know that the South intended to grow cotton and to manufacture it. Last, Root gave a pitch for Atlanta, with its fine climate, its central location within the Confederacy, and its burgeoning population, which he said was fourteen thousand. "The Atlanta Chamber of Commerce would be glad to open a correspondence with your body," Root said in closing. The *Daily Intelligencer* editorialized that merchants should form mercantile associations in every town in Georgia.[25]

Meanwhile, John Beach busied himself representing the firm of Beach and Root in Europe. "The well-known firm of Beach & Root is the first one in this city that has taken this first material step towards mercantile independence," the *Daily Intelligencer* announced on April 24, 1861, following this article with a lengthy letter from a "Southern merchant abroad," signed "B," presumably John Beach. The Atlanta dry goods merchant reported that he had held meetings in London, Liverpool, and Manchester, where he encountered sympathetic listeners. "They don't like the negro," he wrote, referencing the institution of slavery, "but they do like the cotton." "B" assured readers that a single military victory would ensure British recognition of the Confederacy.[26]

By early July, the *Daily Intelligencer* sounded less optimistic about the free trade utopia it had been promising for months. Britain's decision to take a neutral position on the American conflict ended any immediate hope that its navy would aid the South in breaking the U.S. naval blockade, begun by Lincoln in April and rapidly tightening around the southern coastline. The newspaper nonetheless reminded readers, "It is all we ought to expect or desire," for neutrals could trade freely with the South so long as ships did not contain contraband of war. However, when southern cotton planters began participating in a voluntary embargo of cotton exports in an effort to force Britain's hand, the *Daily Intelligencer* responded forcefully that such a threat could "plunge Europe into a civil revolution. Such threats at such a time are out of place. . . . We have enough on our hands without provoking a war with France, Spain and England. Our policy with Europe is not war and bluster, but peace and free trade."[27]

The following week, the *Daily Intelligencer* sounded an alarm, predicting "Danger Ahead" in a column devoted to foreign relations. The newspaper suggested that the South's position was weakening. The North had consuls in every major European city who were busily undermining the Confederacy's position. European nations believed the South intended to use cotton as a threat against them. The Confederacy must assure European governments that the South would not withhold cotton as a form of diplomatic blackmail to force the recognition issue and must state that all foreign goods entering southern ports should be exempt from tariffs. The *Southern Confederacy* took the opposite view, editorializing in favor of using cotton as a diplomatic tool and suggesting that only by withholding cotton would the Confederacy bring Britain into the war on its side.[28]

Public attention soon turned away from foreign policy and toward the military front. On July 21, the Confederacy won a victory at the battle of Manassas, after southern soldiers routed a federal force sent by President Lincoln to put down the incipient rebellion. The battle occurred outside the nation's capital near Bull Run Creek in Virginia, and the victory sent federal soldiers scurrying back toward Washington, D.C.[29]

The 7th and 8th Georgia regiments saw action in the battle. Former Congressman Lucius Gartrell had organized the 7th, winning election as its colonel. The 7th included Company B from Fulton County, Georgia. The Atlanta Grays became part of the 8th Georgia, commanded by Francis Bartow, the man who had appeared at the Athenaeum when news of Fort Sumter reached the city. During the battle, both regiments fought valiantly but suffered significant casualties. Bartow was mortally wounded, his last words "They have killed me, boys, but never give up the fight."[30]

Combat deaths at the battle of Manassas were slight compared with later battles, but shocking nonetheless for Americans on both sides of the conflict: 460 federal and 387 Confederate dead, in addition to several thousand wounded. When news reached Atlanta, the newspapers announced "Glorious Victory" and "Georgia has covered herself with glory!!" but the next day came news of casualties. Those from the 8th Georgia's Atlanta Grays were listed by name in the *Daily Intelligencer* on July 24: thirteen dead and seventeen wounded. Having left Atlanta to such fanfare less than two months previously, the Grays suffered some of the first casualties of war. Two weeks later, the *Daily Intelligencer* advertised for twenty-five men of "sound body and good character" to join the Grays.[31]

The 7th Georgia lost 19 killed and 134 wounded. Among the dead was sixteen-year-old Henry Clay Gartrell from Atlanta, son of Lucius Gartrell. A soldier since May 31, Henry Gartrell received a serious wound during the battle and died one week later. Colonel Gartrell, who suffered a slight leg wound, nonetheless walked more than ten miles to Warrenton, to be at the deathbed of his son. The war that Lucius Gartrell had done so much to bring about now extracted an enormous personal toll. In later years, he could not hear the boy's name without losing composure. William Watkins, a member of the Atlanta City Council, also lost a son in battle, Private Benjamin M. Watkins. City Council minutes record the solemn news that William Watkins would meet the Western and Atlantic train on August 11 to receive the remains of his son. Thereafter, the City Council made plans to transfer home for burial the bodies of Atlanta men killed in the war.[32]

For white people in the South, the victory at Manassas seemed ample indication that God favored their cause. On June 13, 1861, Jefferson Davis called upon all Confederate civilians to observe a day of fasting and prayer. In accordance with the president's edict, the *Daily Intelligencer* closed its offices and issued no newspaper for the following day. The Reverend Henry Hornady of First Baptist Church gave a sermon emphasizing what he called the "righteousness" of slavery and of the southern cause. Other ministers gave similar orations. Fasting days represented a vehicle through which people could build a national identity by coming together and giving religious meaning to the war. This was the first of ten fast days Davis announced during the war, while Abraham Lincoln designated just three. Some southerners interpreted military victory at Manassas as a direct outcome of southerners' collective prayers on June 13. Throughout the region, newspapers invoked God's name in announcing the victory at Manassas, the *Southern Confederacy* stating, "God has most signally favored us, and vindicated our [cause] in the eyes of the world."[33]

The Independence Day holiday called into question whether Confederates should celebrate a holiday for a nation to which they were no longer connected. While the *Daily Intelligencer* believed southerners had greater claim than northerners to the legacy of the patriots of 1776, insisting that the North with its "bloody hands" should refrain from invoking the Founders, nonetheless Atlantans by and large did not celebrate July 4 during this and subsequent years of the war. In 1863, the *Daily Intelligencer* editorialized in favor of February 22—George Washington's birthday—as Confederate independence day.[34]

Schoolteacher Benjamin T. Hunter declined to celebrate in July 1861, writing in his diary without elaboration: "4th of July—no celebration." The twenty-six-year-old Hunter lived in nearby Lithonia but often made day trips to Atlanta with his wife, India, to shop and visit friends. In June he observed a "great many soldiers in Atlanta." A self-described secessionist, Hunter voted for disunion candidates to the secession convention in January and showed his personal devotion to the Confederacy by sewing flags for local regiments and painting a flag for the town of Lithonia, though he did not reveal where the flag appeared. A religious Baptist, he fasted on June 13, as President Davis requested.[35]

When Confederate forces engaged the Union at Manassas, Hunter wrote about "indefinite rumors from Virginia." Hunter read both of the city's daily newspapers in order to keep abreast of news in Atlanta, but neither the *Atlanta Daily Intelligencer* nor the *Southern Confederacy* had reporters on the Virginia battlefield. Subsequently, military news was slow to reach the Gate City and often came in the form of articles reprinted from the *Charleston Courier*, the *Richmond Examiner*, the *Savannah Republican*, and even on occasion the *New York Herald*, a news outlet that southerners preferred over other Yankee papers because its editorial slant favored the Democratic Party.

When it became clear that the Confederacy had won a "glorious" victory, an excited Hunter viewed "trophies" from Manassas provided by an acquaintance he identified as Lieutenant Hull that included "a Yankee overcoat, a pistol etc." He also toured a local foundry that made "rifling" cannon, one of the new technologies that would make the Civil War the deadliest war in which the United States ever engaged. In August, following the birth of Hunter's first child, a daughter named Fannie, he celebrated the momentous occasion by making her a little Confederate flag.[36]

The Gate City Guard, on which the city had lavished enormous attention, including the presentation of a splendid silk flag, did not fight at Manassas or enjoy the accompanying accolades bestowed on the Georgia units. Unsuccessful in efforts to seize Fort Pickens, the Guard received new orders that sent the unit to Virginia on June 1. Stopping in Atlanta on its way north, the Guard retrieved the new Springfield rifles that Governor Brown had insisted must remain in the state while they were stationed in Florida. Upon arriving in Virginia, the Guard, part of the 1st Georgia Regiment, was sent to Staunton, in the Shenandoah Valley, and assigned as rear guard to the soldiers of General Robert Garnett. On July 13, 1861, Union forces under William Rosecrans defeated Confederates at Corrick's Ford in western Virginia, with Garnett dying in the skirmish's aftermath.[37]

At some point, the Gate City Guard was cut off from other Confederate forces. With the proximity of Union troops raising the specter of being taken prisoner, the decision was made to scale the mountains. According to one soldier's letter to his wife, subsequently published in the *Southern Confederacy*, the Guard struggled through difficult mountainous terrain for four days. Unable to navigate their wagons up the steep inclines, the men pushed them off into the valley—and with them, the tents, blankets, and uniforms and hats so brilliantly displayed by the Guard in its April sendoff in Atlanta. The magnificent flag of Josephine Hanleiter also perished. After marching in rainy, mountainous terrain and experiencing what one soldier later described to his mother as "the horrors of hunger," they finally arrived at a hunter's cabin, where they obtained food for the first time since the ordeal began. Many subsequently died of fever or exposure. Several became deranged. Lieutenant Austin Leyden, the ranking officer of the separated group and subsequently promoted to major of light artillery, recruited some Gate City Guard members for a new battalion, but the Gate City Guard itself ceased to exist as a military unit, its one-year enlistees having served their terms of service.[38] Compared with the victory at Manassas, the Gate City Guard's pitiful story presented Atlantans with a stark contrast between the glamorous beginnings and the unglamorous reality of war.

Throughout the South, women played prominent roles during the spring of 1861 as seamstresses and presenters of military flags, but a growing number of women wanted to broaden their contributions to the Confederacy. In Atlanta, Maria Westmoreland took a leadership role in this effort. Westmoreland moved to Atlanta in 1857, when at age seventeen she became the bride of a prominent local doctor, Willis F. Westmoreland. By all accounts, Maria was beautiful and talented. As a student, she excelled in all subjects and hoped one day to become a writer, but like most southern girls she married young and began a family. Maria and Willis Westmoreland shared a passion for Confederate nationalism. They honored the first state to leave the Union by naming their daughter Carolina.[39]

Westmoreland convened a group of women for a preliminary meeting on April 17, 1861. The group determined to focus its efforts on scraping lint for bandages, since the lint that came from linen fabric was widely believed to be especially well suited for the treatment of wounds. The group quickly took up the job of sewing shirts and pants and knitting socks for soldiers, since neither the army nor the Confederate government supplied soldiers with clothing. Military officers and government officials often placed notices in the local newspapers asking women to supply a specific regiment. On May 29, 1861, Atlanta's quartermaster general, Ira Foster, requested that women meet at City Hall to prepare one hundred uniforms for soldiers preparing to leave for Virginia. Local firms Lawshe and Purtell and Ezzard and Greer provided tailors to cut the cloth, which was donated by clothier William Herring. Women supplied their own needles, since the uniforms would be hand-stitched. Sewing machines were in short supply.[40]

By July, Maria Westmoreland had begun to call her organization the Ladies' Soldiers' Relief Society. It recruited socially prominent women, including matrons such as Martha Winship, wife of the iron foundry owner, and Sarah Massey, like Westmoreland a doctor's wife. Many young women of high social standing also participated, including Emma and Ella Neal, whose father owned the finest home in town, and Caroline, Sallie, and Mary Clayton, whose father was a leading secessionist. Financial contributions began to roll in, and Westmoreland soon was proud to announce $176.30 in the treasury. In the aftermath of the battle of Manassas, requests for uniforms came in frequently, and women increased their stitching.[41]

Over time, members of the LSRS began corresponding with women in other parts of Georgia, who sent items to Atlanta for redistribution to the army. Mary Gay lived in nearby Decatur but visited Atlanta frequently during the war. Her circle of friends in Decatur worked with those in Atlanta, for she spoke of a "patriotic cooperation between the citizens of Decatur and Atlanta." Gay did so much relief work during the war that she later recalled, "I did not walk in those days, but ran." She set a personal goal for herself of knitting one sock per day for the soldiers. Mary W. Lewis of Cass County, age seventy-nine, was proud to donate a box of clothing she had made herself. "She desires the Society to distribute it as may seem best," according to the *Daily Intelligencer*, which added this message from Maria Westmoreland: "Let woman do her share; much she has done, much she can do. Sacrifices must be made and labors performed. Are we equal to these?"[42]

Both of Atlanta's daily newspapers gave ample space to the organization to highlight and encourage its efforts. In addition, the *Southern Confederacy* printed editorials ostensibly written by a woman calling herself "Ziola," promoting patriotism, self-sacrifice, and perseverance so that "our Southern Republic" might earn "praise among the nations." In one letter, Ziola advised women to be mindful of their grandmothers' Revolutionary heritage, to live frugally, to help the soldiers and the less fortunate, and to learn how to shoot a gun just in case.[43]

By the fall of 1861, members of the Ladies' Soldiers' Relief Society made hand-stitched uniforms for the Atlanta Grays, Davis Infantry, Fulton Dragoons, Stephens Rifles, Lewis and Phillips Rifles, and Atlanta Volunteers. The women hoped to raise money on a larger scale than collecting dues and asking for contributions, and they talked about holding a fund-raising fair at which members would appear in homespun in order to present an image of frugality and patriotism. In addition, they began to focus their interests locally, out of concern for the economic distress of soldiers' families. Dividing the city into its five wards, teams of women went door to door to learn whether families needed food, clothing, and fuel. Lemuel Grant's wife, Laura, toured the Third Ward and identified sixteen families containing small children. Sidney Root's wife, Mary, toured the Second Ward. By the end of 1861, the Ladies Soldiers' Relief Society could boast an active membership of 150 women and a commitment to helping the community and its locally organized military units.[44]

While Atlanta women organized as benevolent volunteers, Atlanta entrepreneurs began taking steps to increase production of materials needed for
the military. The company of J. M. Holbrook produced hats. In February
1861, before the war began, Holbrook had urged "every true Southerner" to
buy his locally made hats instead of ordering them from New York. By July,
he appealed directly to military companies for business. McNaught and
Ormond advertised their manufactory of buckles for use on knapsacks and
bridles. The Confederate Iron and Brass Foundry of Gallatt and Barnes
promised metal products "at the *shortest* notice."[45]

Governor Brown, an early and vigorous proponent of secession, now
became an equally vigorous proponent of military preparedness. Following a
gunsmiths' convention in Atlanta, Brown endorsed its recommendation to have
machine shops of the Western and Atlantic Railroad manufacture gun barrels.[46]

The *Southern Confederacy* and the *Daily Intelligencer* reported on efforts
to ramp up manufacturing in Atlanta. The *Daily Intelligencer* reported an
upswing in business at Winship Iron Works, which manufactured railroad
freight cars, wheels, and axles. Shops of the state-owned Western and
Atlantic continued to be the city's largest builder of passenger and freight
cars. Tanneries and shoe factories in Atlanta and nearby Decatur and Marietta
were "full of work and increasing their capacity." The *Intelligencer* concluded
with a familiar refrain about the need to "rescue and improve the legacy of
our Revolutionary Sires, from Northern fanaticism and vandalism." In
December, the *Intelligencer* elevated manufacturing to the level of military
glory: "He who engages in a useful branch of manufacture, fights and whips
the Yankees as effectually as he that marches to the field of battle with his rifle
and sabre." The newspaper added, "While bread must be made, clothing and
all munitions of war are equally necessary. Fat stomachs are poor things with
naked backs and defenceless arms." The *Southern Confederacy* echoed these
sentiments. Companies must "extend their limits and facilities, and throw out
their branches until every hamlet shall resound with the clack of the water-
wheel or the puff of the steam engine." The *Confederacy* predicted, "Nothing
but energy is required to render us entirely independent of the North."[47]

At the end of 1861, the Confederacy held elections to endorse or replace
those elected provisionally in Montgomery. Jefferson Davis and Alexander
Stephens won their elections without opposition. Lucius Gartrell decided to
leave the army and seek Atlanta's congressional seat, encouraged to do so by
those who thought he could be more effective in Congress than in the army. He

had performed credibly in the battle of Manassas but had lost his eldest son and his friend Francis Bartow, who was said to have died in his arms. On September 25, 1861, the *Daily Intelligencer* printed a letter from "A Wounded Soldier" who attested to Gartrell's qualifications based on his strong record in the vanguard of Georgia's secession movement and his bravery at Manassas. An opponent for the office alleged that Gartrell was ineligible for the race since the Confederate Constitution forbade anyone "holding any office under the Confederate States" from being a member of Congress. Gartrell's friends, including Robert Toombs, disputed that his position as army officer constituted office holding. The voters agreed. By a large margin, Gartrell won election to Georgia's Eighth District, defeating John H. Jones. Of the state's congressional delegation, his was the strongest public reputation. Congress convened on February 18, 1862.[48]

As fall gave way to winter, life in Atlanta went on as in prewar days. In December 1861, Mrs. J. M. Boring advertised hats for the fall season at her millinery shop on Whitehall Street. Jacob Land advertised for the return of a stray sorrel mule, offering a reward of $10, while B. F. Bennett advertised for the return of a "stray Negro," a mulatto boy named Henry, age ten, who had slipped away from his owner's home on McDonough Street.[49]

Yet Atlantans were beginning to feel the effects of the war. Soldiers from Atlanta had died in combat. Civilian men felt pressure to enlist, bombarded by newspaper ads promising bounties, politicians and clergy preaching civic duty, and schoolgirls waving flags and offering encouragement. A shop on Whitehall Street advertised a new product called the "metallic burial case," featuring a rubber, airtight top, presumably designed to withstand the Georgia heat in transporting battlefield casualties home for burial. On December 1, 1861, the *Southern Confederacy* reported that three hundred Yankee prisoners had stopped at the passenger depot on their way to prison in Alabama, a source of curiosity for Atlanta's Confederate civilians.[50]

Atlanta's women made the commitment to scrape lint, sew uniforms, and raise money. The *Southern Confederacy*'s Ziola continued to deliver advice to the Gate City's female population, assuring women that while they would probably never shoulder a gun, they must be prepared to spin and weave their own cloth, send male slaves to rural areas where they could increase production of food for the armies, and volunteer to help the soldiers. In this emerging vision of Confederate womanhood, the traditional role of women as nurturers of their families must now be secondary to their role in nurturing a political and military cause.[51]

Several key food items were already becoming scarce. One of them was salt. Alvin K. Seago's company sold salt locally. It had wells in Virginia and northern Alabama. By late summer, the *Southern Confederacy* reported that salt supplies were running low because military demands for salt were so high. The Seago Company advised Atlantans to buy as much as they could since the company made military needs its first priority. By fall, concerned about hoarding, Governor Brown insisted that Confederate soldiers in Atlanta, Macon, and Columbus seize salt being sold at prices above $5 per sack. Brown authorized Jared Whitaker, who had resigned as mayor to become commissary general of the Georgia Army, to provide rations of salt to civilians statewide. Two local businesses, Dodd and Brother on Whitehall Street and Hunnicut and Buice on Decatur Street, offered to sell half-bushel sacks of salt to the families of soldiers for $1.25.[52]

Coffee also made news. Imported from Central and South America and the Caribbean, its price rose as the Union blockade tightened. On July 6, 1861, the *Daily Intelligencer*, in an article about "war coffee," advised Atlantans to stretch their coffee supply by mixing grounds in equal measure with toasted cornmeal. The article suggested that the mix would not produce "anything peculiar in the taste." The arrival in Savannah of more than one thousand pounds of coffee via Cuba prompted an article in the *Daily Intelligencer* on December 24, 1861. The newspaper suggested that upcountry families have agents ready to purchase the much-desired commodity. Over time, coffee would become even harder to obtain.[53]

Atlanta's white residents worried about Unionists, Yankee spies, juvenile delinquents, and problems with their "Negroes." Barely a month after Fort Sumter, the *Daily Intelligencer* warned citizens of the Gate City to be on the lookout for spies. As a railroad hub, Atlanta was an obvious target for Union agents. "Be cautious and vigilant," the *Intelligencer* advised, suggesting that proprietors of hotels and boardinghouses, along with police, track down enemies of the Confederacy. The *Southern Confederacy* warned about Unionists, printing a story about a father and son in Tennessee executed by military authorities for burning a bridge. Their fate "should be a warning to others." The *Confederacy* also warned about the number of white boys who seemed to be congregating on Atlanta's streets and at the passenger depot, and suggested that these unchaperoned youths might become tempted by "dissipation and crime" if parents did not exercise more supervision.[54]

White people worried especially about rebellion by slaves. Stories appeared periodically in the newspapers reporting rumors of slave insurrections. On May 11, 1861, the *Intelligencer* reported on an alleged "diabolical plot" in Kingston, Georgia, in which an unnamed man was caught "tampering with negroes." One of the slaves was hanged, but the perpetrator's name was not yet known. "We cannot be too vigilant [in] these perilous times."[55]

Slaves made it a point to learn what they could about wartime conditions and take advantage of opportunities that became available to them. Despite private and public complaints by white people about slaves hiring out their time, the practice continued. Prince Ponder, one of Ellen Ponder's bondspeople, became a shopkeeper. With his owner's permission, he rented a small building in Atlanta, for which he paid $70 per month in rent. Ponder sold shoes, leather, corn, whiskey, "and anything else on which I could make any money." After the war, he claimed to have earned $100,000 from the proceeds of his store, paying Ellen Ponder varying monthly amounts but keeping most of the profits since he did not reveal to her how profitable his store actually had become.[56]

Subjected to a 9:00 P.M. nightly curfew, Atlanta's African Americans found an ingenious way to dodge the restriction. They held dances but called them fund-raisers for Confederate soldiers in order to circumvent the curfew and avoid suspicion. By the end of 1861, both newspapers editorialized against the practice. The *Daily Intelligencer* called the balls a "nuisance," and seemed to object, most of all, to the fact that "a *big buck* negro with a gold watch in his pocket, and a gold *chain* around his neck" acted as master of ceremonies. Two weeks later the *Intelligencer* backed down, noting that Negro balls were being held in other Confederate towns and that each of three such dances held in Atlanta had raised between $15 and $20. The *Southern Confederacy* condemned the balls unequivocally, calling them "an intolerable nuisance."[57]

The year 1861 ended with no clear resolution to the military situation. Nineteenth-century armies did not fight in winter; consequently, both sides regrouped and prepared for the coming spring campaign. The *Daily Intelligencer* printed an article on November 5 under the title "The War— How Long Will It Last?" Conceding that "a skirmish or two" would not bring about "compromise and peace" as many predicted, the newspaper speculated that European nations ultimately would become involved.[58]

Hopes for a direct trade network with Europe dimmed by year's end. The Confederacy was not well served by its diplomatic team, and it faced an uphill battle when pitted against an established U.S. network of diplomats and talented statesmen in Secretary of State William H. Seward and U.S. ambassador to Britain Charles Francis Adams. On December 6, 1861, the *Southern Confederacy* reported that Confederate Commissioner William Lowndes Yancey had spoken to a group called the Fishmongers' Company, lecturing about the importance of Confederate cotton and the right of self-determination. At the same time, it conceded that Ambassador Adams had spoken to a far more important audience of London officials at Guildhall.[59]

In the fall of 1861, following the resignation of Robert Toombs, the Confederacy's new secretary of state R. M. T. Hunter sent diplomats James Mason and John Slidell to Europe to replace Yancey and the others. Mason and Slidell were captured by the Union Navy as they attempted an Atlantic crossing in November, and the incident sparked an international controversy. The *Daily Intelligencer* carried the headlines: "Good News from Europe! England Indignant." Southerners hoped the ensuing diplomatic crisis would lead to British recognition of the Confederacy, if not outright intervention in the American war. Northerners celebrated the capture and imprisonment of the diplomats, while the government of Britain demanded their release under the terms of diplomatic immunity. The Lincoln administration faced a difficult decision, for it could either satisfy northern public opinion by holding the diplomats, or appease the British by letting them go. Wisely, Lincoln released the diplomats.[60]

In the end, the South's efforts to create a transatlantic free-trade zone collapsed, as did its efforts to use cotton as a weapon of diplomacy. Cotton diplomacy failed because of several dynamics. Liverpool warehouses had a surplus of cotton in 1861. Moreover, Britain had been importing cotton from India and Egypt dating back to the 1840s, and importation from these countries increased dramatically during the American conflict. Confederates failed to understand that Europe's economy, unlike its own, was multilayered, with the textile industry being but one aspect, albeit an important one. Finally, Britain imported wheat and corn from the United States, an indication that the Anglo-American economic connection was not limited to cotton.[61]

If Europe failed to become the South's military and economic savior, the South would have to win the war on its own. And in less than one year, prospects appeared bright that the Confederacy might prevail.

4. A City of Considerable Importance

When Savannah's former mayor Charles C. Jones, Jr., visited Atlanta in July 1862, he estimated its population to be seventeen thousand, nearly double what it had been before the war. In just over one year, Atlanta had become an important Confederate city, one that attracted thousands of new residents eager to find employment. The year 1862 marked a turning point in Atlanta's history, for the city soon garnered attention from leaders in Richmond and throughout the South because of its growing importance as a center for transportation, industry, and medical care. Locally, the war confronted Atlanta civilians at every turn. Financial opportunity attracted in-migration, but refugees, inflation, and poverty provided challenges. Nonetheless, Atlanta's value as a Confederate city was incontestable, and some local residents reacted with pride. One young woman who had grown up in the prewar period wrote, "Atlanta is a place of considerable importance now."[1]

Ironically, earlier in the year, Atlantans appeared to be losing enthusiasm for war. With fighting suspended during the winter months, military recruitment fell off even though newspapers emphasized the need for new recruits. A crescendo of voices questioned why Confederate military authorities failed to end the war by entering Washington, D.C., following the battle of Manassas the previous July. The *Southern Confederacy* felt the need to editorialize about the "reckless" men who had lodged this accusation, suggesting they were out of touch with reality. Attendance declined at meetings of the Ladies' Soldiers' Relief Society. On January 7, only 20 of 150 members showed up for a routine meeting at City Hall. Fund-raising also declined. The LSRS brought in only $6.30 in dues for the week of February 11.[2]

Events in the coming months changed the mood in Atlanta. In the early weeks of 1862, few local residents knew the name of Union general Ulysses S. Grant, but he was about to change Atlanta's history forever. A West Point graduate who had left the army in the 1850s, Grant returned to military service at the outset of the war and trained volunteer soldiers in Illinois. In January 1862, he marched them through Cairo, Illinois, and into Tennessee, where he proceeded to attack strategically important Fort Henry on the Tennessee River, then moved on to the more solidly fortified Fort Donelson on the Cumberland River north of Nashville. Fort Henry capitulated on February 6, while Fort Donelson fell to Grant on February 16, clearing the way for the federal army to capture the city of Nashville. Not only was Nashville the first Confederate state capital to fall into Union hands, but it was also an industrial center and like Atlanta a transportation hub. Moreover, Nashville was only 240 miles from Atlanta, linked directly to the Gate City by rail lines through Chattanooga. All of a sudden, a war that seemed remote when it was being fought in Virginia now appeared much closer to Atlantans.[3]

Local newspapers struggled to keep up with military news and often distorted reports about who was winning. On February 16, 1862, the *Southern Confederacy* claimed a "Glorious Victory" at Fort Donelson, later admitting, "The reports from Nashville and Fort Donelson have been as changeable as the wind," and finally lamenting, under the headline "An Outrage," that federal troops had entered Tennessee's capital.[4]

Local leaders moved quickly to prepare for a possible invasion of Georgia. James M. Calhoun won election as Atlanta's new mayor in January. An attorney by training and an opponent of secession, he had run unsuccessfully as a Unionist delegate to the secession convention. Now Calhoun embraced Confederate nationalism publicly, and "there was no better Confederate than he," one of his children later recalled. His sons William L. and James T. Calhoun served in the 42nd Georgia, one as captain and the other as private. An intelligent and reasonable man, Calhoun served ably as mayor for the rest of the war. On February 19, he convened a citizens meeting to discuss military preparedness. He appointed a committee of thirteen members, including many leading citizens, among them William Ezzard,

Joseph Winship, Edward E. Rawson, and George Adair, who now owned and edited the *Southern Confederacy* with J. Henly Smith. Calhoun charged them with creating plans that were "prudent, proper, effective, and necessary in view of present emergencies."[5]

Military events in Tennessee gave Atlanta another new identity. Already an emerging industrial center, Atlanta now became a hospital center. Hundreds of wounded and sick soldiers began arriving in the Gate City by rail. The *Southern Confederacy* noted the arrival of five hundred convalescents on February 25, 1862. L. T. Pim, assistant medical director for the army's Western Department, submitted an article for the local newspapers in which he announced that wounded soldiers would be under the local care of Dr. Willis Westmoreland. He also called for donations of blankets, pillows, clothing, bandages, brandy, and whiskey for the patients and announced the creation of a "Hospital store room" on Decatur Street, where Westmoreland and others could draw supplies as needed. Members of the Ladies' Soldiers' Relief Society staffed this room. Pim reminded Atlanta citizens that they had a responsibility to care for every Confederate soldier "no matter whence he came, or to what division of the army he is attached."[6]

On February 27, Pim issued a letter to Atlanta's citizens announcing that he was "organizing and conducting Hospitals for the sick and wounded" in Atlanta. Determined to establish order in a medical system that included a hodgepodge of public buildings and private homes, Pim issued another directive on March 17 that "sick and convalescent soldiers in private houses" be transferred to army hospitals. As the enormity of caring for wounded soldiers became apparent to Confederate authorities, Dr. Pim began to advertise locally for slaves to work in area hospitals. "We need quite a number of negroes—able-bodied men, and women without children—to serve in our Hospitals," he wrote. Pim asked that Atlantans and those in surrounding areas lease their "spare" slaves, and promised attractive wages to their masters in return. Although this ad appeared continuously, Atlantans inclined to lease their slaves often did so at more attractive wages than those offered by Confederate government hospitals.[7]

Pim hired white women to serve as matrons of these hospitals. Their jobs entailed carrying out doctors' orders, overseeing cleanliness in the wards, and making sure that individual patients received adequate care. In September 1862, the Confederate government standardized the pay scale of female medical professionals, with salaries of $40 per month for chief matrons, $35 for assistants, and $30 for ward matrons. Unfortunately, little documentary record survives to tell the story of Atlanta's matrons, but the name of one matron surfaced in newspaper stories from time to time. Margaret J. Murphy served as chief matron of Empire Hospital. Listed in the 1860 census as forty years old, Irish-born, and the wife of a laborer, the childless Murphy was the right age and marital status to be given a position of responsibility. On August 10, 1862, the *Southern Confederacy* noted her receipt of clothing sent by the Ladies Aid Society of LaGrange, Georgia. On March 20, 1863, an anonymous letter to the editor printed in the same newspaper applauded her hard work, selflessness, and dedication to the men in her care.[8]

With a growing number of wounded soldiers arriving in Atlanta, Martha Winship stepped forward to create a new women's benevolent association called the Atlanta Hospital Association. Winship came from one of Atlanta's most prominent families and was proud of her lineage. Born in 1813, Martha Cook Winship claimed to be the first white child born in Macon, Georgia, while her father, an army major, served at Fort Hawkins during the War of 1812. Married at age fourteen to Isaac Winship, she gave birth to twelve children, then moved with her family to Atlanta in the early 1850s, part of the vast influx of businessmen and industrialists who saw the promise of making money in a rising city. As coowner with his brother Joseph of the Winship Iron Works, Isaac Winship prospered and built his wife a large home north of the city center, surrounded by orchards, gardens, a springhouse, and a bathing pool. Mrs. Winship became a pillar of the congregation at Wesley Chapel Methodist Church. She arrived for weekly services as part of a family entourage and always wore a flowered silk dress over hoop skirts, a tasteful mantilla embellishing her hair. In the winter months, a slave named Sandy carried her foot stove into the church.[9]

Surviving photographs of Martha Winship present the image of a matronly woman with a serious countenance, but the photographs fail to uncover the essence of Martha Winship during the war: her incredible energy, her complete devotion to wounded soldiers in Atlanta's hospitals, and her understanding that nursing was the female equivalent of volunteering to fight. Described as small in stature but also as a "noble, stout-hearted woman," Martha Winship dedicated more than three years to caring for Confederate soldiers. She quickly recognized that Atlanta's hospital facilities did not come close to providing adequate space. Initially, soldiers received care at the Medical College, Gate City Hotel, Hayden's Hall, Grant's Hall, and Kile's

Hall. When these facilities filled up, military authorities left wounded men in tents near the passenger depot. Martha Winship addressed the problem by turning her home into a hospital, moving her family to the first floor and appropriating the entire second floor for wounded men, cramming as many cots as she could fit into its six rooms. With the help of slaves Sandy and Booker, she met incoming trains and transported wounded men to her home via the family carriage. Day and night, she cooked chickens in enormous wash pots to feed the soldiers in her care.[10]

After L. P. Pim discouraged private home care for soldiers, Martha Winship founded the Atlanta Hospital Association and began treating patients via the army's facilities. Although previously active in the LSRS, Winship preferred to create a separate society from among women in her Methodist congregation. Perhaps she also left the LSRS because she wanted to play a leadership role she was unlikely to obtain in the multidenominational society led by Maria Westmoreland. The two organizations shared a common goal of caring for wounded and ill soldiers, but they also shared a healthy rivalry. A third organization called the Saint Phillip's Hospital Aid Society played a smaller role. Its president, the local Episcopal clergyman Reverend A. F. Freeman, designated Mrs. E. B. Walker to serve as "Directoress." The women of First Baptist Church created a Dorcas Society, sewing clothing for soldiers, and its efforts garnered fewer stories in the local newspapers. When the colorful Maria Westmoreland resigned as president of the Ladies' Soldiers' Relief Society after giving birth to a child and was replaced by the competent but less colorful Henrietta Collier, the energetic and vibrant Martha Winship became Atlanta's undisputed doyenne of female benevolence.[11]

Martha Winship understood that volunteer nursing was an act of political partisanship. Like many of the volunteers who joined her Hospital Association, Winship had multiple family members in the Confederate military, including one son, four sons-in-law, and two brothers, one of them a general. She used military nomenclature to inspire women and often spoke to them like a military officer issuing orders. She told them, "You have all enlisted *for* the war" and commanded them to attend organizational meetings on Wednesday mornings. Atlanta women responded to Winship's efforts. In doing so, they gained satisfaction by knowing that their efforts helped wounded and ill men and contributed to the Confederate cause. Nurses also gained a sense of their individual self-worth, apart from their husbands and children. Given as many columns of newsprint as she needed, Winship saw to it that the *Daily Intelligencer* and the *Southern Confederacy* printed the names of individual women assigned to specific tasks, thereby giving public recognition to women whose names rarely if ever appeared in the newspapers before the war.[12]

Atlanta's hospitals and aid societies had treated an estimated thirty-five hundred soldiers when word reached the city that Union and Confederate Armies clashed at Shiloh, Tennessee, on April 6, 1862. Early reports in the *Daily Intelligencer* declared "Complete Victory," after Albert Sidney Johnston's Confederates caught Ulysses S. Grant and his federals off guard and pushed back his lines considerably. Although the *Intelligencer* noted the death of General Johnston, the newspaper continued to print stories about the alleged victory several days after Grant's army forced the Confederates back toward Corinth, Mississippi. In a small article on April 13, the newspaper also noted that Fort Pulaski off the Georgia coast had fallen into Union control but expressed confidence that Savannah "will be defended successfully." The *Southern Confederacy* blamed Pulaski's loss on "the stupidity and folly which have marked the defenses of our coast," insisting that the fort should have been abandoned and its guns moved elsewhere.[13]

In the aftermath of the battle of Shiloh, Martha Winship announced that a new group of wounded would soon "be sent hither to take the places of those who have been restored to health and returned to the post of duty," and Atlanta's hospital volunteers needed to be prepared. Winship urged women in surrounding areas of the South to ship their "Hospital stores" to Atlanta for distribution to areas where the need was greatest. She then proceeded to list the names of individual donors and their donations of cash, food, and clothing. In offering praise for Mrs. Winship, the *Intelligencer* noted that her organization, founded just seven weeks earlier, had already distributed five thousand items of clothing and bed linen, and immense amounts of food collected at their office in the Trout House Hotel. Meanwhile, Dr. Pim appealed to Atlanta women for bed linens, clothing, and goods to be sent directly to Corinth, Mississippi, by Dr. Willis Westmoreland or mailed directly to him.[14]

Because medical science was so limited in the 1860s, the role of Civil War nurse involved nurturing more than it involved treating patients with medical procedures. Nineteenth-century society held women to be inherently more nurturing than men, thus nurses often regarded themselves as superior to doctors as healers. They fed, washed, and bandaged patients and

provided comfort during recovery or encouragement to face death coura-
geously. Interviewed in the early twentieth century as members of the Atlanta
Women's Pioneer Society, these hospital volunteers looked back with pride on
their accomplishments. Delia Foreacre recalled nursing ill and dying patients,
some with severe wounds. She remembered one case in particular, a gravely ill
officer shot in the neck. She helped feed him through a straw. Foreacre came
to regard the officer as a member of her own family, and wrote letters to his
kin, including the sad message of his death. "Southern women became well
acquainted with the horrors of war," she later remembered.[15]

Other women focused on nurturing soldiers with home-cooked
food. Lucy Ivy recalled making endless pots of soup, also taking milk and
sometimes flowers to the soldiers. Mary Wilson unpacked boxes sent from
women in a variety of Georgia locations and distributed the food to local
hospitals. Soldiers especially loved peach puffs made with dried fruit and
sweetened by sorghum. Soldiers were also pleased when they could get fresh
cream and butter. Coffee had become scarce by 1862, so patients drank a
substitute made with dried, mashed sweet potatoes made more palatable
by the addition of cream.[16]

Some women had a reputation for being especially effective in
comforting soldiers. Lucy Cook was among the most popular hospital visitors, for she combined a cheerful countenance with a sympathetic voice and
manner. Helping soldiers to accept impending death became one of the most
challenging roles for the Civil War's volunteer nurses, including those in
Atlanta. Widely held religious views included the notion that a peaceful
death in which the individual accepted his fate might help to ensure a heav-
enly reward. Mary Wilson's role in comforting one soldier in his final hours
led a friend to thank her by buying an ad in a local newspaper. In it, John H.
Lanier thanked Wilson for visiting B. R. Goodrich at Gate City Hospital
before his death and focusing his thoughts "away from this world to things
of a higher and holier character."[17]

Women who volunteered in hospitals witnessed sights and smells they
had never experienced before. Some women could not handle it. Jennie Lines
and her husband returned to Atlanta from an interlude in Greenville, Georgia,
after Jennie's husband found the economic climate there less favorable than
he had hoped. Now the mother of an infant daughter, Jennie was grateful for
a healthy baby and relieved that her husband had found remunerative work
as a typesetter, but she expressed shock in the appearance of wartime Atlanta.

In a letter to her sister-in-law, Jennie wrote, "You have no idea what a place Atlanta is now. So crowded and so *filthy!* It is almost impossible to pass some of the hospitals; the *stench* is *intolerable*." Jennie did not mention working as a volunteer in any of her surviving letters or in her diary. Gertrude Clanton Thomas arrived in Atlanta during April 1862 to visit her husband, a Confederate officer. A wealthy woman from the planter class in Augusta, Georgia, Thomas wrote in her diary approvingly about her well-appointed room at the Trout House Hotel, but expressed astonishment at the conditions she observed on a tour of Empire Hospital. "Oh such a sight it was," Thomas wrote. "I know I should fail if I were to attempt a description of it." She found the atmosphere "unholsome," especially the fact that men were allowed to smoke pipes and were assigned ten to a single room.[18]

In addition to nursing, Atlanta women supported the Confederacy's wounded warriors by sewing and knitting. Groups gathered in locations around town including the storerooms of the benevolent associations, City Hall, and also Calico House, the home of Marcus and Mary Jane Bell and one of Atlanta's architecturally distinct homes. Painted shades of yellow, blue, and red to resemble a popular calico pattern, the house had been designed and decorated by a man trained at creating marbleized paper for the inside covers of books. Like many private homes, Calico House sheltered wounded soldiers early in the war, and later hosted groups of women sewing for the soldiers. Piromis Bell, son of Marcus and Mary Jane and a child during the war, recalled that "the rooms were every day occupied by groups of ladies assisting in the work of packing the boxes, knitting, sewing, and 'pulling lint' to be sent to the medical department of the government for use of the surgeons in the field and field hospitals." Many women worked from their homes and donated their finished products to the relief associations. Sarah Massey learned to knit as a child but had no need of the skill as a grown woman until the LSRS put out a call for socks. She later recalled producing twenty-seven pairs of socks for the Ladies' Soldiers' Relief Society. Sallie Richards, wife of the bookstore owner Sam Richards, sewed "comforts"— ersatz blankets made of used household linens—and took her turn cooking for the soldiers via the LSRS.[19]

In the spring of 1862, the Confederate government commissioned a major hospital complex of forty buildings near the Georgia Railroad on land previously used for farm shows. Called Fairground Hospitals, the facility began receiving patients in September, when five hundred beds became available to house patients formerly cared for at a converted concert hall. For the remaining years of the war, Fairground treated thousands of soldiers from the Western Department, renamed the Department of Tennessee. Following the death of General Johnston in April, Braxton Bragg became commander of the Army of Tennessee and appointed Dr. Samuel Hollingsworth Stout superintendent for all military hospitals under his authority. Evidently, Stout considered making Atlanta his headquarters, though ultimately he chose Chattanooga as his base of operations.[20]

Although medical care improved in Atlanta as the army established more control over its services, inevitably men died in Atlanta hospitals. On May 7, 1862, the *Daily Intelligencer* announced a new policy of printing the names of dead soldiers, on a hospital-by-hospital basis, even including the names of those who died at the passenger depot before being transported to hospital. Throughout the war, the City Council entered interment statistics into its quarterly records. During the first quarter of 1862, records indicate 63 civilian burials at City Cemetery and 157 military burials.[21]

In addition to the capture of Nashville, New Orleans fell into Union hands in late April, and the importance of naval operations to the outcome in both cases was a lesson not lost on Confederate authorities. Landlocked Atlanta, with its rail access and its safe, interior location, became even more desirable as a site for Confederate factories. Confederate authorities began looking at Atlanta as a possible site for relocation of the Nashville Arsenal. Local businessmen and industrialists encouraged the move, understanding that a major government presence in Atlanta would mean contracts for private businesses as well. In June, the City Council appointed a committee of five to assist "Col [James H.] Burton [who] is now in the City with a view of Selecting a Suitable Site for the Confederate States Armory in this or some neighboring City." The Confederate government's decision to accept Atlanta as the site of its new arsenal marks a major turning point in Atlanta's wartime history. As one scholar put it, "Atlanta began its rise as the chief manufacturing and supply center for the Southern armies."[22]

The new Atlanta Arsenal began production in the spring of 1862 under the direction of Colonel Moses H. Wright. A graduate of West Point, he served the U.S. Army at arsenals in St. Louis and New York before the war, then gave his allegiance to the Confederacy. In 1862, he supervised the relocation of the Confederate operation from Nashville, signing a series of contracts with an Atlanta builder named John C. Peck to construct a magazine, twenty-five feet by forty feet, and additional shops including "a building suitable for a laboratory."[23]

Peck was an enterprising man who owned a carpenter shop, a blacksmith shop, and a kiln for drying lumber. He used this equipment in the manufacture of "Joe Brown Pikes." Following the Confederate capitulation at Fort Donelson, the Georgia governor insisted that a soldier with a gun might fail to hit his target, but a soldier with a six-foot staff topped with an eighteen-inch blade could inflict serious damage upon Yankee invaders. After pikes fell out of favor—indeed, became the subject of ridicule at the governor's expense—Peck leased his shops to Colonel Wright for use by the Confederate Arsenal, the contract expiring "one month after the ratification of a treaty of peace." Wright appointed him superintendent of woodwork for the arsenal.[24]

Moses Wright was just twenty-six years old when he arrived in Atlanta, and he ran an operation with a $1.5 million annual budget. Within a year, the arsenal had factories housed in buildings scattered around the city that produced percussion caps, saddles and harnesses, cartridges, and artillery shells. At its peak of production in 1863 and 1864, the Atlanta Arsenal employed nearly fifty-five hundred individuals, a number unmatched by any industrial enterprise in Atlanta during the nineteenth century. Perhaps its most impressive achievement was the production of percussion caps, for the arsenal manufactured forty-one million percussion caps for muskets alone, and another five million for pistols.[25]

The Confederate military also created a Quartermaster's Depot in Atlanta, with Major George W. Cunningham in command. The depot produced jackets, pants, shirts, undergarments, hats, and shoes. Forty shoemakers turned out 150 pairs of shoes daily, but clothing production occurred on an even larger scale. With a labor force of twenty tailors and two trimmers, Cunningham outsourced the sewing to three thousand seamstresses, many of them soldiers' wives who did "piecework." These women worked from home stitching garments by hand. A woman identified by the *Daily Intelligencer* as Miss Pittman acted as superintendent of clothing construction for Cunningham. The newspaper praised Pittman as an "amiable and patriotic" woman who "has given work to hundreds of her needy sex in this city. No one could have done more than she, to carry out the objects of her appointment, or give more general satisfaction to this community." Major Cunningham bragged to authorities that his operation could produce 130,000 jackets and pants per year and even more shirts.[26]

In addition to supplying the Confederate Army with materials, and thousands of Atlantans with jobs, government operations also boosted production at existing companies. In May 1862, Colonel Wright began placing orders with local companies, including Winship Iron Works, owned by the brothers Isaac and Joseph Winship, who constructed railroad freight cars. Lewis Scofield and William Markham, who owned the largest privately run rolling mill operation in Atlanta, made iron rails, gunboat iron plating, and cannon under government contract. J. J. Thrasher made cartridge boxes, cartridge belts, bayonet scabbards, and shoulder straps, while J. B. Langford and Son made cavalry saddles, and S. A. Durand made haversacks.[27]

Several industries relocated to Atlanta from elsewhere in the Confederacy. Hammond Marshall relocated his sword company from Nashville, renaming it the Atlanta Sabre Manufactory. In the Atlanta newspapers, the company advertised swords for cavalry, artillery, and infantry "of the finest temper and finish" and costing $30 to $100. Touring the factory in June 1862, a reporter for the *Daily Intelligencer* praised the production rate of 170 pieces per week. Demonstrating the type of boosterism that characterized Atlanta's newspapers during the war, the *Intelligencer* crowed: "Such enterprises in our midst should meet with encouragement from both Government and people."[28]

James Burton scouted more than just sites for the Atlanta Arsenal when he visited in June. Burton was an investor in a new pistol factory being relocated from the Confederate capital of Richmond. Although Burton ultimately made Macon his home, his partners Edward Spiller and David Burr moved forward with plans to establish their factory in Atlanta. Their contract stipulated that the company would produce 15,000 pistols, with the first 600 to be handed over by February 1863 and 1,000 per month to be delivered after that. Despite the attractive wages they offered, the Spiller and Burr operation struggled to find skilled workmen in wartime, especially after the Confederacy began drafting men into its armies. In the end, the factory produced only 1,532 firearms.[29]

Soldiers needed arms and equipment, but they also needed food, and Atlanta became home to a Confederate smokehouse. In February, Confederate Commissary agent Major F. R. Shackelford and several others submitted a proposal to the City Council that would allow them to construct a facility at the corner of Alabama and Lloyd Streets to cure meat for the army in Virginia, as well as the western army. One soldier's wife wrote to him in July that she had seen "8 or 10 drays hauling bacon to the Depot, they had a dispatch from Richmond, for 1,000,000 lbs (one million)."[30]

Atlanta's transformation from emerging prewar city to wartime metropolis led to dramatic changes. Eventually the city's population reached twenty-two thousand. Thousands of people left other locations in Georgia and elsewhere and made the Gate City their new home. When Sam Richards moved from Macon to Atlanta in October 1861 in order to run a bookstore with his brother on Whitehall Street, he benefited indirectly from Atlanta's manufacturing boom because the Richards bookstore attracted many new customers. Richards admitted in a diary entry on January 9, 1862: "Business is pretty good and the profits *splendid* on what we do sell." However, residence in the wartime city involved challenges, as Richards soon learned. Housing prices were steep. Subsequently, Richards, his wife, and their four children moved in with his brother Jabez, wife Stella, and their two children at their home on Washington Street, an arrangement that both brothers regarded as temporary but that lasted for most of the war. With Sam, his wife, Sallie, and the four children crammed into two rooms, and a sister-in-law who resented their presence, tensions were bound to occur, and they did. Sam confided to his diary on May 25, 1862, "We have quite worn our welcome out here as far as Stella is concerned and Sallie wants to move."[31]

With the fall of Nashville and with other parts of Tennessee in turmoil, Atlanta became home to refugees from central Tennessee. Anna Sehon fled Nashville, along with her husband, John, a military officer now assigned to the Confederate quartermaster's office in the Gate City. "Annie," as she was known among relatives, came from a family of wealth and privilege. Her father, Thomas, was a planter and judge, with sizable real estate and personal holdings. Annie, twenty years old and recently married, often exchanged letters with her older sister Bettie Kimberly, wife of a chemistry professor at the University of North Carolina in Chapel Hill. "You are a little surprised are you not to hear from me at Atlanta," she wrote on March 10, 1862. "I am really here and here I expect to remain until we can drive back the hated enemy and return victorious to our dear old home." She called the capture of Nashville "a sad fact and woeful[,] woeful are its consequences."[32]

Annie had never seen Atlanta before, and she recorded her impressions in letters to her sister. She wrote that Atlanta had the feel of a village, except for its large size, and was filled with frame houses, "sweet little cottages," she called them. But she also discovered that rents were high and servants were hard to find. Nonetheless, John Sehon found a four-room house with a nice front porch for the couple to rent and two domestic servants to help Annie with the house, one of them an "excellent" cook. Annie thought her husband very savvy to have found the house for "such is the condition of Atlanta there is scarcely a house to be found for rent or a servant for hire." Food prices shocked the young matron. A "beefstake" cost seventy-five cents, and a roast could cost as much as $2.25.[33]

The cost of meat concerned many women in addition to Annie Sehon, but the cost of another food staple created greater concern: wheat. Due to a weak harvest, the price of wheat climbed to $17 to $20 per barrel, placing it out of reach for many people. Local newspapers cautioned citizens to use corn. "Proper economy in the use of corn can make wholesome food plentiful for the next twelve months," the *Southern Confederacy* suggested. To ensure that corn remain plentiful, Governor Joe E. Brown issued an executive order that outlawed the distillation of corn into whiskey. Although his central concern was to preserve the food crop, Brown, a teetotaler, probably liked the idea of imposing his abstemiousness on fellow Georgians. At the request of Confederate military and hospital authorities, the governor allowed distillation of corn for medicinal purposes.[34]

In spite of the governor's measure to protect the corn supply, middle- and upper-class southerners regarded corn as the diet of poor white people and slaves. Understanding this, merchants advertised rice flour as an appropriate substitute for wheat or corn. Edward M. Edwardy ran a popular grocery store on Whitehall Street. He supported the relief societies by filling their orders for food items, a practice that revealed he was civic-minded and perceptive enough to realize that this act of generosity was probably good for business. Edwardy ran ads offering "Fresh Rice Flour and Meal at reduced prices," and included recipes for how to make bread and waffles from the flour. Sam Richards, a friend of Edwardy and a fellow merchant on Whitehall Street, learned to appreciate rice flour. Complaining that wheat was too expensive, Richards wrote in his diary, "I like a good rice-flour bread made with buttermilk and soda quite as well as flour bread, at least for awhile."[35]

A growing number of Atlanta residents believed that speculators were causing exorbitant prices for wheat and other commodities. Stories appeared in local newspapers suggesting that speculators hoarded and hid barrels of wheat flour, then released them for inflated prices. One individual sent a letter to the *Daily Intelligencer*, claiming that "Atlanta is cursed with many of these bad men who have . . . carried on their business, not only openly, but with perfect impunity." The *Southern Confederacy* tried to tamp down rumors about speculators by suggesting that there were fewer cases of "unpatriotic speculation and extortion" than many might suppose.[36]

Both of Atlanta's newspapers acknowledged the seriousness of another economic problem during 1862: counterfeiting. By the summer of 1862, problems with the Confederacy's currency raised alarm in the Gate City, and many newspaper stories educated citizens about how to recognize fake government notes. The *Southern Confederacy* told residents to look for roughly engraved notes printed on inferior paper stock. After the newspaper revealed in August that as much as $100,000 in false currency might be circulating in Atlanta, it backpedaled in another story to report that the figure was more like $10,000. Newspapers also reassured Atlantans that the secretary of the treasury, acknowledging the widespread problem with counterfeiting in the Confederate states, would make changes to the printing process in order to make it harder for counterfeiting to occur. The Confederate Congress passed a law imposing the death penalty for those convicted of this crime. Nonetheless, counterfeiting continued to plague the South during the war. The *Daily Intelligencer* suggested that many of the false notes originated in occupied Nashville. By October, another round of articles warned Atlantans about counterfeit notes and cautioned that the new notes were far better quality and harder to detect. In a story citing exchanged Confederate prisoners as a source, the *Southern Confederacy* reported that newsboys in northern cities sold counterfeits on street corners. Both of the local newspapers in Atlanta warned against shinplasters, a type of circulating medium that some businesses accepted as bank notes. Neither newspaper would accept payment of this kind.[37]

Confederate Atlantans also worried about Unionists. Judging by the newspaper coverage of events in 1860–61, by and large Unionists in Atlanta had been ignored. When the early months of 1862 introduced Atlantans to a new reality that included military defeat and food shortages, tolerance for Unionists receded and fear of espionage accelerated. The newspapers led the charge, with the *Daily Intelligencer* warning in February: "Let every true son of the South look out for Spies and Traitors." In subsequent editorials, the *Intelligencer* also declared that men and women of "northern sympathies" should leave the Gate City, including those of native birth and

those of foreign birth. "Too much has been tolerated here already of treasonable language, and, in future, *it must cease.*"[38]

Atlantans had more than treasonable language to worry about when, in
mid-April, word reached the city that Union saboteur James Andrews and a
small group of fellow conspirators had hijacked a locomotive called the
General in Big Shanty (present-day Kennesaw), Georgia, with the eventual
goal of tearing up the track and giving control of the railroad to the Union.
The *Daily Intelligencer* called it "this extraordinary and most audacious
attempt of LINCOLN'S SPIES to rob, burn, and destroy the State [rail]Road."
Although a local engineer named William Fuller thwarted Andrews by
chasing him down as he tried to escape, and the saboteur was executed in
Atlanta, along with seven others, his "audacious attempt" sent chills through
Atlanta's Confederate citizenry. Andrews provided proof that spies were
present in Georgia. Andrews's small band of men destroyed the belief that
Atlanta might remain physically isolated from the military events of war.
James Crew, a railroad employee, wrote to his wife after the hangings,
"would to god I was out of this town until this war was over."[39]

Fears related to the Andrews raid, coupled with concerns about the
federal army in Tennessee, led Mayor James Calhoun to call a citizens
meeting at City Hall in early June. Calhoun suggested that local men form
themselves into companies for the purpose of home defense. Lucius Gartrell,
now a Confederate congressman, wanted to go farther than that. Quickly
inserting himself into a leadership position by suggesting the mayor
appoint a committee of twenty-one to compose resolutions, then persuading
the committee to appoint him its chairman, Gartrell, with his committee,
proceeded to write a series of resolutions designed to shut down the
speech and activities of those who might question Atlanta's Confederate
loyalty. Their resolutions emphasized that there was no room for neutrality
in this war, branded anyone aiding the North a traitor, recognized the
"sublime courage" of the residents of federally occupied New Orleans,
and demanded a Vigilance Committee to help the local police to stamp out
disloyalty in Atlanta. Sidney Root seconded the report and it was adopted.[40]

The appointment of Colonel George Washington Lee to be Atlanta's
provost guard marked another turning point in the city's treatment of
suspected Unionists and spies. The provost guard acted as the Confederacy's
representative overseeing civilians. Lee, a prewar Atlanta saloonkeeper, and
a crass, unpopular man who coveted power, collected a force of five hundred

men under his command, many of them unemployed teenagers and recent conscripts. Lee paid minimal attention to newspaper stories about Unionist women visiting Yankee prisoners, but he did crack down on male dissidents after a suspicious fire near a munitions laboratory. Confederate authorities placed the city under martial law for the month of August, and Lee's men arrested eight or more suspected traitors. Details of the arrests are unclear, including the precise number and identity of those arrested. Lee also hired the wartime proprietor of the Trout House Hotel, a Mr. G. McGinly, as "special detective," and McGinly helped capture Martin Hinton, a local Unionist who attempted to flee the state and got as far as Rome, Georgia. Hinton was believed to be en route to inform General Don Carlos Buell of the movements of Confederate General Braxton Bragg's army. In spite of Lee's efforts, several mitigating factors worked to the favor of Unionists in the city. One was the affluence and social prominence of many Unionists, which probably protected them from arrest. Another was Mayor Calhoun's prewar ties to the Unionists and the mayor's concern about the comfort of Unionists held in jail. A final factor was Lee's unpopularity with many Atlantans and their belief that he wielded too much authority. Nonetheless, by the end of 1862, acts of overt Unionism declined in Atlanta.[41]

Regardless of the challenges faced by Atlanta's Confederate citizens, there was much to cheer about in 1862. Many Atlantans were making money, and the economic growth generated by war industries ended the economic downturn that beset the city during the secession crisis. Beginning in 1862, the Gate City's economic vigor earned accolades locally and regionally. One reporter opined that the city's manufacturing enterprises grew so rapidly that he could not stay on top of all the news. Reporters for the *Daily Intelligencer* and *Southern Confederacy* emphasized the unlikelihood of foreign intervention in the war—the *Southern Confederacy* called such hopes "baseless and delusive"—and the necessity for the Confederacy to achieve economic independence as well as military victory.[42]

Because Atlantans enjoyed full employment, they had money to spend. To feed, clothe, and entertain Atlanta's burgeoning population, new businesses sprang up on the city's principal business arteries, Whitehall and Decatur Streets. A "New Bakery" at Decatur and Lloyd Streets, opened by Mr. P. Giebelhouse, formerly of Savannah, advertised cakes, pies, and bread "always on hand." Another new firm, S. Solomon and Bros., sold hardware, household goods, calico, and other cloth, while the newly formed

Gaar, Niles and Co. advertised food, hardware, and "excellent Smoking Tobacco."[43]

New and existing businesses began advertising "blockade goods" for sale. Often at the forefront of business trends, Edward Edwardy advertised blockade goods in April under the banner "Run the Blockade." Edwardy had five thousand packets of "fresh garden seed," a practical and valuable commodity, given that many Atlantans planted gardens and avoided purchasing high-cost food when they could. In June, J. McPherson and Co., the largest bookseller in the Gate City, advertised five hundred reams of English letter and notepaper as well as 300,000 envelopes. In December, D. Mayer, Jacobe advertised cloth valued at $20,000, while Holbrook and Lawshe offered French Hats obtained despite the blockade.[44]

Atlanta was home to several firms running the blockade via the ports of Charleston and Wilmington. Sidney Root and his partner John Beach, among the earliest Atlanta merchants to begin "importing" from England, were also among the most successful. While Beach set up an office in Liverpool, Root purchased a large lot in Charleston and built a warehouse. Ships entered Charleston after stopping in Nassau and Bermuda. According to a typescript memoir that Root wrote for his children in the 1890s, he allowed the Confederate quartermasters first pick of his cargoes and in one shipment sold thousands of Enfield rifles to government authorities. At the peak of its operations, the firm had, "if I remember correctly, from 19 to 21 ocean steamers." When he was not in England or South Carolina managing the firm's affairs, Root remained a pillar of Atlanta society, acting as superintendent of the Sunday school for Second Baptist Church and singing tenor in the choir.[45]

One steamer owned by Root and Beach was the *Memphis,* and it carried sixty-five thousand yards of English fabric for sale in Atlanta according to one newspaper advertisement in July 1862. An accompanying story in the *Daily Intelligencer* congratulated the firm on its success, willingness to take risks, and sale of blankets, cloth, and paper to the army. For its female readers, the *Intelligencer* cast as patriotic behavior the act of purchasing blockade goods: "Our true Southern women will, doubtless, be ambitious to secure a dress from this successful venture of importers." Sam and Sallie Richards were close friends of Root and his wife, Mary, socialized often, and sang together in the choir at Second Baptist. Sallie Richards bought a calico dress from Root's *Memphis* shipment. Her husband complained about the price, noting she had paid $6.50 for what would have cost $1.00 before the war. For Mrs. Richards, the availability of English cloth must have been a great comfort. Six months earlier her husband had purchased a dress made out of homespun, commenting with satisfaction that it cost only fifty cents per yard and was "neat and strong." While Mrs. Richards's reaction to the homespun dress is unknown, as the fashion-conscious wife of a rising merchant, she undoubtedly preferred not to wear homespun. Additional blockade runners included Richard Peters and the partnership of William McNaught and James Ormond, who ran the Fulton County Export and Importing Company.[46]

Atlanta's Confederate civilians often found city life exciting in 1862. Children like Sam Richards's son Arthur loved to watch the trains coming and going at the rail yards. Hamilton Yancey was thrilled when he received permission from his parents to go to the depot to see captured Yankee soldiers as they traveled through Atlanta on their way to prison. Sarah Massey's son loved to pretend he was a soldier, marching the family slaves around as his army. The children of a Mrs. O'Neal on Decatur Street made an exciting discovery while playing near a small stream close to their house: eighty-one hundred dollar bills, which their mother turned over to Colonel Lee and discovered to be counterfeits.[47]

Children and their parents found pleasure and escapism by attending the theater, and they showed their support for Confederate nationalism by buying tickets to fund-raisers at the Athenaeum. The Atlanta Amateurs performed there often in the first two years of the war, giving benefit performances for the Ladies' Soldiers' Relief Society and for military units including the Jo Thompson Artillery, the Wyly Artillery, and the Leyden Artillery. When the Amateurs gave a performance in April 1862 to celebrate the troupe's first anniversary, the *Daily Intelligencer* noted that they also had performed in Macon, Milledgeville, Augusta, Newnan, and Marietta during the previous twelve months and had raised a total of $9,000.[48]

Maria Westmoreland became a major figure among the Amateurs, one of five women in the twenty-eight-member troupe. Before the war, respectable women like Mrs. Westmoreland did not appear on the stage, but this social barrier was broken in Atlanta and throughout the South as women held musical and theatrical events to raise money for the soldiers. Westmoreland stretched the boundaries of gender propriety even farther, for the Amateurs performed a play she wrote called *The Soldier's Wife*. In 1862, the play was advertised as "written by a LADY of this city," but by 1863 Westmoreland's identity as playwright was publicly revealed when the Amateurs performed another of her plays. *A Soldier's Trials or The Warning Voice* follows the life of a soldier from his departure from home and through the trials of a military campaign. Its debut in March 1863 led the *Southern Confederacy* to praise Westmoreland as a "gifted dramatic writer" and to suggest that her play would "claim a conspicuous place on Southern Stages as long as this war for Southern Independence is celebrated by surviving heroes and their descendants." Although the *Confederacy* also praised the eight-member cast, the newspaper's reviewer suggested that the cast had failed to achieve the kind of "intense feeling" and "emotion" that the audience expected for a drama of this kind. Nonetheless, the debut production raised $500 for the benefit of Atlanta's needy citizens, and subsequent ads for the production billed it as "Mrs. W. F. Westmoreland's Successful Play."[49]

Traveling thespians found enthusiastic audiences in Atlanta. Among the favorites were the Queen Sisters and Palmetto Band from Charleston, South Carolina, who entertained Atlanta audiences for the first time in February 1862 and returned numerous times. Sisters Laura, "Little Fanny," and "Infant Julia" Waldron sang, danced, and acted. When the Queen Sisters returned to Atlanta's Athenaeum for a three-week engagement in July 1862, their act had expanded to include their three brothers, and their tour encompassed Macon, Montgomery, Mobile, and New Orleans. Theatergoers could purchase tickets at all of the area hotels and bookstores at a cost of fifty to seventy-five cents for adults and twenty-five cents for children and slaves. The Queen Sisters' lighthearted comedic performances included such numbers as "Sweethearts and Wives," but over time they became more willing to engage wartime themes. When they came to Atlanta in October 1862, the Queen Sisters performed "The Conscript," which the *Daily Intelligencer* concluded "suits the times," but also reprised their farce "The Two Gregories" in order to provide audiences with the type of lighter fare that spectators expected from them.[50]

Minstrel acts also played at the Athenaeum, including White's Minstrels. Tim Morris earned praise from the *Daily Intelligencer* for his "delineations of the negro character" which "we have never seen surpassed."[51] But if Atlanta audiences were entertained by white men pretending to be black men, they were even more entertained by the African American musician "Blind Tom" Wiggins, who toured Atlanta for the first time in 1861 and played to enthralled audiences many times during the war.

Thomas Greene Wiggins, a slave who was sightless from birth, was born in Harris County, Georgia, in 1849 and sold to James Bethune of Columbus, Georgia, soon thereafter, along with his mother and siblings. As a young child, Wiggins demonstrated an interest in music and a talent for playing the piano that his owner found both puzzling and fascinating. After hearing a piece of music played one time on the piano, he quickly learned to play it from memory. In 1857, he began performing in Columbus, then in the surrounding towns of Macon, Atlanta, and Athens. According to one account, his playing style combined "scientific precision" with "unusual *tours de force*." Wiggins came to Atlanta in December 1861 and performed at City Hall. Sam Richards, who attended with his wife, recorded in his diary that "Blind Tom" "is truly one of the *seven wonders*[,] plays the most difficult operatic music correctly and composes pieces of his own and yet is but 12 years old and little better than an idiot." The *Southern Confederacy* called Wiggins "remarkable," for his talent and for the fact that he never made mistakes.[52]

Today, Wiggins might be diagnosed as autistic, but for white audiences in the 1860s he was a combination of musical genius and sideshow freak. Billed as "Tom, the Little Blind Negro Boy Pianist," Wiggins gave a benefit for Confederate soldiers at the Athenaeum on November 7, 1862, the proceeds given to the mayor for distribution to needy soldiers and their families. In addition to marveling at his brilliance as a pianist, audiences also cheered his original compositions, such as a piece commemorating the 1861 Battle of Manassas, performed before many audiences in the Confederacy, including those in Atlanta. Performances of this piece featured Wiggins's handler Perry Oliver calling out the themes to Wiggins's accompaniment. As Wiggins played softly, Oliver called out, "The eve of battle." As Wiggins played a crescendo, Oliver called out, "The noise of arms and accoutrements" and "General Beauregard's trumpets." To replicate the battle itself, Wiggins alternated the strains of "Yankee Doodle" with "The Cannon," which he simulated while banging the flat of his hands on the lower range of the piano. The piece ended with "The Retreat" and Confederate victory. Blind Tom dazzled audiences with his rendition of this composition. They admired his technical command of the piano and they loved to revisit the South's first military victory of the war. Wiggins's apparent Confederate patriotism relieved their anxiety about slaves' loyalty during the war.[53]

While Tom appears to have composed the piece, he presumably did so at the behest of Perry Oliver and not in spontaneous celebration of Confederate victory, as alleged by Oliver. References to the piece do not appear in public until nine months after the battle, an indication that the piece was carefully crafted after the fact. Wiggins's production may have been modeled after a Yankee battle piece introduced early in 1862 called "L'Union: Paraphrase de Concert," which incorporated patriotic tunes such as "Yankee Doodle" and ended with a thundering rendition of the "Star Spangled Banner." Wiggins began performing "The Battle of Manassas" ten days after "L'Union" played before an audience in St. Louis.[54]

More than anything else, military news excited Atlantans in 1862. In early March, their city hosted the "largest military muster ever held in this county," a clear sign that the apathy of the winter months was giving way to renewed enthusiasm for war. General T. R. R. Cobb, brother of Howell Cobb and a secessionist-turned-general, offered a patriotic speech. By recruiting two new military companies, Fulton County achieved its military quota, thereby avoiding the need for local conscription, which had now become an official policy of the Confederate government.[55]

In the spring and summer of 1862, the exploits of the cavalryman John Hunt Morgan captivated Atlantans, and their fascination with the dynamic leader never waned for the rest of the war. An upper-class Kentuckian who had served in the Mexican-American War, Morgan built a thriving hemp-manufacturing business in Lexington during the 1850s, and supported secession even though the slave state of Kentucky remained loyal to the Union. In 1861, he joined the cavalry and quickly began his rise to fame. With a small band of men, using speed, daring, and the newest technology in repeating pistols, Morgan staged a series of raids behind Union lines and succeeded in seizing supplies, wreaking havoc on bridges, railroads, and telegraph lines, capturing prisoners, and getting his name in the newspapers. For Confederate Atlanta, Morgan seemed to personify the best of southern manhood.[56]

No other military officer captured the imagination of Atlantans the way Morgan did, and their fervent belief that a single cavalry officer and his men could influence the war's outcome led to naive expectations about military victory in the conflict. One letter to the editor in April 1862 suggested that "John Morgan, with a handful of picked men, has done more for the cause of Southern Independence, than whole Brigades." Atlanta men applauded Morgan's military triumphs, praising his gallantry and his apparent indifference to personal glory. Periodically Morgan came to the Gate City, raising money for his cavalry and sometimes recruiting new members. In June 1862 he appeared at the passenger depot, "greeted by a large and enthusiastic throng," according to one account. When called upon to give a speech, Morgan declined, telling the crowd that they must "excuse him, as he was *not a politician*," a response that no doubt further endeared him to residents of the Gate City.[57]

Newspaper editors loved Morgan because his exploits made good copy. The *Southern Confederacy* admitted that its fondness for Morgan was partly grounded in the fact that his raids brought them readers. "The newspaper fraternity owe[s] a heavy debt of gratitude to that gallant partisan leader," one reporter wrote, adding that Morgan furnished the material for reporters to write "spicy paragraphs and interesting articles." The *Daily Intelligencer* reported with great relish about one of Morgan's raids near Gallatin, Tennessee, in which Morgan and an aide disguised themselves in Yankee uniforms and railed against "d[amne]d rebels," then made off with dispatches from a telegraph office that provided the Confederate Army with information about Union troop movements. Often the newspapers resorted to bombast. In an article titled "Morgan the Terror of Yankees," the *Southern Confederacy* alleged that when it came to stealth, cunning, and resolve, "We doubt if the world contains his superior.... He is certainly the Marion of this war," a reference to Francis Marion, the "Swamp Fox" cavalry hero of the American Revolution.[58]

Women found Morgan a romantic figure. Newspaper articles described his personal appearance, including his dark eyes, auburn hair, and "long sandy whiskers." Annie Sehon told her sister that if she were a man, she would like to ride with Morgan because "his life is such a rich [and] varied one." White Southerners also admired Morgan because he was a southern gentleman who respected women's place as noncombatants in a war where their ability to remain out of the fray was increasingly difficult. Morgan reportedly captured several cars of the Louisville and Nashville Railroad in May 1862 and told the terrified Unionist women on the train that they had nothing to fear, for "ladies and their baggage are sacred and to be scrupulously respected.... You are helpless women." According to this account, Morgan then arranged for their safe return to Louisville. Although the newspapers did not make a comparison between Morgan and Union General Benjamin Butler, they may have intended readers to do so. On May 15, 1862, as commander of Union forces occupying New Orleans, Butler issued an order that threatened to treat women who engaged in disloyal behavior as prostitutes. Butler's "notorious" order caused outcry in the South. The *Daily*

Intelligencer printed the order on May 24 and condemned Butler as a "vile, squint-eyed wretch."[59]

Atlanta women showered affection on John Hunt Morgan. Gertrude Grant wrote him a poem published in the *Daily Intelligencer*. Called "Our Partizen Leader," it ends

> 'Tis one great human organ
> One heart, one thought, one mouth—
> Long live our gallant Morgan
> The idol of the South!

Women named their sons after him; Sarah Dye's son John Morgan Dye was born in 1862. Women of the Atlanta Hospital Association, whose critical need as caregivers, cooks, and fund-raisers was constantly impressed upon them by Martha Winship, nonetheless took time away from nursing soldiers to present Morgan with a gold-capped ceremonial cane in June 1862 "in token of their gratitude and admiration of his deeds of daring in defence of our oppressed country." Morgan sent them a reply expressing his thanks and his hope that "the future may prove him more worthy of their consideration and regard."[60]

Above all, Atlantans loved Morgan because he accomplished amazing feats despite seemingly insurmountable odds. During a two-month period beginning July 4, 1862, Morgan, with fewer than one thousand men, rode through the Kentucky towns of Tomkinsville, Glasgow, Lebanon, Springfield, Harrodsburg, Versailles, and Cynthiana, capturing many prisoners and losing only a small number of his own men. Readers of Atlanta's newspapers followed the details avidly. In reporting the "Glorious News" of the capture of Lebanon, the *Daily Intelligencer* alleged that Morgan had caused "Great Tribulation Among the Yankees and Unionists." Throughout the Confederacy, Morgan's success raised hopes that Kentucky might secede from the Union. Morgan encouraged this sentiment among Kentuckians by posting everywhere he went a proclamation telling the people of Kentucky that Confederate independence was "an achieved fact" and imploring them to rid Kentucky of "its detested invaders."[61]

During the summer and fall of 1862, military news also reached Atlanta from battlefields in Virginia, but the news was often frustratingly slow to arrive. Local newspapers looked to the Richmond papers for reports, but often found the most current news by printing the letters and telegrams of

Atlanta soldiers dispatched to their relatives back home, or relatives of Atlantans who lived close to the action.

The *Intelligencer* printed a number of letters from Captain James H. Neal of the 19th Georgia to his father. Neal, a twenty-six-year-old attorney by training, was the son of John and Mary Jane Neal, a couple who had moved to Atlanta in the 1850s and occupied a grand home on Washington Street near City Hall. Its large size and massive Corinthian columns made the home well known to many Atlantans. Captain Neal commanded Company B of the 19th Georgia Infantry, known as the Jackson Guards.[62]

Neal provided details about the series of battles near Richmond, part of a campaign in which Union soldiers of General George B. McClellan staged an amphibious landing on the peninsula between the York and James Rivers and fought their way toward the Confederate capital. Neal's letters to his father did not glorify combat; indeed, Atlantans may have read more details than they wanted to learn about Neal's case of dysentery. Neal's ability to convey the sights and sounds of the battlefield made events seem real for Atlantans. In a letter written on June 3 and printed on June 10, Neal wrote: "The air was thick with shell, shot, grape, and canister, not to mention the number of rifle balls which a large body of infantry were showering into us." As an officer on horseback, Captain Neal was especially vulnerable to being picked off, and he attributed his survival to "the Providence of God." Nonetheless, his regiment suffered heavy casualties, and Neal mentioned some of them by name in his letter. At the end of the day's fighting, the exhausted Neal helped "getting up the stragglers" and then lay down on the wet ground to rest without any blanket or even overcoat. He felt he had "done my whole duty in the fight." The letter of another Atlantan from his daughter in Richmond shared additional information about the fighting around the Confederate capital. When the Confederate commander, General Joseph E. Johnston, suffered a serious wound, President Jefferson Davis transferred command of the Army of Northern Virginia to Robert E. Lee. Though few realized its immediate impact, Lee's appointment was to transform the war militarily and also bolster the morale of Confederate civilians. Two years after the capital city survived a narrow escape, Atlanta found inspiration from Richmond's example.[63]

The fighting near Richmond led to the arrival of more wounded soldiers in Atlanta. Confederate authorities believed that soldiers recovered more quickly if they went home to convalesce. Subsequently, those who could travel often did so. Volunteers set up a series of Wayside Hospitals in or near train stations throughout the Confederacy where soldiers could get food and where their injuries received preliminary care. One traveler from Richmond to Georgia in the fall of 1862 wrote about the presence of wounded men in every rail station he encountered. "At the depot at Richmond, and along the line from there to Augusta, crowds of sick and wounded soldiers are constantly presented. . . . Hence you live amid groans, shrieks, and cries as you travel." John Johnson, post surgeon in Atlanta, placed a notice in the *Southern Confederacy* telling wounded soldiers arriving in Atlanta to go directly to the closest hospital, for the City Hotel, Gate City, Alexander, and Concert Hall Hospitals were not more than 150 yards from the passenger depot. Food was always available at the depot. Soldiers could find clean clothing at the storerooms of the relief societies.[64]

By late summer, Union General John Pope had begun menacing civilians in Virginia, including the threat of expulsion for those who declined to take an oath of allegiance to the United States government. The *Daily Intelligencer* referred to the "brutality" of these "vile invaders"; however, Pope's military campaign culminated in a stunning Confederate victory at Second Manassas in late August. Under the command of General Lee, the Confederate Army of Northern Virginia began its rise to seeming invincibility. In a dramatic reversal of fortunes, the once-threatened Confederate capital was now safe, while Washington, D.C., was "trembling," as the *Intelligencer* put it. Atlantans learned details of the victory from passengers arriving in the Gate City with copies of northern newspapers.[65]

James H. Neal, now a major in command of the 19th Georgia, wrote to his father about Lee's invasion of the Union slave state of Maryland in September. Apparently, Neal came home to recover from his ailments, because he published a letter in the *Daily Intelligencer* on August 19, 1862, indicating that he was preparing to leave Atlanta and offering to carry letters and small packages to Virginia for members of his regiment. Back in the field, in a letter to his father dated September 7, Neal reflected the confidence that Confederates felt during the campaign when he wrote of the "fine fighting soldiers" who made up the army and the "strong force" marching into Maryland. Neal may have also reflected ambivalence about the Confederate Army's mission when he wrote, "This is a magnificent country, and it seems a pity to desolate it by war." General Lee's decision to invade Maryland was controversial among many southerners who believed they were fighting a war to protect their homeland. By invading Maryland, Lee gambled that a victory there might bring Maryland into the war and impress Britain and France, leading to their intervention on the side of the Confederacy. Neal wrote again from Harpers Ferry, which the Confederates captured on September 15, along with eleven thousand prisoners and "a large amount" of food and equipment, according to Neal. He was happy to report that his regiment lost no men from Atlanta, though he barely survived death or serious injury after a shell exploded close to him.[66]

Neal did not write from the scene of the campaign's culminating battle on Antietam Creek near the village of Sharpsburg, Maryland, September 17, 1862. Atlantans waited anxiously for news of the battle, finally learning via the *Southern Confederacy* that while reports were contradictory, there was general agreement that this contest was "the most bloody and desperately contested engagement of the war." The *Confederacy* was correct in its assessment. The fiercely fought battle would be the single deadliest day of the war, with nearly sixty-five hundred soldiers killed outright and an additional fifteen thousand wounded. Although technically neither side won, Lee was forced to retreat because he was deep in enemy territory. Nonetheless, the *Southern Confederacy* chose to declare victory, calling Lee's actions "brilliant" and "successful."[67]

The Virginia military campaigns of 1862 ended with another victory for Robert E. Lee's Confederates at the battle of Fredericksburg on December 13. The Union Army, now commanded by Ambrose Burnside, badly executed an effort to cross the Rappahannock River and attack Lee. Failure to bring the proper equipment needed to transport his army across the river led to delays that allowed Lee to get his army into place in well-entrenched positions. The result was one of the Union's worst losses of the war. For Confederate Atlantans, news of the "decisive victory" of General Lee was tempered by telegraphic reports that General T. R. R. Cobb was one of the battle's casualties. A resident of Athens and member of a distinguished Georgia family, Thomas Cobb had been a leading secessionist and principal speaker at Fulton County's military muster just a few months earlier. The *Southern Confederacy* reported, "All hearts are saddened over the death of Gen. Tom Cobb."[68]

A few weeks earlier, the *Daily Intelligencer* broke away from its Virginia coverage to note the appointment of Lemuel P. Grant as a Confederate captain of engineers. A railroad engineer by training and an Atlanta resident since the 1840s, Grant received orders to construct the Rome and Blue Mountain Railroad, which would connect the Alabama coal mines at Blue

Mountain directly to the state of Georgia. Although a lack of funding ended the project before it even began, the effort underscores Atlanta's importance as an industrial and supply center. In the coming year, Confederate authorities would assign Grant another task, that of building fortifications designed to protect Atlanta from Yankee invasion, and the city's future, which now appeared so promising, would be far less certain.[69]

5. Second City of the Confederacy

By 1863, Atlanta's Confederate civilians enjoyed bragging rights about their city, for Atlanta was now the Confederacy's second-most-important urban center, after the capital, Richmond. Not only was Atlanta the central transportation hub for the lower South, but it was also a major industrial, commercial, and medical center. Annie Sehon, who had moved to Atlanta from Nashville the previous year, wrote to her sister, "Next to Richmond this is the most important place in the South." The *Atlanta Daily Intelligencer* also crowned the Gate City as the Confederacy's number two metropolis, citing Atlanta's thriving businesses and factories and boasting that not even Richmond could surpass Atlanta's commitment to the cause of Confederate independence. Although the first half of 1863 represented the high point of Confederate nationalism in Atlanta, events in the coming months were to test whether a sizable segment of the Gate City's citizenry, notably its growing underclass of women and slaves, might undercut the South's ability to fight the war. One scholar has written, "With respect to women, at least, the Confederate project was seriously off course. . . . A new version of the body politic was taking shape in the South."[1]

Israel Gibbons, a reporter for the *Mobile Daily Advertiser and Register*, found Atlanta to be a fascinating place when he stopped in the city on his way to the military front in Tennessee in 1863. His writing underscored the gritty side of wartime Atlanta, which he characterized as "a great railroad whirlpool . . . where the locomotives are eternally shrieking." According to

Gibbons, the city's streets teemed with people, who "plunge and splash about daily." He saw newsboys running "as fast as they can, screaming as loud as they can" to sell their papers, and slaves carrying luggage from trains to hotels and back again. He described a city littered by the discarded trash of people who bustled through its streets and sidewalks, leaving behind them a trail of "goober-shells and apple peelings." He wrote of the importance of theater to Atlanta's wartime culture: "The plays at the theater [are] nightly joined in by the audiences." The Gate City's economic dynamism made the most vivid impression on Gibbons. "Many stores do a smashing business," he wrote. The auctioneers were "incessantly shouting," and "the all-pervading spirit of the people is trade, trade, trade."[2]

Gibbons's presence in Atlanta spoke to another distinction achieved by the city. By 1863, Atlanta was the news-gathering capital of the lower South. Following on the heels of the Richmond press, which had created its own news agency in the fall of 1862, western journalists met in Macon and later in Augusta, Georgia, during February 1863 and created the Press Association of the Confederate States of America. Its superintendent, John S. Thrasher, formerly a correspondent for the *New York Herald*, toured cities of the lower South before settling on Atlanta as the PA's headquarters. For Thrasher, Atlanta was the obvious choice because the city's "central geographic position," coupled with its existing infrastructure, allowed "communication by telegraph and rail with all parts of the country." The PA provided telegraphic coverage of military news to its member newspapers. Thrasher advertised in a variety of newspapers, including Atlanta's *Southern Confederacy*, recruiting professional reporters and soldiers who might write short pieces for the service. Within a few months, Thrasher had hired twenty journalists and signed up forty-four newspapers, including Gibbons's *Mobile Daily Advertiser*, the *Southern Confederacy*, and the *Daily Intelligencer*. The PA's telegraphic reporting was uneven in quality, sometimes accurate, other times wildly speculative or altogether incorrect, but readers gobbled up the telegraphic reports.[3]

Atlanta's Confederate civilians began the year 1863 optimistic that their effort at nation building would succeed. Opening their copies of the *Daily Intelligencer* on January 1, 1863, they read an editorial filled with pronouncements about "hope for the future . . . triumph over the vandal enemies of our country," and "a peaceful prosperity." The *Southern Confederacy* counseled patience but also offered hope that "a cessation of hostilities, peace, and acknowledged independence" could be achieved in the coming year. The bookseller Sam Richards wrote in his diary about "renewed hope that ere many months the dark tide of War will have passed away, and the blessings of Peace be again restored to us."[4]

President Jefferson Davis made a brief appearance at the passenger depot on New Year's Day, on a return trip to Richmond. Davis was greeted with a "salute of guns" before a carriage whisked him off to a private dinner described as "sumptuous" by the *Daily Intelligencer*. A personal rail car made his return journey a comfortable one. In brief remarks to citizens gathered at the depot, Davis apologized for being fatigued but spoke of Georgia's important role in the war and asked the public to support conscription, a topic the president knew to be controversial.[5] Over time, it was to become even more controversial.

In 1861, schoolteacher Jennie Lines had questioned whether Georgia should leave "Uncle Sam's and Aunt Columbia's care," but now she wrote of her disgust for the United States government and especially its president. She blamed Abraham Lincoln for military deaths: "How many hearts he has caused to bleed! [How] many homes he has desolated!"[6]

Many Atlantans shared Jennie's antipathy for Lincoln, who angered white southerners further by signing into law the Emancipation Proclamation on January 1, 1863. In September, Lincoln had announced the details of his proclamation and his intention to sign it on the first day of the new year. The president's proclamation would free all slaves living in Confederate-controlled areas as of that date. Lincoln did not attempt to alter the status of slaves living in Union states such as Maryland, for he feared that such action might trigger secession. He did not attempt to end slavery in Union-controlled areas of the Confederacy such as New Orleans. As a result, many white people in the Confederacy regarded Lincoln's policy as a cynical ploy. Technically, Lincoln's proclamation freed slaves in Atlanta, for it was part of the Confederacy not under Union control and therefore covered by Lincoln's proclamation. In reality, of course, Lincoln had no power over the status of slaves in Confederate-controlled areas. Nonetheless, in an editorial on January 1, 1863, the *Daily Intelligencer* called Lincoln a "dictator" and concluded, "We laugh to scorn the audacious and bloody design" of the Yankee president. Later that month, the *Intelligencer* reprinted an editorial from the *Chicago Times*, a Democratic newspaper and leading critic of the Lincoln administration. The *Times* concluded that Lincoln's proclamation ended any chance of a negotiated end to the war and allowed the "craziest abolitionism" to achieve "the very acme of its desires."[7]

The *Chicago Times* also suggested that Lincoln's Emancipation Proclamation "unites the people of the South forever." Indeed, support for southern nationalism coalesced among white southerners after Lincoln signed the document. The *Southern Confederacy* concluded, "We are glad he has done this.—We needed something to show our people the real policy of that faithless, perverse and unprincipled nation and people." The high prices brought by slaves further boosted white people's confidence. The *Southern Confederacy* published an article about market prices, including slave prices, in February: "Negroes have greatly advanced . . . since old Abe sticks up to his proclamation." Sam Richards called Lincoln's Emancipation Proclamation a "dreadful ukase," and he predicted that slaves would bring even higher prices when Confederate military victory ended the war and worldwide demand for cotton escalated. The Richards's bookstore business produced such high profits that Sam could afford to invest in city lots, country acreage, and a slave. A few days before Lincoln signed the proclamation, he purchased Ellen, a young teenager he had rented as a domestic servant for several years. Richards was immensely proud to become a slaveowner, for the ownership of human property bestowed a level of prestige on a southern man unlike that of any other type of property.[8]

The *Mobile Daily Advertiser*'s Israel Gibbons wrote of Atlanta's economic vitality, and indeed many businessmen profited handsomely in Civil War Atlanta, including prewar Unionists like Richards who now saw that risks the South took in leaving the Union had paid dividends. In his diary, Sam marveled at the profits he and his brother made in their bookstore business. During February 1863, Sam and Jabez Richards sold goods totaling $6,773.80, their best month ever. One sale struck Sam as particularly astounding. On February 23, the brothers realized $28 on "Pens & Holders" that had cost them only seventy-five cents.[9]

Blockade goods continued to fill Atlanta's shops, leading to profits for the owners of these ships and for businessmen who sold the goods to eager consumers. As part of an update of markets on March 29, the *Southern Confederacy* noted matter-of-factly, "Blockade runners come and go at will to and from Charleston."[10] Atlanta businessmen also earned money from contracts with the Confederate government, including men such as Sidney Root who had been reluctant secessionists. Root and his partner John Beach sold cloth, thread, and blankets to the Confederate quartermaster in Atlanta for use by the army. The grocer Edward M. Edwardy sold huge quantities of food to the Confederate government for patients in Atlanta's hospitals. One receipt signed March 31, 1863, was for $5,888.40 worth of rice sold in casks. The partnership of Richardson, Faulkner sold pots and pans, dishes, and cutlery to the military hospitals, while the Atlanta druggists Hamilton, Markley, and Joyner kept them supplied with medicine. A receipt dated June 18, 1862, for $919.05 included a dissecting case, iodine, and opium. Local newspapers profited by printing government advertisements for workers, conscription information, and notices about deserters from the army. Sam and Jabez Richards sold ledger books to the Confederate government for its book-keeping. The jeweler Er Lawshe billed the Confederate government for the placement and removal of shackles and irons from Union prisoners.[11]

Additionally, local businessmen leased their offices on Whitehall and Decatur Streets and their warehouses on Alabama Street for use by the Confederate government at attractive rents. On August 6, 1863, for example, Sidney Root signed a contract with Quartermaster G. W. Cunningham to rent space for a shoe factory at $225 per month. Edward Edwardy leased space for use by one of the hospitals. McNaught and Ormond held govern-ment contracts for enormous amounts of iron products and pistol caps. They also rented office space to the Confederate quartermaster. John Neal, one of Atlanta's richest citizens, rented a building to the Confederate government for a new hospital. He received $300 per month.[12]

While businessmen earned substantial and in some cases spectacular profits, Atlanta's ordinary citizens struggled. In some families, single women labored to support their children, and in others men did not earn wages that could support their dependents, so wives went to work, and in a growing number of cases so did children. James Bell was thirteen years old when he found employment at Jack's Bakery, a business that produced hardtack, the flour or cornmeal crackers that were the staple of the soldier's diet in the Civil War. James and his younger brother William worked a variety of tasks that included stoking the furnace with wood, "peeling" the crackers out of moulds, and delivering them to hospitals and local camps. The boys' father may have died, for their mother is listed in the 1860 census as a head of household employed as a prostitute.[13]

As Atlanta's largest employer, the Confederate Arsenal included a work-force of men, women, and children. Two arsenal employment ledgers called

"Time Books" survived the war. They cover the period from March 1862 to June 1863. These time books reveal that adult men earned on average from $2.00 to $3.00 per day, with blank cutters and carpenters at the low end and machinists at the high end of the pay scale. Managers earned more. Thomas Hartley was paid $5.00 per day as a foreman at the percussion cap factory, and John C. Peck earned a monthly salary of $120 as superintendent of woodworking. Women rolled and sewed cartridge bags at the arsenal and earned considerably less than men, an average of seventy-five cents per day in 1862. Most of the children employed at the arsenal were between the ages of eleven and fifteen. Boys ran errands for fifty cents per day, while both boys and girls rolled and sewed cartridge bags, earning thirty-five to fifty-five cents per day, the specific amount depending on productivity.[14]

In the absence of surviving family records, it is difficult to make definitive conclusions about the circumstances that led children to work in a government factory, but the 1860 federal census provides clues. Arsenal children whose names can be traced to the 1860 census came from white, working-class families, and their wages undoubtedly helped their parents put food on the table. Virginia Warmick, age eleven in 1862, was the daughter of a stonemason. She earned forty cents per day in June 1862, as did Julia Boswell, also age eleven. Although most child workers appear to have come from two-parent households, Julia's name appears in the census as the daughter of a widowed mother. Siblings are often listed in the time book, testimony to the need for multiple family members to contribute toward family support. Joseph and Amanda Berry were children of a "bar keeper," Robert and Margaret Beavers's father was a laborer, and Rebecca and Elizabeth Head were daughters of a watchman, while Edward and Theodore Grambling and William and Ann Lumpkin were children of carpenters.[15]

Because the two surviving time books cover only fifteen months and may not represent a comprehensive list of employees, the total number of children employed at the arsenal is not known, but their numbers were significant. Colonel Moses Wright, the arsenal's commander, wrote a letter to his counterpart in Macon, Georgia, in August 1862, indicating that he "can work 125 Boys" to help "turn out 75,000 Rounds [of ammunition] per day, if lead is supplied to me." Wright declined to use children in the more dangerous pyrotechnic laboratory, telling Josiah Gorgas, the chief of ordnance headquartered in Richmond, that it was "unsafe to employ *boys* & *girls* in that Department." Wright believed that boys were too inclined to be careless, and he feared the possibility of an accident. Wright's decision may have stemmed from a horrific tragedy at the Confederate States Laboratory in Richmond a few weeks before he wrote to Gorgas. An eighteen-year-old employee named Mary Ryan accidentally set off a series of explosions that killed at least forty-five and wounded twenty-three. Among the dead were children ages ten to twelve.[16]

In October 1862, some of the arsenal's adult employees signed a petition demanding higher wages. Colonel Wright issued an order that alluded to such a petition when he reminded male employees that they were "liable to conscription" and strongly hinted that they should cease complaining. Nonetheless, wages went up in the coming months. Men continued to earn wages that depended upon skill level, with carpenters earning $3.00–3.75 per day, bullet molders $3.00, copper rollers $3.50, gunsmiths $4.00, and machinists as much as $4.75. Enterprising young men could rise through the ranks. Nineteen-year-old Alonzo Jepson, the son of a carpenter at the arsenal named Lemuel Jepson, appears in the time book in June 1862 as an errand boy earning fifty cents per day. In March 1863 he is listed as a machine foreman making $3.25 per day. Adult women who rolled and sewed cartridge bags often earned $1.00 per day by 1863, a pay scale that probably became the government standard, since it matched the earnings of their counterparts in Richmond. However, a particularly skilled worker might earn even more; Mary A. Edwards made $1.60 per day. Many children still worked for wages at or near their pay for 1862, though some brought up their wages. For example, Ann and William Lumpkin earned fifty cents per day in November 1862 and eighty cents per day in March 1863.[17]

Workers at the Atlanta Arsenal were subject to a variety of rules and regulations imposed by Colonel Wright, including the beginning and ending of the workday signaled by bell ringing. Employees could be and were dismissed for all manner of infractions, including the perception that they were dissatisfied with their positions. Male employees knew that if they lost their positions they could be conscripted. Nonetheless, Wright, whose correspondence conveys the sense that he was always in need of more workers, also needed to keep his current employees happy enough to be productive. Lectures about patriotism were not enough. Wright made concessions on occasion to keep the morale of his employees at a reasonable level. In suspending operations at the arsenal on Christmas Day, 1862, he acknowledged the need for employees to visit family and friends, but reminded them to be at their jobs on the twenty-sixth, so that "every shop will be filled as usual on the day following Christmas, showing that spirit that actuates every true lover of his country." Wright allowed a similar day of rest for January 1, 1863, with admonitions to be at work the following day. On February 26, 1863, he suspended operations at the Armory, Carpenter and Machine shops so that employees could attend the funeral of George Eubanks, an arsenal employee who had died of typhoid fever at age forty.[18]

Colonel Wright urged slaveowners to lease their slaves to the arsenal, with wages paid to their owners. Their names appear in the time book, sometimes with the owner's name in parentheses. For example, Joe and Burrill, owned by J. J. Thrasher, earned 96 1/6 cents per day, paid to Thrasher in March 1862, the first month for which records are available for the Atlanta Arsenal. By May and June of 1863, the last months of the time book that survive, slave wages had risen considerably. Joe and Burrill earned $40 per month for Thrasher. Surviving records of the Atlanta Arsenal suggest that slaves made up a relatively small percentage of the arsenal's employees.[19]

Moses Wright ran an impressive operation. With shops all over Atlanta, his arsenal produced a variety of hardware for the Confederacy. In March 1863, Wright wrote to the Atlanta quartermaster, "Artillery, Arms, Equipments, & Ammunition are daily shipped to the Army in large quantities. We all arrange about fifteen drays per day are necessary to receive & ship the stores . . . between the different establishments of the arsenal." Atlanta's railroads shipped massive amounts of equipment and ammunition, some locally made, others passing through the Gate City for reexport to Virginia, Tennessee, or the coast. Wright continued, "Last month, February, I find that the army[']s daily *shipments* . . . amount to from ten to fifteen tons—some days up to twenty five tons—others not so much—to say nothing of the transportation of material & manufactured articles from or to the various establishments of the arsenal."[20]

On February 11, 1863, employees of the arsenal presented a bridle to General Braxton Bragg, the commander of Confederate troops in the West. In a letter to the general, Moses Wright suggested the gift was "a specimen of their *own* handiwork, and a slight token of their Esteem. The Briddle was made entirely by them." Whether Wright ordered his employees to make Bragg's gift is not known; it is known that Bragg was becoming a controversial figure in the Confederacy, for a growing number of southerners questioned his abilities as Confederate commander.[21]

Union forces under General William Rosecrans defeated Confederates under Bragg at the battle of Stones River, December 31, 1862–January 2, 1863. The battle took place in middle Tennessee near the town of Murfreesboro. As they often did, Atlanta's newspapers printed stories that declared a military victory based on what they claimed to be early reports of the battle. The *Southern Confederacy* suggested that Bragg's victorious army would soon reoccupy Nashville before moving on to liberate Kentucky. The *Daily Intelligencer* referred to a victory over "Abolition forces," perhaps in recognition of the fact that Abraham Lincoln had recently signed into law the Emancipation Proclamation. As late as January 10, the *Intelligencer* still insisted that Rosecrans was lying when he wrote a report claiming to have won the battle.[22]

While some Atlantans debated the meaning of the recent military clash, others focused on nursing the wounded men transported daily into the city's hospitals, "by every train," as the *Daily Intelligencer* put it. John Sehon, who worked in the quartermaster's office, anticipated that at least fifteen hundred wounded would arrive by train on one night alone. Colonel G. W. Lee feared such a massive influx of wounded that he appointed a local arrangements committee of six men. The committee's chairman, J. R. Mayson, organized an initial meeting, publishing the date and time in the local newspapers. In a patronizing postscript, he invited the city's female benevolent volunteers to participate.[23]

Martha Winship and Henrietta Collier made no public comment about the appointment of a male committee. With their usual energy and determination, these presidents of the Atlanta Hospital Association and the Ladies' Soldiers' Relief Society organized volunteers, including teams of women assigned to morning and evening shifts cooking food for soldiers arriving at the passenger depot. Like other southern rail stations, this one was now called Soldiers' Rest or Wayside Hospital. Members of the Baptist-affiliated Dorcas Society and the Episcopal-affiliated St. Philip's Hospital Society raised money, made clothing, and knitted socks.[24]

The recent battle placed an enormous strain on Atlanta's hospitals. So many men flooded the city in need of medical care that Fairground Hospital split into two divisions. The first, known as Fairground Hospital No. 1, had a capacity of about 400 patients. Fairground Hospital No. 2 was still under construction in early January but received 127 patients on February 15, 1863. Gate City, Empire, and Medical College Hospitals, also crowded with patients, printed the names and military units of those being treated in their facilities. The newspapers also printed the names of those who died in battle. By 1863, twenty-six hospitals cared for patients in Atlanta.[25]

The fighting in Tennessee also brought another group of Union prisoners to Atlanta. John Sehon predicted the arrival of three thousand prisoners from the Murfreesboro fight. Schoolteacher Benjamin T. Hunter noted in his diary, "Saw a number of Yankee prisoners in Atlanta." At least some of these men spent the winter in Atlanta housed at a military prison. The *Southern Confederacy* printed the names and regiments of men present on January 10, 1863, including those captured by Confederates at Murfreesboro, seventeen men recently captured by General John Hunt Morgan, and "Mrs. E. F. Carter, spy."[26]

The presence of Union prisoners in Atlanta aroused the suspicion of Atlanta's Confederate civilians, some of whom charged that the men were being treated too well at a time when the families of Confederate soldiers struggled to make ends meet. One of the prisoners, Lieutenant William R. Lawrence of the 73rd Illinois, recalled spending the winter of 1863 in Atlanta housed in a "Lodge room" on the third floor of a brick building. He and fellow officers kept themselves busy by listening to Shakespeare's plays read aloud by a fellow prisoner, engaging in calisthenics led by another, and playing games of chess, checkers, and cards. After procuring a fiddle through the help of a Confederate guard, the officers held "stag dances" in which some of them danced as women, others as men. Public outcry about the allegedly lenient treatment of Union prisoners led Provost Marshal Lee to issue statements to the *Daily Intelligencer* denying the rumors and assuring the public that Union prisoners were not allowed to walk the streets of Atlanta "and do as they pleased."[27]

Some Union soldiers died in Atlanta's hospitals and prisons. Their burial at City Cemetery also caused controversy. The arsenal's Colonel Moses Wright fired off a letter addressing this issue to Dr. Joseph P. Logan, who was now in charge of Atlanta's Confederate hospitals. Wright vehemently opposed the burial of Union soldiers with "no *distinction*" being made geographically between "the graves of our Brave men who have died for our cause, and the graves of the worthless invaders of our soil." He added, "This is all wrong—unkind and ungenerous," and he reproached himself for not having "discovered the fact sooner and put a stop to it." The practice did not stop. Several hundred Union soldiers who died in Atlanta hospitals were interred at City Cemetery, buried side by side with Confederates, enemies in life but not in death.[28]

After Bragg's defeat, the armies went into winter quarters, leaving Atlantans time to worry about high rents, food and fuel prices, sanitary conditions, and disease. The lives of Jennie Lines and her husband, Sylvanus, illustrate the challenges faced by Atlanta civilians in 1863, and these challenges threatened to undercut morale among Atlanta civilians in the coming months. The Lineses moved out of their boardinghouse and into a rental home following the birth of their daughter Lillie. In her diary, Jennie expressed gratitude that Sylvanus's job as a typesetter exempted him from conscription, and she expressed relief that Lillie remained in good health. But Lines's diary also reveals the family's problems with escalating prices for housing, food, and fuel, fears related to infectious disease, crime, and the outcome of a military contest that had already lasted far longer than anyone had predicted. Having put aside her diary in 1862, Lines seemed reluctant to take it up again. "I ought to have kept a journal the past year for it has been fraught with strange, sad and frightful incidents in the history of our country," she wrote on January 23, 1863. "This dreadful war which is scourging our land affords a sorrowful theme to write and think upon. I often try to put the subject far from my mind, but there is too much to remind one of the terrible state of our country to forget it for an hour."[29]

Despite the fact that Sylvanus received a raise to $25.00 per week working as a typographer, the couple struggled to make ends meet. Jennie complained of "exorbitant rents" in Atlanta because of the number of refugees moving to the Gate City. To save money, the couple lived outside of town, but they wanted a live-in domestic servant to help with the baby. In letters to family, Jennie outlined her dilemma. She quickly dismissed the notion of hiring a white girl. Social norms dictated that live-in white servants were entitled to personal space, minimally a bed instead of a pallet on the floor. Jennie did not want to be bothered with such arrangements. On the other hand, rental slaves needed no privacy, according to Jennie. To save the most money, she would hire "a *little* negro," because an adolescent would cost too much in rent and clothing. She hired a twelve-year-old slave girl named Beckie for eight dollars per month and proceeded to complain about her constantly. "Like all negro help she is a perfect eye servant," she confided to her diary on January 24, 1863, the expression meaning that she could not let Beckie out of her sight. She certainly did not trust Beckie alone with the baby, and regretted that she could not go to church with Sylvanus because of this. Unfortunately, Beckie left no diary or letters to reveal how she felt about Jennie, but in general, white people who hired slaves had less concern for their well-being than their owners did, and the system of hiring slaves frequently involved separating hirelings from family and friends. Beckie's desire to reconnect with her kin was to complicate her relationship with Jennie in the coming months.[30]

Food costs troubled Jennie. Flour continued to be out of reach for middle- and lower-class families. Jennie was proud of her ability to make a palatable cake from corn and rice meal mixed together. By summer 1863, the Lines family gave up eating meat altogether, except for the occasional soup bone. They subsisted on Jennie's corn and rice cakes, vegetables and fruit from their garden, and the buttermilk that Jennie loved. The spread of disease concerned Jennie even more than the high cost of meat and wheat. Food prices were "not our greatest trouble," she wrote in her diary in January. "If the sword could be stayed, and disease checked, then could our hearts beat with the calmness and hope of other days."[31]

Smallpox terrified Jennie and many other Atlanta residents. Smallpox struck Atlanta in the fall of 1862. Because the disease caused disfigurement, even the rumor of its spread generated stories in the newspapers. In reporting the presence of the disease in surrounding counties in August, the *Southern Confederacy* also noted that the military post surgeon in Atlanta, Dr. Logan, was making vaccinations available to white Atlantans free of charge for a three-day period at City Hall. At other times, citizens were encouraged to seek vaccinations at the military hospitals. When a case of smallpox finally appeared in the city in October, Provost Marshal Lee concealed the patient's identity but ordered his quarantine outside of city limits at a facility that cared for both military and civilian patients. But the growing number of smallpox cases soon made it difficult to quarantine everyone who had the disease.[32]

In January 1863, a group of physicians appeared before the City Council and presented evidence of the "alarming extent to which Small Pox had already spread" in the Gate City. The *Southern Confederacy* reported an estimated one hundred cases. Recognizing the gravity of the situation, the City Council ordered the mandatory vaccination of every resident of Atlanta. The city hired physicians to go door to door in each of Atlanta's five wards. Physicians placed notices in the daily newspapers indicating their appointment by the city and their intention to visit every home.[33]

Doctors wasted no time carrying out their orders, and many citizens complied without hesitation. A physician came to Sam Richards's home on February 8. Frightened of the disease, as were all residents of the Gate City, Richards wrote in his diary a few weeks earlier, "God protect us and keep us from the 'pestilence that walketh in darkness.'" As a previously vaccinated healthy person, Richards was an excellent candidate from whom to extract fresh vaccine material for use on others. Richards complied with the request from a Dr. Raborg to "take matter from and [be] re-vaccinated myself." Annie Sehon embraced vaccination with enthusiasm. She had her six-month-old baby vaccinated and it "took splendidly." She noted, "The small pox is quite bad in Atlanta."[34]

Julia Davidson moved to Atlanta in October 1862 and immediately confronted the difficulties of wartime city life, including Atlanta's smallpox contagion. The wife of Lieutenant John M. Davidson of the 39th North Carolina Regiment, Julia chose to live in Atlanta because her father became a hotel keeper in the Gate City and purchased a small home near Winship Iron Works for Julia and her three children. On February 2, 1863, Julia wrote to her husband about smallpox "scattered pretty thickly over the city." Because there was a case near her house, Julia and the children did not leave their home for nearly a week. Julia took the vaccine and had her children vaccinated.[35]

Some Atlantans feared the vaccine's purity and refused to have themselves inoculated. Sarah Huff was seven years old in 1863. Her father was away in the army and her mother managed a household that included several children and a small number of slaves. In a memoir published in 1937, Huff recalled that people in Atlanta did not approve of the flags that city officials wanted them to fly as warnings of smallpox patients within their households. They also "disapproved of vaccination." Although local physicians, military authorities, and members of city government all touted the vaccine's safety, Sarah Huff's family remained skeptical. The *Daily Intelligencer* published an article that specifically addressed the question of the vaccine's safety, including a discussion about whether contaminated vaccine materials could give a patient "erysipelas or some similar disease." The newspaper concluded that the vaccine was safe so long as vaccine material was taken from a healthy person. Nonetheless, Huff indicated that there were individuals in Atlanta who refused to be vaccinated and who refused to give up visiting the sick.[36]

It is unclear how many slaves received vaccinations in Atlanta. In December 1862, City Councilman Calvin Hunnicutt proposed that the city marshal remove "the negroes known to have been exposed to Smallpox" to be treated by Dr. Westmoreland and quarantined under guard. Subsequent cases came before the Council in which owners asked for restitution from the city for lost wages of these slaves. They were referred to the Inferior Court.[37]

By March, the smallpox contagion had "played out in this city," as the *Southern Confederacy* put it, but other diseases sickened residents of Atlanta, including pneumonia and scarlet fever. Both diseases killed a number of children in the early months of 1863, and those who lost friends and family poured out their personal grief in letters, diaries, even newspaper testimonials. When a teenager named Ellen Luckie died of scarlet fever on February 19, six of her bereaved school friends wrote a tribute published in both of the city's daily newspapers. It lauded her purity, her spirit, and her ability to help them with their homework, especially Latin and French translations. Classmates wore mourning badges for thirty days. After Atlanta's weather turned warmer, cases of dysentery and typhoid fever took the lives of children, with babies and toddlers among the most vulnerable.[38]

The sexton at City Cemetery revealed the vulnerability of children to disease when he recorded interments for the first quarter of 1863. Thirty-six white children and twenty-eight black children under the age of ten years were interred that quarter, along with twenty-seven white and thirty black civilians over the age of ten. Slave children are listed in cemetery records by the owner's name. For example, Joseph Winship's slave Moses, age seven, died from pneumonia on January 24. Slave children under one year of age lack names in the cemetery records, their brief lives recorded only as losses for their owners. An infant belonging to Richard Peters died on January 25 from croup, and Congressman Lucius Gartrell's three-month-old slave died of the same ailment on December 12. The highest number of slave deaths recorded in the African American cemetery records are those of the slave dealer Robert M. Clarke, whose business was located on the west side of Whitehall Street. In newspaper advertisements, Clarke claimed to have "a commodious, well arranged Yard, with every convenience for the health and comfort of slaves," yet twelve children belonging to Clarke died in 1863, often from infectious diseases such as pneumonia, croup, and measles. Held in close proximity while awaiting sale, they probably infected one another.[39]

Because the smallpox epidemic frightened so many Atlantans, the Athenaeum did not hold performances during the first few months of 1863; the reopening of the theater in the early spring provided an opportunity for the *Daily Intelligencer* to reflect upon the importance of music and drama to the morale of Atlanta's civilian population. Atlantans "require in these times of turmoil, and distress, and much suffering . . . amusements of some description," of which theater was their favorite, one reporter wrote on March 24, 1863. Eloise Bridges became the Gate City's most acclaimed actress in 1863, thrilling audiences with her performances as Desdemona in Shakespeare's *Othello*, as Julia in *Hunchback*, and in the title role in *Lucretia Borgia*. John Davis often acted the male lead, including a patriotic drama called *Roll of the Drum on the Battle of Manassas*, a play that allowed audience members to relive the exciting days of the Civil War's first battle.[40]

When Blind Tom Wiggins gave another benefit for sick Confederate soldiers at the Athenaeum in April 1863, an ad for his concert appeared directly above another ad, one for W. H. Henderson, Negro Brokers and Commission Merchants. An untold number of bondspeople went on the auction block in wartime Atlanta. When reporter Israel Gibbons wrote about auctions and trade in Atlanta during his 1863 visit, he may have referenced the slave trade among other types of auctions. Many slave traders in addition to W. H. Henderson sold bondspeople in Atlanta, including Solomon Cohen, A. K. Seago, Whitaker and Turner, Fields and Gresham, B. D. Smith, Inman, Cole and Company, and perhaps the largest of the city's slave brokers, the firms of Crawford, Frazer and Company and Robert M. Clarke.[41]

Atlanta's newspapers printed stories attesting to the high prices brought by slaves. On April 15, the *Daily Intelligencer* contained a story about a slave sale the previous day conducted by Crawford, Frazer. This firm sold a slave waiter for $3,500, a maid for $3,000, and a nine-year-old boy for $2,150, along with "others in proportion." Although slave prices were similar to those in Macon, another Georgia city with wartime factories, the *Intelligencer* bragged that Atlanta had become *the* regional center for slave trading, with buyers and sellers from throughout the Confederacy using Crawford, Frazer. Atlanta was "almost up to Richmond as a negro mart," the *Intelligencer* insisted. The following week, Crawford, Frazer printed an ad with sixty-six slaves for sale, listed by name and description, including Margaret, age forty-two, a cook, and Henry, age twenty-three, a dining room and store clerk. Crawford, Frazer offered several family groups for sale, including Amy, a thirty-three-year-old cook, washer, and ironer, and her six children ages one to thirteen. While traders often listed family groups, they did not hesitate to sell family members separately if a buyer chose not to purchase the entire group. In spite of the newspaper bombast, not all slaves brought high prices. On May 2, 1863, Crawford, Frazer sold Harry and Hannah, slaves estimated to be ages thirty-four and thirty, for a combined price of $3,600. The buyer received a printed receipt attesting to the slaves being "sound of body, [and] of mind."[42]

The high prices that slaves brought at auction were a testament to white people's confidence in the institution's future and to the elevated demand for slave labor. The Confederate government continued to advertise for owners to lease their bondspeople for use in the Confederate hospitals. By the middle of 1863, African Americans made up half of the labor force in Atlanta's military hospitals, most of them cooking, doing laundry, and caring for patients. Their owners received $25.00 per month for men and $15.00 for women. Atlanta's largest hospital, Fairground No. 1, had the largest black workforce, with forty-six individuals on its fulltime roster. Lemuel Grant, now busily constructing fortifications around Atlanta, wanted owners to lease their slaves to him. Moses Wright employed slaves at the arsenal and looked for additional manpower. Ads appeared regularly by Atlantans seeking to hire or purchase slaves. Ads also appeared in Atlanta newspapers placed by those seeking slaves to work in industries located in Columbus, Georgia, and Raleigh, North Carolina, and at the Confederacy's largest iron works, the Tredegar factory in Richmond.[43]

Even as the demand for their labor increased, African Americans faced deteriorating conditions in the city. In January, a male slave was "dreadfully mangled" on a farm outside of Atlanta when he was accidentally hit by an artillery shell from a battery of men who were practicing nearby. In April, a shoddily constructed building intended for slave nurses at Gate City Hospital collapsed, causing serious injury to one slave who was buried in the rubble. So many slaves suffered illness and injury while working on fortifications around the city that Lemuel Grant asked for a government-paid physician to work with him.[44]

Yearning for freedom, understanding the challenges but also the opportunities presented by the war, and increasingly willing to take risks, Atlanta's slaves began running away in growing numbers. The documentary record is sketchy, but newspaper ads for runaway slaves provide clues. In 1862, many ads referenced runaways who came from Tennessee, probably brought to Atlanta by owners fleeing the federal army and/or looking for new economic opportunities in the Gate City. For example, Alvin K. Seago offered $50 in December 1862 for the apprehension of "my boy Dave," who was from Murfreesboro, Tennessee, and "frequently manifested considerable anxiety to be with his wife whom he had left behind." By 1863, slaves were running away from businesses and households throughout the city of Atlanta. Robert M. Clarke advertised for Bill, Daniel, Richmond, and Henry, who "broke out of my [slave] yard" and fled. Slaves also fled after being auctioned to new owners; Lucy Jane ran away from her new owner several weeks after Clarke sold her. A slave named Sam disappeared the same day he was purchased from the auction house of Crawford, Frazer. They disappeared from businesses; a woman named Charity fled from the Atlanta Hotel. Slaves ran away from factories; John and Morris disappeared from the Atlanta Rolling Mill. They ran away from jobs as domestics in family homes, including slaves owned by the city's most prominent families. John Neal advertised for the return of Mary Ellen in January. Er Lawshe lost Jack in March.[45]

Some runaways were captured and returned. Beckie, the rental slave of Jennie Lines, attempted to run away in February 1863. Sylvanus found her "before she got to town, [and] all she gained by the undertaking was a severe whipping." Beckie may have known she would be recaptured, but her desire to see friends and family overcame her fear of punishment. Frank, the slave of Jabez Richards, ran away in September to see his wife, but was picked up east of Atlanta, taken to the Covington jail, and whipped before Richards arrived to reclaim him. Other slaves died trying to run away. In April, Joseph Winship found a dead body in his barn loft on Peachtree Street. The unidentified, unclaimed corpse of an African American male was wedged between bales of fodder, possibly a runaway bondsman seeking refuge.[46]

Slaveowners regarded runaways as "bad Negroes." White southerners believed that slaves were inherently weak in character and prone to misbehavior. In their minds, slavery was a benign institution in which lightly tasked bondspeople received firm but fair guidance from caring white people. According to this notion, slaves were expected to play by the rules, and failure to do so made victims of white owners, not of slaves. When Annie Sehon's sister Bettie offered her the use of a family slave named Pennie, Annie declined because the bondswoman had previously attempted to flee. Annie did not trust a slave who had tried to run away, telling Bettie "I always have this [negative] feeling for a negro that has once run away." After Beckie attempted to run away, Jennie Lines wrote in her diary, "I fear she is a bad negro." Jennie had reason to distrust Beckie. In July, Beckie ran away again, after Jennie sent her away from the house to pick blackberries. Although Jennie predicted that Beckie had gone to visit friends and would return, when she did not do so for several days, Jennie feared that Beckie might have escaped from bondage. Finally, Sylvanus came home one night and reported that Beckie's master had decided to sell her after apprehending the runaway yet again. Although Jennie often described Beckie as "careless and stupid," she found life without a servant difficult. Beckie's fate is not known. She might have been sold privately, or she might have ended up in the "slave yard" of Crawford, Frazer or Robert M. Clarke.[47]

Even when they did not attempt to flee, slaves were becoming harder to control. White Atlantans thought that slaves seemed to be committing more acts of "insolence" toward white people and more crimes, including serious ones. Sam Richards believed that slaves owned by himself and his brother were behaving in an "outrageously impudent" fashion, and he believed that his brother was not treating the matter seriously enough. Richards recorded several instances of whipping his slave Ellen, including once, in May 1862, when she helped herself to some of Sallie Richards's cologne, a repeat offense, and again, in February 1863, when she supposedly stole a spool of thread. Knowing the likely outcome, Ellen decided to assert herself regardless of the consequences.[48]

A variety of legal cases involving slaves engaging in "disorderly conduct" came before the Mayor's Court, the judicial process whereby Mayor Calhoun made decisions about nonviolent crimes. In February 1863, a slave named Bill came before the mayor, charged with disorderly conduct for riding a horse on the sidewalk and "using insolent language" to Mr. and Mrs. G. W. Evans. Mayor Calhoun pronounced Bill guilty and sentenced him to fifteen lashes at the jail, costs to be paid by his owner. Jane, charged with disorderly conduct for "using improper language and behavior to Mrs. Davis in Atlanta . . . & at other times before that time," also guilty, received twenty-five lashes.[49] Some slaves committed serious crimes. In May 1863 two female slaves faced arrest when they attempted to burn a boardinghouse owned by Edmund Holland. Both women were hirelings, whose arson involved throwing smoldering coals under the building. The presence of smoke alerted the owner, who put the fire out before it could cause serious damage. The slaves were hauled off to jail.[50]

City authorities made an effort to enforce laws intended to prevent African Americans from doing business in the city, although the Ponder slaves were apparently exempt from this. A slave named Hannah was indicted in June for selling pies, fined $4.00 by Mayor Calhoun, and ordered to be whipped twenty lashes if she could not pay. White Atlantans did not want free African Americans to reside in their city. The *Southern Confederacy* reprinted a city ordinance, under Mayor Calhoun's signature, that mandated free people of color to pay a fee of $1,000 within ten days of their arrival in Atlanta in order to reside there. While this ordinance remained on the books, it was not always enforced. In May, the city released a free woman named Mary who had been incarcerated along with her children for violating the ordinance.[51]

Problems with food prices, disease, and recalcitrant slaves contributed to a growing sense of pessimism among Atlanta's Confederate civilians, and by the spring of 1863, there were visible cracks in the unity of Confederate Atlanta. Some men continued to make money, including those who owned businesses, factories, and buildings they could rent to the Confederate government. Everyone else seemed to be sliding downward. Julia Davidson found it difficult to make ends meet. She wrote to her husband on February 2 that she had applied for $100, an appropriation that the state of Georgia made available for women who had no income outside of the pay from a husband or brother in the army. Later that month, Julia thanked her husband for sending her cash via a cousin who visited Atlanta but also wrote that she wished she had his watch, for she could then auction it for cash. The war created many challenges for widows like Amanda Lin, who lived on Decatur Street with her three daughters. To keep her only son Charles out of the army, she sent him to the Georgia Military Institute in Marietta, leasing out her slave to pay the tuition. By 1863 she was taking in boarders and complaining "*Times get worse and worse [a]bout something to eat.*"[52]

In addition to the economic woes facing a growing number of Atlantans, the emotional toll of war seemed increasingly apparent. The longing that Julia and John felt for each other comes through in their letters. John wrote in March to Julia, nicknamed "Scrap" because of her short stature, that he missed the pleasure of sleeping in a "comfortable bed with a nice *little Woman.*" John then apologized for "casting any insinuations" of sexual longing. After reading that Atlanta's provost guard might be increased in size to one hundred men, Julia wrote to John. "How I wish you could get a place among them. Can you try?" As the war stretched on month after month, couples found the strain of separation very difficult. "How long will this slaughter of human beings continue[?]" Julia wrote in despair on June 29, 1863.[53]

The war created myriad fears for children. Some of them held jobs to support their families. Children's labor was increasingly in demand as the government conscripted adult men. Advertisements in city newspapers called for women and boys as factory workers. Brown and Hape advertised for workers at their Tooth Factory, and promised liberal wages, since the work "is eminently ARTISTIC" and involved a period of training. Brown and Hape wanted to hire some "worthy young men." Parents worried about children in the workplace and about their safety in Atlanta's busy streets and rail yards. When a boy named Jimmie Grub died after being struck by a train and another child died under similar circumstances the following week, anxious parents redoubled their efforts to protect their youngsters. Benjamin Yancey, a cavalry officer stationed in Virginia, wrote to his son, warning him never to board a moving train and never to "put y[ou]r head out of the windows."[54]

In turn, children worried about their parents. Many children had fathers in the army. After John Davidson had been home for a visit, his young daughter Hattie kept repeating, *"Papa gone gone,"* Julia Davidson wrote. Over time, more children confronted family tragedies involving parents who were ill, wounded, or killed. Piromis Bell's earliest childhood memory was of seeing his father come home on medical leave in 1862 so emaciated by typhoid fever that his four-year-old son barely knew him. Piromis also remembered the death of his Uncle Henry Bell and the funeral at City Cemetery. Mothers died too. Annie and Ethel Richards lost their mother Stella Wheeler Richards to tuberculosis in February 1863. Their bereaved father moved his family to the countryside, evidently having concluded that Atlanta was an unhealthy place. Some children became orphans. In April, Atlantans organized an Orphans' Ball that raised money for the state orphan asylum.[55]

Many Atlantans found ways to cope with adversity, but the city's growing underclass revealed a new willingness to resort to drastic measures. On the morning of March 18, 1863, the cracks in Atlanta's Confederate unity widened perceptibly when a dozen women broke into a butcher shop on Whitehall Street and demanded that the butcher lower the price of bacon below $1.10 per pound. When he refused, one of the women drew a gun and invited her compatriots to help themselves to the bacon. They took meat valued at $200. Additional details about the affair are sketchy, including the identities of the women.[56]

Atlanta officials tamped down the episode hurriedly. City marshal Benjamin Williford arrived soon after the holdup and dispersed the group, suggesting that the women return the next day, when, he promised, he would distribute funds to those in need. Williford did so, collecting $500 and making it available to women who came back to claim it. In reporting the episode, the *Atlanta Daily Intelligencer* treated the women sympathetically. Under the title "Relieve the Distressed," the *Intelligencer* indicated that the women were wives and daughters of soldiers deserving of sympathy. In a series of stories entitled "The Women's Seizures" and "More on Those Women," the *Southern Confederacy* suggested that while a few of the women were genuinely needy, others were simply "bad characters." The *Confederacy* also intimated that the ringleader of the group, described by both newspapers as a tall woman, was actually the wife of a well-paid local shoemaker who did not need to steal food. The *Confederacy* emphasized the importance of respecting the rule of law and warned against violence. However, in a subsequent story, the *Southern Confederacy* backed off its strident tone. Citing the city marshal, the newspaper reported: "We have many poor women in the city who need liberal charity. The majority of them work hard but do not earn enough to meet their necessary wants."[57]

Although the confrontation in Atlanta's butcher shop ended quickly, this episode was the first of several incidents labeled "bread riots" in the Confederacy during the spring of 1863, all of them apparently initiated by women, many of whom were underprivileged. Bread riots also occurred in Salisbury, North Carolina; Mobile, Alabama; and Petersburg, Virginia. Several Georgia cities experienced episodes of looting in the weeks following Atlanta's. Looters in Macon stole calico cloth, while in Columbus armed women broke into a dry goods store and took "whatever they wanted," according to one account. By the spring of 1863, clothing had become nearly as unaffordable as food. The biggest riot in the Confederacy occurred in the capital city of Richmond on April 2 and involved several hundred women, many of them wives of laborers. Looters stole shoes, books, pots, and pans, in addition to food. An appeal from President Jefferson Davis ended the affair, and close to fifty accused rioters were brought before the Mayor's Court.[58]

The riots of 1863 forced state governments and the central government in Richmond to acknowledge women's emergence as political partisans and their willingness to resort to violence when pushed beyond the level of endurance. By 1863, the notion that women sat on the sidelines of war, sheltered by male protectors, gave way to a new understanding that women would not remain passive in the future. Governor Brown, who had already shown a populist instinct when he rationed the state's salt supply in 1861 and protected the corn crop from being distilled into whiskey in 1862, called the Georgia legislature into session nine days after the Atlanta incident. Announcing that "the great question in this revolution is now *bread*," Brown asked for new restrictions on distillers who, after laws prohibiting distillation of corn into whiskey, had turned to other commodities, including potatoes and fruit, items that the governor declared should be available as food not drink. Furthermore, he said, if farmers continued to grow even small amounts of cotton instead of food crops, "the result will be our subjugation by hunger, and the utter ruin of the Confederacy." Brown did not persuade the legislature to prohibit the cultivation of cotton, but he did get a bill outlawing the distillation of a wide variety of food items, including grains like wheat, barley, and millet, vegetables including sweet potatoes, and dried fruit, and sweeteners such as molasses, honey, and sugar cane.[59]

The *Southern Confederacy* framed the situation by posing a question: "Whither are we drifting?" Women, whose support for the Confederacy was believed to be vitally important, took to the streets to protest their plight in March. What would happen next? Instead of articles about flag waving, hospital volunteering, and money raising, Atlanta women now showed up in the newspapers as rioters and also appeared in records of the Mayor's Court. Before the war, women rarely appeared in Mayor's Court records except in cases of prostitution, for which the city issued modest fines, then turned to other matters. In 1863, prostitution cases still appeared, a total of four cases involving eight women, one of them a repeat offender, but Mayor's Court cases now also involved female drunkenness, fighting, and indecent language. On March 27, Eliza Lee was fined for "being drunk and using profane & obscene language in Atlanta." On May 15, Emily Sweatman was found guilty of "using profane language and abusing one Miss McCoy." In these and other cases, fines of $10.00 were levied and failure to pay led to five days of jail time.[60] In addition to Unionists, poor white women and slaves now posed a potential threat to Atlanta's peace, prosperity, and civic unity.

As the spring military campaigns began, stories about "bad Negroes" and "bad women" gave way to reports from the battlefield. In the East, the news was positive. During the first week of May, Robert E. Lee's Army of Northern Virginia won a stunning victory at Chancellorsville, Virginia, against Union forces commanded by Joseph Hooker. For once, the *Southern Confederacy* did not exaggerate when it called the battle "one of the greatest victories of the war." However, in subsequent days the newspaper reported the death of General Stonewall Jackson, Lee's most gifted commander, who had suffered a nonmortal wound, then contracted pneumonia and died the following week. Although Jackson never captured the imagination of Atlantans the way John Hunt Morgan did, his importance to Lee's army was well understood. The *Confederacy* concluded that Jackson's death was "the most serious loss [of a military commander] we have yet sustained."[61]

As it had in 1862, the *Daily Intelligencer* published the correspondence sent by Lieutenant Colonel James Neal to his father John Neal in Atlanta, thus providing newspaper-reading Atlantans with a more personal portrait of battle than the stories supplied by the *Intelligencer*'s Richmond correspondent, who used the moniker "Clio." Neal's regiment, the 19th Georgia, saw heavy fighting at Chancellorsville, and though the battle had been a great success, Neal acknowledged significant Confederate combat deaths in his regiment, including one man from the Gate City. In subsequent days, the *Southern Confederacy* printed lists of men killed or wounded at Chancellorsville, and anxious families searched its pages for news of loved ones. By 1863, this had become a familiar and dreaded ritual.[62]

In the West, all eyes focused on Vicksburg. The last major Confederate fort on the Mississippi River, Vicksburg was now the target of General Ulysses S. Grant and his army. If Grant took Vicksburg, the Union would control the river and isolate Texas, Louisiana, and Arkansas from the rest of the Confederacy. In March, Mayor James Calhoun visited the "Gibraltar of the Mississippi," where his sons Captain William L. Calhoun and Private James T. Calhoun were stationed. James suffered a case of typhoid fever but survived. In April, the *Southern Confederacy* published a letter from Captain Calhoun to his wife in Atlanta attesting to the "fine spirits" of Confederate soldiers stationed in the garrison and their efforts to shell Yankee gunboats menacing the fort.[63]

In May, Grant's siege of Vicksburg generated news reports, coupled with speculation that soldiers of General Joseph Johnston might reinforce the Confederate garrison at Vicksburg, commanded by General John Pemberton. With the Press Association unable to get a reporter closer to the action than Jackson, Mississippi, reports generated by the PA were largely based on interviews with those leaving the Confederate lines. The *Daily Intelligencer* predicted, "Vicksburg will be saved." The *Memphis Appeal*, which became Atlanta's third daily newspaper when it set up shop in the Gate City during early June, contended that "Gen. Pemberton and his forces grow stronger and stronger." Over time, it became harder for newspapers to maintain this optimistic tone, especially when the public listened to "*rumors* at the car-shed," as the *Intelligencer* put it. The arrival of dozens of trains every day made the passenger depot the city's principal venue for gossip and speculation about military affairs. Nonetheless, the *Intelligencer* expressed confidence in the Confederate Army and offered assurances to its readers that the Confederate garrison had abundant rations and could withstand anything the Yankees might attempt.[64]

On June 27, the *Southern Confederacy* acknowledged the tide of public pessimism by running an editorial titled "Can Vicksburg Be Saved?" The story concluded that the South "could better afford to lose almost any other point now held by us and menaced by the Yankees."[65] For Confederate Atlanta, the waiting seemed endless.

6. Difficult Questions and the Search for Answers

On Thursday, July 9, 1863, Atlantans opened their evening editions of the *Southern Confederacy* to learn that the Confederate garrison at Vicksburg had surrendered to General Ulysses S. Grant. For Confederate Atlantans, their worst fears had been realized. In the second half of 1863, Atlantans confronted a shifting military situation, a declining economy, and an increasingly intrusive central government in Richmond. Efforts by the government to enforce conscription, collect taxes, requisition crops, and impress slaves for military use led civilians in Atlanta and elsewhere in the Confederacy to debate the meaning of their experiment in nation building. Should the states cede power to the government in Richmond? Were the sacrifices the war imposed on soldiers and their families worth the fight? "Southerners struggled with competing visions of their political future," one historian has written. "The advocates of centralization argued military necessity," while their critics believed that "the rights of individuals, communities, and states must be maintained at all costs." In the coming months, Atlantans searched for answers, and civic unity became increasingly difficult to maintain.[1]

The defeat at Vicksburg elicited a great deal of public comment, since Atlantans understood the importance of its loss. Amanda Lin wrote to her son Charles on July 10, "We are feeling bad about the Yankees having Vicksburgh." Atlantans knew that the Union now controlled the mighty

Mississippi River, and that Texas, Arkansas, and Louisiana were effectively isolated from the rest of the Confederacy. However, initial reports about General Robert E. Lee's army offered cause for optimism. Lee followed his victory at Chancellorsville with an offensive that took his enormous army into southern Pennsylvania. By planting his army close to Philadelphia and Washington, D.C., Lee hoped to generate opposition to the war among northerners. Rumors flew about the progress of this campaign and were duly noted by the newspapers. One report reached Atlanta that the Confederates had captured the Pennsylvania state capital of Harrisburg. Another had Lee "spreading terror and consternation" among citizens of Philadelphia, Baltimore, and Washington. Yet another, headlined "Our Success," suggested that Lee had captured forty thousand prisoners. Three days later, another proclaimed the "falling back of the Yankees."[2]

None of the reports was true. Lee lost badly at Gettysburg, and this loss in Pennsylvania, coupled with the debacle at Vicksburg, sent ripples of fear through the Confederate States. "Vicksburg has fallen . . . and we hear that the reported glorious victory of Lee's in V[irgini]a is not as great as represented," Annie Sehon wrote to her sister Bettie. "This is certainly the darkest period of our revolution." In the next few months, Confederate authorities worried about whether the South could sustain a political and social consensus to continue the fight.[3]

Ulysses S. Grant paroled nearly thirty thousand Confederate prisoners at Vicksburg, many of whom boarded trains and traveled through Atlanta. Benjamin Hunter, who lived in nearby DeKalb County, made frequent appearances in the Gate City during the summer of 1863 to visit his brother Sam, a patient at Fairground Hospital. On July 25, Hunter wrote in his diary, "The 42nd Ga. Reg. returned from Vicksburg—crowded times in Atlanta," and on the twenty-eighth, "Every train crowded with paroled prisoners from Vicksburg." Among the parolees from the 42nd Georgia were William and James Calhoun, sons of the Atlanta mayor. Like many others, they would violate the parole papers they signed at Vicksburg by rejoining their regiment. In the present crisis, the Confederacy needed all of its available manpower.[4]

Atlantans heard more bad news in early August. General John Hunt Morgan, whose 1862 cavalry raids had inspired so much adulation among residents of the Gate City, executed a series of raids in southern Indiana and Ohio during 1863. With Atlantans feeling "gloomy" in the aftermath of

Confederate losses at Vicksburg and Gettysburg, the *Daily Intelligencer*'s article on July 24 recounting Morgan's exploits provided a "thrill of delight" to its readers. Two days later, Morgan's luck ran out. He was captured near Salineville, Ohio, and incarcerated at a prison in Columbus. News reached the Gate City in early August after the *Intelligencer* copied stories from northern newspapers gleeful over the capture of such a high-ranking military officer. Subsequent articles in the Atlanta papers told the details of his capture and his treatment by prison authorities.[5]

In the summer of 1863, Confederate civilians turned to God to understand their declining prospects. Jefferson Davis announced in July a day of fasting and prayer to be held on August 21. Davis told the southern people to engage in "self examination." He suggested that Confederates suffered from overconfidence and personal faults such as greed. In promoting the fast day, the *Daily Intelligencer* told the people that they must "humble themselves before the Mighty power," for God was testing the Confederate people to see whether they had the will to continue the fight. On Friday, August 21, the *Intelligencer* reminded residents of the Gate City to "repair to their different places of worship" for the Confederacy's fast day, and many did so. Sam Richards closed his bookstore, noting in his diary, "This is our National Fast Day and all business is suspended." Richards and his wife attended services at Second Baptist Church.[6]

The Gate City's three newspapers printed a series of stories in the summer of 1863 designed to reassure Confederate Atlantans and provide them with a vision for the future. Concerned that local women might be questioning whether to continue supporting a war seemingly without end, Atlanta newspapers published editorials specifically aimed at them. In applauding female heroism in one article, the *Daily Intelligencer* singled out for special commendation women's efforts on behalf of the sick and wounded in area hospitals. The *Southern Confederacy* preached personal sacrifice by publishing a poem that paid homage to "The Southern Girl with Homespun Dress," by "author unknown" and intended to be sung to the tune of "Bonnie Blue Flag." The heroine of this poem needed no blockade goods from Paris or London. She was proud to wear homemade clothing to show her patriotism.

> This homespun dress is plain, I know—
> My hat's Palmetto, too—

> But then it shows what Southern girls
> For Southern rights will do.

Another stanza implied that women in homespun were especially attractive to men:

> We've sent our sweethearts to the war,
> But dear girls, never mind,
> Your soldier lad will not forget
> The girl he left behind.[7]

Newspaper editorials aimed at male readers focused on military recruitment. The recent reverses at Vicksburg and Gettysburg should "arouse us to renewed energy and vigor rather than be permitted to overshadow us with the gloomy pall of despondency," according to an editorial in the *Memphis Appeal*. On August 9, the *Intelligencer* reminded readers to love their country and to have patience because victory might take longer than anyone initially thought. The key to Confederate success was enlistment of more men, according to an editorial on August 16.[8]

Efforts to recruit new soldiers succeeded in Atlanta, at least initially. Fulton County held a rally to fill its military quota two weeks after the losses at Vicksburg and Gettysburg. The *Daily Intelligencer* reported that it was well attended. Many ladies signaled their own patriotism with their presence, and the *Intelligencer* predicted that Fulton County would have no trouble enlisting five hundred men, as mandated by the government. Congressman Lucius Gartrell addressed the crowd and spoke of a life-and-death struggle in which an "unscrupulous foe" sought the South's "subjugation and destruction."[9]

Although Gartrell could still command an audience with oratorical fireworks, he also built a quieter reputation in the Confederate Congress as an advocate for soldiers and a supporter of President Davis's policies. The lack of funding blocked his efforts, but Gartrell lobbied to increase the pay of enlisted soldiers and transport home for burial at government expense the bodies of whose who died in service to their country. Gartrell also strongly endorsed President Davis, who was increasingly at odds with the Confederacy's doctrinaire states' rights proponents, including Georgia's Governor Brown. In addition to conscription, which Brown opposed, believing that Georgia's soldiers should fight exclusively for defense of their home state, Davis's policies included efforts to standardize the seizure or "impressment" of food, livestock, and slaves for military use. Although the government paid civilians when it impressed, the amount never approached market value, and the practice was highly controversial. Gartrell considered a run for governor in 1863, understanding that the Richmond government would support him. However, he decided against such a course, and Governor Brown handily defeated two opponents in November. Meanwhile, debate continued among proponents of centralization and those who supported states' rights. Georgia's Alexander Stephens became a vigorous advocate for states' rights, even though he held the office of Confederate vice president.[10]

Despite the efforts of Gartrell and others, the call for military recruitment was not heeded by all men. In the same diary entry in which he noted his participation in a day of religious observance and fasting for a cause to which he adhered, Sam Richards also noted his most recent efforts to dodge the draft. At age thirty-nine, Richards regarded himself as too old to fight and temperamentally unsuited to do so. He did not believe the Confederate government had the right to force him to join. However, the Confederacy needed manpower, and Congress, which initially drafted men as old as thirty-five, raised the age to forty-five. Unlike many men in the Confederacy, Richards had enough money avoid conscription. He hired a substitute, a legal action in both the Union and Confederacy. In March 1863, Richards paid $2,500 to John D. Kugler of Carroll County, Georgia, to take his place in the draft. Substitutes often collected money, then deserted, and within a matter of months Kugler disappeared from the Confederate Army. Next, Richards became a part-time typesetter because printers received an exemption, their work producing newspapers deemed vital to their country. To enhance his chances further, Richards and his brother Jabez purchased a newspaper called the *Soldiers' Friend,* a publication designed to raise morale among soldiers by providing them with inspirational stories, many of them religious in nature. This action earned Richards his coveted draft deferral.[11]

For those without Richards's money, the path to draft resistance was more difficult, and Confederate authorities became increasingly aggressive in tracking down those who attempted to avoid conscription. On August 19, 1863, two Confederate officers accompanied by several additional soldiers appeared at a performance of White's Minstrels at the Athenaeum. They barred the doors of the theater just as the curtain fell on the second act and began systematically checking the crowded hall for individuals who might be draft dodgers. They found half a dozen men and escorted them to military barracks. "No skulkers will be allowed to remain in Atlanta," the *Intelligencer* intoned. The following week, military authorities provided the *Intelligencer* with an alphabetical list of those whose names had been called in an effort to draw public attention to individuals in violation of conscription law. The newspaper also warned citizens to be on the lookout for men who might attempt to forge papers pretending they had hired substitutes. In December 1863, the Confederate Congress voted to end the practice of allowing substitutes.[12]

As military engagements increasingly went against them, Confederates hoped that northern antiwar sentiment might undercut the Union's desire to prosecute the war. Atlanta's newspapers provided coverage of the bloody draft riot taking place in New York City during July and the success of antiwar Democrats in stirring up opposition to the war in parts of the lower Midwest. In the aftermath of the battle of Gettysburg, New York City exploded in violence as working-class men, many of them Irish immigrants who were angered over the prospect of being drafted, viciously attacked African Americans and white people who supported them. Citing the *New York Herald*, the *Intelligencer* noted the violence aimed at the Negro Orphan Asylum and the harassment and even the killing of African Americans in the city. President Lincoln had to divert troops from Gettysburg to quell the violence. Under the headline "Anarchy in the North," the *Memphis Appeal* predicted that draft riots would spread to other areas, a forecast that was largely incorrect.[13]

Ohio Congressman Clement Vallandigham became the most visible and articulate antiwar leader in the North. As the northern citizenry grew tired of a war now in its third year and as antagonism toward Lincoln's Emancipation Proclamation coalesced among Democrats, the "Copperhead" wing of the Democratic Party argued for an end to the war by granting southern independence. Copperhead strength was greatest in Ohio, Illinois, and Indiana, the three most densely populated states of the Midwest. In 1863, Vallandigham sought the governorship of his state and gave speeches disparaging President Lincoln. He advocated resistance to the draft and a repudiation of the Emancipation Proclamation. Military authorities arrested Vallandigham, found him guilty of treason, and sentenced him to prison. Democrats denounced this action, and President Lincoln partially defused the situation by ordering that Vallandigham be banished behind Confederate lines. The *Southern Confederacy* printed many stories about Vallandigham, including one focused on a Copperhead meeting in Newark, New Jersey, where a crowd of Peace Democrats condemned the "illegal seizure and banishment of Hon. C. L. Vallandigham" and the "military despotism" of the Lincoln administration.[14]

Confederate authorities knew that they could not count on northern antiwar sentiment to end the war and also knew that Vicksburg's capitulation drew attention to the vulnerability of cities in the lower South. In response, they ordered Lemuel P. Grant, chief engineer of the Department of Georgia, to build a ring of fortifications to protect Atlanta. On August 17, 1863, he reported "satisfactory" progress in the completion of "small works at the Ferries on the Chattahoochee" River, but in subsequent reports to his superiors, Grant complained of a lack of available labor to complete the job. He sent recruiters into rural counties in Georgia, Alabama, and Mississippi seeking to hire slaves at $25 per month, guaranteeing their transportation by rail to Atlanta, adequate nourishment, and medical care at government expense. The contracts he offered to slaveowners also guaranteed that in the event of death caused by injury or "exposure to the enemy," owners would be compensated the appraised value of their slaves. Grant briefly experimented with hiring slave women and children, but ultimately he concluded that their limited ability to use a pick and shovel made this experiment unsuccessful. As he put it, "women and small negroes of both sexes, have not earned the rations with which they have been supplied. . . . The labor was not satisfactory to me."[15]

Like all those who owned or hired slaves, Grant complained about runaways. He sent a list of seventeen names of men he believed to be runaways to the sheriff of Fayette County, offering to compensate him for his time if he rounded up the missing men, presumably suspecting that they had returned to this county south of Atlanta to see family members. Perhaps because he feared another such episode, Grant allowed a group of slaves from Troup County southwest of Atlanta to visit family for Christmas 1863 with admonitions to "be ready for the [railroad] cars on the morning of the 1st of January."[16]

Despite these difficulties, within three months Grant had enough labor to build a ring of defenses around the Gate City that included a series of redoubts, or small defensive enclosures, linked by rifle pits, each designed to hold five guns. The defensive line was open at the back and Grant sought clarification from his superiors in Richmond about whether they wanted him to enclose the rear with stockades. Grant's preparations would be ongoing.[17]

By fall 1863, panic about the future subsided and a revival of patriotism characterized the Confederate home front. Leading that revival in Atlanta— in addition to the newspapers—was the indefatigable Martha Winship. Although she never overtly challenged male leadership in the Gate City, Winship demonstrated an increasing willingness to take the initiative in planning events to help wounded men and to foster Confederate nationalism. Winship's Atlanta Hospital Association organized a dinner for paroled Vicksburg soldiers, intended no doubt to encourage both their return to Confederate regiments and the overall morale of Atlanta citizens who read about the event in the newspapers. Winship asked women to contribute cash, meat, and vegetables for the occasion, which would take place at Walton Spring, a popular and picturesque spot north of the city center. Winship's committee of organizers included Mrs. Antoinette Gartrell, the congressman's wife; Mrs. Austin Leyden, whose husband led a popular artillery battalion; Miss Jennie Clayton, a daughter of one of Atlanta's socially prominent families; and Mrs. Ellen Ponder, who despite the scandal surrounding her alleged marital infidelities and her separation from her husband, still presided over a large household of slaves on Marietta Street and volunteered her time faithfully to the Hospital Association.[18]

On Saturday, September 5, 1863, Martha Winship welcomed one thousand paroled Confederate prisoners from Vicksburg to a feast prepared by stalwarts of the Hospital Association. Seated at long tables under the shade of large oak trees, the "weather beaten, sun burnt" veterans, some of them wounded and maimed, bowed their heads as the Reverend James W. Hinton, pastor of Mrs. Winship's Wesley Chapel Methodist Church, gave the blessing. The men then feasted on platters of meat, vegetables, bread, pies, and cake while a band serenaded them. After dinner, Governor Brown gave an hourlong address that focused on the consequences of slacking in the war effort, and presaged the speech he would give two months later at his fourth gubernatorial inauguration in Milledgeville. Brown praised women's efforts early in the war, then he suggested that women had shown a recent proclivity to "permit, if not encourage," their menfolk to avoid military service. According to the governor, if Confederates lost the will to fight and negotiated an end to the war, the result would be reunion with the North and "the Yankees taxing the [southern] property to death." If the Yankees won a military victory outright, southerners would lose all of their slaves immediately. As a man of the yeoman class, Brown knew how to appeal to nonslaveowners and in this instance hammered the theme that nonslaveowning Georgians should fight to defeat Yankee invaders of the southern homeland. He disputed the notion that the war was a rich man's war and a poor man's fight, while admitting that rich men had a greater stake in its outcome. He also condemned "union men . . . that may still be in our midst." The *Daily Intelligencer* concluded that the speech was "one of the Governor's happiest efforts," which earned him enthusiastic applause.[19]

Despite the efforts of patriotic civilians, military officials, and government authorities, civic unity became harder to maintain in the second half of 1863. As the governor suggested, Union men represented an ongoing problem. After the fall of Fort Sumter in 1861, most of Atlanta's Unionists publicly supported the Confederacy or kept their Unionist views to themselves. A small number of openly Unionist men and women remained, including William Markham, coowner with Lewis Scofield of the Atlanta Rolling Mill, one of the largest producers of iron products in the South and the largest private industrial endeavor in the Gate City. Neither Markham nor Scofield appears to have harbored antislavery views, since they advertised for runaway slaves in the local newspapers.[20]

The war placed Markham and Scofield in a bind. The Confederate government expected their factory to yield ever-higher output, but both men supported the United States government and therefore felt reluctant to contribute to the Confederate war machine. For a time, they limited the industrial output of their mill, thereby addressing their personal issues of conscience about not aiding the Confederate war effort any more than they had to. However, as the Confederacy's need for industrial goods increased, it became harder to continue this pattern. Moreover, Confederate Atlantans increasingly targeted those whom they regarded as traitors to a sacred cause. Although the details are unclear, at one point during the war an unknown assailant shot Markham as he rode through the darkened streets of Atlanta. He survived the attack. In 1863, Markham and Scofield found a solution to their dilemma. They sold their mill for $600,000 to Trenholm and Frazier, a firm headquartered in Charleston, South Carolina. The Atlanta mill now had a new name that left no doubt as to the loyalties of its owners: Confederate Rolling Mill.[21]

Periodically during the war, Atlantans formed themselves into "vigilance committees" that tracked down and interrogated those of questionable loyalty. Edgy Atlantans read newspaper reports about "a great many spies . . . in our midst, and too much vigilance cannot be exercised." On August 18, 1863, Major J. H. Steele chaired a citizens meeting at City Hall. The meeting followed what had become by now a standard format. The assembled group passed a series of resolutions that recognized the high price of liberty and suggested that "no enemy is more dangerous than the lurking foe in our midst." Another resolution declared that loyal citizens should not make trips "into the enemy's country" and back again. The group then appointed a vigilance committee of fifteen members to investigate disloyalty in the Gate City.[22]

On August 27, readers of the *Daily Intelligencer* learned about the vigilance committee's interrogation of a local merchant named A. C. Wyly, accused of being an "alien enemy." The committee exonerated Wyly of the charges. Wyly's specific attitude toward the war effort is not known. Also unclear is his precise role in a blockade-running enterprise that bore his name, the Wyly-Markham Company. The company included a variety of investors, many of whom were Unionists but some of whom were Confederate civilians, among them Samuel Richards and William Lawshe, the company's president. But the company's mastermind appears to have been its treasurer, a local Unionist named Amherst Stone. Keeping Confederate investors in the dark about plans, Stone plotted to sell a shipload of cotton to the North, instead of Europe. Stone attempted to launch the business on a trip to New York. In an ironic twist of fate, he was arrested while on a side trip to visit family in Vermont. A Union provost marshal suspected Stone of being a Confederate sympathizer and smuggler. He spent time in prison at Fort Lafayette in New York, and the Wyly-Markham Company never got off the ground.[23]

Atlanta civilians worried about the military situation in the West. Union General William Rosecrans, "with a boldness never before attempted by any Yankee General," marched his vast army to the proximity of Chattanooga, a place of vital importance to the Confederacy as a rail center and a city so close to the border with Georgia that it provided a gateway directly into the state. Rosecrans had his eye on Atlanta. He telegraphed the War Department that Chattanooga was "a point of secondary importance to the enemy, in reference to his vital one, Atlanta."[24]

The Confederacy's Army of Tennessee remained under the command of General Braxton Bragg, a controversial general who had earned public censure after he lost at Murfreesboro, Tennessee, during the first week of

January. Anxious Atlantans heard rumors that Bragg's army was falling back and wondered how far back the army intended to go. On September 13, the *Daily Intelligencer* tried to quell rumors that Bragg's army was retreating all the way to Atlanta with the Union Army in close pursuit. "We advise the people to place no credit in the rumors about town." Several days later, the *Intelligencer* reminded Atlantans that they were engaged in a "holy cause."[25]

City authorities struggled to maintain order amid military uncertainty. Refugees poured into Atlanta from a variety of locations, including Tennessee. Wealthy refugees brought their slaves, thereby adding to the concerns of city leaders about controlling the black population. Most refugees were poor whites. Unable to find or afford lodging, many camped at the passenger depot, and some took up residence in empty rail cars. Mayor Calhoun acknowledged the increase in Atlanta's population and the "unusual amount of strangers," many of them impoverished to the point of "desperation." Adding to the turmoil and to civilians' sense of anxiety, state troops awaiting possible deployment jammed Atlanta's streets. The Athenaeum filled seats every night, but theatergoers complained to the mayor about periodic disruptions to the plays caused by unruly soldiers and young boys making snide remarks. In response, Mayor Calhoun closed all of Atlanta's taverns until the military situation stabilized, and he threatened to close the theater if rowdiness continued. The City Council had already taken the precaution of purchasing chests in which to pack city records and arranging for their removal if necessary. Members of the city police formed a military company in case they were needed for the protection of Atlanta.[26]

General Bragg's military plan called for the Confederate Army to abandon the city of Chattanooga in order to protect its railroad supply lines in north Georgia, a strategy that was to provoke public debate in the coming weeks. On September 19–20, 1863, the two armies clashed in the north-western corner of Georgia near Chickamauga Creek. The first day's fighting was inconclusive, but the second decided the battle. Aided by the timely arrival of soldiers detached from Lee's army in Virginia and under command of General James Longstreet, Bragg's army crushed the Union forces. They sent much of the Union Army into a hasty retreat toward Chattanooga, including General Rosecrans himself. It was the most important victory ever achieved by the Confederacy's Western Army. The immediate threat to Atlanta's safety ended and the victorious outcome lifted spirits among

Confederate Atlantans. Under the headline "A Great Battle in Georgia," the *Daily Intelligencer* reported the "glorious consummation of victory to our arms," with the added benefit of many Union prisoners. Although the Confederate General John Bell Hood suffered a serious wound resulting in the amputation of his leg, he was expected to survive.[27]

The battle of Chickamauga marked a turning point for Civil War Atlanta. Few civilians realized it at the time, but the military victory was to bring no long-term gain, and in its aftermath the city fought a losing battle to navigate the challenges presented by incoming wounded soldiers and multitudes of refugees. The battle placed unprecedented strain on Atlanta's hospitals and on the entire medical apparatus of the Confederate Army. Medical Director Dr. Samuel Stout and his staff faced logistical difficulties involving a changing military situation, a lack of funding, and a transportation system that never seemed adequate to the task. Moreover, Stout underestimated the number of casualties that the Confederate Army would sustain at Chickamauga. Wounded soldiers at the battle numbered sixteen thousand to eighteen thousand out of sixty-six thousand engaged.[28]

Atlanta's hospitals contained eighteen hundred beds, but the Gate City now became home to ten thousand sick and wounded men. As quickly as possible, Stout's doctors sent those who were ambulatory to other destinations, including hospitals at Macon, Columbus, and Augusta, and Montgomery, Alabama. Those who were well enough to walk might be sent home on furlough. The rest were spread out among Atlanta's twenty-six hospitals, and private homes carried the overload.[29]

Two weeks after the battle, trains continued to transport wounded to Atlanta even though the city's hospitals already exceeded their capacity. "The wounded soldiers have not quit coming down yet," Georgia Lin informed her brother in a letter. "The place is crowded with them." Confederate authorities took over Atlanta's elite school for girls, the Female Institute, and turned it into Institute Hospital. Students at the school now took their lessons at the Washington Street mansion of John and Mary Neal, and the Neals moved elsewhere. Institute Hospital, like all of Atlanta's medical facilities, quickly exceeded its capacity. The Atlanta Hospital Association placed notices in the newspapers urging women to roll bandages, volunteer as nurses, and contribute food for the soldiers. The *Daily Intelligencer* reported: "The ladies in town are all engaged in the noble work of alleviating the sufferings of our wounded. Heaven speed them in their patriotic task!" The efforts of medical professionals and volunteers saved many lives, but many soldiers were past saving. When the city sexton made his report for the last quarter of 1863, he noted the interment of 743 soldiers at City Cemetery, the largest number buried in Atlanta to date.[30]

In a familiar refrain, family members in Atlanta waited anxiously for word of soldiers who fought in the battle. John Davidson saw the worst sights he had witnessed in the war. In a letter to Julia on September 24, he described the scope of the fighting over a battlefield ten miles long and four miles wide. "The sufferings of the wounded was past my powers of . . . description," he wrote, sharing with Julia the small role he had played in caring for the wounded. Of 240 men in his regiment who fought at Chickamauga, 102 were killed, wounded, or missing in action. John narrowly escaped capture at one point. A. J. Neal, younger brother of James Neal and an officer in an artillery battalion, wrote to his parents to let them know he had survived the battle. A. J. noted, "The dead & wounded are lying thick around me." He called the battle of Chickamauga "the hardest fighting of the war. . . . Men say the New England Yankees do not fight as these men do."[31]

On October 8, President Jefferson Davis paid a surprise visit to Atlanta. Unlike his appearance in early January, this one involved no banquet, no special rail car, and no accolades about his leadership. By the fall of 1863, Davis, once a symbol of Confederate strength, now generated controversy as the head of a government that conscripted men but failed to win the war. Although the purpose of the visit was not announced publicly, Davis stayed in the Gate City a short time before boarding a train for north Georgia, where he conferred with Bragg and the generals who served under him. Bragg did not have the confidence of his officers, for he was a difficult man with limited ability as a commander. His failure to pursue the Union Army aggressively after the victory at Chickamauga was a grave error in judgment that Bragg's generals recognized. At the "council of war" called by Davis, the generals shared their frustration. Davis nonetheless kept Bragg in command, in part because he personally disliked the two possible replacements, Generals Joseph E. Johnston and P. G. T. Beauregard. Davis's handling of the matter exacerbated the command problems in the Army of Tennessee.[32]

Debate over Bragg's generalship dominated discussions in Atlanta's parlors, hotels, and boardinghouses, not to mention conversations among travelers at the passenger depot. Everyone, it seemed, had an opinion about Bragg. While the *Daily Intelligencer* championed the besieged general, the

Southern Confederacy and *Memphis Appeal* were inclined to be critical. In an editorial on October 30, the *Confederacy* criticized Bragg and also Davis for having failed to remove him. The *Confederacy* accused Davis of having "toyed with the danger that hangs over us" through his failure to remove Bragg. The *Appeal* accused Bragg of blaming others for his own failings. Annie Sehon wrote to her sister Bettie about the glorious victory at Chickamauga, predicting, "We will take Rosecrans' entire army," for "we have him so surrounded." Sehon blamed Bragg for his failure to regain control of her native state of Tennessee.[33]

As the military situation continued to raise questions, so did the civilian one. By the second half of 1863, Atlanta had become a city of women, and a growing number of Atlantans acknowledged that women were struggling. A journalist for the *Daily Intelligencer* tried to make light of the situation. He wrote, "Every street, house, garret and cellar appears full of them"; "they go in one ceaseless string all day long," some in "blockade runners' toggery," others in homespun. While the newspaper alleged that all women were determined to "'see the war out,' under Confederate colors," and published additional articles exhorting women to knit fifty thousand socks for the soldiers during the winter, in fact many women and their children lived in abject poverty. By 1863, soldiers' wives could not afford basic necessities. Julia Davidson, an officer's wife, could not afford milk and meat, her children had no shoes, and winter was coming.[34]

The wages that women earned in Atlanta did not sustain them and their families on even the subsistence level. Many women made money by sewing garments for the Confederate government. As early as the fall of 1862, seamstresses complained about affluent women donating their time, therefore taking work away from "poor people [who] are dependent on their daily labor for daily support," as a woman called Isabel wrote to the *Daily Intelligencer*. The *Intelligencer* admitted that "crowds of poor women, many of them who have seen better days, may almost daily be seen patiently waiting their turn to be supplied with a handful of work." The women received "prices, we are informed, that are so low as to reflect discredit upon our Government." Some women waited for long periods before being turned away without any work at all. Many of these women were soldiers' wives.[35]

In early October, the weather in Atlanta turned chilly, leading to public discussion about the fate of poor people in the coming months. The *Daily Intelligencer* reported that boardinghouses were raising their prices. Stores on

Whitehall Street sold new overcoats for $250 and used ones for $100 to $150. Coal could not be found in Atlanta, so families kept warm by stoking fires with wood purchased from rural people who brought wagons into town and sold it by the load or the cord. In October 1863, wood sold in Atlanta for $10 to $15 for a "two horse load" or $20 to $40 per cord. With these high prices, Atlantans had trouble putting both food on the table and wood in the fireplace. The *Memphis Appeal* speculated about the consequences, for "We are approaching a state of things that will inevitably culminate in riots and bloodshed."[36]

Many Confederate cities faced similar circumstances and struggled, as Atlanta did, to cope with an impoverished citizenry. Richmond's wartime population grew to an estimated one hundred thousand in comparison with Atlanta's twenty-two thousand. Richmond's City Council appropriated $150,000 for poor relief between July 1863 and April 1864. In Atlanta, expenditures for "pauper relief," including food and wood, totaled $40,000 during 1863, out of total city expenditures of $113,000, and the mayor acknowledged, "The drain upon the Treasury to supply the wants of the suffering poor . . . has been unprecedented." The *Daily Intelligencer* wondered whether more could be done. In an editorial on October 22, the newspaper suggested that the government should "signify" its intention not to seize any wagons, horses, or wood entering the city of Atlanta for use by the army.[37]

Instead, facing many challenges in its efforts to feed and equip the army, the Confederate government stepped up efforts to seize crops and livestock. Benjamin Hunter joined a cavalry company in August, and the following month his company began impressing horses for use by the Confederate military. On September 20, he recorded in his diary, "Took train in Atlanta and was soon en route we know not where." The following day, Hunter, now in rural LaGrange, southwest of Atlanta, engaged in his "first feat at 'seizing'—was very successful." Hunter's company took "upwards of sixty" horses in one day. In October, Hunter's unit began impressing cattle.[38]

Throughout the Confederacy, impressment and conscription generated public opposition, as did new taxes levied by the Richmond government in May 1863 on income, investments, and proceeds from the sale of items including food and clothing. Southerners who praised small government before the war now complained of intrusive government tax collectors. For some southerners, taxes and impressment became symbolic of an oppressive government seemingly intent on forcing its people into poverty. In the pages of his diary, Sam Richards complained about the impressments of local horses for use in the Confederate cavalry. Even though he owned no horses himself, Richards noted that the army deprived many Atlantans of their carriage horses. "I think it is a high handed and dishonest proceeding," he wrote, "unworthy [of] such a government as ours professes to be." Richards complained as well of high taxes extracted by the Confederate government from merchants such as himself. Happy to earn high profits in wartime, Richards was not happy to pay an installment of $500 in tax for a period from April to July 1863. Given their dissatisfaction with government policy and the increasing difficulties of coping with inflation, high prices, and shortages, some Atlantans felt morally justified in breaking the rules. In a letter to her brother Charles on October 7, Georgia Lin wrote, "I havent any news to write only they are [im]pressing mules, and Ma has got old Fannie hid away to keep them from pressing her." In another letter, she noted that the family had taken in two new boarders, a married couple, to help their finances.[39]

Wartime conditions exacerbated the distinctions between Atlanta's elite and its poverty-stricken masses. Although they could not ignore the war, the city's elite citizens found ways to enjoy themselves even while the world seemed to fall apart around them. Several days after the battle of Chickamauga, Sallie Sehon married Moses Wright, commander of the Atlanta Arsenal. The young couple had an elegant wedding. Sallie wore a dress of white crepe, trimmed with puffs of tulle and artificial flowers along the hemline. According to her sister-in-law Annie Sehon, "Sallie's dress is beautiful, not what Mother wanted to get but much handsomer than I thought could be gotten in the South." Unable to find a suitable hat in Atlanta, Sallie obtained one from Augusta, made of straw and trimmed with white ribbon. Although Annie complained that the supper table did not contain the "luxuries" that prewar Atlanta would have afforded, the bride and groom along with one hundred guests nonetheless feasted on chicken salad, tongue, lemonade, pyramids of jelly and custard, and seven "handsomely iced" cakes.[40]

Affluent young women visited the soldiers in Bragg's army, including eighteen-year-old Sallie Clayton, who took an excursion to Missionary Ridge, Tennessee, in November 1863. The guests of General Bragg, Clayton and her party included her mother and sisters, Julia, Mary, and Caroline. A dozen other relatives also joined the party, among them the wife and daughters of Confederate Admiral Raphael Semmes, a cousin of Sallie's mother. The Clayton-Semmes party knew that General Bragg held a council of war the night before the group departed from Atlanta, but evidently felt that they were entitled to enjoy a pleasurable excursion despite the gravity of the military situation. Apparently, General Bragg welcomed the diversion.[41]

Leaving Atlanta by train late on Saturday afternoon, November 21, 1863, they traveled through the night and arrived at Chickamauga station on Sunday morning. General Bragg sent a military escort to greet them and three horse-drawn ambulances to transport them and their "large hamper of provisions" to his headquarters. The group endeared themselves to the general by asking him to provide autographs for each of them. Bragg said, "rather sadly," Sallie recalled, "that he thought he had not a friend in the world besides his wife," but he provided the autographs when members of the group assured him that they valued his friendship. Bragg entertained the group with a serenade by soldier musicians and planned a trip the next day to Lookout Mountain, where he promised them an opportunity to shoot a cannon.[42] Privileged civilians like the Claytons wanted to play at war.

The trip to Lookout Mountain began on an amusing note and ended on a frantic one. It was Monday morning, traditionally the day when soldiers and civilians did laundry. Traveling in their caravan of ambulance wagons, the Claytons and their guests passed a soldier who was washing his clothes in a tub. The clothes "were evidently all that he had," so comrades of the naked soldier quickly pulled him inside a tent as the ambulances went by. Soon thereafter, the Claytons had to abandon their plan to ascend the mountain when an artillery shell hit the ground near their position. When the ambulances returned to General Bragg's headquarters, the Claytons saw members of the Confederate high command observing the Union forces through field glasses. General Bragg believed the Yankees might be staging a dress parade in honor of General Grant, who had replaced General Rosecrans after President Lincoln blamed Rosecrans for the loss at Chickamauga. However, one of Bragg's officers noted that the litter corps had begun to assemble. Litter bearers carried the stretchers used to transport wounded men from battlefields. This was no dress parade. Sallie's mother suggested the party should depart immediately for the train station. Although General Bragg believed there might be time to eat a meal, a messenger soon arrived to say the party must leave in ten minutes. "At the same time there came the sound of a volley of musketry from the valley below," Sallie remembered. "I think none of us really ran; we only thought we did so." On the return trip, the group had no military escort. They witnessed scenes of "wild confusion" as men grabbed their weapons, assembled, and prepared for combat. A major battle was about to begin.[43]

Residents of the Gate City waited anxiously for news of the military engagement in Tennessee. With Chattanooga located on the rail line just north of the Georgia state line, everyone knew what was at stake. As the *Daily Intelligencer* put it, the battle would decide "whether Georgia is to be overrun by the vandal foe, or whether we shall again possess Tennessee." While acknowledging General Grant's success at Vicksburg the previous year, the newspaper pointed out that this time the Confederate Army was not defending a garrison and was not cut off from its food supply, as it had been in Mississippi. The newspaper placed its confidence in General Bragg and in the Almighty, who "will give us the victory."[44]

Neither Bragg nor the Almighty helped the Confederacy in the Chattanooga campaign. In addition to his own deficiencies as a commander, Bragg was hampered by the decision of President Davis to detach a portion of his army under General Longstreet and send it east in an unsuccessful attack against Union-controlled Knoxville. The *Intelligencer* carried headlines about Bragg's predicament, calling it a "Desperate Struggle" to hold Lookout Mountain. After two days of fierce fighting, General Grant's well-executed campaign forced the Confederates off Lookout Mountain and nearby Missionary Ridge. The defeated Bragg managed to lead his men in retreat to the relative safety of Chickamauga Creek. Hoping to avert panic in Atlanta, the *Daily Intelligencer*, in reporting the Confederate retreat, also reassured the public that Bragg was "fully able to hold the enemy in check." In subsequent days, the *Intelligencer* reported erroneously that Longstreet had captured Knoxville and many prisoners.[45]

With the exception of the *Daily Intelligencer*, General Bragg had little support left in Atlanta. In describing what it called Bragg's "partial defeat" at Chattanooga, the *Intelligencer* also wrote of "confusion, tumult and excitement" in the city of Atlanta as citizens tried to come to terms with what had happened. In the privacy of their homes, some Atlantans predicted their city's eventual capture. Annie Sehon confided to her sister, "It is the opinion of Mr. Sehon and of Father and of every gentleman whom I have heard express himself, that Atlanta will be taken." Annie's older brother George Maney was a brigadier general in Bragg's army. Wounded in the shoulder, he arrived in Atlanta to convalesce.[46]

On December 3, the *Daily Intelligencer* reported that Bragg had been relieved of command "at his own request" and that General William

Hardee now commanded the army until a permanent replacement could be named. Bragg arrived in Atlanta that day by train from north Georgia, then departed again for Newnan, Georgia, where his family resided. Loyal to the end, the *Intelligencer* called him a "distinguished officer" who had won "laurels" during the war. Speculation began immediately about a permanent replacement. The *Southern Confederacy* scooped the *Intelligencer* and the *Appeal* by reporting the appointment of General Joseph E. Johnston, one of the Confederacy's most respected generals whose personal clashes with President Davis had prevented his appointment earlier.[47]

As both armies went into winter quarters, the Confederates near Dalton in north Georgia and the Yankees at Chattanooga, Atlantans held yet another day of fasting, humiliation, and prayer on December 10. Governor Brown called for this fast day, hoping for God's protection against "the storm of invasion, now raging with remorseless fury around us." As Brown no doubt suspected, a growing number of Georgians had begun to question whether God still favored their cause. The *Atlanta Daily Intelligencer* harbored no such doubts. The newspaper insisted that God's favor had kept the Confederacy alive during two and a half years of war.[48]

In the final weeks of 1863 refugees continued to arrive in Atlanta from Tennessee, and since the loss of Chattanooga they also came from various places in Georgia. Mary Mallard moved to Atlanta from Walthourville near Savannah in December 1863, when her husband Robert became minister at Central Presbyterian Church. She and her husband and two children occupied a house provided by their congregation, near the Presbyterian church on Washington Street and next door to Sidney and Mary Root. In letters to her widowed mother in south Georgia, Mallard shared her impressions of wartime Atlanta.[49]

Mallard's arrival at the passenger depot presented her with a picture of crowding and chaos that many had witnessed before her. When the Confederate government needed the railroad cars in which her furniture was transported to Atlanta, her items were "tumbled . . . into the wareroom." Mallard lost a box of candles, which she feared were stolen. Candles were becoming scarce in the city and sold for six dollars per pound, an enormous sum that placed them beyond the means of many Atlantans. As the wife of an important clergyman, Mallard received the support and largesse of members of his congregation, making her situation atypical of Atlanta's newest arrivals. Lemuel Grant and Joseph Logan sent loads of firewood, which the

Mallards needed now that temperatures were in the twenties. Congregants also sent food. Like many in Atlanta, Mary Mallard read a local newspaper and held strong opinions about the recent military campaign. She called the loss at Chattanooga "shameful and most humiliating. . . . I am glad he [Bragg] has been relieved of his command." Mallard also told her mother about the fortifications being constructed in the city, though it troubled her to see so few soldiers. This place is being fortified," she wrote on December 21, "but unless some reinforcements are sent to our army, we will not be very safe. Our only hope is in God."[50]

Mary wrote often about her slave Tenah, whose story illustrates the changing nature of slavery in wartime. Like many other slaves, her life was upended when she moved to Atlanta. Although Tenah relocated because of her owner's new job, many slaveowners moved their bondspeople away from southern coastlines now menaced by the Union Navy or away from advancing federal armies in the South's interior. Pregnant at the time of her arrival in Atlanta, Tenah now lived hundreds of miles from her husband, Niger, owned by Mallard's mother, Mary Jones. But Tenah turned misfortune into opportunity. As childcare provider to the Mallards' son and daughter, Tenah understood her value to Mary Mallard and began immediately to pressure her mistress about finding employment for Niger in Atlanta. In a matter of weeks, Reverend Mallard found a position for Niger at a steam tannery, where he chopped wood to feed the furnaces, and Mary Jones received $33.35 per month for his hire. In February, Tenah gave birth to a baby the couple named Cinda. Although Tenah and Niger did not escape from slavery or profit financially themselves, they did manage to live together as a couple thanks to Tenah's negotiation skills and Atlanta's desperate need for labor in its businesses and industries.[51]

Like Tenah, many African Americans took advantage of wartime conditions to stretch the boundaries of servitude, understanding that manpower shortages coupled with a lack of adequate policing made their apprehension increasingly difficult. Mayor's Court records provide evidence that slaves were getting away with more of what had previously been regarded as prosecutable actions. Although it is not possible to know precisely the size of Atlanta's wartime black population, anecdotal evidence suggests that it rose along with the white population between 1861 and 1864. Yet cases involving African Americans before the Mayor's Court actually declined from thirty-seven in 1861 to twelve in 1862 and thirteen in 1863. Overall, the volume of cases heard by the mayor fell, then rose, from 234 in 1861, to 180 in 1862, to 348 in 1863, with the preponderance of the cases involving charges of drunk and disorderly conduct. By contrast, Savannah's black population generated four times the number of cases before its Mayor's Court during the period 1862–64 compared with the previous period. Atlanta's failure to prosecute blacks represents a judicial system struggling unsuccessfully to cope with urban turmoil caused by wartime pressures.[52]

No one stretched the boundaries of slavery in Atlanta more fully or successfully than Robert Webster, who moved to the city in 1856 with his owner, Benjamin Yancey, brother of the famous secessionist William Lowndes Yancey. Bob Webster claimed to have been born in 1820 at Gadsby's National Hotel, in Washington, D.C. He identified his mother as a mixed-raced woman named Charlotte Goodbrick, a slave owned by John Gadsby, who ran the hotel. Bob Webster identified his father as the famous Massachusetts senator Daniel Webster, a claim that has no corroboration. Nonetheless, Bob took Webster's surname. By the time Bob Webster moved to Atlanta, he had been sold several times and in one instance had been gambled away in a game of cards. In spite of these traumas, Webster became a skilled barber and also earned a reputation as a man who liked to gamble. Benjamin Yancey allowed Webster to buy his time as a barber, in exchange for paying Yancey $150 per year. In Atlanta, he quickly turned a profit, running a barbershop, later two, selling produce and fresh meat as a side business, and also making loans to gamblers, taking jewelry and gold in payment.[53]

During the war, the enterprising slave connected with the city's small but active Unionist circle. A frequent visitor to the city jails, where he shaved prisoners and provided them with haircuts, Webster helped at least one Unionist prisoner to escape by supplying him with the rope used to scale the prison walls. Though risking arrest, he managed to avoid detection by Confederate authorities. Ever the astute businessman, Bob Webster also ran a currency exchange in the jails. Atlanta Unionists who wanted U.S. greenbacks gave Webster their Confederate money, and he traded it for U.S. currency obtained from the prisoners. Again, he eluded detection. Webster used the Confederate currency to purchase such items as tobacco.[54]

In the climate of instability in Atlanta, questions arose about the leadership of Mayor James Calhoun, and those questions included the concerns of white Atlantans about the future of slavery. Although the mayor's personal commitment to the Confederacy was not an issue, Atlantans knew he had been a Unionist before the war, and some of them asked whether he was aggressive enough in apprehending those accused of disloyal behavior. Although Calhoun won his reelection bid in December 1863, the *Daily Intelligencer* opposed him, complaining about his decision to close the Athenaeum and offering its greatest editorial vitriol for Calhoun's failure to prohibit African Americans from hiring their own time and making money. Slaves should not be "allowed the rights and privileges of white men," the newspaper editorialized, also insisting that any reported instance of this conduct must be fully investigated by the mayor. The *Intelligencer*'s complaint suggests that the institution of slavery was breaking down in Atlanta.[55]

As the year 1863 drew to a close, efforts to bolster civilian morale included a concert by Blind Tom Wiggins and a "Grand Entertainment" organized by Martha Winship and her Hospital Association. The event took place at City Hall on Christmas Eve. Winship placed ads in the local newspapers soliciting contributions for the refreshment tables and decorations for a Christmas tree. Ticket sales raised money for the soldiers. Winship also asked Atlanta families to take a few soldiers into their homes so that convalescents might have a break from the dreariness of hospital life.[56]

In an article about Christmas in Atlanta called "Santa Claus Not Dead," the *Intelligencer* condemned "abolitiondom" in the North and "croakers" in the South who cast doubt on the prospects for southern independence. As evidence, the newspapers invoked Winship's "Ladies Fair," with its "elegances and luxuries not surpassed on any previous Christmas Eve." While suggesting that "large proceeds" had been realized, the newspaper did not estimate the number of attendees or tickets sold. Instead it concluded, suggestively, "Thank God, we are not yet the starved race our enemies have us to be!" The *Intelligencer*'s word choice, "not *yet* . . . starved," was an admission of deteriorating conditions in the city.[57]

Tom Wiggins and Martha Winship brought good cheer to some, Atlanta merchants like Beach and Root tempted Atlanta's well-heeled citizens to purchase silk cloth and other luxury items for the holiday season, and the city was spared any large-scale epidemics of disease in the fall and winter months; however, many civilians contemplated the Christmas holiday with little to cheer about. "I think of all seasons Christmas ought to be the merriest and happiest and it is a great privation to me when I cannot have it so," Annie Sehon wrote to her sister on December 23. Jennie Lines was devastated by the death of her only child, an infant daughter Lillie, who succumbed to dysentery in September. On Christmas Day, she wrote in her diary, "Sylvanus and I remembered each other last night and slipped a small token of our great love in each other's stocking. But O! how inexpressibly sad have been our bereaved hearts to-day." The couple tried to be festive by making a nice dinner and, heeding Martha Winship's admonition to show kindness toward individual wounded men, they invited a soldier to enjoy it with them.[58]

The port cities of Savannah, Charleston, Wilmington, and Mobile remained in Confederate hands, much to the relief of Confederate Atlantans. In July, Lieutenant Colonel James H. Neal wrote to his father from James Island, South Carolina, where his regiment, the 19th Georgia, had been transferred as part of an effort to protect the port of Charleston. In a letter reprinted in the *Daily Intelligencer*, Neal told his father that his regiment had pummeled a Union regiment of African American soldiers on July 16, capturing thirteen, killing forty, and suffering only one casualty in the process. Neal wrote that his men followed the Union soldiers until they reached their transports. Neal did not identify the enemy regiment, but it was the Massachusetts 54th, and its efforts that day represented the first combat experience for this African American regiment. Two days after Neal and his men faced the 54th, the unit and its white commander Robert Gould Shaw gained immortality by staging a heroic though unsuccessful assault against Fort Wagner outside Charleston. The regiment suffered 272 casualties, including Shaw. The courage shown by members of the 54th brought accolades to the unit, positive publicity for black recruitment in the North, and increased efforts to bring African Americans into the Union Army. If Neal wrote to his father about the details, the local newspapers did not print the account.[59] In Atlanta, Confederate civilians might feel comforted listening to the concert of Blind Tom playing a Confederate battle anthem, but the war had changed irrevocably, for tens of thousands of black men now wore federal uniforms.

By December 1863, the surge in Confederate nationalism inspired by newspaper editorials, Martha Winship's banquet, and the victory at Chickamauga gave way to pessimism about the future. The surge in wartime prosperity inspired by business profits and high wages gave way to economic hardship. Wealthy slaveowning families like the Neals and the Claytons remained steadfast, as did affluent industrialists like the Winship brothers and their wives, including the seemingly unstoppable Martha Winship. Successful businessmen such as Sidney Root and Richard Peters appeared unwavering too. Everyone else seemed to question whether the sacrifice was worth the cost. Middling businessmen like Sam Richards ignored public pressure and looked for excuses not to fight. Soldiers' wives, including Julia Davidson, wrote plaintive letters to their soldier husbands about deprivation and asked them to find excuses to come home. Single women like Amanda Lin faced renewed challenges that caused her to break the law, refusing to give up her mule to the Confederate Army. Most troubling, a growing underclass in Atlanta lacked adequate shelter, food, and fuel and increasingly demonstrated a willingness to engage in rowdiness and crime. Confederate civilians feared that the institution of slavery was unraveling.

On December 24, the *Daily Intelligencer* reflected on the military situation at year's end. The *Intelligencer* labeled its story "The Pause." The newspaper reminded its readers that Virginians had endured the presence of enemy regiments within their state's borders since the beginning of the war, yet they had successfully fought multiple attempts to take their capital of Richmond. Georgians must now protect Atlanta. "There is work for every one to do," the newspaper intoned. "Men must fight who never dreamed of fighting when the war began." The *Intelligencer* told Atlantans they should place their "trust in an overruling Providence to assist us in the mighty work in which we are engaged."[60] Events in the coming year were to test Atlantans more than ever before.

As "Gate City to the South" in the 1850s, Atlanta built a fine new
passenger depot (left) and a luxury hotel, the Trout House (right, rear).
Library of Congress

A fiery orator and an advocate of secession, Lucius J. Gartrell represented Atlanta in the U.S. Congress and later in the Confederate Congress. Courtesy of the Kenan Research Center at the Atlanta History Center

Many prewar Unionists eventually embraced Confederate nationalism, including businessman Sam Richards and housewife Jennie Lines. Richards image courtesy of the Kenan Research Center at the Atlanta History Center; Lines image courtesy of the Hargrett Rare Book and Manuscript Library, University of Georgia Libraries

Local leaders in Confederate Atlanta included Mayor James Calhoun and Martha Winship, president of the Atlanta Hospital Association. Courtesy of the Kenan Research Center at the Atlanta History Center

Atlantans fell in love with independent cavalryman John Hunt Morgan in 1862. One Atlantan wrote, "John Morgan, with a handful of picked men, has done more for the cause of Southern Independence, than whole Brigades." Library of Congress

Thomas "Blind Tom" Wiggins performed piano concerts many times in Atlanta during the war. His alleged Confederate patriotism relieved white Atlantans' anxiety about slaves' loyalty during the war. Courtesy of the Hargrett Rare Book and Manuscript Library, University of Georgia Libraries

Ellen Ponder's stucco mansion was so extensively damaged by the federal shelling of Atlanta during August 1864 that the house could not be lived in again. The home's position near Confederate breastworks made it a federal target. Library of Congress

General William T. Sherman's expulsion of Atlanta civilians in September 1864 led to a "profound stillness" on city streets, including Whitehall Street. This section of Atlanta would soon be put to the torch. On the left side of the photograph, with figures seated in front, is the Crawford, Frazer slave auction house. Library of Congress

The rapid rebuilding of railroads after the war helped Atlanta to recover economically. Hannibal I. Kimball built a grand hotel, left, to match Atlanta's emerging importance as a postwar city. The hotel served as a backdrop for political and social gatherings. Courtesy of the Kenan Research Center at the Atlanta History Center

John B. Gordon and his wife Fanny were among Atlanta's most important postwar political leaders. John Gordon helped "redeem" the state from Republican rule during Reconstruction, while Fanny Gordon led the Atlanta Ladies Memorial Association. Courtesy of the Hargrett Rare Book and Manuscript Library, University of Georgia Libraries

Carrie Berry Crumley, a child diarist of wartime Atlanta, is buried in Oakland Cemetery's Original Six Acres (1921). Roderick D. Badger is buried in Oakland's African American Grounds (1890). Badger practiced dentistry while he was a slave before and during the war. He also practiced as a free man after the war. Crumley image courtesy of the Kenan Research Center at the Atlanta History Center; Badger image courtesy of the DeKalb History Center Archives

7. Civilian Loyalty in a Time of "Intense Anxiety"

"We are passing through times of intense anxiety," Mary Mallard wrote to her mother on May 27, 1864. Mallard referred to the unending stream of refugees descending on Atlanta, the ceaseless rail cars of wounded soldiers delivered to Atlanta's hospitals, and the fears expressed by civilians who heard frightening reports about the encroaching army of General William T. Sherman. Mallard closed her letter with expressions of hope that "we will enjoy a portion of our summer in peace and quiet." There would be no peace and little quiet in Atlanta during 1864. The city's ability to cope with wartime pressures appeared shaky at best, especially its efforts to maintain law and order. The institution of slavery, already weakening, started to collapse. More and more Atlantans questioned whether the Confederacy deserved their allegiance. One scholar has written, "Loyalty was frequently imperfect, rarely unconditional, and often influenced by circumstance."[1] By 1864, circumstance did not favor loyalty to the Confederacy.

The winter of 1864 was the coldest in thirty years. As temperatures hovered around zero degrees, Atlantans struggled to find warmth. Benjamin Hunter noted in his diary, "Great demand for wood—impossible to keep comfortable." The *Atlanta Daily Intelligencer* joked about the weather, noting "Everything is frozen, from the water to our ink," then changed its tone to address the predicament faced by impoverished civilians. "With the present high price of wood, the poor of the city must suffer terribly." On January 8, the *Intelligencer* reported the death of a Confederate soldier from exposure, left in a "shelter" by his comrades after a night of drinking. Found the next morning by an unidentified black man, he died a short time later. The newspaper reported his name and age without comment. He was John Stancell, age fifty-four.[2]

The appearance of General John Hunt Morgan in Atlanta on February 6, 1864, served as a rallying call for Confederate Atlantans. In early December, newspapers reported his escape from an Ohio penitentiary through an elaborate scheme involving disguises, tunnels, and friends on the outside. Interest in Morgan remained high among residents of the Gate City. In their bookstore on Whitehall Street, Jabez and Sam Richards sold copies of a pamphlet called "Morgan's Capture and Escape." Caught up in the Morgan mania that swept the city, Mary Mallard offered to send her mother a copy.[3]

Because most of Morgan's former soldiers languished in northern prisons, Morgan needed new recruits, and he sent a public letter from his recruiting base in Decatur, Georgia, dated January 1, 1864, and published in area newspapers including the *Memphis Appeal*. "Come at once, and come cheerfully, for I want no man in my command who has to be sent to his duty by a provost guard," Morgan wrote. Efforts began at once to raise money to equip Morgan's cavalry. The Atlanta Amateurs held two "Festival Soirees" to benefit "Morgan's Command" at the Athenaeum. Admirers of Morgan raised additional funds by setting up a subscription table at the Trout House Hotel, where by mid-January they had collected $8,575 out of pledges amounting to $10,000. Patriotic citizens of Savannah, Macon, and Augusta mounted similar efforts.[4]

In January and February, Morgan made appearances in the Confederate capital of Richmond and in Atlanta. In both places, he drew large crowds of enthusiastic civilians. In Richmond on January 10, Morgan and his wife upstaged President Davis and his family when they appeared at St. Paul's Episcopal Church. The Confederate government hosted a reception for Morgan at the Virginia capitol, leading the *Memphis Appeal* to editorialize that no individual had a "personal style" that was more "attractive" to the multitudes than did Morgan. He represented the "dignity and spirit of the revolution" for Confederate independence. Unbeknownst to the public, Morgan held private talks with President Jefferson Davis about whether a Confederate force might be siphoned from General Joseph E. Johnston's army at Dalton and used to invade and liberate Morgan's beloved state of

Kentucky. Nothing came of the plan.⁵ Regardless, to Confederate civilians Morgan represented the hope that feats of daring could still deliver the military victories that eluded the Confederacy on the field of battle.

On January 19, 1864, the Atlanta City Council announced, "We hail with delight" the prospect of Morgan's visiting the Gate City. Mayor Calhoun appointed a committee to plan an appropriate reception. Ultimately, the City Council spent more than $8,000 entertaining Morgan, including a lavish reception, a cost the city could ill afford to pay. Newspapers reported the route of Morgan's trip to Atlanta, including his stop in Columbia, South Carolina, where hundreds of people greeted his arrival and serenaded him at his hotel. In Dalton, Georgia, Morgan visited winter camps of the Confederate Army.⁶

Morgan hoped to inspire renewed support for the Confederacy in Atlanta, and the turnout of several thousand Atlantans who greeted him, his wife Mattie, and members of his staff at the depot on February 6 gave him the platform from which to do so. Sam Richards joined the throng of Atlantans that escorted Morgan and his party from the depot to the Trout House Hotel. Morgan held a special place in the affections of those who saw him that February day. Atlantans admired Robert E. Lee, but they did so from afar; Lee was a distant figure they read about in the newspapers. Morgan was a hero they could see and hear. From the Trout House balcony, Mayor James Calhoun gave a speech welcoming Morgan. In doing so, Calhoun revealed how far he had come since opposing secession three years earlier. Calling Morgan "noble" and "gallant," he spoke of Confederate people's fear that Morgan's capture and imprisonment meant his permanent removal from command. Now he had returned to inspire anew "and make efforts for our independence." In the past, "our brave soldiers have almost performed miracles," Calhoun said, insinuating that Morgan and his men might perform miracles again. Calhoun reminded civilians of their own obligation in wartime. They must provide food and clothing for the army and "should not wait for an officer to come to their houses to hunt subsistence." At the conclusion of the mayor's remarks, Morgan, who did not like public speaking, offered brief words of thanks for the city's hospitality. He then "retired amid the enthusiastic cheers of the vast crowd in the street below." Hoping to fire up a crowd that might have been expecting more of a speech, two of Morgan's officers identified as Colonel W. C. P. Breckinridge and Colonel Robert A. Alston stepped forward to give patriotic addresses. A reporter for the

Memphis Appeal called the speeches "thrilling and soul-stirring," and also
noted that Morgan had "awakened in the bosoms of all those who witnessed
[the event] renewed emotions of patriotic ardor that will not slumber until
our independence is achieved."[7]

Morgan remained in Atlanta for several weeks. Sightings of the general
caused a stir among civilians who admired him. Mary Mallard saw Morgan at
the Episcopal Church on February 21. Impressed by the general's unprepos-
sessing style, Mallard described him in a letter to her mother as "very handsome," and his wife as "very pretty, and I can assure you they are a dashing
couple." Mallard's young daughter Maimie was "in perfect ecstasies at having
seen General Morgan." Mallard reported to her mother that Morgan dressed in
civilian clothing except for his cavalry boots and a black felt hat with a brim
that was turned up on one side. Evidently, Morgan's visit to Atlanta inspired a
new style among Atlanta's elite women that winter and spring, for the *Daily
Intelligencer* reported that "a great many of the Atlanta belles" were seen on
city streets wearing what it described as a Morgan-style hat.[8]

No one knew it at the time, but Morgan's visit to Atlanta was the city's
last major celebration of Confederate nationalism. After Morgan left town,
civilians were left to ruminate about the future of their city, and especially the
military situation, for the Union's vast army in Chattanooga was not likely to
remain there much longer. Of the city's daily newspapers, the *Intelligencer*
wrote most bluntly about the military prospects. In an editorial titled "The
Spring Campaign," printed the day before John Hunt Morgan's appearance
in the city, the newspaper stated, "From present indications, it is very likely"
that Atlanta would be "the main object of the federals in the coming spring
campaign." The newspaper emphasized that Atlanta's importance, "both to
the Federal and Confederate government, cannot be over-estimated," especially its role as rail center. If Atlanta fell to the Union, Yankees would
overrun Georgia, and Alabama and Mississippi would lose their rail connection to the Confederate States. Moreover, Atlanta's railroads carried food
from the lower South that fed all of the Confederate armies.[9] A few weeks
later, Atlantans learned that President Lincoln had appointed Ulysses S.
Grant to command all of the Union armies, and Grant's success at Vicksburg
made him a formidable foe.

As they had done the previous summer, Atlanta's newspapers printed a
series of editorials designed to support the Confederacy and shore up civilian
morale. Many newspaper editorials emphasized the high morale of

Confederate soldiers awaiting the spring campaign and their respect for Johnston. The *Southern Confederacy* noted the "unabated enthusiasm" and the "very fine appearance" of Confederate soldiers at Dalton who had been issued new uniforms. The *Confederacy* implied that well-rested and contented soldiers were whiling away their days listening to music, reporting, "There is scarcely a night but one or more bands of music are on the serenade." The newspaper expressed confidence in Johnston and wanted readers to know that soldiers "idolized" their commander. Letters of A. J. Neal to his family in Atlanta support these notions. On February 3, A. J. Neal sent a letter to his mother expressing satisfaction with the present circumstances. "Our encampment is in the wood on the bank of a fine creek and altogether we have an easier time than ever," he wrote. "The men are getting better and more abundant rations than they have since we have been with Bragg[']s Army." Moreover, the furloughed soldiers brought back provisions from home including bacon and syrup, and many received packages in the mail. The following month, A.J. wrote to his sister Emma, "I never saw this Army in such fine spirits. . . . I anticipate brilliant successes this spring and after a few hard fights a glorious Peace."[10]

Newspapers also made separate appeals to their male and female readers. Men must not become naysayers, whom the newspapers called "croakers," especially those who spread false rumors about the possibility of the Confederate Army retreating south toward Atlanta. "He who is continually croaking is no true man," the *Southern Confederacy* suggested. With the federal army poised to invade Georgia, the *Memphis Appeal* reminded soldiers that they now fought for far more than political rights. Now they fought for their land against what it called the "armed mercenaries of Lincoln."[11]

Women and children had their own roles to play. The *Southern Confederacy* offered praise for women. During three years of war, mothers and their children had learned lessons of "Spartan simplicity of dress and diet." The *Memphis Appeal* adopted a more critical attitude toward female loyalty. The *Appeal* lectured on January 1, 1864: women must "abstain from writing demoralizing appeals to their sons, husbands, [and] brothers in the army, thereby encouraging disaffection, disloyalty, desertion." The *Daily Intelligencer* published a story in early March that it no doubt intended as a cautionary tale to any woman tempted to encourage her husband's desertion. Private Pleasant Smallwood of the 21st Georgia was executed for desertion, leaving behind a wife and eight children who resided in Summerville,

Georgia.[12] These editorial efforts make clear that female loyalty was deemed essential to the Confederate cause and that it was believed to be conditional by this point in the war.

Newspapers added a stronger racial element to their editorials in 1864, for they hoped to convince white residents that defeat at the hands of Yankee invaders would lead to a new racial order. One article played to white people's belief that they had African Americans' best interests at heart by insinuating that Louisiana blacks under federal control were suffering from "cruelty and brutality," becoming "emaciated and sick." Most articles were intended to provoke fear, including the notion that interracial marriage might be a logical outcome of slavery's demise. One story cited an alleged case of a Yankee schoolteacher sent south to educate freed slaves in Vicksburg who married one of her students. Another story involving Vicksburg told of the murder of a "peaceable, unoffending" white man by black soldiers. The *Memphis Appeal* got to the heart of the matter by insisting that "the mad spirit of abolition fanaticism showed a determination not only to run riot with the Constitution and Union as they formerly existed, but to rob the Southern people of their liberties, property and personal rights, and our only salvation lay in war to the death." The editorial concluded with racially charged language. "To succeed is to live as we were born, freemen; to fail is both to live and die slaves."[13]

In spite of the efforts made by local newspapers, loyalty remained a contested issue in Atlanta. Desertion from the army was one manifestation. The Confederate Army of Tennessee rarely granted furloughs to soldiers, for its commanders understood that soldiers allowed to go home might not return to their regiments. During the winter of 1863–64 and especially once the Atlanta campaign began, a growing number of soldiers deserted. Before the campaign began in May, Fulton County lost 102 men, more than 5 percent of the county's soldiers in the Confederacy's western army. Some of these men deserted to the enemy. Others went home, not because they were "croakers" but because their sense of duty to family trumped their sense of duty to the Confederacy. Sometimes these soldiers deserted in response to desperate pleas from their wives, who struggled to keep farms going and children fed. Statewide, 3,368 Georgians left the ranks and 11,000 evaded the draft or found exemptions.[14]

Unionist families with sons of draft age found ways to get them out of the city. In 1863, Marcellus Markham, whose father, William, sold the rolling mill he owned with Lewis Scofield rather than continue to make supplies for the Confederacy, helped his son escape from Atlanta. First, the elder Markham secured his son's release from conscription by interceding with a Confederate official in Richmond "who was obligated to him," then he sent Marcellus north with a suitcase filled with money, including U.S. currency and gold. Young Marcellus traveled to Richmond, then forded the Rappahannock River into Maryland, where corrupt provost marshals picked him up and demanded money in exchange for his release. Markham's suitcase contained at least $15,000, and he was happy to part with some of it in order to secure his freedom. Once released from capture, he used his connections to have his captors arrested and brought to justice.[15]

Even Confederate civilians of unassailable loyalty began quietly moving their sons out of harm's way, unwilling to sacrifice promising young lives for a sinking cause. Claiming that he was worried about his only son, Johnny, age fourteen, running away to join the Confederate Army, Sidney Root sent the boy to England aboard one of his blockade runners, the *Lady Sterling*. David Mayer's son Morris, age sixteen, went to Germany to visit family, paying $150 in gold for his ticket on a blockade runner that traveled via Wilmington and the Bahamas. Younger siblings stayed home, their draft status not in question.[16]

Some adult civilians defected to the North. John C. Peck abandoned Confederate Atlanta at some point in early 1864, moving to Minnesota ostensibly because of his health. An asthmatic who had moved to Atlanta in 1858 seeking a warmer climate to help his medical condition, Peck quickly established himself as a successful carpenter and contractor. In 1862, he was happy to make money from the Confederate government when the South's economic and military prospects appeared bright. He built a number of shops that made up the Atlanta Arsenal, manufactured Joe Brown Pikes, and superintended woodwork for the arsenal. In 1864, Peck's loyalty shifted and he decided to leave. A man who had moved to Atlanta for the warm climate six years earlier now announced that he needed a cold climate. As an ostensibly patriotic builder for the Confederacy, Peck was able to find safe passage out of the city without arousing suspicion, and he remained in Minnesota for the duration of the war. Four months after the conflict ended, Peck returned to Atlanta, where he immediately began making money as a building contractor.[17]

Peck did more than leave in 1864. He provided Union General George Thomas with detailed descriptions of Atlanta's fortifications and its arsenal. Having built the latter, Peck was well qualified to describe its location and dimensions. He also revealed to General Thomas that Atlanta's government buildings were not well guarded and might easily be destroyed. He further noted the scarcity of coal in the city, indicating that machine shops struggled to find an adequate supply.[18]

Throughout the war, a network of Unionists and spies operated in Atlanta. Their shadowy lives are often difficult to trace, but their presence was more than a figment of Confederate authorities' imagination. Among the best-documented Unionists in Atlanta was Cyrena Stone, who kept a diary for seven months beginning in January 1864. In the diary, she changed her name to Abby and disguised the names of all of her friends, fearing that her Unionism might be unmasked. Cyrena attended church at Central Presbyterian even after fellow parishioners refused to speak to her. She wrote in her diary disdainfully about sermons that contained a decidedly Confederate tone. Although she did not identify the pastor by name, presumably she referred to Robert Mallard when she wrote that "victory was prayed for as usual," then acknowledged that the minister told his congregation that if Atlanta fell, they must be resigned to God's will. In the meantime, they should loan their carriages for use transporting the wounded. Cyrena tended her home and property to the northeast of Atlanta's city center with the aid of slave domestics, but without the aid of her husband, Amherst, who had left Atlanta the previous year in an effort to begin a blockade-running endeavor.[19]

By 1864, Atlanta's Unionist circle was largely a female one since most men, like Cyrena's husband, had left for the North. Even female Unionists had to be careful. When they held meetings and sang patriotic songs in the privacy of Cyrena's home, they no doubt did so softly, in order to avoid drawing attention to their presence. When they tended to Union prisoners in local hospitals, they do so warily, and sometimes surreptitiously. To deflect attention from their mission, Unionist women ministered to Confederate patients before quietly moving to Yankee men, offering small amounts of food and words of comfort.[20]

Her gender protected Cyrena from conscription, but male Unionists who chose to stay in Atlanta struggled to find ways to avoid military service. Charles Bohnefeld, an immigrant from Germany who was the city's principal coffin maker, did a booming business in 1864. Ads for "C. Bohnefeld, Cabinet-Maker, Manufacturer of Coffins" appeared regularly in all of Atlanta's newspapers. Bohnefeld's shop on Luckie Street near Walton Spring produced seven to ten coffins weekly, according to a petition he sent to

Governor Brown asking for his exemption from the draft. Bohnefeld alleged that he was Atlanta's only maker of coffins for civilians, the military having its own shop. Bohnefeld was not conscripted.[21]

Even among citizens who supported the Confederacy, high prices and shortages raised questions about present and future loyalty, not only in Atlanta but also in other cities. In Charleston, civilians ate rice but found meat, butter, and salt in short supply. In the South's interior, corn remained the staple. The *Daily Intelligencer* ran a story on February 11, 1864, predicting a bountiful harvest of both wheat and corn, telling readers, "There is plenty in the land," with harvests predicted in just 120 days. The problem was a lack of food in the meantime, and a longer than normal cold season made the planting of household gardens and the survival of livestock problematic. In early February, Sam Richards had the family's "big calf" slaughtered in order to provide meat for his family, a decision that was also grounded in the fact that he could no longer afford to buy feed for the animal. In late April, Richards had to replant his beans, cucumbers, and okra because the seeds of his first planting did not germinate. Jennie and Sylvanus Lines could afford basic foodstuffs but not meat. The "nice little pig" they purchased in the fall had frozen to death during the unusually cold winter. Jennie wanted to obtain a replacement, and some chickens too, but "it costs so much to buy them I expect we shall have to do without them." The Huff family ate biscuits when they could grow wheat and find a way to thresh it; otherwise, they subsisted on fried cornbread. They also grew sugar cane as a sweetener for a coffee substitute they made from parched corn. Sarah Huff, a child eight years old in 1864, wrote many years later, "In those hard fights for bread it was victory or starvation."[22]

Newspaper stories focused on high prices. The cost of food in Atlanta had increased so precipitously that the Trout House and the Atlanta Hotels now charged $10.00 for a single meal in their dining halls. In 1862, Cornelius Hanleiter had paid seventy-five cents to share a room with another officer at the Trout House and an additional seventy-five cents for breakfast at nearby Washington Hall. Costs for staple food items became exorbitant. By the end of March, corn sold for $10.00 per bushel, peas for $15.00 per bushel, and sweet potatoes for $20.00 per bushel. Newspapers speculated about whether farmers were holding back their produce in an effort to force up the prices they would receive at market. One disgruntled citizen wrote to the *Memphis Appeal,* revealing an understanding about the connection between basic subsistence for its civilians and the Confederacy's ability to continue the military fight. "These high prices are wrong, foolish, and are sapping the life blood from the poor people's patriotism," wrote "A Tennessean." High prices injured the goal of Confederate nationalism as much as did Yankee invaders, "by causing the poorer classes, to a great extent," to call for "peace upon almost any terms."[23]

Cyrena Stone observed growing war weariness among Atlanta's poorest citizens. In the pages of her diary, Stone described the visit of a woman who called on her in January and wept at the prospect of her husband being drafted. The woman did not know how she would feed their five children. The eldest child, a teenage daughter, already helped to support the family by walking two miles into the city to obtain "Government sewing," and often stopped to rest at the Stone residence. After several months, her earnings allowed her enough profits to purchase a pair of shoes, but many of Atlanta's poorest citizens went without or wore shoes made from cloth. Stone also noted that some impoverished women wore dresses made of flour sacks. The *Southern Confederacy* described the plight of pieceworkers who crowded the trains from Decatur and Stone Mountain as they came to the Gate City daily to receive and deliver articles of soldiers' clothing. Sometimes trains were so crowded that women had to stand during the entire trip.[24]

Similar scenes played out in other Confederate cities, and the efforts of local philanthropists helped to a limited degree. In Savannah, businessmen distributed rice and sugar to impoverished women. In Richmond, the City Council created a supply store whose agents sought inexpensive produce outside the city. In Mobile, seventy-four businessmen formed a supply association that purchased food in rural areas and sold it at cost to needy citizens. In Atlanta, Joseph Winship and William Barnes published an appeal to "Help the Poor" on behalf of the Atlanta Mutual Supply Association, formed in November 1863 to aid the destitute. The organization hired agents in southeastern Georgia to find modestly priced food that the railroads offered to transport to Atlanta without charge. Winship and Barnes called upon farmers around the state and citizens in Atlanta and elsewhere to spare a modest amount of cornmeal or bacon "or anything to eat," and to do so in the name of helping the poor, including soldiers' families.[25]

The Confederate government at Richmond responded to high prices by devaluing Confederate currency 33.3 percent effective April 1, 1864. The *Southern Confederacy* inserted a handy table in its April 5, 1864, edition so that its readers could see old values and new; Mary Mallard enclosed a copy in a letter to her mother. The *Daily Intelligencer* praised the new $10 bill with its "well executed" engraving. On the other hand, the *Memphis Appeal,* while assuring its readers that the Confederate treasury secretary had the authority to make this move, nonetheless predicted that the devaluation would not help struggling businessmen. Sam Richards did not feel reassured. Richards had invested $12,000 in Confederate Bonds in part because he could pay his taxes by doing so. The bookseller joked that "under the late law that will probably be the amount necessary" to pay taxes. Concerned about both the economic situation at home and the military situation in North Georgia, Richards wrote, "It is a time of perplexity now."[26]

In early April, the Atlanta Typographical Union took collective action to improve the financial situation of its members by striking for higher wages against Atlanta's daily newspapers. Sylvanus Lines served as the union's president, one of eight officers elected in January. By walking off the job after management refused to consider their demand for a 50 percent increase in wages, the strikers shut down all of Atlanta's newspapers. The strike lasted one week. The day after it ended, John H. Steele, editor of the *Daily Intelligencer,* wrote an article indicating that while he understood the printers' demands, he deplored the suddenness of their actions and their alleged unwillingness to negotiate. Nonetheless, the printers were in a position to win their fight. Atlanta newspapers would not have an easy time finding replacement typographers, and all parties involved in this labor dispute knew it. Steele did not reveal details about the settlement reached, but did state, "Each [side] will strive" to keep the *Intelligencer* "afloat in perilous times— perilous in a financial, as well as warlike aspect." In apologizing to its readers for its first-ever suspension, the *Memphis Appeal* promised not to raise subscription rates.[27]

Most Atlantans lacked access to collective bargaining and some of them resorted to extralegal means to stay afloat. The previous year, struggling women had broken the law by collectively holding up a butcher shop on Whitehall Street; in the spring of 1864, struggling Atlantans resorted to individual and collective acts of theft. Newspapers reported a series of burglaries in the spring of 1864, with food and clothing as the thieves' principal booty. Winter pants now cost $150, and yard goods to make a simple calico dress ran $108. In late March, thieves pried open the window of a home on Peachtree Street under cover of darkness and made off with $2,000 to $3,000 worth of food, including sacks of flour and rice, sugar, and syrup, along with tobacco and jewelry. The same week, burglars used a false key to enter the clothing store of William F. Herring on Whitehall Street and steal an estimated $5,000 worth of goods. The following month, thieves broke into two stores on Whitehall Street, hauling away bolts of calico cloth, pairs of shoes, and leather. According to a newspaper account, "The robbers left the most valuable articles, only taking such as they could easily conceal, or dispose of to avoid detection." A more likely scenario was that thieves sought necessities, not valuables. Observing the problems of poverty in the city and no doubt reacting to newspaper stories of theft, Cyrena Stone noted in her diary, "Calico is ten and twelve dollars a yard. Is it any marvel that crime and prostitution are so common?" On March 30, the *Southern Confederacy* noted that fifty white men had been arrested for theft since the first of January.[28]

Thieves stole vegetables from gardens and chickens and other poultry from private homes. With "diminutive" cabbages selling for $6 per head in Atlanta's market, vegetables began disappearing from local gardens, some taken by men dressed as soldiers. In March, Robert and Mary Mallard lost two turkeys, several roosters, and a dozen chickens, pilfered in the night by a thief who broke the hinges off their henhouse. "Things are coming to fearful pass in this city," Mary Mallard told her mother. "The exceptions are those who have not been robbed." Barrels of flour and sides of bacon disappeared from the storehouses of the Mallards' friends. Mary attributed the thefts to slaves who hired their own time and those impressed to work for Colonel Lemuel Grant in building Atlanta's fortifications. She also complained about the inefficiency of Atlanta's police force. But African Americans were themselves the victims of crime. The *Memphis Appeal* reported a black man being held up by gun-wielding white men and robbed of $40 as he came to Atlanta from Dalton. The perpetrators were not apprehended.[29]

Atlanta's newspapers reported a variety of stories involving children committing crimes. While journalists attributed these episodes to moral lapses and a lack of adult supervision, the children undoubtedly acted from necessity, perhaps desperation. The problem of young boys on Atlanta's streets created ongoing concerns. Newspapers reported about boys engaging in gambling and other illicit pursuits, and one news story suggested that the problem cast the entire city in a bad light. "Oh, Atlanta . . . how long until thy morals are renovated?" The city's newsboys fleeced customers by charging them fifty cents for a newspaper when the cost was supposed to be twenty-five cents. The

Memphis Appeal wanted its customers to know they should not pay more than twenty-five cents and that newsboys made a "handsome profit" from selling the papers at this price, a claim that was an overstatement at best. The *Daily Intelligencer* printed similar cautionary letters to its readers about newsboys overcharging. Girls also engaged in crime. The *Southern Confederacy* reported an apparent scam in which a young girl showed up at the post office, opening mail from boxes and extracting small amounts of money before slipping away. Caught in the act and questioned about her family, she changed her story several times, eventually identifying her mother as an employee of a local hotel. "How much more degrading it is to feel that female depravity is scarcely a whit behind that of the opposite sex," the *Confederacy* concluded.[30]

Adults were responsible for most of the city's crimes. Farmers coming to the city to sell produce became easy prey for thieves. Five white men disguised as blacks robbed a Henry County man of his freshly butchered pork as he traveled to Atlanta's market in February 1864. Crime such as this threatened Atlanta's survival, for if farmers stopped bringing their goods to market, Atlanta's citizens could not be fed. While much of Atlanta's crime resulted from economic necessity, some of it can be attributed to wartime chaos and cheap liquor. With the streets crowded with refugees and soldiers looking for a break from the monotony of winter quarters, violence occurred on a regular basis. In mid-January, a group of men belonging to Waddell's Artillery Battery slipped away from the army without permission, traveled to Atlanta, and "drank freely of liquor" in a Decatur Street tavern. A drunken squabble ensued in which someone fired a gun, killing a private named William Shays. In reporting this story, the *Daily Intelligencer* suggested that murders occurred weekly in the Gate City, and rarely were the perpetrators brought to justice.[31]

In decrying the problem of crime in Atlanta, the *Memphis Appeal* noted the public's "universal" query, "'Where was the police!'" In spite of the *Confederacy*'s report of fifty arrests for thievery, it was becoming more and more difficult to maintain law and order in Atlanta. The City Council doubled the size of Atlanta's police force during the war, from fourteen members to around thirty. With most able-bodied men serving in the military, it was next to impossible to find qualified policemen, and Atlanta's law enforcement officers were routinely dismissed by the mayor and City Council for drunkenness, sleeping on the job, stealing from prisoners, and general incompetence. The City Council voted to fire twenty-two men for one offense or another during the war years.[32]

Many suspected criminals were never apprehended, and those who were caught often avoided conviction. Superior Court records for Fulton County, 1861–64, reveal the largest number of wartime cases involved larceny, robbery, and forgery. Of ninety-nine recorded cases, eight defendants were found not guilty, eight were convicted, and the other defendants had their case dismissed, or their outcomes are unrecorded. The *Daily Intelligencer* may have been correct in its estimate that murders occurred weekly in Atlanta, but only ten murder cases landed in Superior Court between 1861 and 1864, and only one led to conviction.[33]

Understanding the gravity of the situation, General Marcus J. Wright, the new commander of the Post of Atlanta, stationed soldiers on street corners to maintain order in the Gate City. Civilians were now required to carry passports identifying them as legitimate residents. While supporting the cause of law and order, the *Daily Intelligencer* disliked the presence of military police on every corner, calling the new a system "perfect humbug." In March, the city marshal called a meeting with the plan of organizing citizen patrols to supplement the efforts of Atlanta police. Sam Richards, now enlisted in a branch of the Georgia militia called the Press Guards, also took his turn as a citizen policeman.[34]

No issue better symbolized the toll of war in Atlanta than the closing of the Athenaeum by its owner, James Williams. Given the potential for rowdiness at the Athenaeum, the mayor was reluctant to grant permits for groups to perform there, and Williams could not afford to pay taxes without performers paying him. Beginning in March 1864, the building was used only for auctions. Understanding the theater's importance to the cultural life of Atlanta, the *Intelligencer* deplored a state of affairs in which the building that once proudly boasted Shakespearean plays now served as a venue for auctioning goober peas and slaves. The Athenaeum was a victim of bad economic times and uncontrolled crime. Its closing left the Gate City without a theater or major cultural venue of any kind.[35]

With a federal army perched on Georgia's doorstep waiting for spring weather to allow military campaigning, Confederate Atlantans speculated about the future of slavery. In some ways, the institution of slavery seemed to continue much as it had before the war. Slave auctions went on as usual. Although Atlanta's large auction house, Crawford, Frazer, dissolved in January when Robert Crawford bought out his partners Addison and Thomas Frazer, Crawford ran the Atlanta slave mart himself. Crawford advertised frequently as both a buyer and seller of slaves, and told clients who lived outside of Atlanta that he would gladly send his elderly porters Andrew and Antony to the depot to pick up house servants, waiters, blacksmiths, carpenters, and those he called "young fellows" and "young women."[36]

The Confederacy's conscription of white men, combined with military defeat and a vast Union army camped at Chattanooga, led to public discourse about whether or how to make maximum use of slave men in the army. Slave labor was in high demand. As they had for the past two years, Atlanta's hospitals solicited slave labor to help with a variety of tasks. Colonel Lemuel Grant impressed slaves to build Atlanta's fortifications. Mary Mallard was grateful that her mother's slave Niger was not taken. Evidently, Mallard's slave named Charles (Niger's father-in-law) was impressed. Cyrena Stone hid four black men in her cotton house. They feared impressment, telling Stone that slaves who worked on the fortifications "are dying up" from overwork and undernourishment. The *Daily Intelligencer* wanted to see black men used more extensively in the Confederate Army and published a detailed proposal that would employ black men as teamsters, wheelwrights, blacksmiths, cooks, hospital nurses, shoemakers, and "engineer laborers." The proposal would theoretically free up forty thousand white men to fight. But the *Memphis Appeal* warned of potential disaster if field hands were removed from cultivating and harvesting crops that would feed Georgia's people. Instead, the newspaper suggested that thousands of refugees now congregating in Atlanta might be recruited.[37]

Concerns about slave uprisings preoccupied Atlanta's white residents from the beginning of the war, and by 1864 their concerns grew to alarm. In late January, the *Daily Intelligencer* reported a story under the headline "Disgraceful and Outrageous." On a Sunday, traditionally the day of rest for blacks and whites, a group of sixty "negro fellows and boys," along with fifteen white men and boys, were engaged in cockfighting near the Confederate Rolling Mill. When military guards approached, a scuffle took place during which several men fired guns, including guards but also "some of the negroes." Readers of the *Daily Intelligencer* would have understood the gravity of this situation. Negroes with guns? A *group* of armed black men in the midst of Atlanta? In the melee, one black man was killed and a white boy suffered a wound to his hand. Thirty-two blacks were carted off to the city jail to be whipped before being returned to their masters. "This outrageous incident is a lesson to the authorities here," the *Daily Intelligencer* reported. "The *dandy* and '*buck negroes*' in this city have for some time past manifested a spirit, and displayed a bearing that *must* be subdued; if not, we may look out for serious troubles."[38]

In the current climate, African American tradesmen and professionals had to watch their backs. The *Memphis Appeal* protested when, during early April, a black man allegedly came to market to sell vegetables at "three to four times as much as the retail prices of the same articles in the Augusta market during the present week." The newspaper suggested, "The rascal ought to have been driven from the market place, and his vegetables distributed among the various hospitals." Bob Webster managed to stay out of an argument that took place in his barbershop between two white boys, one of them a seventeen-year-old and the other only twelve. Evidently, the two argued over a bet, culminating in the older boy shooting the younger one. He was apprehended and taken to jail. Webster's name appeared in the newspaper only as the owner of the shop where the incident took place.[39]

Roderick D. Badger continued to practice dentistry from an office located at 3 Marietta Street, around the corner from where Robert Crawford sold slaves. Badger was widely regarded as the city's most skilled dentist, but his success antagonized some white people. Minutes of the Mayor's Court on February 12, 1864, reveal that Mayor James Calhoun dropped charges against a man identified as Thomas Chastin for "Malicious mischief" involved in "cutting down a sign by Roderic, a slave whose master allowed him to put it up." The minutes contain no additional details, but "Roderic" may have been Roderick D. Badger. Four days after the incident described in Mayor's Court records, Badger placed an ad in the *Southern Confederacy* under the heading Dentistry: "The friends and acquaintances of R D Badger will remember that his Office is still on Marietta street," and "he would be pleased to see them as usual."[40]

In Atlanta and in other cities of the Confederacy, slaves were running away in droves. As in previous years, some ran from Atlanta and some were suspected of running to Atlanta. What is striking about the newspaper ads for runaways in 1864 is the number of owners who placed ads seeking the return of multiple slaves, offering substantial amounts of money as rewards, and anticipating that slaves were running to the Union Army. For example, a man named E. Steadman who lived near Covington, east of Atlanta, offered $900 for the return of Anthony, Jerry, Lewis, Isaac, Ned, Aleck, Webster, Tony, and Joshua, all of them between the ages of eighteen and thirty and heading toward the Union lines. Steadman believed that these slaves might be passing through Atlanta. J. C. McManus of Marietta, Georgia, offered $1,000 for the return of Jesse and his wife Delia, who were thought to be "making their way for the enemy" with forged passes. Sometimes, white owners offered enormous rewards for the return of a single slave. Such was the case with twenty-three-year-old Lavonia, who ran away or was stolen in Walton County, Georgia, during June and for whose return P. E. McDaniel offered a reward of $500.[41]

As the cold winter of 1864 gave signs of ending, Atlantans wondered what was in store for the Confederacy and for their city during the spring military campaign. Lucius Gartrell wanted to play a role in defending his state. He decided to end his political career and resume his military one by organizing a brigade to fight for home defense. In a letter to Confederate Secretary of War James Seddon on March 5, 1864, Gartrell indicated that he would seek men ages seventeen to eighteen and forty-five to fifty. Evidently, the former congressman had an easier time recruiting younger men, for he admitted to Seddon, "I find the young men disposed to come promptly forward, but the men over forty-five, with few exceptions, refuse to volunteer, giving as a reason that it will be time enough to do so when called out by the order of the President." Gartrell informed Seddon that he had twenty companies "in process of organization." Gartrell or his surrogates advertised in Atlanta newspapers seeking recruits. Gartrell received the rank of brigadier general.[42]

When Atlantans scanned their newspapers for updates about the military situation, they read about "sham battles" taking place within the Confederate and Union Armies. These exercises prepared soldiers for battle, instilled confidence and pride, and impressed civilians and newspaper reporters. General John Bell Hood, a corps commander under General Johnston, staged a drill followed by a sham battle in March. "The drilling was superb," wrote a correspondent for the *Southern Confederacy*, "and the troops were put through various difficult evolutions in a manner which reflects great credit upon Gen Hood." Next, the sham battle occurred, complete with bellowing cannon, staff officers "dashing about," and an infantry charge. The *Daily Intelligencer* concluded, "The whole affair was very imposing and drew forth the warmest praise from all who were present." Eugenia Goode, a young woman from a prominent Atlanta family who served as secretary to Martha Winship's Atlanta Hospital Association, attended the sham battle as a member of a party of young people who traveled on the Western and Atlantic Railroad to Dalton. At the time, Goode was engaged to marry Major Joseph Morgan, so her trip to Dalton allowed a brief visit with her fiancé. Goode recalled many years later that the faux battle presented an "awe inspiring" scene. However, the image it conveyed of Confederate military invincibility was soon put to the test. A few weeks later, Goode recalled, "General Johns[t]on's army commenced that famous retreat which will live in song and story when gallant deeds are recounted."[43]

General William T. Sherman commanded the Union Army's campaign to capture Atlanta, chosen by Ulysses S. Grant to conquer and possess the Confederacy's second most important city. A West Point graduate whose prewar military career was as unimpressive as that of Grant, Sherman reentered the army at the start of the war and served under Grant at Shiloh, Vicksburg, and Missionary Ridge. The red-haired, quick-tempered Sherman won Grant's confidence with his brilliant mind, boundless energy, and absolute determination to carry out military orders. Moreover, the two men had become close friends, and Grant trusted Sherman implicitly. Sherman came to Georgia well equipped to defeat his enemy. He had three armies estimated at sixty thousand to seventy thousand men by Atlanta newspapers. Johnston's army had sixty thousand men. Because he was in enemy territory, Sherman would need to remain tethered to the Western and Atlantic Railroad for supplies.[44]

Atlantans learned news of the military campaign via the city's daily newspapers, which had correspondents with the army, in addition to employing the efforts of the Press Association. Citizens also heard rumors from civilians arriving at the passenger depot and from wounded soldiers in Atlanta hospitals. Throughout the campaign, Atlantans believed that a "great battle" would decide the fate of their city. During the early weeks of the campaign, the city's daily newspapers took the editorial position that the Confederates would not be outgeneraled by Sherman or outfought by his army. The *Memphis Appeal* put it this way: "Gen. Johnston chose his ground . . . and will hold it." The newspapers also insisted, as they had in the past, that God favored the Confederate cause. "The God of Battles is with us," according to the *Daily Intelligencer*. Nonetheless, the City Council, anticipating military burials in the spring campaign, quietly appropriated $5,000 to expand the boundaries of City Cemetery.[45]

During the prelude to the Atlanta campaign, the newspapers reported on the activities of General Nathan Bedford Forrest. Like John Hunt Morgan,

Forrest was a cavalry commander who menaced the Yankees in the western theater of the war. Forrest's victory over Union forces at Fort Pillow, Tennessee, in mid-April had been largely missed by Atlantans because it occurred during the newspaper strike that brought all news reporting to a halt. In late April and May, however, newspapers reported details of Forrest's victory in capturing an important federal fort in Tennessee. The *Memphis Appeal* applauded Forrest's "daring achievement," calling it a "severe blow to the enemy," while the *Daily Intelligencer* characterized the Yankee army as being "dismayed and demoralized" in its aftermath. The *Southern Confederacy*'s coverage also included reports that Forrest's men had gunned down soldiers in the garrison, including African American troops who had dropped their arms and attempted to surrender, but the *Confederacy* dismissed the allegations by calling them a "romantic version of that affair." Likewise, the *Memphis Appeal* denied "any wanton massacre or disregard of the rules of warfare."[46] As Atlantans waited for positive news from General John Hunt Morgan, Forrest became the darling of the newspapers.

Atlantans also waited anxiously for news from the Confederate Army in Virginia. On May 7, telegraphic communication about the progress of General Robert E. Lee's army brought news of a victory at the Wilderness against Union soldiers commanded by General Grant, who had gone east to fight Lee while leaving Sherman in charge of the Atlanta campaign. Confederates received more good news from Virginia the first week of June, when Lee's forces defeated those of General Grant at Cold Harbor. In a frontal assault that failed to make a dent in Lee's lines, Grant lost thousands of men, a horrific slaughter that generated negative publicity for the Union high command. The *Memphis Appeal* called it "a signal and bloody repulse." Having failed to break the Confederate lines, Grant subsequently settled in for a lengthy siege outside of Petersburg south of Richmond. The *Southern Confederacy* accused Grant of leaving behind guns in favor of building trenches with shovels and spades and called the Union commander "Useless Spade Grant."[47]

In spite of ongoing predictions of a climactic battle to decide Atlanta's fate, General Sherman had no intention of giving Confederates a chance to fight on those terms. Instead, the Union commander moved slowly to the south, careful to protect his supply lines on the Western and Atlantic Railroad. He staged a series of flank attacks, beginning when federal forces under General James McPherson launched a flanking movement southwest of

Johnston's forces at Dalton during the week of May 7. Residents of the Gate
City knew that the long-awaited campaign had finally begun when they saw
the *Daily Intelligencer*'s headline on May 1 indicating that Confederate pickets
had been driven in. The *Intelligencer* reported that a large force was moving
in the direction of Dalton and that "a great battle will soon be fought." In
subsequent weeks, Union prisoners confirmed that Sherman would not fight
but instead would flank the Rebels. Sherman kept his focus on the Confederate
railroads, understanding the need to seize key rail junctions before claiming
the ultimate prize, Atlanta.[48]

On May 12, General Johnston abandoned Dalton and retreated sixteen
miles to the south at Resaca. Atlanta newspapers did not learn the news
immediately because a storm disrupted telegraphic connection between
north Georgia and the Gate City. However, the *Memphis Appeal* predicted
optimistically that despite "severe fighting," Sherman would soon retreat to
Chattanooga and send the bulk of his force to bolster the forces of General
Grant.[49]

The *Appeal*'s prediction proved incorrect. Sherman's soldiers faced men
from Hood's command at Resaca and drove them back, May 14–15. Among
the wounded was Captain William L. Calhoun, the mayor's son, who was
shot in the hip and subsequently transported to his parents' home in Atlanta
for treatment. The *Daily Intelligencer* had a reporter on the scene at the battle
of Resaca who revealed the gravity of the military situation. Previous reports
suggested that Sherman had sixty thousand to seventy thousand men. Now,
the newspapers reported that Sherman had more than one hundred thousand
men who fought "with desperate earnestness."[50]

The armies' movements caused uproar in Atlanta. "An immense number
of wagons and provisions are being sent" to the front, Mary Mallard wrote to
her mother on May 14, and in another letter she described the horribly
wounded men arriving and being carried on litters at the passenger depot,
"bearing all their sufferings without a groan." Kate Cumming, a nurse with
the Confederate Army, arrived in Atlanta on the morning of May 16 and
went straight to the army's Receiving and Distributing Hospital, where an
estimated seven hundred to eight hundred wounded had recently arrived.
"That morning was one of the gloomiest I ever passed," Cumming noted in
her diary, for the Atlanta hospitals treated "dirty, bloody, weary" men, many
with serious wounds to their heads and faces. Hospitals cleared out their
wards of men felled by illness in order to make way for the wounded soldiers

who began arriving in the city, along with scattered groups of Union prisoners. Within days, newspapers started printing columns of names of the wounded.[51]

The efforts of hospital volunteers impressed Cumming, who noted that many women engaged in the most emotionally wrenching types of nursing work, including changing the bandages of wounded men. Volunteers worked in appalling conditions. Every Atlanta hospital was filled to capacity, and more wounded arrived on every train. With everyone focused on the wounded, no one had time to clean the wards, and the sight of it shocked Cumming despite her years of experience as a nurse. "Sickening" is the word she used to describe the piles of bloodied rags used to dress wounds and sheets used to cover patients who underwent amputations. Many female volunteers focused on nourishment, bringing large quantities of milk, coffee, lemonade, and wine to the passenger depot. Volunteers also set up a depot at the Athenaeum, where women gathered to receive and sort supplies.[52]

Although city officials had previously resisted requests to turn City Hall into a hospital, Governor Joseph E. Brown's insistence on creating a separate facility for members of the Georgia militia led to the creation of Brown Hospital at City Hall. Despite the governor's orders to the contrary, this facility also cared for Confederate soldiers during the Atlanta campaign. Its surgeon reported two to eight deaths per day out of a hospital population of several hundred.[53]

As news reports arrived in Atlanta about renewed fighting in north Georgia, Atlanta's claim to lawfulness, tenuous even before the fighting began, now became even more so. A reporter for the *Daily Intelligencer* captured a sense of the raucousness when he wrote about "the continuous stream of wagons" that filled Atlanta's streets. "The noise of their wheels is deafening; the shouts of the drivers mingle with the roar. Laughs and yells, calls and greetings, newsboy's cries and braying of mules and the whistle of the iron horse, all combine to make a very Bedlam of this Babel." Performances by the Atlanta Amateurs, who were given special permission to use the Athenaeum, and Tom Wiggins at City Hall raised money for wounded soldiers, but also provided outlets for bad behavior. The *Intelligencer* complained about men showing up at one concert accompanied by women of *"notoriously bad character,"* and cited the city marshal in threatening consequences if prostitutes came to City Hall again. Kate Cumming thought Atlanta was "the most wicked place in the world."[54]

Sam Richards needed to get away from Atlanta's crowded, dirty, cheerless streets. On a Sunday afternoon after church, he took his wife and children to City Cemetery to reflect on the meaning of what was happening around him. What he saw that day caused Richards to record his sentiments with uncharacteristic depth and emotion. It was "the saddest sight that I have ever seen," Richards wrote in his diary on May 15, an "*acre* of fresh-dug graves that are filled by dead soldiers, the result of this terrible war. Not a blade of grass left growing there. And still the work of destruction goes on." Richards, who supported the Confederacy but never glorified military conflict, now felt uncertain and anxious while awaiting news from the front.[55]

As Sherman's army continued to press Johnston's Confederates with steady flanking movements—"to retire in this direction," as the *Memphis Appeal* put it diplomatically on May 22—refugees from north Georgia fled in panic, clogging roads and adding more displaced people to Atlanta's already crowded passenger depot, hotels, and streets. Among the new arrivals were citizens of Rome, Georgia, a city recently overrun by Yankees. Cyrena Stone noted a "wild day of excitement" on May 24, as trains thundered in and out of Atlanta, refugees arrived and left, and Atlantans began to make difficult decisions about whether to stay in the Gate City and protect their property or leave for a potentially safer place. Stone, whose house northeast of the city center was close to Lemuel Grant's breastworks, feared the future without her husband's protection but had nowhere else to go.[56]

Local clergy, including Henry Hornady and William T. Brantley of First and Second Baptist Churches, Central Presbyterian's Robert Mallard, Harwell Parks of Trinity Methodist, and David Mayer of the Hebrew Benevolent Association, published "An Appeal to the Benevolent" begging the public to donate money to help "those who have been driven from their homes in the Northern portion of this State." These people were now "in a most destitute condition." The clergymen did what they could to find food and shelter for these desperate people, and the newspapers published editorials urging the public to treat refugees with sympathy and generosity. "Our city is full of them," noted the *Intelligencer* on May 27. "How sorrowful their position. How desolate their hearts. . . . Reader, deal kindly with them."[57]

On May 17, General Marcus J. Wright held a bimonthly inspection of local troops on Marietta Street, accompanied by band music. The soldiers included workers at the Atlanta Arsenal and members of the local fire companies. Despite the newspaper accolades in reporting the event, neither Mayor

Calhoun nor Governor Brown believed Atlanta had enough defenders. Both leaders issued proclamations calling upon able-bodied men to defend their state. With his usual rhetorical flourish, Brown insisted, "He who remains at home now, may soon occupy it as a slave or be driven from it."[58]

By the second half of May, newspapers adopted a new interpretation of military events in Georgia. Having once suggested that Confederates would not cede ground to the federal army, the newspapers now predicted that Johnston retreated because he was looking for the best terrain on which to stage a major battle. "Our last news is that the army has fallen back in the neighborhood of the Etowah [River]," Mary Mallard wrote to a relative on May 20, then added, "General Johnston has issued his battle order saying that he will now give battle and will fall back no further." However, the *Daily Intelligencer* soon reported that the armies had shifted again. Sherman's army had crossed the Etowah River and now marched in the direction of Marietta, news that triggered alarm among Atlantans. Marietta was a rail stop that many Atlantans knew well and a clear barometer of how close the enemy now came to the Gate City itself. Four days later, the *Memphis Appeal* reported "commotion" in the city of Atlanta because citizens claimed they could hear cannon fire in the distance. Sam Richards heard the sounds and described a week of "great excitement in our city." Richards added, "May God deliver us from our blood-thirsty foes."[59]

By early June, even the *Daily Intelligencer* dropped any pretense that the Union Army could easily be stopped. In predicting the possibility of enemy raids on Atlanta, the newspaper felt the need to "sound an alarm that the people may awake to a stirring sense of their danger." The newspaper urged Atlanta civilians to clean and load their guns and keep them close at hand in case they had to face the Yankees themselves. The newspaper even suggested that the Confederate Army might be pushed back all the way to the Chattahoochee River, six miles from the city. The newspaper insisted that such a retreat would not represent any "sign of weakness." Three days earlier, the *Intelligencer* reported that the young cadets at the Georgia Military Institute in Marietta had passed through Atlanta and now stood ready to defend the city. Amanda Lin's son Charles, whom she had carefully kept away from conscription by enrolling him in the military school, now wore a Confederate uniform.[60]

A. J. Neal's letters to his parents and siblings reveal a change in tone from his messages of February and March. Neal served in Hoxton's Battalion of the Marion Light Artillery. Writing from a location near Resaca on May 15, he still expressed the same confidence in God's favor toward the Confederate cause and still believed that a grand battle would decide the campaign. But Neal admitted, "I am well nigh worn out—fighting all day and running or working all night." By the first week of June, Neal cited Confederate skirmishers in Dallas who reported the Yankees had "destroyed everything," including livestock and food, leaving civilians there in "great distress." Just north of Marietta, Neal reported the Yankees drove in Confederate skirmishers, brought up their lines and took possession of Confederate breastworks. "They came up waving their infernal flags and cheering as if they had captured all Rebeldom," Neal complained in a letter to his father.[61]

Mayor Calhoun set aside June 10, 1864, as a day of fasting and prayer. In regard to this event, the Atlanta City Council passed a resolution that "the Lincoln Government has concentrated two of the largest armies ever seen on this continent, the one under the leadership of Gen'l Grant to besiege Richmond ... and the other under Gen'l Sherman to invade Georgia and capture Atlanta, 'the citadel of the Confederacy.'" Although religious citizens like Sam Richards observed the occasion, many did not. By June, Atlanta had become a city "in a state of siege," as the *Daily Intelligencer* put it. Adding to newspaper reports about advancing armies, crime, and crowding, the *Mobile Advertiser*'s reporter who wrote under the byline "Shadow" now predicted Atlanta's imminent fall and characterized its citizens as "bewildered" and "panic-stricken." The *Intelligencer* pushed back, calling the *Advertiser* sensationalist and unpatriotic. Nonetheless, Atlanta was a city in chaos. During the day, sentinels stationed on street corners tried to keep order, and insisted on checking the passes of every citizen who walked by. At night, law-abiding civilians dared not go near Decatur and Whitehall Streets, for drunken soldiers and stragglers from the army filled the area with their alcohol-induced brawling and thieving. Under the headline "Drunk," the *Southern Confederacy* claimed that there had been more intoxicated men on city streets the previous evening than ever before, including a number of military officers. Revelers kept up their howling and yelling until midnight. City authorities, including police, failed to curtail drinking and lawlessness.[62]

Confederate civilians in Atlanta wondered what African Americans knew and how they might react to the shifting military situation. A slave woman came to visit Cyrena Stone in early June "to see how I was coming on." Stone identified the woman as "Aunt Cherry," though she probably changed her name as she changed those of others in the diary. Aunt Cherry told Stone that she did not plan to leave her owners, for "we black folks is going to be free— the Bible says so—and I think the time is mighty near."[63] By June 1864, it was only a matter of weeks.

8. The Barbarous War

On a hot, humid night in July 1864, Sam Richards pulled out his small clothbound diary and penned an entry. Richards worried about the military situation, which did not look promising. The Confederate Army had failed to stop the onward march of General William T. Sherman and his army, and Sherman now aimed enormous artillery guns that rained a "great many shells" into neighborhoods throughout Atlanta, including Richards's own. Levelheaded and rational, Richards avoided panic but did express frustration that General Sherman engaged in warfare against civilians, including women and children. Richards called it "a very barbarous mode of carrying on war."[1] The barbarous war had no end in sight. By the summer of 1864, conversations about business profits, military strategy, even loyalty to state and region no longer mattered to Richards and other Atlanta civilians. Instead, they focused on survival amid deteriorating conditions. When General Sherman aimed his guns at the city, Atlanta began to implode.

Five weeks before Richards's lament, on June 14, Atlantans opened their daily papers to see black-bordered columns of newsprint; Lieutenant General Leonidas Polk had been killed by Yankee artillery. With the armies now massed northwest of Atlanta near Kennesaw Mountain, Generals Joseph Johnston and William Hardee, along with Polk, had held a conference on nearby Pine Mountain. While observing Sherman's army, they suddenly realized that the enemy had artillery trained on them. Just as they broke up the meeting, a shell hit Polk, killing him instantly. Although Polk had a poor record as general, Confederate civilians held him in high regard, for he personified their values of military leadership and Christian service. A graduate of West Point in the 1827, Polk left the army to become a planter, clergyman, and later a bishop in the Episcopal Church. He joined the Confederate Army in 1861 and quickly won an appointment as major general. During the Atlanta campaign, Polk also provided religious counsel and personally baptized Generals John Bell Hood and Joseph E. Johnston.[2]

According to news reports, Atlantans were "thrown into gloom" upon hearing the news that the beloved general had fallen. Mayor Calhoun sent a delegation of civilians to the depot to receive Polk's remains. The train arrived early in the morning, and a solemn tolling of bells marked the occasion. Polk's body lay in state at St. Luke's Episcopal Church until noon, when the casket left Atlanta, transported by rail to Augusta, where Bishop Stephen Elliott conducted the funeral and presided at the burial. Thousands of Atlantans paid their respects to Polk by filing past his casket at St. Luke's. A Confederate flag draped the coffin, also embellished with white roses and magnolia blossoms. Many of the silent mourners paused to take a flower or leaf, apparently desirous of keeping a memento of the general. The crowd then formed a line of mourners to accompany the coffin back to the rail station.[3]

Military events soon refocused the attention of Atlantans on the living. In late May and early June, Dr. Samuel Stout evacuated hospitals in Marietta and concentrated his base in Atlanta, further indication that the military situation was deteriorating. Stout struggled to find an adequate number of doctors and staff for the hospitals, and vegetables for patients. Concerns about scurvy, a terrible disease characterized by lethargy and bleeding through the skin and gums, led doctors to solicit vegetables as a preventive. Via the newspapers, Stout asked the public to share their vegetables with the South's wounded heroes. By May, the weather turned warm, allowing Stout to supplement existing hospitals with tents in which soldiers could be treated. In Atlanta, post surgeon Dr. Joseph Logan put out a special order that surgeons in Atlanta's hospitals use tents for incoming patients and construct "rough sheds made of such material as can be obtained." He added, "Preparations admit of no delay."[4]

With the armies now situated near Kennesaw Mountain, Atlantans wondered whether a major battle would soon decide their fate. The *Daily Intelligencer* warned that Sherman wanted to occupy the Gate City by the Fourth of July. Earlier in the war, Atlanta newspapers had placed their faith in miraculous efforts by John Hunt Morgan and his cavalry. Morgan was in Kentucky, where his current efforts did not match the successes of earlier years, but Nathan Bedford Forrest and his mounted men, now engaging the enemy in Mississippi, might rescue them. If Forrest attacked the rear of Sherman's army and menaced his supply lines, the *Intelligencer* suggested, "one well-directed blow struck by Forrest ... would insure Southern Independence."[5]

On June 27, General Sherman ordered a frontal assault against a well-entrenched Confederate Army on Kennesaw Mountain. With complete confidence in himself and his men, Sherman believed that the Confederate defensive line was stretched too thin and might be penetrated. At 8:00 A.M., the Yankees began firing their cannon at Confederates, and an hour later infantry attempted to storm the Confederate lines, climbing, firing, and leaving dead and wounded comrades in their path. At one point, gunfire triggered fires in front of Confederate General Daniel Govan's brigade, opening up the possibility that wounded Union soldiers could be burned alive. The two sides declared a brief cease-fire to remove the wounded before the fighting continued. By late morning, it was clear to commanders on both sides that the Confederates had prevailed. Sherman wanted to resume the fight, but his generals talked him out of it. He lost three thousand men to the Confederates' seven hundred. General Johnston had won his first major victory of the Atlanta campaign.[6]

Atlantans waited anxiously for news from the front. Although the newspapers had trouble getting details, they reported on June 28 that the Confederates had won a clear victory with relatively small loss of life. The Yankees sent their infantry "seven lines deep" up the hilly terrain, the *Memphis Appeal* noted, and the enemy was "repulsed with heavy loss." A reporter with the Press Association counted five hundred ambulances descending the mountain carrying Yankee wounded. Word of the Confederate victory came as "Glorious News." The *Daily Intelligencer* quickly assumed yet another editorial position about the campaign; Confederate victory at Kennesaw Mountain had "infused new life into our gallant army." Confederate civilians also cheered. Mary Mallard wrote reassuringly to her mother on July 1, "The last disaster to Sherman has been a very serious affair."[7]

The cheering did not last long. After several days spent burying their dead, the armies began to move again, with Sherman resuming his flanking maneuvers, pushing Johnston's army south toward the Chattahoochee River and Atlanta. Sherman's chief of engineers, Orlando M. Poe, lingered another day. Poe ascended the mountain on July 3 and surveyed the landscape with a spyglass. He could see the Gate City clearly from the mountaintop, and pictur-esque scenery stretched out before him as far as the eye could see. Writing in his diary, what struck Poe most vividly was the tableau of the two armies. "The Scenery was beautiful," Poe wrote, "and when combined with the powerful Armies scattered over it formed an ensemble, witnessed but once in a lifetime."[8]

As Atlantans learned the news of yet another federal advance, many began to leave the Gate City "on every train," as Sallie Clayton put it. John and Mary Jane Neal took their children to their plantation in Pike County, Georgia. Amanda Lin took her daughters to Opelika, Alabama, where they had relatives. Predicting Atlanta's ultimate fall, John Sehon moved Annie and their children to the town of Covington, east of Atlanta, during the first week of June. Annie, whose brother George Maney led a brigade that saw some of the worst fighting on Kennesaw Mountain, was happy to learn of his safety but now feared for her children. John Sehon owned two factories in the Gate City, one that manufactured candles and the other that he rented out. For some time, he had been trying unsuccessfully to sell both establishments. He worked in Atlanta during the week and visited his family on the week-ends. "O Bettie how I wish I could know the fate of Atlanta," Annie wrote to her sister on July 4. "We hear every day of the retreat of our army and the advances of the Federals and the general opinion is that the great battle of the war is to be fought on the Chattahoochee River seven miles from Atlanta." Annie, now the mother of two young boys, nursed her son Johnny through a frightening case of diphtheria that spring. The child survived, but Annie was exhausted and pessimistic about the military situation. She feared a future of "poverty and hardships" for southerners. She wished she could raise her children in Europe, "away from the land of revolution."[9]

For those who remained, Martha Winship responded with a special appeal on behalf of the Atlanta Hospital Association. Since the beginning of the war, Winship worked quietly and behind the scenes to help wounded and ill soldiers. Never challenging male leadership publicly, Winship nonetheless grew in stature and confidence. Recruiting female volunteers from throughout the city, she organized fund-raisers and meetings to promote the well-being of soldiers and the political cause of Confederate nationalism. On June 26, Winship issued another appeal in the Atlanta newspapers. This time she addressed her remarks to "Citizens of Georgia." Winship's use of the term is revealing, for she made no gender-based distinctions about volunteers and implied that women, like men, were "citizens." Winship asked for contributions of vegetables to soldiers in hospital, noting that warm weather and abundant rains meant that "gardens and fields are teeming" with produce.[10]

Atlantans who stayed in the city during June faced deteriorating conditions. In spite of the departure of some residents, Atlanta remained a city jammed with civilians. The weather turned stiflingly hot, making the crowded streets dusty and difficult to navigate. Women "float[ed] like birds of gay plumage flashing in the sunlight" as they visited the post office or the stores on Whitehall Street, according to a reporter for the *Daily Intelligencer* writing on the thirtieth. Soldiers also filled the streets, including smartly dressed officers and threadbare privates. Newsboys and goober venders plied their trades. African Americans were also present, and the *Intelligencer* objected to their having better clothing than some of the whites, and also criticized their presence in groups on Atlanta's streets, and outward show of confidence. Did slaves believe that their liberation was imminent? The newspaper made no such suggestion but did end its discussion of racial issues with "God defend us."[11]

Sanitary conditions worsened in the city, and with the recent heat wave, the stench emanating from Atlanta's streets became almost unendurable. A slaughter pen on the city's west side produced a noxious odor for a quarter-mile. Government stables caused a "disgraceful manure sink" at the corner of Alabama and Whitehall Streets, one of the city's central business intersections. The unsightly "green, slimy scum breeds pestilence and death" and produced a horrible stench, according to one news report. No doubt it also contaminated the city's water supply and contributed to the deaths of civilians from typhoid fever during the hot summer. Recognizing the health risk posed by public privies, the City Council ordered the removal of two of them deemed to be a threat to sanitary conditions in the city. At night, rats came out. By summer, rats had become such a menace that the *Southern Confederacy* offered helpful advice about how to catch them: fill a tall stone jar two-thirds full with water, into which rats would crawl during the night, and, unable to crawl back out, would drown.[12]

As June gave way to July, Atlantans faced the prospect of an advancing Union Army, and those who dedicated their time to helping refugees and wounded soldiers faced a monumental task. One woman wrote to her mother about "frightful times" with "a great many refugees . . . gone down the railroad and there is a heap in Atlanta just [living] in tents." On June 30, a group that called itself the Executive Aid Association reported that 618 refugees received food daily. After the City Council considered and declined to appropriate $5,000 to aid the refugees, the Ladies' Soldiers' Relief Society called upon residents of the city to contribute food, noting that most of the refugees were women and children "in very destitute circumstances." Women should also help wounded soldiers by contributing food, wine and cordials, bandages, and cotton and linen cloth. Because of delays at the passenger depot that caused problems getting wounded soldiers to hospitals, the decision was made to create a new hospital by pitching tents at City Park located between the railroad tracks and Decatur Street. The new hospital would relieve pressure on the depot. To ease pressure on the hospitals, ambulatory soldiers would be furloughed. As the armies began to move again, Atlanta hospitals received more than 200 wounded soldiers per day.[13]

On July 4, Atlantans learned that the Confederate Army had begun another "retrograde movement" toward the Chattahoochee River. Sherman's army occupied Marietta the previous day and his soldiers reportedly burned at least one factory. "The enemy is now at the doors" of Atlanta, as the *Daily Intelligencer* put it, while also advising citizens of the city to avoid panic, and have the same devotion and courage that citizens of Richmond had when their city faced threats from the Yankees on multiple occasions. "Again we say to our people, *stand firm!*" The *Southern Confederacy* praised Atlantans for their calm demeanor in the face of probable battle. "Atlanta will not and cannot be abandoned," the newspaper proclaimed. Even Atlanta's mothers and children must do what they could to keep the Yankees at bay, though the newspaper stopped short of suggesting that women and children should fire guns. On July 6, the *Confederacy* reported the Yankee position as two miles north of the Chattahoochee and less than nine miles from the Gate City.[14]

And then the presses of the *Southern Confederacy* and the *Daily Intelligencer* went silent. Staffs of the two newspapers packed up and retreated to Macon, leaving the *Memphis Appeal* as Atlanta's sole news outlet, other than "dame rumor" at the passenger depot. One reporter for the *Appeal* wrote copy while listening to artillery fire from the front and hoped for reinforcements to come to General Johnston's aid. However, with or without aid, "the spirit of a people can never be subdued when fighting for life, liberty and the right of free self-government." Atlanta would prevail.[15]

On July 5, workers at the Atlanta Arsenal began packing and removing the final pieces of heavy machinery that once had powered Atlanta's industrial juggernaut. For more than a month, the arsenal's commander, Moses Wright, had been quietly moving "*surplus stores* & ammunition not needed here" to arsenals at Macon and Augusta. Wright also moved his two "Cap forming Machines, in good order," to Macon. The production of percussion caps had been the arsenal's greatest success. Wright waited as long as possible before sending the machinery out of the city. He feared that if he accelerated the process it would lead to panic among civilians, and Atlanta's future was very uncertain at that point. On July 5, Wright wrote to his counterpart in Macon, indicating that he was shipping all of the remaining machinery to Augusta and stores to Macon, and two days later, he informed General Johnston's chief of staff that he had "all my machinery down and ready for shipment." If Johnston's army defeated Sherman, the equipment could be returned to Atlanta.[16]

Confederate authorities also began evacuating Atlanta's hospitals. Doctors continued to evaluate patients but now sent them on to other locations. Henry C. Lay, an Episcopal clergyman who ministered to soldiers in the Army of Tennessee, witnessed the removal. "The [railroad] cars were laden with sick and wounded," he wrote to his wife. "Every ghastly wound, limbs just amputated a few hours before, men dying on the platform . . . an awful sight." Fairground Hospitals, the city's largest medical complex, relocated to Vineville near Macon. Empire, Polk, Institute, and Grant hospitals also moved there. Determined to keep nursing patients, Martha Winship moved her Atlanta Hospital Association to Vineville, renaming it Vineville-Atlanta Hospital Association. In the process of evacuating, most of the organization's records were lost. Within a few weeks, Mrs. Winship had organized a theatrical fund-raiser and appealed to the public in Macon to support wounded men now being cared for in the area.[17]

With the arsenal emptied and the hospitals evacuated, another round of civilians departed the city. A Confederate commissary officer named Joseph Semmes wrote to his wife, "With some exceptions the people who remain are either those who are unable to leave, or who will be pleased with the presence of a Yankee army," in other words Unionists. The passenger depot was packed with civilians trying to leave town, many of them women coping without men. Catherine Bellingrath traveled with her five children, including a baby, Theo. They shared a boxcar filled with thirty-seven people and their possessions. Emma Prescott also left. She traveled to Atlanta from Decatur with her children in a rockaway carriage and then took the train to Macon.

"The excitement at the Depot was simply awful," she recalled. Her vivid memory was one of crowds, crying children, and complete pandemonium, as panicked adults attempted to leave the city as quickly as possible.[18]

Mary Mallard and her family left the city as well. As recently as July 1, Mallard had assured her mother that the family did not worry about the city's imminent danger, but the evacuation of Atlanta's hospitals caused the Mallards to change their minds. They feared that delay would jeopardize their ability to find rail transportation for themselves and their possessions. An accident nearly derailed the trip, for the wagon that carried them and their furniture to the passenger depot stalled suddenly, throwing Mary, her husband, Robert, and their young children to the ground. Others survived with minor bruises, but Mary dislocated her collarbone, an injury that caused her great pain. The Mallard family traveled to Augusta in a boxcar, and Mary's husband arranged for a rocking chair to provide her a modicum of comfort.[19]

On July 8–9, federal soldiers of General John Schofield began to cross the Chattahoochee River near Isham's Ford north of Atlanta. Encountering only minimal resistance from Confederates, they waded across in a shallow spot. At that point, General Johnston retreated again, quickly sending his army across the river and burning bridges behind him. Sherman's army followed in hot pursuit, divided into several wings, one aimed to the south in the direction of Newnan with the goal of destroying the Atlanta and West Point Railroad, another headed to the east toward Decatur with the plan of cutting the Georgia Railroad connecting Atlanta with Augusta.[20]

Buoyed by their success, Union soldiers expressed satisfaction when they could finally see Atlanta on the distant horizon. "We are in sight of Atlanta and can see the people on the streets with our [spy] glasses," wrote Lieutenant Charles Harding Cox of the 70th Indiana. "The city will be in possession of Sherman in less than a week I think." Others expressed frustration that the campaign was taking so long. One Union soldier wrote, "In Georgia there is nothing but hills and bushes and rebbles plenty." Union soldiers had not been paid since January. Now they anticipated a long rest, a hot meal, and the money they had waited so long to receive.[21]

Barely a week after Sherman's soldiers crossed the river, President Jefferson Davis fired Joseph Johnston and placed John Bell Hood in command of the Army of Tennessee. Despite his "retrograde movements," Johnston had been a popular figure with his soldiers and the public; thus the president's decision led to criticism. In letters home, Confederate soldiers shared their disappointment with the news. One soldier wrote to a sister, "You have no idea what gloom is cast over the Army when we heard of the change." However, A. J. Neal took an impartial stance when he wrote to his father that soldiers had not expected the change in command, but "I cannot regard it as [a] calamity. Johnston has never stood well with the [Davis] Administration and he has obtained no favors in this campaign."[22]

Atlanta civilians worried less about the fairness of Davis's decision and more about whether their safety was in question. "The enemy draws nearer and nearer . . . to our city," Sam Richards confided to his diary. "All of a sudden Gen Johnston has been *relieved* of command of the Army and Gen Hood or 'Old Pegleg' as the soldiers style him placed in command." Hood, who lost a leg at the Battle of Chickamauga, had a reputation as a fighting general, and some Atlantans thought the best way for the army to defend their city was to stand and fight.[23]

Hood did so at Peachtree Creek, five miles north of Atlanta, on July 20. The morning of the battle, the *Memphis Appeal* issued its final edition in Atlanta, another attempt to rally citizens and soldiers in support of the cause. "Everything—life, liberty, property, and the independence of the South; the security of our homes, wives, mothers and children—all depends upon the heroism of the men whose toils may be terminated by a brilliant victory." Brilliance eluded General Hood at Peachtree Creek. Hoping to drive the Yankees back across the creek and north of the Chattahoochee River, Hood ordered an attack, but the poorly executed fight collapsed when the Yankees refused to be pushed northward. The failure of Hood and his army brought no gain at all and casualties that the Confederacy could ill afford.[24]

Two days later at the battle of Atlanta, the two sides clashed again. General Hood believed he had found a point of weakness in the federal line, and he sent William Hardee's corps on a night march through the center of Atlanta, hoping to attack federals under James McPherson currently positioned in the vicinity of Decatur. Atlanta civilians, seeing thousands of soldiers marching down Peachtree Street in the middle of the night, feared that their city was being abandoned. At 4 A.M., Sam Richards heard gunfire in the direction of Decatur, then saw prisoners marching through town. Richards concluded that General Hardee had succeeded in flanking the federal army. Richards's optimism was premature. Hardee's men headed south on McDonough Road, then turned to the northeast in the direction of Decatur. The ensuing battle took place east of City Cemetery on the afternoon of July 22. Soldiers on both sides suffered and died in the sweltering heat, but Hood's Confederates suffered greater losses: 5,500 casualties compared with federal losses of 3,722, making this engagement the bloodiest fight of the campaign. Hood's army had failed for the second time to break the Union Army's lines. General McPherson's ambush and death while traveling on an unprotected road provided little consolation to Confederates.[25]

Military events produced "complete hubbub," as Sam Richards put it. Julia Davidson wrote to her husband on the twenty-first, "They are fighting all round." Julia wondered how she would feed her children, for "there is not a bit of *provisions* in the city . . . what are we to do who have to remain—starve to death?" The slave barber Robert Webster and his wife Bess were robbed of jewelry by Confederate soldiers claiming to be searching for runaway slaves. The Websters sought shelter in the barn of Unionist Cyrena Stone, but Stone's home near the city's breastworks made it unsafe, and the Websters helped her move to a safer location in the home of her friend Emily Farnsworth. "I went from room to room—not knowing what to do, or where to go; what to save—if any thing could be saved, or what to leave," wrote a distraught Mrs. Stone on July 21. Before departing, she helped a Confederate soldier's wife by forging the furlough papers of her husband so that he did not have to return to the army. After completing the task, Stone carefully packed her books in a closet, locked the door and left. Her final diary entry on July 22 ended in the middle of a sentence.[26]

On the night of July 22 looting broke out on Whitehall Street. Thieves took paper goods and $30 cash from the Richards's bookstore. Sam also noted the departure of "our last newspaper," the *Memphis Appeal*, and the closing of the post office and all of the city's churches. Though Sam did not mention it, the City Council stopped holding meetings on July 18, when it levied fines yet again for policemen who failed to show up for work. At its previous meeting the Council voted to send "City Mules out of reach of the invading enemy" and to authorize the mayor to remove "valuable records and papers" of the city if he deemed it necessary.[27]

Civilians coped with difficult and in some cases tragic circumstances. Sallie Clayton left Atlanta for the safety of a relative's home in Alabama, but her parents stayed in the Gate City to nurse Sallie's sisters Mary, Julia, Kate, and Augusta, who suffered from typhoid fever probably caused by poor sanitation in the city. Isolating the girls in two rooms, two in each bed, the distraught parents moved between the rooms caring for their girls. Three of them recovered, but Augusta, called "Gussie" by the family, died on July 22. An apparently healthy girl just a few weeks previously, Gussie had helped her mother pack clothing and curtains in anticipation of their departure. Adding to the parents' agony, they were unable to get to City Cemetery because of the fighting in its immediate environs. Denied the comfort of a proper funeral, they buried Gussie in their backyard.[28]

On July 23, Richards noted in his diary, "We have had a considerable taste of the beauties of bombardment today. The enemy have thrown a great many shells into the city and scared the women and children and *some* of the *men* pretty badly." Civilians now realized that Sherman intended to bomb them into submission. One shell hit the street near the Richards house, throwing gravel onto the windows. While Sam served a shift as a volunteer policeman, his wife, Sallie, pulled the children's beds onto the floor behind the chimney, hoping to protect the children from Union artillery. The Clayton home took a direct hit from an artillery shell, which burst in a dressing room that connected directly to the room where several of the Clayton daughters convalesced. William Clayton made the decision to move his entire family to the vault of the Merchants' Bank for safety. They remained there "until the firing quieted down," according to Augusta King, William Clayton's sister, who came from Athens to help nurse the ailing girls. Sarah Huff and her family found shelter in the basement of Richard Peters's abandoned flour mill.[29]

A. J. Neal's artillery battery was assigned to a location near the Ponder mansion. Although Ellen Ponder left Atlanta to take refuge in Macon, her home became a target of the Union artillery since it was perched next to the spiked timber "chevaux-de-frise" and trenches of the Confederate lines. On August 4, A.J. wrote a letter to his sister relating the news that he had survived the recent battles, and describing the destruction to Atlanta caused by Union artillery. "In some parts of town every house has been struck a dozen times," A.J. wrote. Union fire soon rendered the commodious Ponder residence a pockmarked shell. The Neal family home also suffered damage, for A.J. slipped away from his post, toured the family residence, and reported to his sister that two shells had entered the house, one passing through the parlor and the other through the bedroom of their brother James. Two weeks later A. J. Neal was dead, killed by a Yankee sharpshooter. He was twenty-six years old. James Neal wrote to his parents to convey the sad news that their "Family Circle" had been broken.[30]

In the coming weeks, Sherman increased his artillery barrage aimed at the Gate City. He wrote to Ulysses S. Grant, telling him he did not plan to attack the city's defenses because they were "too strong." Instead, he would shell the "heart" of the city, four thousand rounds in order to make "a desolating circle around Atlanta." Sherman then ordered Generals George Thomas and Oliver Otis Howard to maintain a relentless cannonading on Atlanta. Union artillerists relished the task. In a letter to his sister, one soldier bragged, "Our guns can shell the city at their leisure, having fine range." Another wrote to his parents proudly, "Our men are throwing hot shot in the City" at a rate of one shell every five minutes. Fannie Beers, a Confederate nurse who arrived at the passenger depot in the midst of heavy shelling, experienced the new federal policy firsthand. From the train, Beers heard a series of explosions and saw one shell cause serious damage to a brick store near the depot. "I was paralyzed with extreme terror," she recalled, before regaining her composure and quickly exiting the train.[31]

It is difficult to know how many civilians remained in the city by the last week of July, but clearly some stayed because they had nowhere else to go. Others worked for the city, or they hoped to protect their personal or commercial property. Some stayed because they did not believe or chose to ignore warnings about the likely danger. To protect themselves, civilians built a variety of bombproofs, some of them dugouts or "gopher holes" in their gardens, in other cases holes dug in cellars and covered with metal, wood, or in at least one case, bales of cotton.[32]

Years later, Atlantans recalled the fearful times they endured under Yankee fire. David Mayer owned a store on Whitehall Street. Mayer was a leader in Atlanta's small Jewish community, and he opened the family cellar to another Jewish family who were refugees in Atlanta. Both families shared these cramped quarters for three weeks. The Mayers' bombproof, as the cellar was termed, was covered with several bales of cotton, which muffled the noise but posed a potential fire risk. Cornelia Venable, her mother, and her children slept in a dugout in their garden. The tiny shelter had enough room for the children to lie down, but the adults had to sit up. After four weeks, Venable's husband, who remained in the city because he served as clerk of the court and took charge of protecting Atlanta's city records, moved the family to a house on Washington Street, where he believed they would be safer, away from businesses and factories at the city center. Mrs. Venable finally had a chance to sleep on a mattress on the floor, "and I believe I slept the sweetest sleep I ever enjoyed in my life." Lucy Kicklighter and her family had more comfortable accommodations. They took shelter in the bombproof of her neighbor Mrs. Ware. Five or six feet deep, this shelter contained amenities including a carpet and chairs.[33]

Julia Davidson moved with her mother and young children to a home on Marietta Street owned by a local doctor. During periods of heavy bombardment, the Davidsons took refuge in the basement of a neighboring house, sometimes fleeing for shelter in great haste when the bombing began. "God grant it may cease," she wrote to her husband on July 26, also noting the death of a Confederate soldier struck dead in Ellen Ponder's yard. For Julia, the cost of war had become too high. She urged her husband to desert, come home, and care for his family. "I beg of you please do not return to your command." John did not comply.[34]

Living underground was alternately frightening and boring. Otto Braumuller was eleven years old when the shelling of their city forced him and his mother into a backyard dugout. For several nights Otto sat next to the door of their dugout and observed the shelling. "They made a beautiful fireworks display," he recalled, until the shelling came a little too close to home for comfort and he retreated inside. Lucy Ivy and family lived in a cellar under the store of A. C. Wyly at the corner of Pryor and Peachtree Streets. Each day before dawn, Lucy emerged from her hiding place and cooked enough food to last the day, then retreated to the cellar until she repeated the process. At one point, an elderly woman stopped by and "begged us to take her in." She identified herself as a fortune teller and offered to tell their fortunes if the family shared its cellar. Her presence allowed the family a temporary reprieve from the tedium of living underground.[35]

Carrie Berry was nine years old when the Yankees began shelling her city. Precocious and inquisitive, she decided to keep a diary of her experiences. Carrie spent her tenth birthday in a cellar. "This was my birthday," she noted on August 3. "But I did not have a cake [because] times were too hard." Like most civilians who lived in shelters, Carrie was sometimes bored and sometimes scared. "How I wish the federals would quit shelling us so that we could get out and get some fresh air," she wrote in exasperation on August 11. It seemed to comfort Carrie to know that her sacrifice was somewhat like that of the Confederate soldiers who had to stay in ditches. Other times, Carrie was terrified. One morning while playing outside, she heard "a very large shell filled with balls" fall next to the garden gate and burst. "The pieces flew in every direction. . . . I never was so frightened in my life." Carrie headed for the cellar.[36]

The following week, Carrie's parents moved the family to a larger cellar where the children were encouraged to run and make noise, so Mama "can't he[ar] the shells." The children's play calmed Mrs. Berry's nerves, but nothing could allay another of Mrs. Berry's fears, that fire might burn the house down. Fires started by hot, dry weather and Yankee shells were a daily occurrence. For Atlantans living in cellars, there was no end in sight. "The shells get worse and worse every day," Carrie wrote.[37]

In early August, the *Daily Intelligencer* began publishing again in Macon and provided expatriate Atlantans with news about the shelling of their city. Eyewitness accounts came from Isaac Pilgrim, the *Intelligencer*'s foreman. On August 6, Pilgrim reported damage to buildings caused by Yankee artillery. Not surprisingly, Union gunners aimed at the railroads. Pilgrim reported that twenty shots hit the Western and Atlantic roundhouse, damaging it significantly. The Winship Iron Works suffered serious damage, along with houses in its vicinity. The Trout House Hotel received one shot, "tearing it up considerably," but a shell that struck Charles Bohnefeld's Coffin Shop caused little damage. Wesley Chapel was struck by five shells, which left the church "horribly mutilated" and its parsonage "considerably damaged." Attempting to put a positive spin on deteriorating circumstances, the *Daily Intelligencer* wanted readers to know that some of Atlanta's leading citizens remained in the city, including William Markham, David Mayer, and James E. Williams.[38]

Inevitably, civilians died in the shelling. One was Solomon Luckie, a free black man who ran a barbershop in the Atlanta Hotel. Luckie had the misfortune to be aboveground at just the wrong moment. An artillery shell hit his leg, and although a physician amputated the wounded limb, Luckie died of shock a short time later. A woman identified as Mrs. Smith died when a shell struck her as she ironed some clothing. J. F. Warner and his young daughter died when struck by an artillery shell while they slept at their home near the Atlanta gasworks. The *Daily Intelligencer* marveled that so few civilians were killed. Sam Richards estimated that twenty people died in the shelling. Dozens more were injured. Richards had some close calls himself. A shell hit his store. Another passed through the backyard of his home on Washington Street near City Hall. Yet another of "these terrible missiles" passed through the roof of his church and lodged near the front wall, having traveled close to the place where Sallie Richards sat during choir practices. Richards began moving his remaining stock of books from the Whitehall Street store to the Richards home on Washington Street, since Whitehall Street with its warehouses and government offices was a target of the Union artillery. He also dug his bombproof three feet deeper and created a barricade of dirt-filled boxes. In addition to serving as a volunteer policeman, Richards did militia detail. On August 28, he spent the morning unloading army wagons from rail cars and assembling them. Richards found some measure of solace in attending church services at the Episcopal and Methodist churches, both of which reopened for brief periods.[39]

In mid-August, Sherman's army increased its shelling of the city. On the night of August 18th, the *Daily Intelligencer* reported "constant shelling of the city" and "heavy skirmishing and cannonading" during the day. A shell struck and killed Francis Hale, an employee of the Western and Atlantic Railroad. Soldiers told other tragic stories to family members in their letters home. Joe Semmes wrote to his wife that Yankee guns caused fires that burned houses. A surgeon told Semmes that he had personally performed many amputations on civilians, including children, since the shelling began. On August 23, the *Intelligencer* reported the worst shelling yet seen. An explosion at a house on Peters Street killed a cavalry officer and two children, wounding others. Because stores stopped selling provisions in late July, destitute civilians now sought help from the army. One brave civilian volunteer who stayed in Atlanta to help the poor estimated that one thousand families remained in the city, four thousand individuals in all, and General Hood's army handed out fifteen hundred rations per day. Without revealing its sources, the ever-optimistic *Intelligencer* alternately reported stories of shelling with stories about a possible armistice between Confederate and U.S. governments, even rumors that Sherman might be retreating.[40]

On August 24, Isaac Pilgrim wrote that the Yankees "rained shell into the city" for twenty-four straight hours. The shells fell throughout the city. Most of the businesses along Whitehall Street were damaged extensively, if not destroyed. Warehouses on nearby Alabama Street containing cotton, tobacco, and lard caught fire, creating enormous conflagrations that spread to surrounding buildings. In earlier periods of bombardment, the city's firemen, assisted by slaves and soldiers, had managed to contain the fires, but this time, cisterns in the city were dry and many firemen had left the city. In reporting the shelling, the *Daily Intelligencer*'s reporter called it "a day of more excitement than has ever been witnessed in Atlanta."[41]

The following day, the federal army suddenly stopped shelling Atlanta. Civilians slowly emerged from their hiding places and hoped that the tide had turned in their favor. Carrie Berry wondered whether Sherman's army might be headed back to Tennessee. Sam Richards took a walk on Marietta Street to survey the damage caused by several weeks of bombing. "The city is badly cut up," he wrote on August 29. Others took advantage of the opportunity to leave Atlanta. Many years later, Augusta King recalled riding on the last train out of the city. She traveled on the only spot she could find, seated atop five hundred muskets being removed so that they would not fall into Yankee hands. Even though she needed to travel east, she could find only transportation south to Macon. She saw "dreadful sights" along the way, including dead and dying soldiers left near the tracks, a band playing the melancholy song "Lorena," and a whippoorwill chanting its mournful tune.[42]

After several days without shelling, Confederate soldiers, who were just as puzzled as civilians about what was going on, concluded that Sherman and his men had been repulsed. A. T. Halliday served in the Confederate Army defending the city. On August 26, he visited Atlanta and wrote about it in a letter to his wife. "I feel more confident and hopeful this morning about the salvation of Atlanta than I have since I have been here. Everything is as still as death in our front." Halliday claimed that deserting Yankee cavalrymen told their captors, "Sherman is compelled to fall back for the want of supplies." Halliday found it sobering to see the damage done to Atlanta by Sherman's big guns. "There is scarcely a house but what is riddled."[43]

Some Atlanta evacuees returned to the city. "The Yanks stopped shooting at the city last Friday & a good many of the citizens here are returning," wrote Martha Winship's son-in-law Josiah Flournoy on August 28, but "Sherman wants to cut us off at Jonesborrow & take the city with his forces from above at the same time." Flournoy was correct. Sherman's men moved to the south of Atlanta and pummeled Confederates when William Hardee's men attacked them near Jonesboro on August 31. Federals then cut the last remaining rail line into Atlanta. A federal soldier wrote triumphantly to his wife a few days later, "Hood has been outgeneraled this time."[44]

On the night of September 1, General Hood ordered the evacuation of Atlanta. Government stores of cornmeal were opened to the public and quickly claimed, as hungry Atlantans descended on the stores to take what they could. Hoping to keep valuable commodities away from the Yankees, departing Confederates blew up an eighty-one-car ordnance train, along with five locomotives. The blasts continued for more than thirty minutes, the reverberations causing glass to break in Atlanta homes and frightening civilians in a twenty-mile radius. Unaware of the cause of the blasts, some Atlantans feared that Yankees finally descended upon their city. When they realized that Confederates lit the fires, they stared in wonder at what one young woman described as "a most beautiful spectacle. . . . The Heavens were in a perfect glow."[45]

At midnight, Sam Richards's friend Thomas West came to the back gate of the Richards home on Washington Street and told him that the militia had been called out, headed south toward McDonough. Richards and West had a decision to make; would they fight for the Confederacy? Neither man agonized very long. Richards went to the depot and took three sacks of cornmeal. He would stay home.[46]

During the late morning of September 2, Mayor James Calhoun with a small group of citizens, including Unionists William Markham and Robert Webster, rode out Marietta Street past Ellen Ponder's pockmarked mansion and the city's breastworks. They met with a Union officer Calhoun later identified as Colonel Coburne, actually Colonel John Coburn. "The fortune of war has placed Atlanta in your hands," Calhoun began, according to a formal statement he later wrote for the Yankees. He asked for military protection for civilians and their property. The Union officer replied that the U.S. Army did not intend to "make war upon non-combatants or on private property"; however, Coburn did not put this promise in writing, an oversight Calhoun was to regret. With the formal surrender of the city, Union soldiers entered Atlanta and raised their regimental flags above City Hall. A few hours later, General Henry Slocum arrived at the Trout House Hotel and telegraphed the news to Washington: "General Sherman has taken Atlanta."[47]

Blue-coated soldiers soon filled the city, and looting began. Soldiers and civilians, including slaves, broke into stores on Whitehall Street. Soldiers wanted tobacco more than anything. One soldier wrote home, "We have confiscated lots of Tobacco, I got 750 Cigars & 50 to 75 Large Plugs [of] Tobacco." Civilian looters were a cross-section of Atlanta's dispossessed humanity. Hundreds of ragged, barefoot women robbed stores, taking what they pleased, and giving vent to years of deprivation and suffering. Slaves celebrated something even more fundamental than food. They celebrated freedom. On this and on subsequent days, African Americans filled the streets, waving and shouting in celebration, offering thanks to God that the long-rumored, long-awaited arrival of the Yankees finally had occurred.[48]

African Americans also took advantage of the federal army's arrival to flee from slavery, or, as the *Atlanta Daily Intelligencer* put it, "remain with the Yankees." Sam Richards wrote in his diary, "Our negro property has all vanished into air," and also noted that federal soldiers were telling slaves that they were free. Richards saw his brother's slave Sally on the street acting "as independent as can be." Two male slaves owned by the brothers were rumored to be in the city, and Sam's teenaged slave Ellen disappeared from his diary and presumably from his life. Mary, a slave owned by Carrie Berry's family, departed five days after the federal army arrived. "Mary went off this evening," Carrie wrote matter-of-factly, "and I don't expect that she will come back any more." Sidney Root's slaves sought protection from the Union Army. Before leaving, a slave named Patience stole enough flour, coffee, and sugar to sustain her for many weeks, a fact that Root recorded with some bitterness, because Patience had been Mrs. Root's slave since her mistress was three years old, and Sidney Root regarded her as a "petted" family servant. A few slaves chose to remain with their former owners, including Henry, owned by Sidney and Mary Root, who remained with them for decades after the war as a paid employee. Silvery, slave to Ann Cozart Harralson, stayed with the family during the postwar period as well.[49]

In the ensuing days, Union soldiers shared impressions of Atlanta with family members. Many commented on the damage to buildings. Rufus Mead of the 5th Connecticut was struck by the number of bombproofs throughout the city, but suggested that one hundred civilians had died nonetheless from the shelling. Others focused on the positive. "Atlanta is a very pretty place surrounded with woods," a soldier in the 123rd New York wrote to his mother. In a letter to his wife, Orlando Poe described Atlanta as an attractive town, though the buildings were "a good deal injured by our shot." Poe regretted the shelling, which "did no good at all." As an engineer, he believed that some of the warehouses and other buildings destroyed in the shelling could be useful to the Union Army now. Poe sent his wife a flower he picked in Atlanta. General John Geary described Atlanta's trees and shrubbery but was also struck by the City Cemetery, which was "almost a wonder. . . . It contains nearly 10,000 newly made graves filled principally by rebel losses in the late battles."[50]

Soldiers were impressed by Lemuel Grant's fortifications. Diarist Henry Stanley called them "the most formidable I have ever seen." Public buildings also impressed the soldiers. George Lawson of the 45th Illinois saw Atlanta's passenger depot on a tour of the city and called it "a magnificent structure." George M. Patton of the 98th Ohio was impressed with Fairground Hospitals, a "splendid place" that could accommodate a multitude of wounded and sick men. John Lockman of the 119th New York thought the Trout House was "quite a hotel," but also "very aptly called after its owner whose fishy name & scaley prices are known" in the region.[51]

Once they got over their initial shock at the Union takeover of their city, some Atlantans began to think the Yankees might not be so bad. Looting stopped, and on Sunday, September 4, Union soldiers filled Atlanta's churches. Afterward, many soldiers stopped at private homes, asking for a cooked meal and offering to pay for it. Sallie Richards obliged, as did others. "The Yankees have not molested us much at the house, they have generally behaved pretty well," Sam Richards admitted. Carrie Berry wrote, "I think I shall like the Yankees very well." The Yankees even reopened the Athenaeum for a fund-raiser to help a widow who needed money for her passage north. The "Celebrated Brass Band of the 33rd Massachusetts Volunteers" played, and General Sherman attended.[52]

Confederate Atlantans soon changed their opinion of General Sherman, for he ordered their expulsion from the city. Civilians could go north or south, and for those who were southbound, he promised a ten-day truce. In his memoirs, Sherman wrote that he wanted the measure to serve as a warning to the entire Confederacy that "we were in earnest" to subdue the South and to end the war. Sherman's decision generated immediate controversy even among some Union officers. Colonel William Le Duc, a prewar friend of Sherman and a Union quartermaster who now occupied the abandoned home of Richard Peters, told a colleague to warn Sherman that "this order won't read well in history." Mayor Calhoun protested the order, writing to Sherman that poor women and children should be allowed to stay in the Gate City because of the "extraordinary hardship" that the expulsion order created. No one debated the issue of hardship. Many Union generals could testify to the suffering of Georgians during the campaign. General John W. Geary wrote to his wife about seeing an emaciated woman with her "starving child, so poor as scarcely to live." As an act of humanitarianism, the army began providing rations for hungry Atlantans estimated at two thousand to three thousand per day.[53]

General Sherman chose Atlanta's grandest home for his headquarters, the former residence of John and Mary Jane Neal located on Washington

Street near City Hall. The house with its massive Corinthian columns was leased to the Female Institute at the time that Sherman moved in, the Neal family having moved to their plantation in Pike County. Sherman spent much of his time in the coming weeks sitting on the porch reading newspapers, answering correspondence, and receiving visitors. Unionist Joshua Hill from Madison, Georgia, was among the guests. Hill later carried a personal invitation to Governor Joe E. Brown from Sherman. The federal commander invited Governor Brown to pay him a visit, hoping to parlay Brown's well-known states' rights proclivities into negotiations for the state to separate itself from the Confederacy and withdraw from the war. Brown declined Sherman's invitation.[54]

From its headquarters in Macon, the *Atlanta Daily Intelligencer* struggled to keep up with military events as they developed. On September 6, the newspaper gave credit to General Sherman for winning the Atlanta campaign by "genius, wise military strategy, and with overwhelming numbers." The *Intelligencer* assigned partial blame to President Davis, suggesting that he might have come up with a better military plan to prevent the downfall. The newspaper made no effort to downplay the immense destruction of Atlanta, especially the loss of 150 rail cars along with several engines. The "promiscuous pillaging" of Sherman's men made the situation far worse. Regarding Sherman's expulsion order, the *Intelligencer* believed that it should bring condemnation from "enlightened generous hearted [citizens] throughout the world." The *Intelligencer* also noted the death of General John Hunt Morgan, killed in Greenville, Tennessee, on September 4, after a Unionist twelve-year-old boy told the federal army of Morgan's whereabouts. Morgan had been a symbol to Confederate Atlantans, a man whose personal courage and success against seemingly steep odds buoyed their spirits when the military situation seemed otherwise grim. Morgan's name "will remain forever identified with the history of our revolution."[55]

Atlantans bitterly resented their expulsion but had little choice other than to make plans about where to go. Mary Root and her daughter Florence went south to Griffin and then to Macon. Root's home was searched by federal soldiers, who knew that her husband had made money running the blockade. Mrs. Root managed to move some family possessions to the home of her parents nearby, then hid $200 in gold as well as diamonds inside the head of her daughter's favorite doll Gerty. The Yankees never found Gerty's hidden contents. They did locate three bottles of Madeira wine that Sidney

Root had carefully hidden. Root and Jefferson Davis planned to drink a toast to Confederate independence when the war ended. Now, Root was in Nassau and Davis was struggling to keep the Confederacy alive.[56]

Mary Root's sister Elizabeth and her husband, Edward E. Rawson, an Atlanta city councilman, decided to go north to Iowa, where they had family. The Rawsons' daughter Mary wrote an account of her family's departure from Atlanta. Parting with "home servants" was difficult. A house slave named Charlotte evidently had not yet separated from her former owners, for she cooked the white family one last meal before bidding them goodbye. In a gesture that was both formal and familiar, she shook Mary's hand. En route to Iowa, the Rawsons stopped in Chattanooga, where a member of their party politely asked an African American man they encountered to bring some water. He said he would, took their bucket, and never came back. White people were beginning to get a sense of a new racial order descending on the South.[57]

Yankee authorities allowed some Atlantans to transport large items or quantities of goods northward. Sam Richards and his family went to New York City, where both Sam and Sallie had family. He financed their trip by selling furniture to Yankee officers and holding a small amount of gold. The Yankees allowed him to carry off much of the remaining contents of his bookstore, which he sold at auction in Louisville on his way north. Otto Braumuller and his mother secured a rail car to transport two pianos and sold them in Nashville. While there, they met up with Otto's father, who had left Atlanta before the siege. As they continued north toward Louisville, thieves held up their train and robbed the family of their cash, but fortunately Mrs. Braumuller had hidden $800 in gold in her clothing, and it was not found.[58]

Many southbound civilians traveled to the town of Rough and Ready in convoys of wagons during the ten-day truce. When the wagons reached Rough and Ready, the travelers and their provisions changed to Confederate wagons and continued to Lovejoy's Station and other points to the south. More than sixteen hundred Atlantans traveled south in this manner, among them Mrs. Calendar Bell and her teenage sons, who had once worked in a factory that made hardtack for the army. When their convoy reached Macon, James and William Bell immediately found employment at the Confederate bakery there. Sam Richards's brother Henry and his wife and child joined the exodus, as did Joseph Winship's wife, Emily. Some Atlantans carried considerable baggage. Jeremiah Trout, who had built the magnificent hotel now occupied by Yankees, left with a party of two adults and five children, plus sixty packages. Laura Grant, accompanied by two children, left with one servant and fifty packages. Her husband, whose fortifications were often admired by enemy troops but in the end did not protect the city from General Sherman, had already evacuated to Augusta, where he hoped to protect the city and its manufacturing operations.[59]

Although some Atlantans left with possessions, numerous "exiles of Atlanta" had nothing; they lived in abject poverty, many of them homeless, some of them hungry. Fund-raisers held by women in Macon and Milledgeville raised money to feed them, but their efforts did not adequately address the need. Because Macon housed the greatest number of Atlantans and was too crowded and economically burdened to handle the numbers, the *Daily Intelligencer* suggested that exiles be repatriated to southwest Georgia, or possibly to Florida and Alabama. A story on September 28 suggested that the state might assist in the building of a "Home" near Gordon, Georgia, on the Central Railroad.[60]

Today, scholars continue to debate the ethics of Sherman's expulsion order. Those who focus on the extreme poverty of southbound Atlantans tend to be critical. One historian called the expulsion "an act virtually without precedent in the war." More recently, scholars have pointed to Sherman's relative leniency in allowing Atlantans to transport considerable amounts of baggage. Union soldiers carried out Sherman's order "with as much regard for the civilians as circumstances allowed. . . . The expulsion was hardly devoid of humanity," according to one author, who also noted that some Atlantans managed to elude the army's orders to leave.[61]

Macon continued to serve as home for many expatriates, and Jefferson Davis made an appearance there during late September. The beleaguered president addressed an audience at the Baptist Church and defended his decision to appoint General Hood to command, stating that he knew that Hood would "strike an honest and manly blow for the city, and many a Yankee's blood was made to nourish the soil before the prize was won." Davis then suggested that the Confederacy could defeat the Union if furloughed soldiers returned to their regiments and mothers let their teenage sons enter the army. Davis insisted that Sherman would soon be forced to retreat, just as Napoleon had from Moscow in 1812, for Yankees could not protect their supply lines forever. While the president's speech received a polite reception, Atlantans had heard these arguments many times before, from politicians, from military officers, and from newspaper editors. Most refugee Atlantans had more pressing concerns than war strategy, including where their next meal was coming from and whether they were safe in Macon. Would Macon's Confederate Arsenal be Sherman's next target?[62]

Predictably, the fall of Atlanta generated finger-pointing on the part of civilians whose loyalties clashed before, during, and now after the Gate City's fall. Alexander Wallace, who raised one of Atlanta's first regiments, wrote a letter to the *Atlanta Daily Intelligencer* in which he condemned Unionists as "traitors and spies who infested Atlanta, of whom William Markham was the chief." According to Wallace, Markham had convinced Sherman to issue an "order of outlawry" against him. Moreover, Wallace's son George was captured as part of John Hunt Morgan's command near Greenville, Tennessee. While others in the group were exchanged, George Wallace was currently held in Atlanta, "barefooted[,] nearly naked and in every way destitute" according to his father, who believed that Markham was to blame. In the coming weeks, Markham and others identified by the *Intelligencer* as "mongrel curs" left Atlanta for the North and safety. Markham sent part of his family north accompanied by a federal officer who had obtained a thirty-day furlough.[63]

The emptying of Atlanta created a "profound stillness" in a city once characterized by the hustle and bustle of mercantile activity and more recently by the ear-splitting sounds of gunfire. The summer heat continued into September, and a thick layer of dust cast a ghostly pall over the bomb-damaged buildings and warehouses of Whitehall and Alabama Streets. However, the area around City Hall teemed with activity as Union soldiers constructed temporary housing near the former seat of Atlanta's government. Soldiers used the basement of Robert Mallard's Central Presbyterian Church to slaughter beef for their meals and turned the Sunday school rooms into stables for their horses. Mary Mallard wrote to her mother, "It grieves me to think of our beautiful church being desecrated" by the "horrible" Yankees.[64]

In early October, reports reached Atlanta's refugee community in Macon that Hood's army was in the vicinity of Marietta, heading north. Hood would take his army into Tennessee, hoping to lure Sherman away from Georgia. Although the *Southern Confederacy* suggested that Hood's presence in Tennessee created "alarm" in the North, in fact, Hood and his army, a mere skeleton of its former size, were to be defeated twice before year's end and virtually annihilated by troops that Sherman detached from his command in Atlanta.[65]

On November 15, the guessing game about Sherman's military intentions in Atlanta ended when the *Daily Intelligencer* informed its readers that Sherman's army had begun the systematic destruction of the Gate City. As reported by the *Intelligencer*, Yankees destroyed everything that the army could not carry as it headed south from the city, the ultimate destination unknown to Confederates at the time. "We cannot imagine how the place can be more effectually destroyed than it has been," one reporter noted forlornly. Even before Sherman's intentional burning, arsonists had started fires around town. One soldier noted in his diary, "A portion of Atlanta was set on fire by some malicious rascals" in the night. Arsonists lit fires on the north side of town resulting in considerable damage. To discourage further such actions, General Henry Slocum offered a reward of $500 for anyone turning in a perpetrator.[66]

Orlando Poe, Sherman's engineer, ordered his men to tear down the passenger depot, which was *"rammed down . . . no fire or powder applied,"* according to the account of Major Henry Hitchcock, an assistant adjutant general. Sherman gave orders to destroy all the railroad depots, warehouses, machine shops. Hitchcock stood and looked in wonder as Whitehall Street's already bomb-damaged businesses and warehouses went up in smoke. He described a process whereby bursts of smoke were followed by dense black puffs, then by "tongues of flames." Hitchcock estimated that the fires were visible from fifty miles away. Decatur Street also burned, including the Athenaeum and the Trout House Hotel, twin symbols of Atlanta's prewar prosperity and modernity, both of them symbols of Atlanta's wartime civic pride. "The city has done & contributed probably more to carry on & sustain the war than any other save perhaps Richmond," Major Hitchcock continued. "We have been fighting *Atlanta* all the time, in the West: have been capturing guns, weapons &c &c marked '*Atlanta*' & made here, all the time: and now since they have been doing so much to destroy us & our Govt we have to destroy them."[67]

9. Rebuilding, Reconstruction, and the New City

On July 6, 1865, the *Atlanta Daily Intelligencer* carried a brief report about Independence Day festivities in Atlanta that included federal soldiers marching through the Gate City's streets before being reviewed by General E. F. Winslow. The newspaper provided few details about the event and no discussion about who attended. However, the *Intelligencer* also carried an account from General Winslow about the repair and reopening of the Western and Atlantic Railroad, which had been damaged in the war. The railroad that helped to launch Atlanta as a city in the 1830s, then provided a gateway for Sherman's army to capture it, now, once more, linked Atlanta to "direct communication with the Northern States."[1] By the summer of 1865, the war had ended in Confederate surrender and Atlantans had started returning to the city. Ironically, the four-year war fought by Confederates to preserve plantation slavery had revealed the South's cities as major drivers of the region's economy. In the postwar period, railroad transportation hubs like Atlanta were to eclipse port cities as economic engines of a New South. Newspaper editors encouraged the South's postwar rebuilding and often focused attention on young businessmen who emerged after the war. In Atlanta, however, many successful entrepreneurs were the same men who made their mark during the 1850s and profited handsomely in the first half of the Civil War. While it might appear that they gambled and lost when they cast their lot with the secessionists, most of them landed on their feet after the war, and so did their city.[2] Atlanta's phoenixlike rebuilding impressed many visitors, including northern journalists and even European travelers, but the triumphal narrative of postwar Atlanta fails to reveal another aspect. While some Atlantans prospered, others struggled, including freed slaves, single women, and children of both races. For these disadvantaged residents, postwar Atlanta was not the promised land.

Atlanta had a long and difficult road ahead. Significant portions of the city had been destroyed either by bombardment or by fire. One visitor noted, "The burnt district of Richmond was hardly more thoroughly destroyed than the central part of Atlanta." In addition to all of the buildings associated with the city's four railroads, the commercial buildings on Whitehall and Alabama Streets were reduced to rubble. "I regret to be the harbinger of bad news," a business associate wrote to William McNaught, then reported bluntly, "your stores are destroyed."[3]

A sizable portion of the city had burned. Fire destroyed all of the hotels except the Planters' Hotel, where angry secessionists had burned Lincoln's effigy in 1860. Several churches went up in flames, among them the recently constructed St. Luke's Episcopal. Many homes burned, including Lucius Gartrell's home east of the city center. To the north, fire destroyed the home of Martha and Isaac Winship. Even those whose houses survived Sherman's fires suffered damage from Union artillery or vandalism. Ellen Ponder's stucco mansion was so extensively damaged that it could not be inhabited again. Richard and Mary Jane Peters lost much of their furniture to a thief who sold it to the Yankees. Some houses were torn down so that housing could be constructed for Union soldiers. Even the cemetery suffered damage. According to a report sent to Governor Brown by General W. P. Howard of the militia, the federal army grazed horses at City Cemetery; soldiers broke funerary objects and stole silver nameplates from graves.[4]

By December of 1864, many Atlanta exiles had either heard or read reports about the damage of their city, expressing shock and sadness at the news. In addition to the destruction of buildings, the city was littered with tons of trash and other debris, including the bones of dead horses, cannonballs, and shell casings. A friend's account of Atlanta led Cornelius Hanleiter to write, "His account of affairs in Georgia, and especially about Atlanta— My old home—is truly heart-rending."[5]

Some Atlantans never returned to the Gate City. Martha Winship and her husband lost everything, including the home and garden Martha prized so highly and the iron foundry Isaac ran with his brother Joseph. The Winships made their postwar home in Macon, and Martha devoted her time to placing headstones on the graves of Confederate soldiers. She died in 1882 at age sixty-eight. Annie Sehon, who arrived in Atlanta during 1862 after fleeing federally occupied Nashville and who fled her Atlanta home two years later ahead of the advancing army, died in August of that year. During the war, Annie nursed her husband and young son through several bouts of illness. Like so many Atlantans in the hot summer of 1864, she contracted typhoid fever, and she died at the age of twenty-two shortly after the family reached what it thought would be a safe haven in Augusta. Cyrena Stone survived the war, though her house, burned by Yankees, did not. Her husband became a Republican politician in Savannah, but Cyrena evidently found postwar life in Georgia not to her liking, for she returned to her native Vermont and died in 1868 from an unknown illness at age thirty-eight.[6]

The diaspora caused by Sherman's advancing army during the spring and summer of 1864 led civilians to fan out across the United States, and those who settled in the North complained of feeling unwelcome, out of place, and impoverished. Jennie Lines, her husband, Sylvanus, and their sixteen-month-old daughter, Daisy, settled in New Haven, Connecticut, where Sylvanus's widowed sister ran a boardinghouse. In December 1865, Jennie wrote in her diary for the first time in two years. She was grateful to have a daughter to replace the one who had died in Atlanta. She was happy to live in comfort away from the upheaval of wartime Atlanta. She complained about newspaper reports describing the "idleness" of freedpeople in the South. Nonetheless, she missed home. "We have been very homesick," she wrote, adding, "I think we shall eventually return South." Lines also resented her family's impoverishment caused by war. Seeing the throngs of Christmas shoppers in New Haven only accentuated her own dependent, impecunious state. Jennie and Sylvanus could afford only a few modest gifts. "We felt the inconvenience of a shallow purse," Jennie admitted.[7]

Sam Richards and his family lived in New York City, where they changed apartments several times seeking cheaper rent. Richards earned a little money when he worked at D. Appleton Company selling books during the Christmas season, but the job did not last, forcing Sam and his wife, Sallie, to economize whenever they could. The Richardses sampled a variety of churches in an effort to seek religious inspiration in troubled times. In February 1865, Sam expressed a longing for his old congregation at Second Baptist in Atlanta, noting "Alas! for the pleasant services and our plain church at Atlanta and the pleasant social choir reunions. . . . We cant feel at home in this land."[8]

David Mayer and his family also lived in New York, but none of them enjoyed the city. Like other Atlantans in the North, they felt like strangers in a foreign land. Mayer's son Solomon complained about bullies at school who sometimes chased him home because he was a "little Rebel boy." The Mayers eventually returned to Atlanta, encouraged to do so by friends including Lucius Gartrell and Joseph E. Brown.[9]

Ten-year-old Carrie Berry and her family had managed to avoid being expelled, and she witnessed the Yankee fires that destroyed parts of the city. On November 16, 1864, she wrote that the family stayed up through the night in an effort to protect themselves and their property. Their property was spared, but it nonetheless "looked like the whole town was on fire," she wrote. Carrie thought the Union soldiers "behaved very badly. . . . We were glad when they left for no body knows what we have suffered since they came in." Carrie was thrilled when her cousin Marcellus Markham returned to Atlanta in June 1865. Marcellus, who had left Atlanta with a carpetbag stuffed with cash, managed to avoid Confederate conscription and to return home safely from self-imposed exile in New York. "Oh how glad we were to see him," Carrie wrote.[10]

When news of Confederate surrender reached exiled Atlantans, they expressed a range of emotions. James Ormond left Atlanta for New York, while his family visited relatives in Canada. Ormond conveyed a sense of relief when writing to his wife; he wanted to "begin life anew" with his united family after the cessation of hostilities. Sam Richards, also in New York, consistently expressed the belief that "a righteous God" would never allow northern victory over the Confederate states, but when he picked up a newspaper and learned of Robert E. Lee's surrender, he expressed resignation to God's apparent will. "So now there seems to be nothing more for the South to do but make the best terms they can and give up," he wrote in his diary.[11]

Five days later, Richards learned the startling news that President Abraham Lincoln had died by the hand of an assassin. Richards articulated the view of many when he wrote, "I have no great love for Abraham Lincoln . . . but I abhor such crimes as assassination." In Atlanta, civilians expressed similar sentiments. Louisa Crew wrote in her diary, "President Lincoln assassinated by Booth. I regret his death exceedingly." Even the *Atlanta Daily Intelligencer,* returned from exile in Macon and now publishing again in the Gate City, called Lincoln's murder a "fearful tragedy."[12]

Atlanta's rebuilding process began as soon as the Yankee fires died out in November 1864, but the city and its mayor faced a daunting prospect. Not only was Atlanta a city in ruins, but it was also a city with an empty treasury. Although the City Council authorized Mayor James Calhoun to borrow money, Confederate money had little to no value, and U.S. greenbacks could not be found in late 1864. By June 1865, the situation improved when the City Council issued $20,000 in bonds in denominations ranging from twenty-five cents to $10. These bonds helped fund the city and acted as a kind of substitute currency.[13]

By the spring of 1865, a few enterprising businessmen operated commercial endeavors in Atlanta. The former slave Bob Webster barbered and shaved Atlanta's white men from a shop he had run before and during the war. A saloon reopened on Decatur Street to serve the city's thirsty clientele. More important, wagons filled with produce began entering the city again, selling their wares to eager patrons. Octavia Hammond wrote to her friend Mary Adair, "Country wagons keep us supplied even cheaper than Augusta" with ample quantities of bacon, flour, eggs, potatoes, and cornmeal. "There seems to be a plenty of everything." Like many families, the Hammonds had departed the city in great haste the previous year, leaving behind possessions that disappeared in their absence. Hammond regretted the loss of the family's piano and practical items like their wash pots, but was thrilled to find three green chairs, a battered old bedstead, "half of a bureau and a half of an extension dining table."[14]

Race relations in the city prompted a great deal of speculation. When they arrived in Atlanta during September 1864, federal soldiers told slaves they no longer had to stay with their masters, but the Thirteenth Amendment had yet to be ratified, thereby leaving Atlantans both black and white with uncertainty about slavery as a legal matter. Most Atlantans knew Bob Webster, whose current position of independence surprised no one. But what of other African Americans? Octavia Hammond spotted Mrs. Adair's former slave Nancy on the street. "I have seen her passing the house several times wagging under a bag of meal in the rain, and cold, almost naked," she wrote to Adair. On one occasion, Hammond approached the former bondswoman asking if she belonged to Mrs. Adair. Nancy said no and walked on. Mrs. Adair's other domestic, a woman named Hannah, had not been seen. Hammond wrote, "I expect Hannah has 'gone up the spout' long ago."[15]

Louisa Crew, wife to Atlanta railroad employee James R. Crew, purchased a slave for $50 in gold while traveling in Lawrenceville, Georgia, in May 1865, several weeks after Confederate surrender. "I think the institution [of slavery] about gone," Crew confided to her diary, but the slave "has not a relative in the world[,] seems affectionate [and] well disposed." Mrs. Crew could not resist a bargain. She took the young woman to Madison, Georgia, where Crew had family, away from the meddling of the federal army.[16]

Readers of the *Atlanta Daily Intelligencer* saw a variety of articles addressing racial issues. One article titled "Painful and Strange" described the death of an "old freed-woman" found lying dead on the side of the road. Her kinfolk said proudly "*She perish to def, sur, but she free.*" While her relatives celebrated the life of a slave who lived long enough to enjoy several months of freedom, the *Intelligencer* used the case as an opportunity to emphasize the need for freedpeople to work; otherwise, they would "perish" like the old woman on the wayside. The same issue of the newspaper carried a story that Atlanta's white population no doubt regarded with alarm. In "Negro Suffrage," the *Intelligencer* discussed the "exciting question of negro suffrage" that is "the absorbing one now in the North."[17]

Liberated from farms and plantations throughout the South, African Americans now thronged to Georgia cities, including Atlanta, and the resulting challenges involving work, education, and race relations led Congress to create the Freedmen's Bureau. This agency helped freedpeople negotiate work contracts, establish bank accounts, and find educational opportunities in their new environment. Oliver Otis Howard, who had once commanded a wing of Sherman's army in Georgia and now led the Bureau, demonstrated a heartfelt commitment toward advancing the rights of former slaves in the South. However, Bureau officials in individual states showed varying levels of dedication to his mission. General Davis Tillson led the Bureau in Georgia, and Colonel George Curkendall served as Atlanta's subassistant commissioner. On Christmas Day in 1865, Curkendall gave a speech to a crowd of two hundred African Americans who gathered at City Hall. Curkendall emphasized the concept of self-help and not government handouts. Former slaves must work hard in order to earn honest wages, he said, and highlighted his personal work ethic. For those who could not find immediate employment, the Freedmen's Bureau operated a camp near Atlanta. It housed and fed an estimated 650 people on a temporary basis, but its efforts never met the need, and Curkendall emphasized that the government could not support any of them for the long term. Few white people heard the speech.[18]

Barnwell's city directory provides a snapshot of Atlanta's shifting demographics. According to a census ordered by the City Council, 10,940 white people resided in Atlanta. Of that number, 928 were widows and orphans, about half of them widows and orphans of Confederate soldiers. Atlanta's black population was 9,288. In 1860, blacks had accounted for 20 percent of Atlanta's population; now they made up nearly half, and African Americans lived in each of the city's five wards.[19]

For the most part, Atlanta's white residents remained fearful about the new racial order that was evolving around them. They were especially wary of the black men in uniform who made up part of the army's garrison encamped on Peachtree Street just north of the city center. The *Daily Intelligencer* alleged that members of the 138th U.S. Colored Troops engaged in robbery or other lawful behavior. Although the newspaper's editorial perspective always favored white people's views, in this instance the *Intelligencer* also printed letters of denial from white officers who commanded the regiment. Nonetheless, the newspaper contributed to an unflattering image of African Americans, including an article describing the departure by rail of some members of the 138th and the emotional response of black Atlantans who witnessed the event. The *Intelligencer* called the scene "ludicrous and pathetic." One citizen who saw Negro troops on Atlanta's streets in the late fall of 1865 expressed the view of many whites when he wrote, "I wish they were all some where else."[20]

White people alleged that blacks were lazy and unwilling to work. Sam Richards wrote in his diary about the difficulty in finding servants in postwar Atlanta. On September 9, 1866, he wrote, "We have two new servants," and then on November 17, "We have another servant on trial named *Louisa*, being the *fifth* since we began to keep house about a year ago. . . . They 'endure for a time' only, and soon spoil and pass away." Elizabeth Hanna visited Atlanta for the first time in 1866 and stayed at the only hotel to survive the war, the Planters' Hotel, now renamed American Hotel. The accommodations were basic but acceptable to Hanna; what surprised her was the lack of black staff to serve clients in the basement restaurant. Although a small black child ran a mechanical fly brush, guests were expected to serve themselves condiments from what she described as "a revolving disc-like arrangement," what might be called a lazy susan in later years. "This was certainly a very ingenious way of meeting the new conditions imposed by emancipation," Hanna concluded, while also decrying the "lack of proper service."[21]

Atlanta's African Americans interpreted the situation in a different way. At the same time that white people decried "indolence" and expected deference from former bondspeople, black people celebrated freedom, insisted on moving where they pleased, enjoying family life unencumbered by white people's control, and establishing patterns of religious worship in their own churches. Moreover, blacks wanted access to education, political rights including the vote, and opportunities for economic advancement on their own terms and without the harsh discipline that characterized slave labor.[22]

While often preoccupied with racial issues, white Atlantans also focused on economic opportunity. The wagon trade had been one of Atlanta's most important economic drivers before and during the war. In October 1865, the city opened a new market. Although it was "hastily gotten up" and rudimentary in appearance, the building would serve the purpose until a second, more permanent structure could be opened in February of the following year. These markets fed Atlanta's growing population, helped farmers get back on their feet, and provided much-needed tax revenue for the city.[23]

Atlanta's commercial men moved back to the city and immediately built or rebuilt businesses, seemingly as ambitious as ever. Sam Richards and his family returned from New York in August 1865. As renters rather than owners of retail space on Whitehall Street, Richards and his brother and business partner Jabez suffered minimal financial losses in the war, and they quickly began earning money again selling books from a storefront on Peters Street. Other businessmen started new businesses. William McNaught and James Ormond, previous owners of a commission business in Atlanta and a blockade-running concern called the Fulton Exporting and Importing Company, rode the crest of Atlanta's postwar building boom by creating a successful hardware firm that sold building supplies. Alfred Austell bought a large lot on Decatur Street that once had housed the Trout House Hotel and erected a four-story business house.[24]

George Adair lost his newspaper, the *Southern Confederacy*, when his troubled finances forced him to sell in 1863, and he lost his home in the federal burning of Atlanta; nonetheless, Adair returned to start over. He opened a general commission business in Atlanta, engaged in commercial real estate, and ran an auction business. Among other transactions, he sold lots along Marietta Street that made up the old Ponder estate, land that now became part of Atlanta's new street railway. Founded in 1871 by a group of stockholders that included Adair, Richard Peters, and Lewis Scofield, the Atlanta Street Railroad Company opened its first line in September 1871 using mule-drawn streetcars. By replacing the wartime eyesore of the Ponder estate with

Atlanta's first mass-transit system, commercial men symbolically destroyed an icon of wartime Atlanta to make way for the modern city. Atlanta's business elite were always happy to mix personal profit with civic pride. In this instance, Adair exploited his position with the streetcar company to enhance his auctioneering business by offering free rides to locations where he held auctions. The new streetcar line was conveniently located near the homes of Richard Peters and George Adair.[25]

The rebuilding and reopening of all four of Atlanta's railroads contributed significantly to a resumption of trade. The railroads all sustained significant damage during the war. Confederates retreating ahead of Sherman's army destroyed locomotives and boxcars. Union soldiers destroyed track by prying loose the iron rails, then heating and twisting them into "Sherman neckties." By the summer of 1866, little more than a year after the war ended, railroad workers had succeeded in repairing and reopening all four lines. This impressive feat gave Atlanta an edge against competitors in the state and the region. Several years later, an Englishman who visited Atlanta en route from Charleston to New Orleans noted that the rebuilt city "has sprung up entirely from being a great railway centre. 'Get to Atlanta,' said a Yankee to me, 'and then you can get anywhere else on God's airth.'"[26]

Changes to the nature of cotton production also contributed to Atlanta's resurgence. Before the war, cotton "factors" in coastal cities had handled the transportation and sale of raw cotton to mills in the North and in Europe. After the war, cotton brokers replaced factors. Brokers operated from offices in rail centers like Atlanta, for railroads, not ships, provided the most efficient access to northern cities. It took years for the American South to recover its place in the international cotton trade, since European mills began importing cotton from India and Egypt during the war.[27]

Reporters from the North who descended on the city to chronicle its resurgence could scarcely contain their enthusiasm. "The burnt district of Richmond was hardly more thoroughly destroyed than the central part of Atlanta," wrote Whitelaw Reid. Yet in the months following the war, four thousand mechanics quickly found employment as Atlanta's economic engine cranked back into gear. Sidney Andrews, who reported for the *Chicago Tribune* as well as the *Boston Advertiser*, was even more effusive. Andrews called Atlanta a "new city" where "business is springing up with marvellous rapidity." He estimated that Atlanta had two hundred businesses by the end of 1865, and the city needed more work than it had laborers to fill the need. Andrews believed that even the booming northern metropolis of Chicago could not compare with what he witnessed in Atlanta. Andrews understood what was at stake. "The one sole idea first in every man's mind is to make money," he wrote.[28]

Inevitably, not all of Atlanta's businessmen prospered after the war. Cornelius Hanleiter, a pioneer citizen of prewar Atlanta, onetime member of the City Council, and prosperous owner of Franklin Printing, fell on hard times. A series of financial setbacks, including the sale of his printing house, led him to earn a meager postwar living as superintendent of the Bethesda Orphans' Home near Savannah. Alvin K. Seago, who ran a commission and grocery business in Atlanta and made profits by selling salt during the war, began his business anew after the war. Seago attributed his business success to his ability to remember the names of every customer. In spite of his personal touch, Seago's business failed, a shocking turn of events for Atlantans who believed him among the city's most solid and business-savvy citizens. Sidney Root lost an enormous amount of money when his blockade-running business collapsed in 1865. Along with his business, Root lost the desire to engage in business speculation. Instead, he moved to New York so that his children could be well educated, and finally returned to the Gate City when he retired in 1873.[29]

Atlantans turned for leadership to many of the same men who had led them before and during the war. Like their prewar counterparts, Atlanta's postwar mayors and city councilmen included men of wealth and standing in the community. Between 1865 and 1873, four of the city's seven mayors owned property valued at more than $20,000, placing them at the top of the economic scale in the city. Approximately half of City Council members owned property valued between $5,000 and $20,000, and 20 percent owned more than that amount. Atlanta's commercial men had a stake in their city's physical and economic recovery. As they had before the war, they took turns running for and being elected to positions of political power.[30]

In 1866, James Calhoun stepped down as mayor, replaced by another of Atlanta's leading citizens, James E. Williams, a commission agent and owner of the now-destroyed Athenaeum theater. In his inaugural address, Williams paid homage to those who died in the war, to the surviving citizens "almost penniless and houseless," and to the daunting task ahead in rebuilding public buildings, streets, gas and fire departments, and City Cemetery. Williams also struck a note of optimism when he said, "We may still cherish the hope that there is in store for us a bright future."[31]

The ranks of Atlanta's lawyers and doctors filled with the same men who had served before the war. Lucius Gartrell returned to Atlanta in the spring of 1865 and quickly became a respected member of the criminal bar. Resigning from the Confederate Congress in 1864, he recruited men for a brigade that bore his name and fought against Sherman's army in South Carolina. After laying waste to south Georgia and capturing Savannah in December 1864, Sherman next marched into South Carolina, the state where secession had begun. Gartrell's success in recruiting men late in the war was not matched by military success in the field, for he suffered a wound that sidelined him for the rest of the war. By July 1865, Gartrell advertised his law practice in the *Atlanta Daily Intelligencer,* his office with partner T. W. J. Hill located on Alabama Street. In later years, Gartrell trained the next generation of criminal attorneys by teaching the subject at Oglethorpe University, which established its Atlanta campus in the early 1870s.[32]

The Atlanta Medical College suspended operations as a school and served as a hospital during the war; it restarted an educational mission after the war. Prewar faculty members John and Willis Westmoreland and Joseph P. Logan, who served as Confederate physicians during the war, resumed their roles as faculty members when the conflict ended. They were joined by Dr. Samuel Stout, previously the medical director for the Army of Tennessee. In August 1866, the Atlanta Medical College granted degrees to twenty-eight new physicians.[33]

The city continued to rebuild its infrastructure. In 1866, Atlanta constructed a new jail and hired thirty-two policemen, many of them Confederate veterans anxious for paid employment. The Atlanta Gas Light Company, which had lost its plant when Sherman's men fired the city in November 1864, reinstated gas service in September 1866. Sam Richards wrote in his diary, "The city is partially lighted up tonight with gas for the first time in several years."[34]

Atlanta's Board of Trade, founded in 1860, when Sidney Root called it the Chamber of Commerce, collapsed during the war and reconvened in 1866. With its headquarters in the building that housed George W. Jack's confectionery on Whitehall Street, the Board of Trade attracted a large gathering at its initial postwar meeting on April 4, 1866. The assembled businessmen issued a resolution that paid homage to "the great and constantly increasing commerce" in Atlanta, and the need for "uniform negotiations and union of action in the promotion of its mercantile interests." A committee of five drew up a "code of regulations" for the new organization, which elected William W. Clayton as its president. Members of the new organization included the iron foundry owner Joseph Winship, bookseller R. M. McPherson, and businessman Marcus Bell.[35]

The war left Atlanta's financial institutions in ruins. The Georgia National Bank helped to launch the city's economic recovery. Located near the railroads on Alabama Street and constructed by the United States government, the bank had local directors including William W. Clayton, Edward E. Rawson, and John Collier. Always anxious to boost Atlanta's economy, the *Intelligencer* on April 4, 1866, applauded the bank and recommended it to the people of Atlanta. "As a depository, and as a fiscal agent; in the purchase of exchange, in negotiating loans, making collections of debts in this and other States; it is what Atlanta has needed and what she has now got. Our business men we trust will profit by it."[36]

Cultural life in Atlanta also returned in 1866 when rival businessmen constructed two auditoriums as venues for theater, opera, and public lectures. The larger of the two, the three-story brick Bell-Johnson Opera Hall, was opened on Alabama Street by Marcus Bell and George Johnson. Sam Richards noted in his diary that Atlantans saw their first Italian opera in October 1866. The event triggered "Opera fever" in the city, but the $2 entry fee kept Richards at home.[37]

By the time Barnwell's *Atlanta City Directory* was published in 1867, Atlanta's economic rebirth was clearly evident. Barnwell noted that the City Council licensed 338 businesses in the second half of 1865. Within two years, Atlanta boasted 250 businesses, most of them housed in brick buildings constructed along the principal business streets: Whitehall, Alabama, Decatur, Marietta, and Peachtree. The city rebuilt two market houses, constructed a bridge across the Western and Atlantic and Macon and Western Railroads, and provided land on which the Macon and Western constructed a new depot. In the evenings, Atlanta glowed with gaslights. Although the iron foundry created by William Markham and Lewis Scofield had been destroyed by Yankee soldiers, a group of investors constructed a significant new foundry near the Western and Atlantic Railroad. Seven machine shops also operated in Atlanta.[38]

Atlanta's affluent residents could not ignore national politics, and they waited with anticipation to learn what direction national policy would take under the leadership of Abraham Lincoln's successor, the Tennessean Andrew Johnson. On May 29, 1865, Johnson issued an Amnesty Proclamation negating the wartime Confiscation Acts, legislation that allowed for the seizure of property belonging to Confederate civilians. But the president's proclamation excluded those with taxable income exceeding $20,000. A small number of Atlantans fell into this category, including Richard Peters, Atlanta's wealthiest citizen, who had made money as a railroad and real estate investor. However, wealthy people in Atlanta and elsewhere quickly learned how to circumvent the law by applying for presidential pardons. Although his land holdings had dropped dramatically during the war, Peters still owned city property worth more than $100,000. Peters returned to Atlanta in September 1865 and quickly resumed his active schedule as a wheeler and dealer. The Georgia Railroad, on whose board of directors he served, constructed a fine new brick depot at the corner of Alabama and Lloyd Streets with a third-floor board of directors meeting room that gave Peters and his fellow directors a fine view of the city and Stone Mountain.[39]

In keeping with Atlanta's established pattern, Richard Peters took his turn serving on the City Council, winning election in 1867. He filled the position of a former councilman with ties to City Treasurer J. T. Porter, who resigned under pressure after allegations that he had embezzled money from the city treasury. Peters chaired the city Finance Committee, which held increased power to oversee income and expenditures after the Porter scandal tainted, though did not directly implicate, the mayoralty of James Williams. Eager to place Atlanta on a sound financial footing both because of his sense of civic duty and because he had purchased city bonds for himself at 8 percent interest, Peters exercised considerable power over city finances. Like many nineteenth-century businessmen, Peters did not believe that city government should be burdened by supporting a large number of dependent, impoverished people. He initiated a resolution on the City Council that garnered unanimous support, one that congratulated the superintendent of Atlanta's Alms House for his "very efficient and economical management."[40]

Peters played an even more important leadership role when Atlanta's businessmen faced a decision regarding federal Reconstruction policy. Congress passed a series of Reconstruction Acts that imposed military rule on the South. Dividing the former Confederacy into five military districts, each of them commanded by a general, Congress also decreed that states would not be readmitted to the Union unless they gave voting rights to black men.[41] Atlanta's men of commerce faced a decision of major consequence. Would they acquiesce in congressional Reconstruction or would they fight it?

On March 4, 1867, just two days after passage of the first Reconstruction Act, a group of Atlantans met at City Hall to discuss the "political troubles which now agitate the country." Understanding that legislation would soon be forthcoming from Washington, a group of concerned citizens including Joseph Winship, Alfred Austell, Edward E. Rawson, Samuel P. Richards, and Reverend Henry Hornady called for the meeting. Hundreds of citizens responded by packing the building "to its fullest capacity," according to the *Daily New Era,* which joined the *Daily Intelligencer* as a leading postwar Atlanta newspaper. Richard Peters chaired the City Hall meeting and appointed Henry P. Farrow to chair a committee charged with drafting resolutions. Farrow's committee acknowledged that the people of Georgia had recently waged "unsuccessful warfare against the Government of the United States" and recommended that "the people of Georgia should promptly and without the least hesitation accept the plan of restoration recently proposed" by the Republican Congress. Additionally, Farrow's committee warned that "all passion and prejudice should be forthwith cast aside . . . or we will yet lose rights and interests which we now enjoy."[42]

After Farrow spoke in favor of his resolutions, a group of men led by Luther J. Glenn proposed a different set of resolutions. Glenn and his followers believed that the Peters-Farrow contingent showed too much submission to congressional will. At this point, the meeting disbanded amid chaos, as proponents of neither camp could attain a clear dominance over the meeting. The *Daily New Era* called it "a scene of confusion and excitement . . . which has been rarely if ever equaled in this city." Richard Peters adjourned the meeting, announcing it could reconvene at 7:00 P.M.[43]

Luther Glenn and those who joined him in a breakaway session represented men who had a great deal invested in the old regime. Glenn had served Fulton County at Georgia's secession convention and later entered the Confederate Army. Wounded at the battle of Fredericksburg, he never fully recovered the use of his left arm. After Sherman's soldiers departed from the Gate City and Confederates reclaimed control, Glenn became commandant of the military post of Atlanta. Lucius Gartrell joined Glenn's breakaway session and presided, aided by Robert Alston, a former member of John Hunt Morgan's cavalry. This group passed resolutions calling upon Georgians to "remain quiet" about Reconstruction legislation, thereby retaining "their self-respect, manhood and honor." Another resolution expressed their desire for the U.S. Supreme Court to rule on the constitutionality of congressional

Reconstruction. By implication, they hoped the Court would overturn the Reconstruction Acts.[44]

That evening, Peters's supporters again took the hall, and former mayor James Calhoun introduced a motion to accept the Farrow resolutions and to forward them to Georgia's governor and the U.S. Congress. The assembled group adopted the Farrow resolutions with a unanimous vote, but only after Peters refused to allow the Glenn-Gartrell faction to participate. Peters and the main body of participants wanted to send an unequivocal message about Atlanta's position on Reconstruction. Although Peters, Calhoun, and others clearly signaled their assent to federal government power, they drew the line at African American participation at their meetings. At least seventy-five black men attended the morning session. Asked whether they might vote, they were told by Peters that they could not do so.[45] Nonetheless, their presence at the meeting and their demand for inclusion in the political process reveals the changing nature of politics in the South. African Americans now claimed the rights of citizenship. They made up nearly half of Atlanta's population, and efforts to limit their participation would not go unopposed.

A second meeting on April 20 added further support to the notion of citizen acquiescence in Reconstruction. At this meeting, Richard Peters, James Calhoun, and an array of local luminaries including George Adair and J. J. Thrasher were joined by prewar Unionists Nedom Angier, Lewis Scofield, and William Markham. The meeting issued a report that endorsed cooperation and reconciliation and appealed to Atlanta's citizenry based on the need to move beyond "our present unsettled and paralyzed condition." The unity that this meeting presented to citizens of Atlanta reveals how fully former Confederates and former Unionists in the city now cooperated in support of a common business-based vision for the city's future. The consensus that characterized Atlanta's business class before the war had been reestablished, and on the surface at least, Atlanta's men of commerce had put the war behind them. In the 1880s, a dynamic young journalist named Henry Grady was to claim the spotlight as Atlanta's leading spokesman for economic modernization, but businessmen of Atlanta's wartime generation laid the groundwork. They would let nothing stand in their way. One scholar has written, "Atlantans were not content to simply let prosperity come—they went out and grabbed it."[46]

The city's reaction to the arrival of General John Pope provides the best indication of leaders' acquiescence in congressional Reconstruction.

Pope, who was assigned to command the Third Military District, encompassing Florida, Georgia, and Alabama, made Atlanta his headquarters. He oversaw the drafting of a new state constitution giving the vote to African American men. During the Civil War, Confederate civilians had expressed outrage toward Pope, who as Union commander in Virginia during 1862 showed a marked disregard for civilian property and safety. Nonetheless, in 1867 a delegation of Atlantans welcomed Pope at the depot and escorted him to the National Hotel. Immediately, they began to lobby Pope to hold a constitutional convention in Atlanta, where they hoped their city's advantages in transportation, hotels, and restaurants would lead to its selection as the new state capital. To further this cause and to signal their cooperation with Reconstruction, one hundred members of the business community held a banquet at which they toasted *"Our Pope*—May he prove to be as infallible as he is powerful." Pope then spoke. He expressed his thanks and also his surprise at the apparent warmth of Atlantans' greetings. In truth, white Atlantans swallowed their pride and accepted reality. Sam Richards wrote in his diary, "Gen Pope is our ruler. We are invited to form new State Constitutions giving the negroes the right of suffrage, and I suppose we shall *have to do it.*"[47]

Another indication of Atlanta business leaders' adeptness in handling Reconstruction issues came when Unionist James L. Dunning formed an organization called the Lincoln National Monument Association and presented the City Council with a petition calling for a statue of Abraham Lincoln to be erected in the city. Dunning had made no attempt to hide his Unionism during the war and had been imprisoned briefly. He ran up a U.S. flag in celebration when Sherman's soldiers entered the city in September 1864. After the war, he worked for the Freedmen's Bureau as an agent for Fulton County.[48]

Dunning submitted his petition to the Atlanta City Council on September 20, 1867. At the behest of Councilman Richard Peters, Mayor James Williams appointed a committee of three to look into the matter. The committee consisted of Peters, Edward E. Rawson, and Alexander Mitchell, all of them prominent businessmen dedicated to moving their city toward renewal and economic growth, none of them interested in provoking tension with the North. The committee reported to the Council the following week, suggesting that the city appropriate money to purchase a ten-acre tract near City Cemetery and quite close to the location where more than five thousand

Confederates had died at the battle of Atlanta two years earlier. In return, the committee wanted the Lincoln National Monument Association to spend $750,000 to $1,000,000 improving the land as park space. Peters and the others knew that Dunning was unlikely to raise that amount. Their negotiations were undoubtedly intended to kill the project through subterfuge. Nonetheless, City Council proceedings and its vote of six to four in favor of the plan created a brief firestorm. The *Daily Intelligencer* railed against a plan that might lead to Lincoln's image being planted "over the mouldering bones" of Confederate soldiers. As Peters and the others had foreseen would happen, the furor quickly died when Dunning failed to raise the money.[49]

General Pope's presence in Atlanta encouraged the growth of Georgia's nascent Republican Party, which began as a coalition of prewar Unionists, federal appointees including Freedmen's Bureau agents, and missionaries who came to the South to help freedpeople. Because most of these individuals lived and worked in cities, Republicanism emerged in Georgia's metropolitan centers. An important step in the process was the formation of the Georgia Equal Rights Association, which began following a convention of freedmen held in Augusta during January 1866. John E. Bryant spearheaded the group. A Freedmen's Bureau agent, Bryant lost his job when it became clear that the Georgia Equal Rights Association endorsed a political agenda. Agents were not supposed to engage in politics. Branches of the Union League also formed in Georgia after the war and became an important part of the new Republican coalition. The League had begun during the war as a group of northerners who supported the Lincoln administration's vigorous prosecution of the war. It organized in the South when it began attracting support from among Unionist whites in the northern part of the state. General Pope helped the party by ordering a voter registration drive. Voters would then go to the polls to decide whether they approved the idea of a new constitutional convention, and if so, they would vote for delegates to represent them.[50]

Georgia's Republican Party formally began on July 4, 1867, with a meeting in Atlanta. The party drew its support from among newly registered African Americans, including Harrison Berry, whose pamphlet *Slavery and Abolitionism, as Viewed by a Georgia Slave* had once been used by proslavery whites to justify the institution's continuation. Now, in addition to political activism, Berry took aim at those who alleged blacks' inferiority by publishing a tract touting their achievements in ancient African societies. In addition to blacks, Georgia's Republican Party also recruited yeoman whites of north Georgia and the

Wiregrass region of south Georgia. Some of these whites had been Unionists. Many suffered from economic problems, including indebtedness and poor harvests, and they were suspicious of a planter class that had led them into a disastrous war. Georgia Republicans held a trump card that gave them hope for the future. Former Governor Joe E. Brown embraced the party, although the level of his enthusiasm was debatable, since he largely avoided speaking at Republican events. Prominent Atlanta Unionists including William Markham, Nedom Angier, and James Dunning also publicly affiliated with the party. Atlanta Republicans gained another voice when the *Daily New Era* newspaper, previously Democratic, became a Republican organ in October 1866 after Dr. Samuel Bard became its proprietor.[51]

Despite choosing an Atlanta venue for their opening convention, Republicans soon turned for leadership to a group of men from Augusta, including John Bryant as the party's new secretary and Rufus Bullock, who quickly emerged as the party's leading light. Bullock had moved to the state in 1859 and served the Confederate government as a quartermaster during the war. He now championed economic development and interracial harmony. Bullock's star rose during the constitutional convention.[52]

Fulton County's delegation to the constitutional convention included Nedom Angier and James Dunning, who resigned from the Freedmen's Bureau in order to serve. Republicans dominated the proceedings, in part because so many Democrats boycotted the delegate vote in protest against the state's emerging interracial democracy. Although none of Atlanta's delegates were men of color, African Americans accounted for 37 of the convention's 170 delegates, making the group that assembled in Atlanta City Hall on December 9, 1867, the state's most inclusive political body ever to convene up to that time. The convention met for more than three months.[53]

The convention produced a progressive new constitution for the state, including measures for debt relief, homestead exemptions, married women's property rights, and public education. The latter would be financed by poll taxes, liquor taxes, and taxes on exhibitions. The new constitution also promoted economic development, including subsidies for railroad building. It guaranteed suffrage for all men; however, convention delegates rejected a provision that guaranteed to all qualified voters the right to run for political office. Twenty-nine African American delegates joined in this decision, perhaps because they assumed that members of their race already enjoyed this privilege. It proved to be a grievous mistake.[54]

Before the convention concluded its proceedings, the Atlanta City Council met and passed a resolution requesting that the convention move the state capital from Milledgeville to Atlanta. To help its case, the Council offered legislative meeting space rent-free for ten years. Because Atlanta's railroads made the city more widely accessible than Milledgeville and because of Atlanta's economic importance, the convention immediately adopted the measure. On February 29, Sam Richards wrote in his diary, "The *fifth* Saturday in February! When shall we see another? Atlanta has been promoted to the dignity and importance of being the Capital of Georgia by ordinance of our great Convention on the past week so that if the people ratify the Constitution, this is a *Capital* place." The voters did ratify the constitution, and Atlanta's bid to become the state capital ended in victory. In 1861, Atlanta had failed in its efforts to become the Confederacy's capital despite an organized effort from the business community. As Georgia's new seat of political as well as economic power, the Gate City took another step toward becoming the principal city of the lower South. The legislature established temporary headquarters at City Hall. The City Council sounded a note of triumph when it offered thanks to the Constitutional Convention for "locating the Capital of Georgia in our thriving city" and suggested that Atlanta deserved to become Georgia's capital because of "the Spirit of the people of the Gate City."[55]

Although Georgia Republicans were clearly on the ascendancy, the Constitutional Convention revealed an emerging schism in their ranks between Radicals from the Augusta Ring, who wanted greater emphasis on rights for former slaves and help for distressed farmers, and Moderates, who were more likely to cooperate with Democrats. Nonetheless, the Radicals succeeded in nominating Rufus Bullock for the governorship. Bullock defeated the Democratic candidate John B. Gordon, the handsome and charismatic former Confederate general who was involved with the state's Ku Klux Klan. By this point, General George G. Meade had replaced Pope as military commander in Atlanta. Meade took measures to assure peaceful elections, forbidding armed gatherings at political rallies and ordering the Freedmen's Bureau to assure African American voters of their political rights. Although Bullock won the election with a plurality of more than 7,000 votes, he lost Fulton County by 1,914 to Gordon's 2,357. Voters in the state and in Atlanta ratified the constitution at the same time. In this instance, Atlantans sided with the majority, but narrowly, 2,229 to 2,019.[56]

The era of Republican dominance in Georgia was brief and fractious. In September 1868, a coalition of Democrats and Republican Moderates voted to expel African American legislators from Georgia's House and Senate, citing the state constitution's lack of a provision that upheld black office-holding along with voting. Despite the protests of Governor Bullock, twenty-nine members of the House and three from the Senate lost their positions. In Atlanta, where African Americans now made up close to half of the population, efforts to win political representation followed a difficult path. In two of Atlanta's five wards, the Third and Fourth, blacks constituted a majority. To prevent their political rise, local Democrats persuaded the Georgia legislature to change election laws in the city so that City Council elections were city-wide instead of ward by ward. This change diluted the black vote. A city ordinance adding a poll tax to voting procedures further discouraged African American political participation. However, the U.S. Congress, angered by Georgia's antidemocratic policies, reinstated Reconstruction, which Congress had lifted following the ratification of the new state constitution, and Henry Holcombe, a Republican legislator from Atlanta, introduced a law that restored ward-by-ward voting. Governor Bullock signed the bill in 1870. In the Georgia legislature, expelled members were reinstated.[57]

These actions cleared the way for Atlanta to elect its first black members of the City Council. Councilman William Finch moved to Atlanta in 1868. Before emancipation, Finch had been a slave owned by Joseph H. Lumpkin, chief justice of Georgia's Supreme Court. A tailor by trade, he left the Lumpkin family in 1865, affiliated with the Equal Rights Association, and opened a tailoring business on Atlanta's Whitehall Street. In 1870, he owned property valued at $1,000. As a prosperous and literate man in a city where the vast majority of blacks were impoverished and illiterate, Finch was a natural fit to run for the City Council. His residence in the Fourth Ward's black neighborhood called Shermantown and his membership in its most important religious congregation, Bethel Church, also helped.[58]

Finch was joined by another black member, George Graham from the Third Ward, whose illiteracy limited his ability to play a significant role on the City Council. However, Finch served on the Street Committee, which controlled a sizable portion of the city's annual budget. He was a strong voice in promoting public education, which Atlanta voters had approved in a referendum the previous year, but which the Council had been slow to act upon. Finch was also conscientious about the constituent service aspects of his job, introducing petitions from African American organizations that wanted to hold festivals in City Hall, and sometimes calling attention to individuals who needed help from the Relief Committee. Occasionally he battled Democratic Councilmen, as he did when they tried to extend Mitchell Street in such a way that it would have bisected Atlanta University. Founded in 1865, Atlanta University had constructed both a dormitory and a classroom building that might have been demolished if Finch had not stopped the street extension. Finch's single term on the City Council was clearly an important one, and all the more noteworthy given that fewer than a dozen African Americans won these positions in Georgia's larger cities.[59]

By the mid-1870s, more than 75 percent of Atlanta's African American men worked in unskilled jobs, notably construction, while the vast majority of African American women found work as domestic servants and laundresses. However, a small number of black men achieved success in business and the professions. Roderick Badger reestablished his dentistry office at 6 Peachtree Street, after first fleeing to Chicago at the end of the war. Fulton County tax records from the mid-1870s show Badger as the city's wealthiest African American, with property valued at $5,600. Badger also served as a community leader, accepting a position as secretary to the Atlanta branch of the National Freedman's Savings and Trust Company. Badger's decadelong residency in Atlanta and his standing as a professional man no doubt gave the bank credibility in the minds of many freedpeople. Freedman's Savings and Trust advertised for deposits of "Five Cents and Upwards" and promised interest paid three times a year. By 1870 the bank had deposits of $8,371, and three years later its deposits reached $379,900. Along with William Finch and D. D. Snyder, Badger also represented Fulton County at the Republican National Convention that renominated Ulysses S. Grant for the presidency in 1872.[60]

In addition to Badger, a small number of African American business and professional men achieved moderate success. They included grocers Tom Foster and James Tate, drayman Crawford Monroe, physician Henry Bauldin, and barbers Dougherty Hutchins and Robert Webster. Already a successful businessman by the time the Civil War ended, Webster broadened his real estate and business interests after the war. In 1867, he opened a "Large and Elegant Bathing House" next to his Decatur Street barbershop. In a rare show of interracial camaraderie, Webster's former owner, Robert Yancey, now a resident of Athens, came to visit and stayed overnight in Webster's house. Webster was careful to protect his business interests even if it meant appearing disloyal to his race. When the U.S. Congress passed the Civil Rights Act of 1875 in an effort to end segregation in public places, Webster wrote a letter to a local newspaper. "I keep a barber-shop for white men— have shaved no negroes, and even under the civil rights bill no negro can have his face scraped," he wrote. Then he added, "I want my colored friends to know that, in their places, I am their friend, and that out of their places, I am not their friend."[61]

While a few black men earned modest profits during the postwar period, a few white men achieved fabulous wealth. Hannibal I. Kimball was principal among them. A New Englander who found success before the war as a carriage maker, Kimball moved to the South as a so-called Carpetbagger when George Pullman hired him to develop his sleeping car business in the region. Kimball was a man of big talent, big ambition, and questionable ethics. Arriving in Atlanta during 1867, he quickly allied himself with Governor Rufus Bullock, and he used this association to secure a contract to build Atlanta's first state capitol. He purchased a partially constructed opera house from its bankrupt builder for $31,370, completed the capitol building in just four months, and then leased it to the state. The building opened on Marietta Street, January 9, 1869, earning accolades from some Georgians and cries of extravagance and shoddy workmanship from others. Meanwhile, the legislature balked at the governor's decision to give an advance payment of $54,000 to Kimball without its approval. State Treasurer Nedom Angier, once a Bullock ally and now an enemy, tried unsuccessfully to stop payment to Kimball. The Bullock-Kimball imbroglio led to public controversy that played out in the newspapers and in committee hearings. The issue was finally resolved in early 1871, when Kimball repaid the $54,000 Bullock had given him and the state purchased the building for $380,000, paid to Kimball in city bonds.[62]

Unfazed by the controversy, Kimball proceeded with his next project, the construction of a hotel designed to provide luxury accommodations for visitors. Constructing his hotel near the passenger depot on land once occupied by the modest Atlanta Hotel, Kimball ignored calls to keep the Atlanta name and instead honored himself by calling the new structure H. I. Kimball House. However, Kimball did not mind sharing a modest amount of his largesse with other Atlanta businessmen, and his decision to do so helped to soften potential resentment from local entrepreneurs when Kimball emerged as the city's most successful mover and shaker. Kimball purchased land from auctioneer George Adair and additional parcels of land from Richard Peters and John P. King. Although he selected a New York architect to design the structure, Kimball hired local contractor John C. Peck as his builder. Peck, whose shifting loyalties during the war led him to leave the state in 1864, was back in town, and like all returning Atlantans he was eager to make money.[63]

The Kimball House dwarfed the prewar Trout House in size and ostentation. Kimball chose the fashionable and ornate Second Empire style for his Atlanta hotel. Inside, a vast open space featured galleries on several floors. Frescoes by a painter named Berdretti embellished the walls. The hotel's six floors contained 317 rooms that could accommodate as many as one thousand people. For four dollars per night, guests enjoyed hot and cold running water, steam heat, and gas lighting, and a staff of one hundred to serve their meals and clean their rooms. Kimball brought furniture and some of the staff, including maids and a French chef, from New York. Shops on the premises sold tobacco, drugs, flowers, and newspapers.[64]

The Kimball House dominated the city. Politicians held meetings in its commodious lobby, businessmen brokered deals over meals and cocktails in its restaurants, and social events including wedding parties, dances, and fund-raisers took place in its ballroom. Beginning in 1873, a group calling itself the Mystic Brotherhood staged annual Mardi Gras–style festivities, with local attorney Logan Bleckley acting the role of Rex in the first instance and Lucius Gartrell taking it the next. The Kimball House provided bragging rights for Atlantans who were proud that the Gate City boasted the largest and most impressive hotel in the South. A reporter for the *New York Times* who spent the night at the Kimball House wrote that "the pride and boast of the traveler through Atlanta, as well as of the citizens of the place, is the magnificent Kimball House, a hotel that need fear no rival in any part of the land."[65]

While businessmen made money in the postwar building and commercial boom, Atlanta's less affluent residents waited for their own share. Impoverished blacks and whites suffered in postwar Atlanta, the result of wartime dislocation, the rapid influx of poor people to the city, and the vicissitudes of postwar capitalism. An army officer's wife who distributed clothing to hundreds of impoverished women in the summer of 1865 recalled "a very sad sight. They looked all yellow and starved, and were scarcely covered by rags." Unable to find housing, many poor people lived in abandoned rail cars and shacks made of discarded timber and pieces of metal roofing. Some lived in army tents left by Sherman's army. It might have reminded elderly Atlantans of the city's prewar Slabtown except that postwar indigent communities largely coalesced on the city's periphery instead of its center. The same *New York Times* correspondent who wrote so effusively about the Kimball House also noted without elaboration: "Some thirty orphans of Confederate soldiers gave a concert here the other night. The attendance was slim."[66]

During its tenure in the state, the Freedmen's Bureau distributed rations to the needy, and for a time, it ran a hospital in Atlanta to serve poor blacks. By 1868, however, the Bureau began to withdraw from Georgia, part of a national policy of downsizing the organization. The Bureau's edicts to local authorities regarding care for the indigent often fell on deaf ears. The city's suffering citizens were all too visible to Atlanta's more affluent classes. Impoverished children seemed to be everywhere, including those who scavenged for stray bullets from the battlefields around the city and sold them to scrap-metal dealers. With their earnings, Sarah and John Huff kept their family from "near-starvation." The *Daily New Era* complained about hordes of children begging on Atlanta streets. Most of the beggars were little girls, and their story was always the same: "Mister, Ma say for you to gin me five cents to buy some meal. She hain't had nothing to eat to-day an' she's sick." The newspaper called these beggars "little wretches" and wanted them off the streets, housed at the city's Alms House or put to work. But the Alms House never had enough space to handle the need. According to the *Daily Intelligencer,* which published an investigative article about the institution in 1867, the Alms House sheltered only 130 of Atlanta's neediest white citizens, most of them women and their children. Although the city provided them with rudimentary housing and rations, the residents' tattered clothing shocked the reporter who wrote the story.[67]

Shortages of food and fuel were most acute in cold weather months, and affluent residents made nominal efforts to help. Every winter, businessmen donated cords of wood to the destitute. In January 1869, for example, the distribution of thirty-five cords "went off briskly," according to one report. Affluent women staged a series of Calico Balls in the late 1860s and early 1870s. Attendees paid $1 per ticket. Women were expected to eschew dresses of fine fabrics and instead to dress in simple "costumes" made of plain calico, men to don scarves made of the same fabric. The next day, women would meet again and donate their used dresses for poor people, selected on the basis of home visits to ensure their virtue and genuine need. Nellie Peters and her mother, Mary Jane Peters (daughter and wife of Richard Peters), as well as Maria Westmoreland, who founded the first women's relief group during the Civil War, became organizers of the Calico Balls. The events raised modest sums. In 1871, for example, the women netted $212.[68]

Though Atlanta once housed twenty-six hospitals to treat Confederate soldiers, the postwar city had no municipal hospital to treat anyone, rich or poor, white or black. Efforts by a coalition of philanthropic women and local clergy to construct a "Soup House and Charity Hospital" stalled when the City Council failed to take action on the proposal. The *Daily New Era* castigated the Council for its failure to act and used a tragic example to illustrate its point. In February 1871 a man was fatally injured when he was struck by a train on a Friday night and local physicians called to the scene struggled to find a place for the unfortunate man to spend his final hours. In a stinging editorial on the twenty-sixth, the *Daily New Era* asked, "In the name of *humanity* are we *never* to have a City Hospital? We build railroads, fair grounds, Kimball houses, depots . . . capitol buildings, &c, while our poor die in the streets."[69]

Reformers did make progress in their efforts to educate Atlanta's children, addressing a pressing need that failed to make headway before or during the war. Initially, the impetus came from missionaries who journeyed to Atlanta after the war, some of them as members of organizations and others as individuals. In 1867, a middle-aged Moravian woman named Elizabeth Sterchi opened a private school for white Protestant children. With the help of several assistants, she volunteered her services on Saturdays teaching five hundred poor children of the city. Although Sterchi called her venture Home Mission School, many Atlantans disparaged it as the "Ragged School" because of the extreme poverty of its students. Nonetheless, Sterchi felt a great sense of pride when her students learned basic skills. Her efforts as a seamstress and the small donations she received from sympathizers allowed her students to wear patched but clean clothing, and she taught them to use good hygiene. Sadly, because of their circumstances, students often left Sterchi's school after a relatively short time, the boys to take jobs as laborers and factory workers, the girls to work as nurses and in shops.[70]

The American Missionary Association helped to start a program for educating African Americans in Atlanta. The AMA responded to calls for help from Georgia's Freedmen's Bureau. Leading the charge in Atlanta were a Minnesota clergyman named Frederic Ayer and his wife, Elisabeth. Before moving to Atlanta in 1865, they had acted as missionaries to Native Americans in Minnesota. Some of Atlanta's first classes for African American children took place in the African Methodist Episcopal Church located at Wheat and Butler Streets, the future site of the Fourth Ward's Bethel Church. Frederic and Elisabeth Ayer and their colleagues received help from the Freedmen's Bureau in the form of rations, but in the first year their students suffered from inadequate clothing, insufficient school supplies, and a lack of heat at the church and other buildings where classes were held. By 1867, funding had improved, pupils enjoyed learning in a new chapel building and two-story brick school, and black enrollment in Atlanta climbed to fifteen hundred children. Among the pupils were Henry and Joseph Flipper, previously the slaves of Ellen Ponder, now freed from bondage and eager to learn. The sudden death of Frederic Ayer and his wife's decision to move back to Minnesota represented a setback for the black education movement and triggered a period of grieving within the African American community. "An immense throng of colored people and some whites" accompanied Ayer's casket to City Cemetery, according to one account.[71]

Public education came to Atlanta in 1872. Although the Georgia Constitution of 1868 included provisions for public education and Atlantans elected a board of education the following year, a combination of factors including organizational and funding problems caused delays in implementing the plan. City Councilman Charles W. Wells objected to the notion of taxpayers funding a system that included black as well as white children. Ultimately, Atlantans of many backgrounds and professions came together in support of education. Members of the Board of Education in the 1870s included businessmen David Mayer and Edward Rawson and former governor Joseph E. Brown, who presided over the board as its president. They divided the city's white children into three districts based on its wards, which now numbered seven. Representatives of the city's two black schools agreed to turn them over to the Atlanta School Board. Grammar schools included boys and girls; in high school the genders separated into Boys' and Girls' High. Girls' High moved to the Neal mansion on Washington Street in 1873 and used the structure for the next fifty years. Atlanta schools remained racially segregated until the mid-twentieth century, and African Americans could not advance beyond the primary grades. Efforts by former city councilman William Finch and Reverend Frank Quarles to build a high school for blacks went nowhere, although Finch succeeded in persuading the city to subsidize secondary education for a small number of African Americans at Atlanta University.[72]

Atlanta's commercial men understood the need for public schools. Without them, idle young men with no purpose in life all too often engaged in petty crime and became impoverished adults. These circumstances threatened stability and made Atlanta compare unfavorably to other metropolitan areas, for business leaders knew that Savannah, Augusta, Nashville, and Charleston had established public schools before Atlanta. However, the Gate City had ongoing issues with water quality, sanitation, and poverty that leaders failed to address.[73] Members of the business elite, like their counterparts around the nation, regarded poverty not as an issue to be solved by government but as one best left to churches and private charities. Atlanta's impoverished citizens were an eyesore, but in comparison with their Civil War counterparts, they must have seemed passive.

Abbie M. Brooks moved to Atlanta from Nashville in 1870, hoping to improve her economic circumstances, and her experiences reveal some of Atlanta's ongoing challenges. The forty-year-old single woman appears to have changed her name from Lindley to Brooks, perhaps because she gave birth to an illegitimate daughter in the 1850s and wanted to move to a new location where her shameful past would not be known. Leaving her daughter with foster parents in Ohio, Brooks moved first to Nashville, then to Atlanta, where she rented a room from a Mrs. Rachel Keith in Ward Five. Apparently, Keith ran a boardinghouse that served white and black women. Occasionally, racial tension resulted in open conflict, as it did one day in May when a boarder gave a glass of lemonade to a black woman before a white woman named Lou received hers. Brooks left the room "before the affair terminated," but when she returned, "Lou was saying anything but her prayer. I remarked Ladies you have heard and read of the doctrine of Abolitionism, but never saw an exemplification before."[74]

Brooks earned a meager living selling religious books, maps, and pictures of Robert E. Lee and Stonewall Jackson. She disliked the work, which involved canvassing the city's neighborhoods and factories. In the pages of her diary, Abbie found an outlet for her occasional feelings of satisfaction and her more frequent feelings of resentment, for she found life as a saleswoman exhausting, demeaning, and often humiliating when her efforts brought only rude responses from individuals she solicited. At the

Phoenix Planing Mills, she sold one map but also endured the hostility of the mill's proprietor, who regarded her "coldly." "Times seem hard and money tight," Brooks concluded after realizing that Atlanta was not an easy place to earn a living. Aside from her efforts to earn money, the city did not impress her, especially its iconic business corridor, Whitehall Street. On an oppressively hot day in July, Brooks complained of the stench there caused by Atlanta's "foetid sewers and pools of filth."[75]

As the city continued to grapple with sanitation and social issues in the postwar world, Reconstruction ended in Georgia. Rufus Bullock's vision of economic development and racial cooperation collapsed in the wake of corruption charges and party squabbles, including the defection of Joe E. Brown. The former Georgia governor now reclaimed his previous political affiliation in the face of Republican decline and Democratic resurgence. Evidence of graft in Bullock's administration alienated voters of both parties. When Democrats calling themselves Redeemers won majorities in the Georgia's legislature in 1870, the Republican governor resigned and left the state, just a few days before the new House and Senate convened for the 1871 term. Had he stayed, Bullock would have faced certain impeachment and conviction. In 1877, Bullock returned to Atlanta to face criminal charges of corruption, but the passage of time and the triumph of Democratic politics made Bullock less a subject of public anger. He pleaded not guilty to charges that he had given outlandish sums of state money to Hannibal Kimball and his brother Edwin. One charge specifically accused Bullock of bilking the state of $42,500 for rail cars purchased but never received from a company in Tennessee with ties to Edwin Kimball. Lucius Gartrell led the defense team, and even the anti-Bullock *Atlanta Constitution* acknowledged that the attorney's "abilities as a great criminal advocate" helped Bullock's case. Gartrell's public stature as a former Confederate general probably helped as well. In any event, Bullock was acquitted of both charges. The Kimball brothers, like Bullock, left the state after Hannibal's bankruptcy in 1871.[76]

On January 12, 1872, Georgia was formally "redeemed" from Reconstruction when Democrat James M. Smith became the state's governor, replacing Benjamin Conley, who had served out the rest of Bullock's term. The *Atlanta Constitution*, now Atlanta's leading newspaper, drew a contrast between Smith's inauguration, which attracted "Georgia's best sons and fairest daughters," and that of Rufus Bullock four years earlier, with its "immense concourse of negroes and its small attendance of whites." The

Constitution celebrated an end to Bullock's "dynasty of corrupt adventurers" and ended the article, "Thank God Georgia is redeemed." With Bullock now gone, the Republican Party faded into oblivion statewide. Atlanta did not elect another African American to the City Council until the twentieth century. The all-white City Council rejected efforts of African Americans to integrate the city's police force. Atlanta's cultural venues were either closed to blacks or segregated. Blacks could attend shows at DeGive's Opera House only if they sat in the colored gallery. They could not stay at the Kimball House. Employment opportunities were limited to low-paying menial work. One visitor to Atlanta who had complained in 1866 about a lack of African American domestic servants in a local hotel expressed satisfaction upon seeing black servants when she returned in 1874.[77]

The following year, Democrats celebrated another victory with the election of John B. Gordon to the U.S. Senate. Gordon had a personal profile that was tailor-made for the Redeemers. Originally from north Georgia, he moved to Atlanta in 1854 to practice law. During the war, Gordon raised his own company, the Raccoon Roughs, and quickly rose through the ranks as an officer, beginning the war as a captain and ending as a major general. No less a figure than Robert E. Lee expressed admiration for Gordon. After the war, Gordon resided at Sutherland, an estate located a few miles east of Atlanta. From this base, he helped to organize the Ku Klux Klan in Georgia to suppress the black vote. Often described as "tall and commanding," with dark hair and a smartly clipped mustache and beard, Gordon was frequently accompanied in public by his handsome wife, Fanny, who traveled with him during his wartime military campaigns and supported his postwar political aspirations. Together they made a striking couple. In 1868, Gordon began his political career when he ran for governor but lost to Rufus Bullock. Five years later, he won a Senate seat. For many Georgians, John B. Gordon personified the qualities of courage and sacrifice, for he had suffered multiple wounds at the battle of Antietam and thereafter bore a scar on his left cheek. At the same time, Georgians viewed him as a skilled and visionary political leader for the New South, who would help them liberate the South from federal control, allowing them to determine their fate without the interference of a black electorate.[78]

On January 17, 1873, Gordon delivered to the Georgia General Assembly an address that reinforced the principles of Redemption, emphasized the notion of the Confederacy having fought for honorable principles, and cast the South in the role of victim of an overreaching federal government. In a statement that would have played well to an audience at the outset of the Civil War, Gordon proclaimed that the patriots of 1776 fought the American Revolution to establish a series of "independent and sovereign States." By extension, Gordon implied that the South had fought for a similar lofty goal. His failure to mention slavery as a cause of the war signaled a new interpretation of the conflict whereby Gordon and other interpreters of the South's "Lost Cause" ignored slavery's role and replaced it with the abstract concept of states' rights. Without mentioning President Ulysses S. Grant by name, he acknowledged the Republican chief executive's reelection in November 1872, while also condemning the overreaching national government and a "solid wall of sectional prejudice built up by the war." Gordon turned next to the issue of the South's future. "What are we to do," he asked rhetorically, then answered the question. The best course for Georgia's future lay in economic development. Gordon wanted direct trade with European nations, with Georgia's ports at Savannah and Brunswick receiving "all the commodities of Europe." Gordon also advocated industrial development and efforts to attract immigrants from Europe. Finally, he suggested that the South establish ties with the West, since western people were the South's natural allies. In the postwar South, Gordon promised, Georgia could achieve "higher prosperity than ever before."[79]

Atlantans held a party at the Kimball House to celebrate Gordon's election. Few could have missed the symbolism, for the magnificent hotel built by a Republican Carpetbagger now provided the backdrop for a celebration of Democratic triumph. According to the *Atlanta Constitution*, prominent citizens packed the hotel's multistory galleries, including "stately matrons and gay and fascinating belles." When the band played "Dixie," the assembled guests "burst forth in applause." In his brief remarks, Gordon paid homage to the fellow Democrats he had defeated in the Senate election, including the venerable Alexander H. Stephens.[80]

Gordon said nothing about the matrons and belles who filled the Kimball House to honor him that night, yet a few days earlier the *Constitution* had printed an article about women in a different setting. The article focused on the woman suffrage movement, which had begun in upstate New York during the 1840s and gained new energy and purpose after the war, as northern advocates of rights for women gave speeches and drafted petitions to Congress demanding women's empowerment. Suffragists attracted public attention when the national Republican Party platform in 1872 promised to treat the subject with respect. After the election, the party quickly dropped the issue. The *Constitution* dismissed the notion of voting women as "tinsel and counterfeit" but acknowledged what it saw as a legitimate topic for discussion: women's economic place in the postwar period. Women needed greater employment opportunities—"more vocations," as the newspaper put it, beyond the agricultural pursuits that had sustained Georgia families for generations. Though the point was left unstated by the *Constitution*, its readers understood that women's plight resulted in large part from the war that killed so many of their fathers, husbands, brothers, and sons, and physically and emotionally incapacitated many others.[81]

Gordon's speech at the Kimball House made no reference to race relations. Although racial politics had preoccupied Atlanta's business elite since the end of the war, in their eyes, the topic lost its immediacy when the Redeemers took power. Yet nine days before the Kimball House reception, forty to fifty African Americans met at Atlanta City Hall to discuss the possibility of organizing a group to emigrate to the West. Throughout the South groups of "exodusters" held similar meetings to decide whether African Americans might find better economic opportunity and less racial prejudice outside of their states or region. Willis Holmes chaired the meeting, and Zac Rice served as secretary, both of them identified in the *Constitution* as African American. The meeting ended with passage of a resolution endorsing emigration to the West for "all the poor whites and negroes . . . as soon as practicable." This resolution prompted one African American to write to the *Constitution* warning potential emigrants to beware of attempts to manipulate them. George McKinney suggested that unethical recruiters seeking cheap labor hoped to lure black workers to the West, where they would end up "among strangers and without money or friends." McKinney believed that "we had best remain where we are known."[82]

In postemancipation Atlanta, African Americans made identifiable gains, including access to rudimentary public education, and, briefly, limited office-holding and the right to claim City Hall as a venue in which to hold public meetings. As time went on, they faced a future with minimal access to economic advancement and minimal access to the political sphere. Impoverished women of both races faced some of the same challenges. For members of Atlanta's Democratic Party and for successful businessmen attending the Kimball House reception, the future looked bright. For African Americans and for poor white women and their children, there were no easy answers.

10. Remembering and Forgetting

July 4, 1867: "The celebration of this day in Atlanta was surrendered almost entirely—if not *wholly* so—by our citizens to the negro population, who appeared upon our streets in a high state of enthusiasm in immense throngs from early morn to a late hour in the evening." So wrote a reporter for the *Atlanta Daily Intelligencer,* who also noted that white people "looked from their windows" but did not participate in the festivities, excepting a few white Republicans. Two months earlier, the same newspaper reported that a "large number" of white women gathered at City Cemetery to decorate the graves of Confederate soldiers. Women of the Atlanta Ladies Memorial Association began a tradition the previous year, one that involved assembling garlands and ceremonially laying them on the soldiers' graves at City Cemetery. In Atlanta, blacks held annual celebrations of freedom on the Fourth of July, and whites celebrated the Confederacy's Lost Cause on Confederate Memorial Day, April 26. A tradition of separate commemorations in Atlanta had begun, commemorations that reveal racial differences over the meaning of the Civil War. African Americans celebrated freedom and interpreted Atlanta's defeat and destruction by Union soldiers as part of a process that led to black liberation from bondage. White Atlantans celebrated the renewal of their city after its victimization by an invading army. Lost in white people's narrative of the war was the role that slavery played in causing it and the role that social conflict played within it.[1]

While Atlanta's white population continued to ignore the Fourth of July as they had during the war, African Americans used the holiday as an opportunity to celebrate freedom, equality, and liberation from slavery, and to organize politically in support of the Republican Party. On July 4, 1867, "a large assemblage" of African Americans met at City Hall. One of the morning's speakers was Amherst Stone, whose wife kept a secret Unionist diary during the war. Stone now supported the Republican Party in Savannah but journeyed to his former home in Atlanta to organize on behalf of the party. Tunis Campbell also spoke. As a black activist with the Republican Party in coastal Georgia, Campbell was beginning his political ascent in 1867. He was to be elected a delegate to the state constitutional convention and serve as state senator before Redemption ended his political career in the state. Representatives of Atlanta's five wards participated in the July 4 rally, each ward represented by a separate name and motto. The Third Ward's Lincoln Union Republican Club had the motto: "Our Emancipator. A Nation mourns his loss." The Fifth Ward's Saxton Union Republican Club held a banner that said, "Georgia's History: The Birth of Liberty, July 4th, '76, The Death of Slavery, July 4th '67." The day's festivities also included band music, reading of the Declaration of Independence, and a "grand pyrotechnic display." In his diary, Sam Richards complained that the "Glorious Fourth has been celebrated here today chiefly by a crowd of negroes . . . and renegade white men."[2]

After Reconstruction ended, July 4 celebrations became less political and more social in focus. Groups of "excursionists," sometimes several thousand in all, took trains to Atlanta, spent the day and returned home in the evening. On these occasions, they visited food booths near the depot that featured lunch items along with cold lemonade and watermelon. Local African Americans celebrated the Fourth with parades, sporting events, and barbecues in black neighborhoods and parks.[3]

Over time, celebrations of "Emancipation Day" on January 1 gained popularity among black Atlantans. While white people often spent January 1 observing the long-held tradition of calling on friends to mark the new year, black people marched in parades, sang, and celebrated the anniversary on which President Lincoln signed the Emancipation Proclamation. Because illiteracy remained an ongoing challenge in the black community, oral communication continued to be integrally important for disseminating information about the memory of the war and its legacy to future generations.

Emancipation Day celebrations generally culminated in a program held at the state capitol or in a local church, beginning with a benediction, followed by reading of the Emancipation Proclamation by a respected member of the community, speeches, and music. Addresses on these occasions emphasized a variety of themes. In 1890, at Lloyd Street Methodist church, the audience passed resolutions condemning the recent lynching of African Americans in Jesup, Georgia, and Barnwell, South Carolina. Additional resolutions called upon Atlanta's white churches and the "white press" to "denounce these outrages, in the name of the constitution of this state, and of the United States."[4]

Often the speeches emphasized racial uplift. In 1897, "every negro in Atlanta" attended the thirty-fourth anniversary of the Emancipation Proclamation, according to one account. Bishop Wesley Gaines, who had helped to found Atlanta's Morris Brown College for former slaves, offered the benediction, followed by choral music performed by students of another African American school in Atlanta, Clark University. President Richard R. Wright of Savannah State University gave a speech emphasizing the need for parents to raise their children with proper values so that they would live upright lives in adulthood. His argument mirrored that of Booker T. Washington, the influential president of Tuskegee Institute in Alabama, who advocated for black economic self-help. On the fortieth anniversary of the Emancipation Proclamation in 1903, a large gathering took place at Ebenezer Baptist Church. Reverend H. H. Proctor, pastor of the black First Congregational Church, gave a speech that emphasized the need for blacks to climb out of poverty. "One white man on Wall street could buy us out twice," he declared. Proctor urged members of the audience to work hard and acquire skills necessary to earn more money.[5]

For Atlanta's white population, Confederate Memorial Day became the occasion for reflection, remembrance of the dead, and interpreting the war that had devastated their state and region. When Jefferson Davis visited Atlanta on the way to his inauguration in 1861, he had spoken about southern economic independence, since the region's cotton "clothed the world," and about spreading southern boundaries to include parts of the Caribbean and northern Mexico. Implicit in his argument was the spread of slavery to these areas. After the war, white southerners, including Atlantans, ignored slavery's role, instead focusing on the abstract concept of states' rights as the war's central cause. Over time, they also began the process of reconciling with the North. As a result, the historian David Blight concluded, "Racial legacies, conflict itself, the bitter consequences of Reconstruction's failure to make good on the promises of emancipation . . . had been *seared clean* from the nation's master narrative."[6]

Gradually, white people resumed the celebration of July 4, with the Spanish-American War of 1898 providing the biggest inspiration. America's decision to declare war on Spain over the issue of Cuban independence led to an upsurge in patriotism throughout the United States. Southerners lined up to volunteer for service, and immense publicity accompanied the role of Confederate cavalryman Joe Wheeler, who became a major general of volunteers thirty years after his Civil War military career ended. The Spanish-American War began in April, and on July 4 white people turned out to celebrate in Atlanta, optimistic that the war would end in victory for the United States. "It has been many long years since the glorious anniversary of American independence has been so generally celebrated in the south," one reporter noted, and predicted, "henceforward a return of the day will be marked by a more earnest display of patriotism." Two years later, it was clear to the *Atlanta Constitution* that celebrations of the national birthday would be permanent fixtures among white Atlantans, for "we are now brethren of a united country." A parade, followed by patriotic orations, capped the festivities in 1900.[7]

Organizations of women dedicated to honoring the graves of Confederate men began in the Civil War's immediate aftermath; the Atlanta group was one of seventy such organizations that formed in subsequent years. Mary Williams of Columbus, Georgia, began the memorialization movement in Georgia with an appeal published in the *Columbus Times* during March 1866. Williams appealed to white women of the South to spend one day annually in collecting flowers and laying wreaths at "the graves of our martyred dead." Williams insisted that the tradition must be "handed down through time as a religious custom of the South."[8]

Many members of the Ladies Memorial Associations were the same middle- and upper-class women who volunteered as nurses and fund-raisers for the Confederacy during the war, and the ALMA's first members included Maria Westmoreland, Sallie Clayton, and Eugenia Goode Morgan, all veterans of benevolent work during the war. In the postwar period, educated, elite women in the North sought access to higher education, opportunities to earn money, and in some cases political rights, but southern white women felt constrained by tradition. The Ladies Memorial Associations offered an outlet for civic activism and leadership, but one that fell within the bounds of socially acceptable behavior.[9]

The war taught women about the perils of depending on men for protection; nonetheless, women risked social isolation if they chose postwar lifestyles that veered away from benevolent work and toward lives of independence. One example is provided by Maria Westmoreland, who struggled more than most Atlanta women to reconcile her understanding of traditional expectations with her ambition to attain public prominence. Westmoreland founded the Ladies' Soldiers' Relief Society in 1861 and also earned public attention as a playwright whose wartime works were performed on the stage in Atlanta. In 1871, Mrs. Westmoreland traveled to New York, accompanied by her husband, in order to meet with representatives of G. W. Carlton and Company, publishers of her forthcoming novel *Heart-Hungry*. A second novel, *Clifford Troupe,* came out the following year. In addition, she wrote articles for the *Atlanta Constitution* commenting on timely subjects relating to women's appropriate sphere, issues that were generating debate across the nation. Through the fictional voice of "Aunt Tabitha," dispensing advice to a younger female relative, Westmoreland condemned "free love," the scandalous notion of couples loving outside of marriage. She suggested that women's economic advancement would occur when they gained access to education, including admission to colleges and universities, and Westmoreland specifically advocated the admission of women to the University of Georgia. While suggesting that women were not yet ready to become voters, she left open the possibility of their enfranchisement by writing, "I do not doubt but that female suffrage will become a law sooner than either you or I expect."[10]

In the fall of 1873, Mrs. Westmoreland moved to New York for the winter in order to pursue her literary career. She took her children but not her husband, the surgeon and professor of medicine Willis Westmoreland, who remained in Atlanta. In addition to a series of articles she wrote for the *Atlanta Constitution* about life in Gotham, she lectured to audiences in northern cities on topics including women's educational opportunity and heroines in history. Press accounts praised Westmoreland's pleasing appearance, fine speaking voice, and presence in the North as a sign of sectional reconciliation. But like other southern women writers who struggled to earn acclaim in the postwar period, Westmoreland came to understand the limits of women's access to the public stage. She largely faded from view by the end of the 1870s. Although the two novels went through several editions, critics panned them, and speaking engagements appear to have dried up. Her marriage may have collapsed, for Maria did not attend her daughter's Atlanta wedding in 1882, and she is not buried next to Willis, who died a much-respected member of Atlanta's medical community in 1890. Maria died six years later.[11] As for Westmoreland's cause of winning access to higher education, women did not gain admission to the University of Georgia until 1918, two years before women won the right to vote nationally.

Atlanta's first celebration of Confederate Memorial Day occurred on April 29, 1866. After placing notices in Atlanta newspapers to alert the public, the women walked to City Cemetery and placed their floral tributes on the graves of the estimated four thousand soldiers. The Reverend Robert Quarterman Mallard offered a simple prayer. In subsequent years, Atlantans celebrated on April 26 (the anniversary of General Joseph E. Johnston's surrender of the last major Confederate army in the field) or May 10 (the death date of Stonewall Jackson). Often the date was determined by whether a suitable number of flowers had bloomed in time for the April date.[12]

Because the tradition of decorating Confederate graves began during the military occupation of the South, women's leadership role in these affairs was crucial, for their efforts could effectively hide the appearance of political intent. Women did not vote and allegedly did not have political views. No one wanted to reignite secession sentiment after the war, but many wanted to glorify the "Lost Cause" with its celebration of southern military efforts and the exclusion of slavery as a cause of the war. Some members privately opposed federal rule in the South. At a meeting of the ALMA in June 1866, Colonel Robert Alston addressed the group and charged it with honoring fallen men. He did not mention slavery as a cause of the war or women's conflicted feelings about Confederate nationalism during the war. Instead, Alston declared that southern soldiers had fought to preserve the Constitution "in its original purity." He praised Atlanta's women for bearing "cheerfully" the sacrifices that the war forced upon them. He also expressed his disgust with the "Radical majority" that "now rules our land" and hoped that "this march of fanaticism" could be stopped. The ALMA's official history reveals how successfully the organization dodged any appearance of interfering in politics. The U.S. military raised "no objection" to the work of the Memorial

Association. General George G. Meade even attended one of the Confederate Memorial Day ceremonies.[13]

In 1868, Fanny Gordon won election as president of the organization. Gordon's rise as a public figure corresponded with her husband's political ascent. Just as John B. Gordon became Atlanta's most important political symbol of Confederate history, his wife became Atlanta's premier symbol of female patriotism. Fanny Gordon made an excellent role model for Confederate womanhood. Married to John at age seventeen, she gave birth to six children in the next twenty-two years. Mrs. Gordon did not live in Atlanta during the war, choosing instead to travel with her husband during his military campaigns. Her personal sacrifice and her well-publicized nursing efforts following her husband's nearly fatal wounds in 1862 elevated her public image to that of model wife and Confederate heroine in Atlanta.[14]

Although Fanny Gordon wielded considerable influence within her family, her public role was that of helpmeet to her husband's career. Well into the twentieth century, newspaper and magazine stories celebrated the beautiful Fanny Gordon as an ideal woman. When she died at age ninety-three in 1931, one obituary included these words: "Mrs. Gordon was a noble exemplar of all those graces, qualities of character, and fidelities of conduct that the world has long associated with illustrative southern womanhood." Even after her death, Fanny's sterling reputation offered popular reading for women and girls, with articles like "The Bride of the Gray Chevalier" (1938) and "Mrs. John B. Gordon: Heroine of the Confederacy" (1955). By contrast, stories of Martha Winship and Maria Westmoreland were largely forgotten in Atlanta.[15]

The Atlanta Ladies Memorial Association needed a celebrity to help its fund-raising efforts, and it got one in Fanny Gordon. Although the group initially focused on cleaning up the cemetery and decorating graves each spring, the ALMA also took on a more ambitious goal: the disinterring of Confederate soldiers buried near the site of the battle of Atlanta and other locations around the city, to be reinterred at City Cemetery. Similar efforts to rebury soldiers took place across the South, fueled by anger at the federal government for appropriating money for seventy-four cemeteries in which to bury Union dead while refusing to make similar efforts to honor Confederates. To accomplish their goal, members needed to raise a significant amount of money, and the women worked assiduously to organize speeches, suppers, and socials, supplementing this fund-raising with additional money raising within individual churches.[16]

By 1869, the women had raised enough money to begin the process of disinterring soldiers. Since wood was scarce in Atlanta, members of the ALMA traveled to Stone Mountain to secure a source of material for constructing caskets, and supervised the removal of bodies within a ten-mile radius of the city. Most of the approximately three thousand dead they recovered had been buried in shallow trenches, in some cases as many as ninety bodies per grave. The total cost of the removal was $6,000.[17]

Building upon its success, the Ladies Memorial Association focused its efforts on fund-raising to erect a monument to Confederate dead in Atlanta, now numbering sixty-nine hundred. As fund-raising efforts commenced, the ALMA debated whether the monument belonged in the city center to honor Atlanta soldiers or at the cemetery to honor all Confederate casualties. A public meeting at City Hall and a secret ballot decided the issue in favor of the cemetery. Evidently, Mrs. Gordon disagreed with the decision, but as a traditional southern woman, she protested the vote by resigning as president rather than by articulating her position before a public audience. Mary Cobb Johnson replaced her as president and held the position until 1881. As the sister of two leading Confederates, General Howell Cobb and General T. R. R. Cobb, she bore an impeccable Confederate pedigree.[18]

The death of Robert E. Lee in October 1870 provided an opportunity for members of the Ladies Memorial Association to lay the cornerstone for their Atlanta monument at a time of public grieving for the Confederacy's most celebrated leader. As Lee's funeral procession was taking place in Lexington, Virginia, Atlantans paid their respects by closing businesses and factories and forming a procession at the capitol on Marietta Street, then marching to City Hall square. The procession included an estimated five thousand individuals, men of every "party, race, or color," according to the *Atlanta Constitution*. Among the group of marshals leading the procession was Roderick D. Badger, the African American dentist. Next in line were members of fraternal organizations, followed by students of Oglethorpe University, members of the press, the Atlanta Typographical Union, and Joseph E. Brown, who now served as chief justice of the state's Supreme Court. Members of the General Assembly came next, followed by Fulton County representatives, the mayor of Atlanta and city councilmen, firefighters, and private citizens, who brought up the rear. The crowd at City Hall was estimated at ten thousand and was believed to be the largest ever assembled in the Gate City.[19]

John B. Gordon was the featured speaker on that sunny, clear day. Gordon had known Lee well. He spoke movingly of Lee's personal traits of modesty and Christian service before turning to Lee's military role in the Civil War. "Lee was never really beaten," Gordon insisted, ignoring the battle of Gettysburg and other examples. "Lee could not be beaten! Overpowered, foiled in his efforts he might be, but never defeated until the props which supported him gave way." In this emerging narrative of Civil War defeat as explained by Gordon and other speakers in the former Confederate states, the South had not lost militarily; it had been overpowered by superior numbers of soldiers and better equipment. According to the *Atlanta Constitution*, Gordon "electrified" the audience. After the City Hall speech, members of the ALMA adjourned to the cemetery for the laying of the cornerstone. A sealed box inside contained a variety of objects, including a Confederate flag that was intended to be "never polluted by Yankee touch," a picture of General Lee, coins, newspapers, and the names and badges of the women in the Atlanta Ladies Memorial Association.[20]

In 1874, stonemasons completed the Confederate monument, and another public ceremony, an even grander one, occurred that April. This time, dignitaries rode in carriages, including members of the Ladies Memorial Association. Spectators traveled to the cemetery in the city's streetcars, one line of which terminated at City Cemetery. An estimated fifteen thousand individuals packed the cemetery that April day, including children from Atlanta's elementary and high schools, who helped to decorate the graves. In its coverage of the event, the *Atlanta Constitution* did not mention the participation of African Americans. The newspaper did print an illustration of the monument, which took the shape of an obelisk, an ancient symbol of eternal life. Constructed of Stone Mountain granite and three stories high, the monument bore the words "Our Confederate Dead." Members of the ALMA decorated the statue with a cross made of evergreens interwoven with flowers. Below were the names of Lee, Jackson, and then two illustrious Georgians who died in the war: Francis Bartow of Savannah, killed at the first battle of Manassas, and T. R. R. Cobb of Athens, who died at the battle of Fredericksburg. Less than a decade after the end of the war, memories of the once-celebrated John Hunt Morgan had grown dim. Morgan's ambush and death following a lackluster military campaign consigned him to obscurity in postwar Atlanta.[21]

Over the years, walking to the cemetery gave way to riding in carriages and streetcars, and later in automobiles, but annual pilgrimages to City

Cemetery for Confederate Memorial Day remained a fixture in Atlanta. In the 1890s, women of Atlanta raised funds again to unveil an enormous monument commemorating the three thousand unidentified Confederate soldiers buried at Oakland. They called the work the Lion of Atlanta and modeled it after a similar statue in Lucerne, Switzerland, dedicated to the memory of Swiss Guards who had tried to defend the life of Marie Antoinette. Atlanta's version features a wounded lion lying on a Confederate flag, with "Unknown Confederate Dead" chiseled on its base.[22]

Groups of Confederate veterans took part in the ceremonies on April 26, 1894, including the Sons of Confederate Veterans and members of the Gate City Guard. Once the city's favorite military unit, the Gate City Guard had disbanded after its rout and the deaths of members in western Virginia during 1861. The Guard reorganized after the war, and fifty members, once again clad in "handsome uniforms," made up part of the procession. No mention was made of the Guard's inglorious past.[23]

During the 1894 ceremony, Henry H. Carlton, a Confederate veteran and U.S. congressman from Athens, addressed the crowd on the topic of the ALMA's efforts over the previous thirty years, including the memorialization of unknown Confederate dead and the organization's efforts to honor individual soldiers buried at the cemetery by replacing their rotting wooden headstones with marble ones. Carlton also delved into the politically sensitive issue of Confederate President Jefferson Davis. Following the war, Davis had been imprisoned for two years without being tried, an emotional issue for many white southerners. By the 1890s, Davis had come to personify the suffering that all Confederate southerners believed they had endured in the postwar period, and Carlton cited Davis's "cruel imprisonment at Fortress Monroe, simply in order to break the proud spirit of our southern people." When Carlton finished his speech, ALMA President Fannie Milledge gave the signal to unveil the monument, cannons delivered a thirteen-gun salute, and a band played "Dixie." The assembled crowd cheered and applauded for several minutes.[24]

By 1894, many members of Atlanta's wartime generation had already died. James Calhoun, Atlanta's mayor from 1862 to 1866, died in 1875, one year after the unveiling of the Confederate obelisk. Calhoun is buried in the oldest part of the cemetery, known as the Original Six Acres. His tombstone correctly identifies him as a "faithful lawyer" and an "honorable public man." In life, he was far more than that, a voice of political moderation amid the chaos of wartime Atlanta.

Over the ensuing decades, Atlanta's other wartime civilians died and were buried at City Cemetery, renamed Oakland Cemetery in the 1870s. Today, Confederate monuments dominate the cemetery, along with row after row of identical tombstones for the thousands of individual Confederate soldiers buried during the war. Collectively, they remind modern visitors of the nearly incomprehensible human cost of the Civil War.[25] In keeping with their central roles in postwar commemoration, General John B. Gordon and his beloved Fanny are interred near the obelisk and the Lion. Although Confederate memorials and the grave of Margaret Mitchell draw the greatest public interest today, the graves of Atlanta's wartime civilians also tell an important part of the city's story.

John Neal lived until 1886, a few months before his ninetieth birthday, and was buried in the Original Six Acres. Like most men of wealth buried at Oakland, Neal has a large marker, this one engraved with a quotation attesting to his good name. Neal supported the Confederacy unwaveringly and sent two of his sons to fight in the war. The Neal family, like so many others, suffered terrible loss in wartime. Both Neal sons died in the war's final months, A.J. in the trenches around Atlanta in August 1864 and James in the final weeks of the war in North Carolina. The grieving parents selected a horseshoe-shaped double marker for these sons, uniting them with a funerary symbol normally used for married couples.[26]

Many of Atlanta's entrepreneurs built themselves fine monuments and mausoleums that attest to their financial success in life. Richard Peters died in 1889. To preserve a record of his accomplishments, he dictated his memoirs to his daughter Nellie Peters Black, who became an important Atlantan in her own right as a reformer and clubwoman. Peters purchased six plots in one corner of the Original Six Acres to ensure that members of his family would hold a prominent place in the cemetery just as they had held prominent places in city life during the nineteenth century. Richard Peters was involved in every important milestone in Atlanta's wartime and postwar history, from his decision to cast his lot with secessionists in 1860, to his profits from the sale of a steam engine to the Confederate government, and finally to his postwar role in rebuilding the city and creating its streetcar system.

Wealthy Confederate civilians are not the only ones who built tombstones to match their importance; those with less enthusiasm for the Lost Cause also left monuments. Bell Tower Ridge is located in the center of the cemetery on its highest ground. Because of its beautiful views, families found

Bell Tower Ridge the most desirable property on which to purchase burial plots after the war.[27] Nedom Angier and William Markham chose side-by-side burial plots for themselves and their families, separated only by a small path. Unionists before and during the war and Republicans after, they managed to both endure and prosper in the postwar period. Their story is also part of Atlanta's Civil War legacy.

John C. Peck is buried in the section of Oakland called Hogpen Corner because the land was farmed before it was used for burials.[28] Peck lived until 1906. Befitting his profession as a builder and his success as a contractor, Peck or his descendants constructed a fine mausoleum to honor him for eternity. Embellished with elaborate wrought-iron doors on the outside and a lovely stained-glass window with his initials J.C.P. on the inside, the mausoleum offers no clues about Peck's constantly shifting loyalties in the war.

East of the Confederate monuments at Oakland is the area known as Jewish Flat. Atlanta's small prewar and wartime Jewish population buried its dead within an area purchased for their use by David Mayer, president of the Hebrew Benevolent Association, in the Original Six Acres. In the 1870s, the city's growing Jewish population needed additional space and purchased land in the southern section of the cemetery.[29]

The African American Grounds are located at the northeast end of the cemetery. Slaves buried before and during the war in the Slave Square, part of the Original Six Acres, were exhumed and reinterred after the war in a vast stretch of the cemetery designated for poor people buried at city expense. Slave Square was replotted for white burials. Somewhere in the Potters' Field section of the African American Grounds is the grave of Bill, the last known slave to be buried in the cemetery. The graves of men, women, and children from the slave yard of Robert Crawford who died of disease during the war are also there, and so are many thousands of other African Americans. One of them is Robert Webster, who to the end of his days insisted that he was the son of Senator Daniel Webster.[30] But there are also monuments located in the African American Grounds, including the tombstone of Roderick D. Badger, who died in 1890. In the 1850s, Badger defended himself against efforts of white dentists to shut down his practice. In the 1860s, the sign was torn from his office and he prevailed again, determined to practice his profession. At Oakland, his tombstone proclaims to all visitors that he was "Dr. Roderick D. Badger."

Many children died during the war, but diarist Carrie Berry survived and lived until 1921; her grave in the Original Six Acres brings us back to the oldest part of the cemetery. The diary that Carrie kept as a ten-year-old amazes modern readers with its clarity and insight. Ten years after the war ended, Carrie married William Macon Crumley. Like his wife, he had witnessed remarkable scenes in the war, for he enlisted in the Confederate Army at the age of fourteen and served three years as a courier for General Joseph B. Kershaw. Sadly, Carrie and William's son lived through the horrors of another conflict, the twentieth century's first deadly world war. William Gregg Crumley, a graduate of Georgia Tech and the Atlanta College of Physicians and Surgeons, volunteered with the British and later the American Army, serving at hospitals in England, France, and Belgium. Returning home to visit his parents in December 1915, he told a local newspaper reporter, "Sherman didn't have the proper word[s] to describe war," then portrayed the horrifying scenes he witnessed of soldiers killed or severely injured by attacks of chlorine gas. Regardless of the danger, Dr. Crumley returned to the field and was himself the victim of a gas attack at Flanders in 1916. He never fully recovered his health. In 1924 he committed suicide, a tragedy that generated front page news in Atlanta. William's siblings buried him next to their parents at Oakland.[31]

Today, the modern city of Atlanta and the Civil War meet at Oakland Cemetery. Heritage groups continue to honor Confederate soldiers, often gathering around monuments that have drawn visitors since 1870. But Atlanta has also moved on. In one corner of the previously all-white Original Six Acres, Atlanta's first black mayor is buried. Maynard Jackson, the great-grandson of slaves, was elected in 1973 and served three terms. His election resulted from changing demographics in the city, a shifting political land-scape, and the Civil War's liberation of his ancestors from bondage. When Jackson died in 2003, the city offered his family a burial plot in the Original Six Acres, an offer that would not have been made to the Jackson family when Maynard Jackson Sr. died in 1953. Reflecting racial change, Oakland is now an integrated cemetery and one where visitors can take tours of both the historic Confederate sites and the historic African American Grounds. Although today's visitors to Oakland often find it a peaceful refuge, a bustling metropolis lies just outside its gates. Looking north and west, one sees the modern skyline of Atlanta, with office towers, hotels, hospitals, and college campuses. In addition to slavery's abolition, urban Atlanta is part of the "changing wind" that transformed the city during the Civil War.

Notes

ABBREVIATIONS

AC	*Atlanta Constitution*
ADI	*Atlanta Daily Intelligencer*
AHA	Atlanta Hospital Association
AHC	Atlanta History Center, Kenan Research Center
ALMA	Atlanta Ladies Memorial Association
ANDE	*Atlanta New Daily Era*
AWI	*Atlanta Weekly Intelligencer*
Breman	Breman Jewish Heritage and Holocaust Museum, Atlanta, Ida Pearle and Joseph Cuba Archives and Genealogy Center
CR	*Confederate Records of the State of Georgia*, 6 vols., ed. Allen D. Candler (Atlanta: Chas. P. Byrd, 1909)
DHC	DeKalb History Center, Decatur, Ga.
Duke	Duke University, Durham, N.C., David M. Rubenstein Rare Book and Manuscript Library
ECU	East Carolina University, Greenville, N.C., J. Y. Joyner Library
EMU	Emory University, Decatur, Ga., Manuscript, Archives, and Rare Book Library
GCG	*Gate City Guardian*, Atlanta
GDAH	Georgia Division of Archives and History, Morrow, Ga.
LC	Library of Congress, Washington, D.C., Manuscript Division
LSRS	Ladies' Soldiers' Relief Society, Atlanta
MA	*Memphis Appeal*, Atlanta (1863–64)

NA   National Archives, Washington, D.C.
OR   *The War of the Rebellion: A Compilation of the Official Records of the*
              Union and Confederate Armies (Washington, D.C.: Government
              Printing Office, 1880–1901)
RG   Record Group
SC   *Southern Confederacy,* Atlanta
UGA   University of Georgia, Athens, Hargrett Rare Book and
              Manuscript Library
UNC   University of North Carolina, Chapel Hill, Southern Historical
              Collection, Wilson Library
WML   Washington Memorial Library, Macon, Ga.

PROLOGUE

1. Sarah Huff, *My 80 Years in Atlanta* (Atlanta: n.p., 1937), 55; Gaines
M. Foster, *Ghosts of the Confederacy: Defeat, the Lost Cause, and the Emergence of
the New South 1865–1913* (New York: Oxford University Press, 1987), 39–40;
Ren Davis and Helen Davis, *Atlanta's Oakland Cemetery: An Illustrated History
and Guide* (Athens: University of Georgia Press, 2012), 4, 105.

2. Georgia Historical Society, Historic Marker, "Burning of Atlanta."

3. Oakland Cemetery Alphabetical List of Interments, AHC.

4. Samuel P. Richards, *Sam Richards's Civil War Diary: A Chronicle of the
Atlanta Home Front,* ed. Wendy Hamand Venet (Athens: University of Georgia
Press, 2009).

5. Lin Family Papers, AHC.

6. Oakland Cemetery Collection, AHC.

7. Jim Cullen, *The Civil War in Popular Culture: A Reusable Past*
(Washington, D.C.: Smithsonian Institution Press, 1995), 67.

8. Margaret Mitchell, *Gone with the Wind* (New York: Scribner, 1964);
Darden Asbury Pyron, *Southern Daughter: The Life of Margaret Mitchell* (New
York: Oxford University Press, 1991), 310–11.

1. GATE CITY TO THE SOUTH

1. Stephen H. Long quoted by Richard Peters in *Richard Peters, His
Ancestors and Descendants, 1810–1889,* ed. and comp. Nellie Peters Black (Atlanta:
Foote and Davies, 1904), 25; James Michael Russell, *Atlanta, 1847–1890: City
Building in the Old South and the New* (Baton Rouge: Louisiana State University
Press, 1988), 14–28; Timothy J. Crimmins, "The Atlanta Palimpsest: Stripping
Away the Layers of the Past," *Atlanta Historical Journal* 26 (1982): 13–32; Thomas

H. Martin, *Atlanta and Its Builders: A Comprehensive History of the Gate City of the South*, 2 vols. (Atlanta: Century Memorial, 1902), 1: 37.

2. Franklin M. Garrett, *Atlanta and Environs: A Chronicle of Its People and Events*, 2 vols. (Athens: University of Georgia Press, 1954), 1: 236–37, 250–53; *Pioneer Citizens' History of Atlanta, 1833–1902* (Atlanta: Byrd, 1902), 136–37; Russell, *Atlanta, 1847–1890*, 27.

3. Garrett, *Atlanta and Environs*, 1: 247–48, 268–71, 295–96, 334; Martin, *Atlanta and Its Builders*, 1: 114–21; Donald S. Hart, "The Mood of Atlanta, 1850–1861," *Atlanta Historical Bulletin* 15 (Summer 1970): 24.

4. Russell, *Atlanta, 1847–1890*, 46–49; *Pioneer Citizens' History of Atlanta*, 116–19; *Atlanta American*, April 16, 1922, in Lucian Lamar Knight Scrapbook, vol. 23, 117, GDAH.

5. Russell, *Atlanta, 1847–1890*, 40–44; Martin, *Atlanta and Its Builders*, 1: 100, 134.

6. Typescript reminiscences of Lucy Hull Baldwin, UNC; Russell, *Atlanta, 1847–1890*, 40–42.

7. Clarence L. Mohr, *On the Threshold of Freedom: Masters and Slaves in Civil War Georgia* (Athens: University of Georgia Press, 1986), 190–94; Watson W. Jennison, *Cultivating Race: The Expansion of Slavery in Georgia, 1750–1860* (Lexington: University of Kentucky Press, 2012), 270; Russell, *Atlanta, 1847–1890*, 71.

8. Patrick H. Calhoun, "Reminiscences of Patrick H. Calhoun," *Atlanta Historical Bulletin* 1 (April 1931): 42–43; Richard C. Wade, *Slavery in the Cities: The South, 1820–1860* (New York: Oxford University Press, 1964), 143–46.

9. Henry Ossian Flipper, *The Colored Cadet at West Point: An Autobiography* (New York: H. Lee, 1878), 7–10; E. P. Ponder to William Ponder, April 4, 1850, William G. Ponder Papers, GDAH.

10. Flipper, *The Colored Cadet at West Point*, 7–10; Jonathan D. Martin, *Divided Mastery: Slave Hiring in the American South* (Cambridge: Harvard University Press, 2004), 161–87. The practice of self-hiring also is discussed in David E. Paterson, "Slavery, Slaves, and Cash in a Georgia Village, 1825–1865," *Journal of Southern History* 75 (2009): 879–930.

11. *Williams' Atlanta Directory, City Guide, and Business Mirror* (Atlanta: Lynch, 1859); *AWI*, December 2, 1854; Frederic Bancroft, *Slave-Trading in the Old South* (Baltimore: J. H. Furst, 1931), 248.

12. Atlanta City Council minutes, September 1 and 11, 1854, AHC.

13. Atlanta City Council minutes, July 15, 1859, AHC; *Williams' Atlanta Directory*, misidentifies Badger's first name as Ralph; Henry S. Robinson, "Robert

and Roderick Badger, Pioneer Dentists," *Negro History Bulletin* 24 (January 1961): 77.

14. Atlanta City Council minutes, September 1 and 11, 1854, June 6, 1856, AHC. The *Southern Confederacy* newspaper reprinted the 1859 ordinance during the Civil War. See, for example, April 15, 1863. Jennison, *Cultivating Race*, 307–8, reports twenty-five free blacks in 1860.

15. Sarah Massey reminiscences in *Atlanta Journal*, December 5, 1909; Cornelia Venable reminiscences ibid., August 1, 1909; Russell, *Atlanta, 1847–1890*, 29; Crimmins, "Atlanta Palimpsest," 15–26.

16. Russell, *Atlanta, 1847–1890*, 73–74; Garrett, *Atlanta and Environs*, 1: 206.

17. Atlanta City Council minutes, July 28, August 4, 1854, AHC; Martin, *Atlanta and Its Builders*, 1: 115, 126; Garrett, *Atlanta and Environs*, 1: 265–66, 372–73, 396–97, 437; Russell, *Atlanta, 1847–1890*, 73–74.

18. In a reminiscence published in the *Atlanta Journal*, March 7, 1909, Lula Cozart Harralson recalled the fine homes and churches and the overall prosperity of 1850s Atlanta; Martin, *Atlanta and Its Builders*, 1: 115–18; Garrett, *Atlanta and Environs*, 1: 361–70; Atlanta City Council minutes, September 1, December 19, 1854, AHC.

19. *ADI*, March 1, 1855; Garrett, *Atlanta and Environs*, 1: 382.

20. Russell, *Atlanta, 1847–1890*, 49–53; *Pioneer Citizens' History of Atlanta*, 230–32.

21. *ADI*, December 2 and December 30, 1854; Garrett, *Atlanta and Environs*, 1: 375.

22. Garrett, *Atlanta and Environs*, 1: 375–77. Atlanta City Council minutes mention Dr. James F. Alexander and Dr. Willis Westmoreland along with John Westmoreland as founders. See September 22, November 11, November 17, 1854, AHC.

23. *ADI*, November 11, 25, December 16, 1854, and July 25, 1860 (restaurant); *AC*, April 8, 1894.

24. Garrett, *Atlanta and Environs*, 1: 509.

25. George C. Lawson to My dear Wife, November 12, 1864, George C. Lawson Collection, AHC.

2. UNIONISM AND SECESSIONISM IN THE GATE CITY

1. William J. Cooper, *We Have the War upon Us: The Onset of the Civil War, November 1860–April 1861* (New York: Knopf, 2012), xiv, 22.

2. Donald S. Hart, "The Mood of Atlanta 1850–61," *Atlanta Historical Bulletin* 15 (Summer 1970): 22; Robert Gibbons, "Life at the Crossroads of the

Confederacy: Atlanta, 1861–1865," *Atlanta Historical Journal* 23 (Summer 1979): 13; Ralph Benjamin Singer, Jr., "Confederate Atlanta," Ph.D. diss., University of Georgia, 1973, 34.

3. Gartrell talked about his legal career in an interview with Charles Lanham in 1858. See Georgia Congressional Correspondence, UGA. See also Supreme Court, State of Georgia certificate of admission to the bar for Gartrell, May 4, 1848, Lucius J. Gartrell Papers, UGA; Samuel Joseph Lewis, Jr., "The Life of Lucius Jeremiah Gartrell," M.A. thesis, University of Georgia, 1947, 3–7, 35–38; *ADI*, March 2, 1861; Stephanie McCurry, *Confederate Reckoning: Power and Politics in the Civil War South* (Cambridge: Harvard University Press, 2010), 11.

4. *AWI*, October 28, 1854; *ADI*, February 14, 1858.

5. *American Colonization Society v. Lucius J. Gartrell*, 23 Ga. 448 (1857); Robert Toombs to Alexander H. Stephens, August 15, 1857, in *The Correspondence of Robert Toombs, Alexander H. Stephens, and Howell Cobb*, ed. Ulrich Bonnell Phillips (1913; rpt. New York: Da Capo, 1970), 420. Census slave schedules show Gartrell with thirteen slaves in 1850 and twenty-seven in 1860; U.S. Federal Census, 1850, Wilkes Co., and 1860, Fulton Co., Ga.

6. Lucius J. Gartrell, "Speech of Hon. L. J. Gartrell, of Georgia, in the Defence of Slavery and the South, Delivered in the House of Representatives, January 25, 1858," *Congressional Globe*, part I, I session, 35 Congress, 399; Lucius J. Gartrell, "The Dangers of Black-Republicanism, and the Duty of the South" (n.p.: Lemuel Towers, 1860).

7. Gartrell, "The Dangers of Black-Republicanism."

8. *ADI*, February 6, 1860. The House eventually elected William Pennington as speaker.

9. *Pioneer Citizens' History of Atlanta, 1833–1902* (Atlanta: Byrd, 1902), 289–91; James Calhoun quoted in Marc Wortman, *The Bonfire: The Siege and Burning of Atlanta* (New York: Public Affairs, 2009), 96.

10. *Pioneer Citizens' History of Atlanta*, 313–15; First Presbyterian Church, Atlanta, Membership Records and Minutes of Session, 1858–1874, AHC; Markham quoted in Thomas G. Dyer, *Secret Yankees: The Unionist Circle in Confederate Atlanta* (Baltimore: Johns Hopkins University Press, 1999), 4–5, 14–15, 45.

11. *ADI*, January 16 and February 6, 1860; Dyer, *Secret Yankees*, 30–33.

12. *ADI*, February 6, April 13 and 14, 1860.

13. Ibid., May 5, 1860.

14. Ibid., May 11 and 21, 1860.

15. *ADI* printed Gartrell's speech over two days, July 17–18, 1860.

16. Ibid., May 21, 1860.

17. *Southern Christian Advocate* quoted in *ADI*, March 10, 1860; Oakland Cemetery Collection, AHC.

18. Harrison Berry, *Slavery and Abolition, as Viewed by a Georgia Slave* (Atlanta: Franklin, 1861), iv. Regarding the argument about northern workers, see Kenneth S. Greenberg, *Honor and Slavery* (Princeton: Princeton University Press, 1996), 85–86.

19. Berry, *Slavery and Abolition*, 9, 19, 27, 37.

20. Ibid., iv–viii. Henry C. Hornady became pastor of First Baptist Church of Atlanta in 1858; *Pioneer Citizens' History of Atlanta*, 331–32; Elizabeth Fox-Genovese and Eugene D. Genovese, *The Mind of the Master Class: History and Faith in the Southern Slaveholders' Worldview* (Cambridge: Cambridge University Press, 2005), 490–91.

21. Berry, *Slavery and Abolition*, 10, 13, 15–16, 28; *ADI*, May 22, 1861; Clarence L. Mohr, "Harrison Berry: A Black Pamphleteer in Georgia during Slavery and Freedom," *Georgia Historical Quarterly* 67 (Summer 1983): 189–205.

22. *ADI*, October 19, 1860, November 1, 1860.

23. William W. Freehling, *The Road to Disunion: Secessionists Triumphant, 1854–1861* (New York: Oxford University Press, 2007), 429.

24. Alexander H. Stephens to J. Henley Smith, August 30, September 12, September 30, and October 13, 1860, in Phillips, *Correspondence*, 493, 496, 500–502; *New York Herald*, September 29, 1860; Thomas E. Schott, *Alexander H. Stephens of Georgia: A Biography* (Baton Rouge: Louisiana State University Press, 1988), 298–301.

25. *ADI*, October 31, 1860, and November 2, 1860; Franklin M. Garrett, *Atlanta and Environs: A Chronicle of Its People and Events*, 2 vols. (Athens: University of Georgia Press, 1954), 1: 474; James L. Huston, *Stephen A. Douglas and the Dilemmas of Democratic Equality* (New York: Rowman and Littlefield, 2007), 176–77.

26. *ADI*, November 7, 1860.

27. Frank Towers, *The Urban South and the Coming of the Civil War* (Charlottesville: University of Virginia Press, 2004), 159, 196, 208–9; Jacqueline Jones, *Saving Savannah: The City and the Civil War* (New York: Knopf, 2008), 122–23; Anthony Gene Carey, *Parties, Slavery, and the Union in Antebellum Georgia* (Athens: University of Georgia Press, 1997), 228–29.

28. *ADI*, November 8, 1860 (two stories); Dyer, *Secret Yankees*, 29, 36–37; Testimony of Nedom L. Angier, U.S. Claims Commission Approved Claims,

1871–1880, RG 217, NA. After the war, the Southern Claims Commission compensated southern Unionists for property used by the U.S. government in wartime.

29. Diary of Jennie Lines, November 8, 20, and 27, 1860, UGA. Jennie's diary was published as *To Raise Myself a Little: The Diaries and Letters of Jennie, a Georgia Teacher, 1851–1886,* ed. Thomas Dyer (Athens: University of Georgia Press, 1982).

30. *ADI,* November 12, 1860; Diary of Jennie Lines, December 27, 1860, UGA.

31. Diary of Jennie Lines, November 20, 1860, UGA; Atlanta City Council minutes, January 11 and 23, 1861, AHC.

32. Freehling, *The Road to Disunion,* 22–24.

33. Gartrell, "The Dangers of Black-Republicanism"; *ADI,* November 1 and 8, 1860.

34. *GCG,* February 11, 1861. Regarding New Orleans, Frank Towers noted, "White supremacy, sectional loyalty, and the promise of a better economy under the Confederacy—appealed to wage-earning voters." See *The Urban South and the Coming of the Civil War,* 200.

35. Sidney Root, "Memorandum of My Life," 1–6, AHC.

36. Ibid., 6; Sven Beckert, "Emancipation and Empire: Reconstructing the Worldwide Web of Cotton Production in the Age of the American Civil War," *American Historical Review* 109 (2004): 1416.

37. *Richard Peters, His Ancestors and Descendants, 1810–1889,* ed. and comp. Nellie Peters Black (Atlanta: Foote and Davies, 1904), 7–14, 19–29.

38. Samuel P. Richards, *Sam Richards's Civil War Diary: A Chronicle of the Atlanta Home Front,* ed. Wendy Hamand Venet (Athens: University of Georgia Press, 2009), 38–39 (December 8, 1860).

39. *ADI,* November 6 and 10, 1860. Historian Stephanie McCurry called the Minute Men's activism "tactically brilliant." See *Confederate Reckoning,* 47–49.

40. *ADI,* November 13 and 30, 1860.

41. Ibid., November 3, 1860.

42. Ibid., November 19, 1860; Gartrell, "The Dangers of Black-Republicanism."

43. *ADI,* December 3, 6, and 10, 1860.

44. William W. Freehling and Craig M. Simpson, eds., *Secession Debated: Georgia's Showdown in 1860* (New York: Oxford University Press, 1992), vii–xxi, 56, 148, 158.

45. Ibid.; McCurry, *Confederate Reckoning,* 55–59; Elizabeth R. Varon, *Disunion! The Coming of the American Civil War, 1789–1859* (Chapel Hill: University of North Carolina Press, 2008), 294.

46. *ADI*, December 12, 1860.

47. Ibid., December 22, 24, 27, and 31, 1860.

48. Ibid., January 2 and 4, 1861; Douglas telegram in Ulrich Bonnell Phillips, *The Life of Robert Toombs* (New York: Macmillan, 1913), 211; Michael P. Johnson, "A New Look at the Popular Vote for Delegates to the Georgia Secession Convention," *Georgia Historical Quarterly* 56 (1972): 257–75; Carey, *Parties, Slavery, and the Union*, 234–35.

49. Michael P. Johnson, *Toward a Patriarchal Republic: The Secession of Georgia* (Baton Rouge: Louisiana State University Press, 1977), 108–9, 113–17.

50. Ibid.; Carey, *Parties, Slavery, and the Union*, 238; Freehling, *The Road to Disunion*, 484; Cooper, *We Have the War upon Us*, 129.

51. *ADI*, January 23 and 25, 1861.

52. Ibid., January 17 and 26, 1861; Warren Campbell to My Dear Father, April 19, 1861, Henry S. Campbell Papers, EMU.

53. *ADI*, January 29, 1861; Warren Campbell to father, October 1, 1861, Henry S. Campbell Papers, EMU. Whether he joined or was drafted, Campbell ended up a private in Company F (Hall County, Ga., Hall Light Guards), 43rd Georgia Regiment, from September 4, 1862, until May 12, 1865. He survived the war and died in 1904; Lillian Henderson, ed., *Roster of Confederate Soldiers of Georgia, 1861–1865*, 6 vols. (Hapeville, Ga.: Longino and Porter, 1959), 4: 674.

54. Atlanta City Council minutes, January 11, February 15, 1861, AHC; *GCG*, February 21, 1861.

55. Diary of Jennie Lines, December 3 and 29, 1860, UGA.

3. THE RISE OF A CONFEDERATE CITY

1. Anne Sarah Rubin, *A Shattered Nation: The Rise and Fall of the Confederacy, 1861–1868* (Chapel Hill: University of North Carolina Press, 2005), 11.

2. Sidney Root, "Memorandum of My Life," 6, AHC; William J. Cooper, Jr., *Jefferson Davis, American* (New York: Knopf, 2000), 160, 275.

3. *GCG*, February 16, 1861; *ADI*, February 18, 1861; William J. Cooper, *We Have the War upon Us: The Onset of the Civil War, November 1860–April 1861* (New York: Knopf, 2012), 189.

4. Jacqueline Jones, *Saving Savannah: The City and the Civil War* (New York: Knopf, 2008), 128; Root, "Memorandum of My Life," 7, AHC. Stephens told Root that fifty thousand volunteers should be able to repel any federal force sent against the South; Atlanta City Council minutes, March 11, 1861, AHC; *SC*, March 13, 1861; *ADI*, March 12, 1861.

5. Ralph Benjamin Singer, Jr., "Confederate Atlanta," Ph.D. diss., University of Georgia, 1973, 70–72. Joseph Allan Frank and George A. Reaves analyze a kind of social contract between volunteers and their local communities in *Seeing the Elephant: Raw Recruits at the Battle of Shiloh* (Urbana: University of Illinois Press, 2003), 54–57.

6. *ADI*, April 1 and 2, 1861; Henry Clay Fairman, *Chronicles of the Old Guard of the Gate City Guard, Atlanta, Georgia, 1858–1915* (1915; rpt. Easley, S.C.: Southern Historical Press, 1986), 7–13.

7. *Pioneer Citizens' History of Atlanta, 1833–1902* (Atlanta: Byrd, 1902), 364–65; Fairman, *Chronicles*, 8, 12–13.

8. *SC*, April 1, 1861; *ADI*, April 2, 1861; Fairman, *Chronicles*, 19–26; *Pioneer Citizens' History of Atlanta*, 160–61; Stephanie McCurry, *Confederate Reckoning: Power and Politics in the Civil War South* (Cambridge: Harvard University Press, 2010), 88–96; George C. Rable, *Civil Wars: Women and the Crisis of Southern Nationalism* (Urbana: University of Illinois Press, 1989), 50. See also Cornelius Hanleiter Papers, AHC.

9. Sarah Conley Clayton, *Requiem for a Lost City: A Memoir of Civil War Atlanta and the Old South*, ed. Robert Scott Davis (Macon, Ga.: Mercer University Press, 1999), 42–43; *SC*, April 1, 1861; *ADI*, April 2, 1861.

10. *SC*, April 13, 1861.

11. Typescript reminiscences of Sarah Massey, Atlanta Women's Pioneer Society, AHC, and also in *Atlanta Journal*, December 5, 1909; Jones, *Saving Savannah*, 130–31.

12. Sarah Huff, *My 80 Years in Atlanta* (Atlanta: n.p., 1937), 7–9.

13. *GCG*, February 23, 1861.

14. *ADI*, April 16 and 30, 1861.

15. *SC*, May 23, 1861; Rubin, *A Shattered Nation*, 14–15; Benedict Anderson, *Imagined Communities: Reflections on the Origins and Spread of Nationalism*, rev. ed. (New York: Verso, 2006), 37–46.

16. *ADI*, May 25, 1861. See April 24, 1861, for a discussion of the Free Trade Rifles.

17. William C. Davis, *Rhett: The Turbulent Life and Times of a Fire-Eater* (Columbia: University of South Carolina Press, 2001), 406, 434, 445, 464; William C. Davis, ed., *A Fire-Eater Remembers: The Confederate Memoir of Robert Barnwell Rhett* (Columbia: University of South Carolina Press, 2000), 32–46.

18. *ADI*, March 14 and March 21, 1861; Howard Jones, *Union in Peril: The Crisis over British Intervention in the Civil War* (Chapel Hill: University of North Carolina Press, 1992), 27–29; D. P. Crook, *The North, the South, and the Powers,*

1861–1865 (New York: Wiley, 1974), 27–28; William Lowndes Yancey to Benjamin C. Yancey, July 15 and August 15, 1861, Benjamin C. Yancey Papers, UNC.

19. *SC,* March 4, 6, and 19, 1861.

20. *ADI,* March 26 and 28, 1861. The *Daily Intelligencer* further suggested that the British, French, and Spanish would break the northern blockade because of the tariff. See June 11, 1861.

21. Ibid., February 15 and March 23, 1861; *Richmond Dispatch* quoted in *GCG,* March 1, 1861.

22. *ADI,* March 22, 1861.

23. Ibid., April 27, 1861; Daniel Hamilton, "The Confederate Sequestration Act," *Civil War History* 52 (2006): 373–408.

24. *ADI,* May 18 and June 15, 1861; Emory M. Thomas, *The Confederate State of Richmond: A Biography of the Capital* (Austin: University of Texas Press, 1971), 22–23.

25. *ADI,* June 25 and July 3, 1861.

26. Ibid., April 24 and July 25, 1861.

27. Ibid., July 12, 1861; Howard Jones, *Blue and Gray Diplomacy: A History of Union and Confederate Foreign Relations* (Chapel Hill: University of North Carolina Press, 2010), 39, 49, 119–20, 157.

28. *ADI,* July 19, 1861; *SC,* August 1, 1861.

29. Donald Stoker, *The Grand Design: Strategy and the U.S. Civil War* (New York: Oxford University Press, 2010), 40–42.

30. *SC,* July 25 and 27, 1861; Francis Bartow quoted in G. Moxley Sorrel, *Recollections of a Confederate Staff Officer* (New York: Neale, 1905), 33; Ray Roddy, *The Georgia Volunteer Infantry, 1861–1865* (Kearney, Neb.: Morris, 1998), 71–80.

31. *ADI,* July 23, 24, and 25, August 8, 1861; *SC,* July 23, 24, and 25, 1861. Roddy, *The Georgia Volunteer Infantry,* 78, reports a total of 41 killed, 159 wounded from the 8th Georgia Regiment.

32. Lucius Gartrell Personality File including letter written by his daughter Carrie Gartrell Blount, dated September 1940, AHC; Lillian Henderson, ed., *Roster of the Confederate Soldiers of Georgia, 1861–1865,* 6 vols. (Hapeville, Ga.: Longino and Porter, 1959), 1: 846; Roddy, *The Georgia Volunteer Infantry,* 72; Atlanta City Council minutes, August 11 and November 25, 1861, AHC.

33. *ADI,* June 13, 1861; *SC,* July 24, 1861; Harry Stout, *Upon the Altar of the Nation: A Moral History of the American Civil War* (New York: Viking, 2006), 47–49, 66.

34. *ADI*, June 28, 1861, July 4, 1863.

35. Diary of Benjamin T. Hunter, January 2, February 18, March 16, April 2, June 3 and 13, July 4, 1861, AHC.

36. Ibid., July 21, 22, 23, 26, 27, 30, August 8, October 4, 1861.

37. Fairman, *Chronicles*, 28–35.

38. Ibid.; E. B. Long, *The Civil War Day by Day: An Almanac, 1861–1865* (New York: Da Capo, 1971), 93–94; J. M. Blackwell to wife Emily Blackwell, July 21, 1861, rpt. in *SC*, July 28, 1861. See also *SC*, July 23 and December 4, 1861; Walter Wiley to "dear Mother," July 25, 1861, rpt. in *ADI*, August 6, 1861. See also *ADI*, July 24 and 25, 1861.

39. Mary T. Tardy, *Southland Writers: Biographical and Critical Sketches of the Living Female Writers of the South* (Philadelphia: Claxton, Remsen and Haffelfinger, 1870), 448–50.

40. *SC*, July 17, 1861; *ADI*, April 17, May 29, June 15, August 1 and 4, 1861; Sarah Yancey to Benjamin C. Yancey, September 6 and 14, 1861, Benjamin C. Yancey Papers, UNC.

41. *ADI*, July 19 and 26, August 5, September 12 and 24, 1861; *SC*, July 17, 1861.

42. *ADI*, August 6 and 8, 1861; Mary A. Gay, *Life in Dixie during the War* (1897; rpt. Decatur, Ga.: DeKalb Historical Society, 1979), 42, 115.

43. *SC*, April 27, June 6, 1861.

44. *ADI*, September 12, 24, and 27, 1861. *SC*, January 10, 1862, reported 150 members in the organization. A group of businessmen also organized to help families via the Soldiers' Relief Fund. This group disbanded in September 1861; Singer, "Confederate Atlanta," 77.

45. *ADI*, February 2, July 30, September 1, 1861; *SC*, December 15, 1861.

46. *CR*, 2: 108–9; Mary A. DeCredico, *Patriotism for Profit: Georgia's Urban Entrepreneurs and the Confederate War Effort* (Chapel Hill: University of North Carolina Press, 1990), 24–25.

47. *ADI*, May 17 and 22, December 8, 1861; *SC*, September 6, 1861; DeCredico, *Patriotism for Profit*, 25–26.

48. *ADI*, September 25, October 9, December 21, 1861; Samuel Joseph Lewis, Jr., "The Life of Lucius Jeremiah Gartrell," M.A. thesis, University of Georgia, 1947, 80–82; *OR*, series 1, vol. 2, 477.

49. *SC*, December 3, 5, 15, and 29, 1861.

50. Ibid., September 25, December 1, 1861.

51. Ibid., September 28, 1861; Drew Gilpin Faust, *Mothers of Invention: Women of the Slaveholding South in the American Civil War* (Chapel Hill: University of North Carolina Press, 1996), 17.

52. *SC*, August 24, December 1, 4, 5, 17, 28, and 29, 1861; *ADI*, August 31, November 23, December 27 and 31, 1861; Singer, "Confederate Atlanta," 99–101; Joseph E. Brown Order, November 20, 1861, in *CR*, 2: 145.

53. *ADI*, July 6, December 24 and 28, 1861.

54. Ibid., May 15, 1861. The *SC*, December 21, 1861, reported the names of the executed men as Henry and Jacob Harman.

55. *ADI*, May 11, 1861; see also March 14, 1861.

56. Testimony of Prince Ponder, U.S. Claims Commission Approved Claims, 1871–1880, Southern Claims Commission, RG 217, NA.

57. *ADI*, December 13 and 28, 1861; *SC*, December 21, 1861.

58. *ADI*, November 5, 1861.

59. *SC*, December 6, 1861; Crook, *The North, the South, and the Powers*, 29.

60. *ADI*, December 18, 1861; Crook, *The North, the South, and the Powers*, 99.

61. Jay Sexton, *Debtor Diplomacy* (Oxford: Clarendon, 2005), 136–38; Jones, *Blue and Gray Diplomacy*, 119–20.

4. A CITY OF CONSIDERABLE IMPORTANCE

1. Charles C. Jones, Jr., to Reverend C. C. Jones, July 25, 1862, in *The Children of Pride: A True Story of Georgia and the Civil War*, ed. Robert Manson Myers (New Haven: Yale University Press, 1972), 937–38; quotation from Mary Lin to Bud Lin, February 19, 1862, Lin Family Papers, AHC.

2. *SC*, January 10 and February 14 (LSRS), February 16 (recruitment), February 27 and March 1, 1862 (Manassas).

3. William S. McFeely, *Grant: A Biography* (New York: Norton, 1981), 13–15, 50, 95–104.

4. *SC*, February 16, 23, and 25, 1862.

5. Ibid., January 17 and February 20, 1862; Patrick H. Calhoun, "Reminiscences of Patrick H. Calhoun," *Atlanta Historical Bulletin* 1 (April 1931): 43.

6. *SC*, February 25 and March 1, 1862.

7. Ibid., March 1, 7, and 8, 1862 (slaves); *ADI*, March 2 (Pim letter) and 31, 1862 (Pim hospital directive).

8. *SC*, August 10, 1862; *ADI*, March 20, 1863; U.S. Federal Census, 1860, Fulton Co.; Jane E. Schultz, *Women at the Front: Hospital Workers in Civil War America* (Chapel Hill: University of North Carolina Press, 2004), 20–21, 33, 40.

9. Obituary in *Macon Telegraph and Messenger*, June 13, 1882; Mattie Cook Flournoy (granddaughter of Martha Winship) to Mrs. Jones, undated, and *AC*, September 28, 1890, in Winship-Flournoy Family Papers, AHC; *Atlanta Sunday*

American, April 16, 1922; Mary Callaway Jones, typescript biography of Mrs. Isaac Winship, prepared in 1938 for the Historical Archives, Georgia Division, United Daughters of the Confederacy, WML; Schultz, *Women at the Front,* 47.

10. Discussion of hospitals in *ADI,* February 25, 1862; *Atlanta Sunday American,* April 16, 1922; Mattie Cook Flournoy to Mrs. Jones, undated, in Winship-Flournoy Family Papers, AHC.

11. *ADI,* April 27 (Saint Phillips), June 27, 1862 (Collier); *SC,* March 9, April 18, June 18, 1862 (AHA) and October 28, November 27, 1862 (Dorcas).

12. *ADI,* April 15, June 27, September 3 and 17, 1862 (tasks); *SC,* September 6 (tasks) and 7, 1862 (quotation); Libra R. Hilde, *Worth a Dozen Men: Women and Nursing in the Civil War South* (Charlottesville: University of Virginia Press, 2012), 15, 58; General Philip Cook was Winship's brother.

13. *ADI,* April 8, 13, and 19, 1862; *SC,* April 13, 1862.

14. *ADI,* April 15 and 16, May 1, 1862; *SC,* April 16 and 17, 1862.

15. Typescript reminiscences of Delia Foreacre, Atlanta Women's Pioneer Society, AHC; Gerald F. Linderman, *Embattled Courage: The Experience of Combat in the Civil War* (New York: Free Press, 1987), 28–29.

16. Typescript reminiscences of Lucy Asenath Pittman Ivy and Mary Wilson, Atlanta Women's Pioneer Society, AHC.

17. Lucy Cook described by Mary Wilson in typescript reminiscences of Mary Wilson, Atlanta Women's Pioneer Society, AHC. *MA,* October 6, 1863. Drew Gilpin Faust, *This Republic of Suffering: Death and the American Civil War* (New York: Vintage, 2008), 22.

18. Jennie Lines to sister [Maria Akehurst], August 13, [1862], Akehurst-Lines Family Papers, UGA; Ella Gertrude Clanton Thomas, *The Secret Eye: The Journal of Ella Gertrude Clanton Thomas, 1848–1889,* ed. Virginia Ingraham Burr (Chapel Hill: University of North Carolina Press, 1990), 202–4.

19. Typescript reminiscences of Sarah Massey, Atlanta Women's Pioneer Society, AHC; Piromis H. Bell, "The Calico House," *Atlanta Historical Bulletin* 1 (May 1930), 28–30. Calico House was located at corner of Wheat and Collins Streets. Samuel P. Richards, *Sam Richards's Civil War Diary: A Chronicle of the Atlanta Home Front,* ed. Wendy Hamand Venet (Athens: University of Georgia Press, 2009), 96 (March 5, 1862); see also 107. *SC* discussion of sewing on November 9, 1862.

20. *ADI,* May 20, 1862; *SC,* September 24, 1862; J. M. Johnson to Dr. S. H. Stout, May 5, 1862, Samuel Stout Papers, EMU; biographical material on Stout in *Texas Medical Journal* [1903], ibid.; Atlanta City Council minutes, July 11, 1862,

AHC; Jack D. Welsh, *Two Confederate Hospitals and Their Patients: Atlanta to Opelika* (Macon, Ga.: Mercer University Press, 2005), 12–32.

21. *ADI*, May 7 and 12, 1862; Atlanta City Council minutes, April 4, 1862, AHC. Of civilian burials, forty-eight were white civilians and fifteen were African American.

22. Atlanta City Council minutes, June 27, 1862, AHC; Mary A. DeCredico, *Patriotism for Profit: Georgia's Urban Entrepreneurs and the Confederate War Effort* (Chapel Hill: University of North Carolina Press, 1990), 35.

23. Contracts, Nashville and Atlanta Arsenals 1862–64, RG 109, ch. IV, vol. 78, NA. Regarding Wright's background, see Matthew W. Norman, *Colonel Burton's Spiller and Burr Revolver: An Untimely Venture in Confederate Small-Arms Manufacturing* (Macon, Ga.: Mercer University Press, 1996), 40.

24. Contracts, Nashville and Atlanta Arsenals 1862–64, RG 109, ch. 14, vol. 78, NA; *Pioneer Citizens' History of Atlanta, 1833–1902* (Atlanta: Byrd, 1902), 279–80; Joseph H. Parks, *Joseph E. Brown of Georgia* (Baton Rouge: Louisiana State University Press, 1977), 186.

25. James Michael Russell, *Atlanta, 1847–1890: City Building in the Old South and the New* (Baton Rouge: Louisiana State University Press, 1988), 103–4; Norman, *Colonel Burton's Spiller and Burr Revolver*, 40.

26. *OR*, ser. 1, vol. 23, pt. 2, 759–69; *ADI*, February 25, 1862.

27. Contracts, Nashville and Atlanta Arsenals, 1862–64, RG 109, ch. IV, vol. 78, NA; DeCredico, *Patriotism for Profit*, 36–37; *OR*, ser. 1, vol. 6, 625–26.

28. *ADI*, June 6, 1862, and company ad on December 9, 1862.

29. Norman, *Colonel Burton's Spiller and Burr Revolver*, 27, 35, 97–98, 130. The factory was located between Calhoun and Butler Streets.

30. Atlanta City Council minutes, February 21, 1862, and Louisa Rice to Zacariah A. Rice, July 5, 1862, Zacariah A. Rice Correspondence, AHC.

31. Richards, *Sam Richards's Civil War Diary*, 88 (January 9, 1862) and 113 (May 25, 1862).

32. Annie Sehon to Bettie Kimberly, March 10, 1862, John Kimberly Collection, UNC. John Sehon's name appears occasionally in census and other records under alternate spellings, including Schon, Schor, and Schow. The *SC* discussed refugees in Atlanta on March 1, 1862.

33. Annie Sehon to Bettie Kimberly, March 29, May 27, 1862, John Sehon to Bettie Kimberly, June 9, 1862, John Kimberly Collection, UNC.

34. *SC*, March 4, April 19, August 30, October 17, 1862; *ADI*, June 26, October 23, 1862; "A Proclamation," Governor Joseph E. Brown, February 28, 1862, in *CR*, 2: 202–7; Parks, *Joseph E. Brown of Georgia*, 188–90.

35. *SC*, April 2, July 20, 1862 (Edwardy); *ADI*, May 15, 1862 (relief societies); Richards, *Sam Richards's Civil War Diary*, 169 (March 21, 1862).

36. *ADI*, March 30, 1862; *SC*, April 3, 1862.

37. *ADI*, July 30, August 7 (death penalty), September 2, 1862 (how to detect); *SC*, July 23, August 31 (engraving), September 2 (amount in circulation) and 13 (how to detect), October 5 and 7, 1862 (North's role). For shinplasters, see *ADI*, August 27, September 23, 1862.

38. *ADI*, February 11 and 16, 1862; Thomas G. Dyer, *Secret Yankees: The Unionist Circle in Confederate Atlanta* (Baltimore: Johns Hopkins University Press, 1999), 95.

39. *ADI*, April 15, June 8, 1862; James R. Crew to wife, June 18, 1862, James R. Crew Collection, AHC. See also Cornelius Hanleiter diary, April 13 [1862], AHC; Russell S. Bonds, *Stealing the General: The Great Locomotive Chase and the First Medal of Honor* (Yardley, Pa.: Westholme, 2008), 89–260.

40. *ADI*, May 9, 1862.

41. *SC*, May 28, June 19, August 9, October 19 and 21, 1862; *ADI*, June 4, October 4, 1862; Dyer, *Secret Yankees*, 98–114.

42. DeCredico, *Patriotism for Profit*, 38. Foreign intervention discussed in *SC*, February 12, 1862, and *ADI*, March 26, 1862.

43. *ADI*, November 16, 1862 (bakery and Gaar); *SC*, December 16, 1862 (Solomon).

44. *ADI*, April 10, 1862 (Edwardy), December 10 (Mayer) and 11, 1862 (Lawshe), *SC*, June 26, 1862 (McPherson).

45. Sidney Root, "Memorandum of My Life," 7–18, AHC; John D. Pelzer, "Liverpool and the American Civil War," *History Today* 40 (March 1990): 46–52.

46. *ADI*, July 3, 13, and 18, 1862; Richards, *Sam Richards's Civil War Diary*, 87–88 (January 2, 1862) and 120–21 (July 27, 1862); Russell, *Atlanta, 1847–1890*, 96.

47. Richards, *Sam Richards's Civil War Diary*, 175 (May 3, 1863); Hamilton Yancey to Benjamin C. Yancey, September 13, 1861, Benjamin C. Yancey Papers, UNC; typescript reminiscences of Sarah Massey, Atlanta Women's Pioneer Society, AHC; *SC*, October 31, 1862.

48. *ADI*, February 12, March 22, April 29, May 2, 1862; *SC*, May 1, 1862; Peg Gough, "On Stage in Atlanta, 1860–1870," *Atlanta Historical Society Bulletin* 21 (summer 1977): 53–54.

49. *ADI*, May 2, 1862; *SC*, March 14, 1862, June 1, 1863; Drew Gilpin Faust, *Mothers of Invention: Women of the Slaveholding South in the American Civil War* (Chapel Hill: University of North Carolina Press, 1996), 27.

50. *ADI,* February 27, July 3 and 18, October 10 and 23, 1862; *SC,* February 27, July 1 and July 10, 1862.

51. *ADI,* August 9, 1863.

52. Richards, *Sam Richards's Civil War Diary,* 85 (December 19, 1861); *SC,* December 20 and 21, 1861; *Atlantic Monthly* (November 1862): 583; "Blind Tom as Seen by His Mother, Charity Wiggins," *Columbus Magazine,* July 31, 1941, in Ella Mae Thornton, "Blind Tom" Collection, UGA; Geneva Handy Southall, *Blind Tom, the Black Pianist-Composer* (Lanham, Md.: Scarecrow, 1999), 1–2.

53. *SC,* November 7, 8, and 13, 1862; Thomas Wiggins, "The Battle of Manassas," *Popular Marches, Battle Pieces Etc. for Piano or Organ* (Chicago: L. S. Brainard's Sons, 1894), a copy available in Ella Mae Thornton, "Blind Tom" Collection, UGA. Wiggins's powers of imitation also included speech. He could allegedly imitate the speeches of Robert Toombs, Alexander Stephens, and Stephen A. Douglas; Deirdre O'Connell, *The Ballad of Blind Tom* (New York: Overlook Duckworth, 2009), 68–69, 107–9, 117–22.

54. O'Connell, *The Ballad of Blind Tom,* 118–20.

55. *SC,* March 6, 1862 (two articles).

56. *ADI,* November 2, December 30, 1862; James A. Ramage, *Rebel Raider: The Life of General John Hunt Morgan* (Lexington: University Press of Kentucky, 1986), 20–29, 32–33, 44–50, 95–106.

57. *SC,* June 4 and 15, September 6, 1862 (ad for recruits for Morgan's "MOUNTED MEN"). *ADI,* April 15, May 21, 1862, also reported Morgan in Atlanta.

58. *SC,* February 27, March 22 ("terror"), 25 ("spicy"), July 24, 1862; *ADI,* November 19, 1862; Ramage, *Rebel Raider,* 111–18.

59. *ADI,* April 8, 1862 (Morgan's appearance), May 21 and 24 (Butler); *SC,* May 21 (train) and 23 (Butler), 1862; Annie Sehon to Bettie Kimberly, May 27, 1862, John Kimberly Collection, UNC; Alecia P. Long, "(Mis) Remembering General Order No. 28: Benjamin Butler, the Woman Order, and Historical Memory," in *Occupied Women: Gender, Military Occupation, and the American Civil War,* ed. LeeAnn Whites and Alecia P. Long (Baton Rouge: Louisiana State University Press, 2009), 20–23.

60. *ADI,* June 5 (Morgan's visit), 10 (poem), and 11, 1862 (cane); *SC,* June 11, 1862. John Morgan Dye, 1862–64, is buried at Oakland Cemetery.

61. *ADI,* July 23, 1862. *SC,* August 9, 1862, printed a copy of Morgan's proclamation. Ramage, *Rebel Raider,* 91–106.

62. Lillian Henderson, ed., *Roster of the Confederate Soldiers of Georgia, 1861–1865,* 6 vols. (Hapeville, Ga.: Longino and Porter, 1959), 2: 705. Neal was

elected major in June 1862, lieutenant colonel in January 1863, and colonel in August 1863.

63. *ADI*, June 10, 1862. See also June 8, 1862. *SC*, June 27, 28, 29, 1862; Gary W. Gallagher, *The Union War* (Cambridge: Harvard University Press, 2011), 89–90.

64. *ADI*, September 17, 1862; *SC*, July 15, 1862.

65. *ADI*, August 21, 1862 ("vile invaders"), September 3, 1862 ("trembling"), September 5, 1862 (northern newspapers). Oath of allegiance discussed in Edward L. Ayers, *In the Presence of Mine Enemies: The Civil War in the Heart of America, 1859–1863* (New York: Norton 2003), 293.

66. *ADI*, August 19, September 21, October 1, 1862.

67. *SC*, September 23, 1862; *ADI*, September 26, 1862; James M. McPherson, *Crossroads of Freedom: Antietam* (New York: Oxford University Press, 2002), 3–5.

68. *ADI*, December 16, 1862; *SC*, December 16, 1862.

69. *ADI*, November 20, 1862; Ralph Benjamin Singer, Jr., "Confederate Atlanta," Ph.D. diss., University of Georgia, 1973, 145–46.

5. SECOND CITY OF THE CONFEDERACY

1. Annie Sehon to Bettie Kimberly, March 31, 1863, John Kimberly Papers, UNC; *ADI*, January 25, 1863; Stephanie McCurry, *Confederate Reckoning: Power and Politics in the Civil War South* (Cambridge: Harvard University Press, 2010), 132.

2. *Mobile Daily Advertiser and Register*, September 24, 1863.

3. "Report of the Superintendent of the Press Association, May 15, 1863," in *The Press Association of the Confederate States of America* (Griffin, Ga.: Hill and Swayze, 1863), 37–39; Ford Risley, "Wartime News over Southern Wires: The Confederate Press Association," in *Words at War: The Civil War and American Journalism*, ed. David B. Sachsman, S. Kittrell Rushing, and Roy Morris, Jr. (West Lafayette, Ind.: Purdue University Press, 2008), 152–56.

4. *ADI*, January 1, 1863; *SC*, January 1, 1863; Samuel P. Richards, *Sam Richards's Civil War Diary: A Chronicle of the Atlanta Home Front*, ed. Wendy Hamand Venet (Athens: University of Georgia Press, 2009), 158 (January 1, 1863).

5. *ADI*, January 3, 1863.

6. Diary of Jennie Lines, January 21, 1861, January 23 and February 16, 1863, UGA.

7. *ADI*, October 3, 1862, January 1, 1863, and *Chicago Times* quoted ibid., January 24, 1863; *SC*, December 9, 1862.

8. *Chicago Times* quoted in *ADI*, January 24, 1863; *SC*, January 9, 1863. See also February 1, 1863. Richards, *Sam Richards's Civil War Diary*, 145 (December 27, 1862) and 158 (January 1, 1863); Walter Johnson, *Soul by Soul: Life inside the Antebellum Slave Market* (Cambridge: Harvard University Press, 1999), 81–82; Edward L. Ayers, *In the Presence of Mine Enemies: The Civil War in the Heart of America, 1859–1863* (New York: Norton 2003), 354–55.

9. Richards, *Sam Richards's Civil War Diary*, 165 (February 23, 1863); David R. Goldfield, *Cotton Fields and Skyscrapers: Southern City and Region, 1607–1980* (Baton Rouge: Louisiana State University Press, 1982), 82.

10. *SC*, March 29, 1863. Amanda Foreman, *A World on Fire: Britain's Crucial Role in the American Civil War* (New York: Random House, 2010), 738, notes that 70 percent of blockade runners avoided capture during the war, with 90 percent succeeding in 1861 and the blockade tightening over time.

11. Confederate Papers Relating to Citizens or Business Firms, M346, NA. The individual businessmen and firms are filed alphabetically: *Atlanta Daily Intelligencer* (roll 28); Beach and Root (roll 50); Edward M. Edwardy (roll 277); Hamilton, Markley, and Joyner (roll 396); Er Lawshe (roll 574); McNaught and Ormond (roll 642); John Neal (roll 733); Richardson, Faulkner (roll 856).

12. Ibid., Beach and Root (roll 50); Edward M. Edwardy (roll 277); McNaught and Ormond (roll 642); John Neal (roll 733). Regarding the varied business interests of McNaught and Ormond, see Mary A. DeCredico, *Patriotism for Profit: Georgia's Urban Entrepreneurs and the Confederate War Effort* (Chapel Hill: University of North Carolina Press, 1990), 37–38.

13. "What James Bell Told Me about the Siege of Atlanta," July 11, 1935, Wilbur Kurtz Papers, AHC. U.S. Federal Census, 1860, Fulton Co.

14. Time Book, Atlanta Arsenal, April–June 1862, RG 109, vol. 1 (ch. IV, vol. 84); Time Book, Atlanta Arsenal, March 1862–June 1863, RG 109, vol. 1 (ch. IV, vol. 81), NA. Time Book ledgers were purchased at the Richards brothers' bookstore.

15. Ibid.; U.S. Federal Census, 1860, Fulton Co.

16. Moses H. Wright to R. M. Cuyler, August 10, 1862, Ordnance office, Atlanta, Ga., Letters Sent, April–October 1862, RG 109, ch. IV, vol. 12; Wright to Josiah Gorgas, May 2, 1863, Atlanta Arsenal, Letters and Telegrams Sent April–July 1863, RG 109, ch. IV, vol. 11, NA; U.S. Federal Census, 1860, Fulton Co.; Ernest B. Furgurson, *Ashes of Glory: Richmond at War* (New York: Knopf, 1996), 188–89. Women also died in munitions accidents in Jackson, Miss., Washington, D.C., Waterbury, Conn., and Allegheny, Pa.; Mary Elizabeth Massey, *Women in the Civil War* (Lincoln: University of Nebraska Press, 1994), 148.

17. Moses W. Wright Special Orders, October 4, 1862, Orders and Special Orders, Atlanta Arsenal, March 1862–November 1863, RG 109, ch. IV, vol. 77; Time Book, Atlanta Arsenal, April–June 1862, RG 109, vol. 1 (ch. IV, vol. 84); Time Book, Atlanta Arsenal, March 1862–June 1863, RG 109, vol. 1 (ch. IV, vol. 81), NA; Drew Gilpin Faust, *Mothers of Invention: Women of the Slaveholding South in the American Civil War* (Chapel Hill: University of North Carolina Press, 1996), 90. George C. Rable, *Civil Wars: Women and the Crisis of Southern Nationalism* (Urbana: University of Illinois Press, 1989), 133–35, notes that in Richmond, in December 1863, wages rose for women who rolled and sewed cartridge bags, and that pay later rose for women who sewed uniforms. Atlanta Time Books do not survive for the period after June 1863.

18. Moses W. Wright Special Orders, December 24 and 31, 1862, February 26, 1863 (funeral), May 21, 1863 (discharging employee), Orders and Special Orders, Atlanta Arsenal, March 1862–November 1863, RG 109, ch. IV, vol. 77, NA; Oakland Cemetery Collection, AHC.

19. Time Book, Atlanta Arsenal, March 1862–June 1863, RG 109, vol. 1 (ch. IV, vol. 81), NA. The figure of $40 for the two slaves represents their wages in May 1863; the writing in the June 1863 book is not legible.

20. Moses H. Wright to Major Jas Leckham, March 13, 1863, Letters and Telegrams Sent, Atlanta Arsenal, May 1862–January 1863, RG 109, ch. IV, vol. 10, NA.

21. Moses H. Wright to General B. Bragg, February 11, 1863, ibid.

22. *SC*, January 3, 1863; *ADI*, January 3 and 10, 1863.

23. *ADI*, January 6, 1863; *SC*, January 4, 1863; Annie Sehon to Bettie Kimberly, January 3, 1863, John Kimberly Papers, UNC.

24. *ADI*, January 11, 1863; *SC*, January 3, 4, and 6, 1863.

25. Jack D. Welsh, *Two Confederate Hospitals and Their Patients: Atlanta to Opelika* (Macon, Ga.: Mercer University Press, 2005), 15–17; *SC*, January 4 and 6 (wounded) and 8, 1863 (dead). Oakland Cemetery Collection contains a list of individual soldiers who died in each of Atlanta's twenty-six hospitals.

26. Annie Sehon to Bettie Kimberly, January 3, 1863, John Kimberly Papers, UNC; *SC*, January 10, 1863; Benjamin T. Hunter diary, January 10, 1863, AHC.

27. Lawrence's account, written in 1907, is in the collection of William Henry Newlin, Miscellaneous Manuscript Collection, LC; *ADI*, February 5 and May 9, 1863.

28. Moses H. Wright to J. P. Logan, October 24, 1863, Letters Sent, Commander of the Troops at Atlanta July 1863–May 1864, RG 109, ch. II, vol. 186, NA. Ren Davis and Helen Davis, *Atlanta's Oakland Cemetery: An*

Illustrated History and Guide (Athens: University of Georgia Press, 2012), 114, note that all but sixteen of the Union soldiers were reinterred at the National Cemetery in Chattanooga or elsewhere after the war.

29. Jennie Lines to sister Anna, December 2, 1862; diary of Jennie Lines, January 23 and 24, 1863, Akehurst-Lines Family Papers, UGA.

30. Diary of Jennie Lines, January 24, 1863, Jennie Lines to Maria Akehurst, December 2, 1862, Akehurst-Lines Family Papers, UGA; Ira Berlin, *Generations of Captivity: A History of African American Slaves* (Cambridge: Harvard University Press, 2003), 221–22.

31. Jennie Lines to sister Anna, March 16 and July 29, 1863; diary of Jennie Lines, January 24, 1863, Akehurst-Lines Family Papers, UGA.

32. Diary of Jennie Lines, January 25, 1863, UGA; *SC*, August 17, September 5 (cases elsewhere); August 22, November 14 (vaccinations); October 21, November 13 (Atlanta cases); November 18, 1862 ("more dreaded"). See also *ADI*, September 7 and 9, 1862, February 13, 1863; Michael Willrich, *Pox: An American History* (New York: Penguin, 2011), 119.

33. Atlanta City Council minutes, January 23 and 30, 1863, AHC; *SC*, January 25, February 7 (Dr. Brown), and 26, 1863; *ADI*, January 27, 1863 (Calhoun's edict, Dr. Thurman).

34. Richards, *Sam Richards's Civil War Diary*, 161 (January 25, 1863), 163 (February 8, 1863); Annie Sehon to Bettie Kimberly, January 3, 1863, John Kimberly Papers, UNC.

35. Julia Davidson to John Davidson, November 4, 1862, February 2, 1863, in Jane Bonner Peacock, "A Wartime Story: The Davidson Letters, 1862–1865," *Atlanta Historical Journal* 19 (1975): 9–11, 25–26, 38–39. This article reprints letters in their entirety. Hereafter cited as "Davidson Letters."

36. Sarah Huff, *My 80 Years in Atlanta* (Atlanta: n.p., 1937), 53. Huff wrote about an outbreak in 1865, but her sentiment was held by some Atlantans in 1863; *ADI*, January 29, 1863. Erysipelas is an illness characterized by fever and skin inflammation. On February 6, 1863, City Councilman James Williams suggested that buildings in which a smallpox sufferer lived be required to fly a red flag; see City Council minutes, AHC; Willrich, *Pox*, 90–92.

37. Atlanta City Council minutes, December 26, 1862, February 6, 1863, AHC.

38. Oakland Cemetery Collection, AHC; *ADI*, February 26, 1863, and *SC*, February 27, March 15, 1863.

39. Oakland Cemetery Collection, AHC. During the period 1861–64, 498 slaves were buried at City Cemetery, and 286, or 57 percent, of them were

children ages sixteen and under; Alexa Benson Henderson, "Paupers, Pastors, and Politicians: Reflections upon Afro-Americans Buried in Oakland Cemetery," *Atlanta Historical Bulletin* 20 (Summer 1976): 43–45. For Clarke's ads, see, for example, *SC*, October 3, 1862, and January 3, 1863.

40. *ADI*, March 24, April 8 and 9, May 1 and 3, 1863. Additional actresses who played in Atlanta included Jessie Clarke (*ADI*, June 25, 1863), Virginia Kemble (*ADI*, November 14, 1863), and Annie Deland (*SC*, June 18, 1863).

41. *SC*, January 3 (R. M. Clarke); March 5 (A. K. Seago); April 5 (W. H. Henderson); April 24 (Inman, Cole); May 1 (B. D. Smith); May 14, 1863 (Fields and Gresham); *ADI*, October 20, 1862 (Cohen), March 5 (Crawford, Frazer), September 1, 1863 (Whitaker and Turner).

42. *ADI*, April 15, 16, and 21, 1863; Crawford, Frazer & Co. slave receipt, Crawford, Frazer & Co. Papers, AHC. Benjamin T. Hunter diary, March 3, 1863, AHC, recorded the sale of three slaves in nearby DeKalb County for $2,300–2,600; Richard W. Iobst, *Civil War Macon: The History of a Confederate City* (Macon, Ga.: Mercer University Press, 1999), 280. On slave families being separated by auction, see Johnson, *Soul by Soul*, 122.

43. See, for example, *SC*, May 17, 1863 (Moses Wright ad); *ADI*, March 3 (hospitals), August 9, September 23, December 29, 1863 (Raleigh, Columbus, Richmond); Clarence L. Mohr, *On the Threshold of Freedom: Masters and Slaves in Civil War Georgia* (Athens: University of Georgia Press, 1986), 128–33.

44. *ADI*, January 13, April 5, 1863; Moses F. Wright to Colonel J. F. Gilmer, August 18, 1863, Letters Sent, Commander of the Troops at Atlanta, July 1863–May 1864, RG 109, ch. II, vol. 186, NA.

45. *ADI*, January 28 (Mary Ellen), June 28 (Sam), December 16, 1863 (John, Morris); *SC*, December 3, 1862 (Dave), March 1 (Jack), May 3 (Lucy Jane) and 5 (Bill, Daniel, Henry), June 30, 1863 (Charity).

46. Diary of Jennie Lines, February 8, 1863, UGA; Richards, *Sam Richards's Civil War Diary*, 196 (September 19, 1863); *SC*, April 18, 1863.

47. Annie Sehon to Bettie Kimberly, December 24, 1863, John Kimberly Papers, UNC; diary of Jennie Lines, February 8, July 1, 11, 24, 25, 28, 29, 1863, UGA; Johnson, *Soul by Soul*, 146.

48. Richards, *Sam Richards's Civil War Diary*, 109 (May 5, 1862), 154–55, 165–66 (February 28, 1863).

49. Mayor's Court, February 23, 1863 (Bill), and April 24, 1863 (Jane); see also May 7 (Frank) and 15, 1863 (Sim), AHC.

50. *SC*, May 20, 1863.

51. *ADI*, May 31, June 13, 1863; *SC*, April 15, 1863.

52. Julia Davidson to John Davidson, February 2 and 14, 1863, "Davidson Letters," 39–44; Mary Lin to Bud Lin, December 10, 1862, Amanda Lin to Charles Lin, first week of 1863, Georgia Lin to Charles Lin, September 29, 1863, Lin Family Papers, AHC.

53. Julia Davidson to John Davidson, February 2, June 29, 1863; John Davidson to Julia Davidson, March 21, April 22, 1863, "Davidson Letters," 38–39, 50–51, 59–61.

54. *ADI*, February 4, 1863; *SC*, February 11, 1863; Mary Lou Yancey to Benjamin C. Yancey, September 24, 1861, and Benjamin C. Yancey to Hamilton Yancey, October 2, 1862, in Benjamin C. Yancey Papers, UNC.

55. Julia Davidson to John Davidson, June 29, 1863, "Davidson Letters," 60; Piromis H. Bell, "The Calico House," *Atlanta Historical Bulletin* 1 (May 1930), 30; Richards, *Sam Richards's Civil War Diary*, 164 (February 15, 1863). Stella Wheeler Richards was Jabez's second wife to die from the disease. She died at age twenty-four; Oakland Cemetery Collection, AHC; *ADI*, April 4, 1863; James Marten, *The Children's Civil War* (Chapel Hill: University of North Carolina Press, 1998), 116–17, 185–86.

56. *ADI*, March 19, 1863; *SC*, March 20, 1863.

57. *ADI*, March 19, 1862; *SC*, March 20 (two articles) and 24, 1863.

58. *ADI*, April 5 and 9, 1863; *Macon Daily Telegraph*, March 31, 1863; *New York Times*, April 5, 1863; James M. McPherson, *Ordeal by Fire: The Civil War and Reconstruction* (New York: Knopf, 1982), 410; Rable, *Civil Wars*, 106–11; McCurry, *Confederate Reckoning*, 169–71, 180–82; David Williams, Teresa Crisp Williams, and David Carlson, *Plain Folk in a Rich Man's War: Class and Dissent in Confederate Georgia* (Gainesville: University of Florida Press, 2002), 80–90; Furgurson, *Ashes of Glory*, 195.

59. *CR*, 2: 370–72; McCurry, *Confederate Reckoning*, 88–89, 178, 197–98; Joseph H. Parks, *Joseph E. Brown of Georgia* (Baton Rouge: Louisiana State University Press, 1977), 233–36.

60. *SC*, March 20, 1863; Mayor's Court, February 13, March 27, July 3, December 18, 1863 (prostitutes); March 27, May 15, 1863 (disorderly conduct), AHC.

61. *SC*, May 10 and 12, 1863. The *ADI*, May 12, 1863, announced news of Jackson's death in an article bordered in black.

62. *ADI*, May 13 and 14 (Neal letter), 1863; *SC*, May 13, 15, 17, 1863.

63. *SC*, March 11, April 25, 1863 (William Calhoun's letter to his wife dated April 17); Henderson, *Roster of the Confederate Soldiers of Georgia*, 4: 606–7; Patrick H. Calhoun, "Reminiscences of Patrick H. Calhoun," *Atlanta Historical Bulletin* 1 (April 1931): 43.

64. *ADI,* May 23 ("will be saved"), June 2 (rumors), 4, 6, 11, and 16, 1863; *MA,* June 9, 1863; Risley, "Wartime News over Southern Wires," 155; B. G. Ellis, *The Moving Appeal: Mr. McClanahan, Mrs. Dill, and the Civil War's Greatest Newspaper Run* (Macon, Ga.: Mercer University Press, 2003), 222–24.

65. *SC,* June 27, 1863.

6. DIFFICULT QUESTIONS AND THE SEARCH FOR ANSWERS

1. The surrender of Vicksburg actually occurred several days earlier but was reported in *SC,* July 9, 1863, and *ADI,* July 10, 1863. Samuel Carter III, *The Final Fortress: The Vicksburg Campaign 1862–63* (New York: St. Martin's, 1980), 294–302; quotation from George C. Rable, *The Confederate Republic: A Revolution against Politics* (Chapel Hill: University of North Carolina Press, 1994), 193–94.

2. Amanda Lin to Charles Lin, July 10, 1863, Lin Family Papers, AHC; diary of Jennie Lines, July 11, 1863, UGA; Julia Davidson to John Davidson, July 17, 1863, in Jane Bonner Peacock, "A Wartime Story: The Davidson Letters, 1862–1865," *Atlanta Historical Journal* 19 (1975): 64–65, hereafter cited as "Davidson Letters"; *ADI,* July 2, 9 (two stories), and 12, 1863; *MA,* July 13 and 14, 1863; Orville Vernon Burton, *The Age of Lincoln* (New York: Hill and Wang, 2007), 181–82.

3. Annie Sehon to Bettie Kimberly, July 13, 1863, John Kimberly Papers, UNC; Rable, *The Confederate Republic,* 205.

4. Benjamin T. Hunter diary, July 9, 18, 25, 28, 1863, AHC; Carter, *The Final Fortress,* 302. Jack D. Welsh, *Two Confederate Hospitals and Their Patients: Atlanta to Opelika* (Macon, Ga.: Mercer University Press, 2005), includes a CD listing patients at Fairground.

5. *ADI,* July 24, August 4, 7, 11, 15, 1863; James A. Ramage, *Rebel Raider: The Life of General John Hunt Morgan* (Lexington: University Press of Kentucky, 1986), 171–87.

6. *ADI,* July 30, August 21, 1863; Samuel P. Richards, *Sam Richards's Civil War Diary: A Chronicle of the Atlanta Home Front,* ed. Wendy Hamand Venet (Athens: University of Georgia Press, 2009), 193 (August 21, 1863); George C. Rable, *God's Almost Chosen Peoples: A Religious History of the America Civil War* (Chapel Hill: University of North Carolina Press, 2010), 270–77.

7. *ADI,* August 13, 1863; *SC,* May 9, 1863.

8. *MA,* July 15 and 24 (quotation), 1863; *ADI,* August 9, 11, 16, 1863.

9. *ADI,* July 17, 1863. Gartrell's sentiments come from his letter to the editor on July 19, but no doubt the speech and letter contained similar thoughts.

10. Ibid., January 9, 1863; Samuel Joseph Lewis, Jr., "The Life of Lucius Jeremiah Gartrell," M.A. thesis, University of Georgia, 1947, 84–88. The possibility that Gartrell might challenge Governor Brown is discussed in Robert Toombs to Alexander H. Stephens, March 2, 1863, and Brown to Stephens, May 21 and 29, 1863, in *The Correspondence of Robert Toombs, Alexander H. Stephens, and Howell Cobb*, ed. Ulrich Bonnell Phillips (1913; rpt. New York: Da Capo, 1970), 611, 617, 618; Joseph H. Parks, *Joseph E. Brown of Georgia* (Baton Rouge: Louisiana State University Press, 1977), 251–53. For an in-depth discussion of impressment, see Bruce Levine, *The Fall of the House of Dixie: The Civil War and the Social Revolution That Transformed the South* (New York: Random House, 2013), 193–202, 206–7.

11. *ADI*, July 24, 1863; Richards, *Sam Richards's Civil War Diary*, 166 (March 4, 1863) and 193 (August 21, 1863).

12. *ADI*, August 20 and 29, September 16, 1863; Mary Mallard to Mary Jones, January 6, 1864, in *The Children of Pride: A True Story of Georgia and the Civil War*, ed. Robert Manson Myers (New Haven: Yale University Press, 1972), 1133–34.

13. *ADI*, July 19 and 22, 1863; *MA*, July 18 and 20, 1863; Iver Bernstein, *The New York City Draft Riots: Their Significance for American Society and Politics in the Age of the Civil War* (New York: Oxford University Press, 1990), 18–72.

14. *SC*, June 11, 1863. See also June 15, 1863; James M. McPherson, *Ordeal by Fire: The Civil War and Reconstruction* (New York: Knopf, 1982), 374–77; Wood Gray, *The Hidden Civil War: The Story of the Copperheads* (New York: Viking, 1942), 108–9, 145–53.

15. Slave requisition form signed by L. P. Grant, George F. Obear Collection, AHC; Grant to Colonel J. F. Gilmer, August 17 and 24, 1863; Grant to John W. Hunt, August 24, 1863; Grant to Chas. F. Williams, August 24, 1863; Grant to D. M. Haydin, October 19, 1863, Lemuel P. Grant Collection, AHC.

16. Lemuel P. Grant to Sheriff of Fayette County, November 12, 1863; Grant to W. H. Cooper, Sheriff of Troup County, December 17, 1863, Lemuel P. Grant Collection, AHC.

17. Lemuel P. Grant to J. F. Gilmer, October 30, 1863; Grant to R. P. Rowly, November 4, 1863, Lemuel P. Grant Collection, AHC; "The L. P. Grant Papers," *Atlanta Historical Bulletin* 6 (February 1932): 32–35; Lee Kennett, *Marching through Georgia: The Story of Soldiers and Civilians during Sherman's Campaign* (New York: HarperCollins, 1995), 117.

18. *ADI*, September 2, 1863; *MA*, August 10, 1863. On the revival of patriotism in the Confederacy, see Rable, *The Confederate Republic*, 207. On

women's roles, see Drew Gilpin Faust, *Mothers of Invention: Women of the Slaveholding South in the American Civil War* (Chapel Hill: University of North Carolina Press, 1996), 93–94, and Libra R. Hilde, *Worth a Dozen Men: Women and Nursing in the Civil War South* (Charlottesville: University of Virginia Press, 2012), 58.

19. *ADI*, September 8, 1863; *MA*, September 4, 1863; Parks, *Joseph E. Brown of Georgia*, 253–56; Harold Lawrence, ed., *Methodist Preachers in Georgia, 1783–1901* (Tignall, Ga.: Boyd, 1984), 248–49.

20. Thomas G. Dyer, *Secret Yankees: The Unionist Circle in Confederate Atlanta* (Baltimore: Johns Hopkins University Press, 1999), 29, 77.

21. Ibid., 77–80; Mary A. DeCredico, *Patriotism for Profit: Georgia's Urban Entrepreneurs and the Confederate War Effort* (Chapel Hill: University of North Carolina Press, 1990), 36–37.

22. *ADI*, August 16 and 20, 1863.

23. Ibid., August 27, 1863; Dyer, *Secret Yankees*, 115–34.

24. *ADI*, September 10, 1863. General Rosecrans quoted in Peter Cozzens, *This Terrible Sound: The Battle of Chickamauga* (Urbana: University of Illinois Press, 1992), 33.

25. *ADI*, September 13 and 19, 1863.

26. Ibid., September 15 and 20, 1863; Atlanta City Council minutes, July 17 and 31, August 28, 1863, January 1, 1864 (Calhoun), AHC; Tera W. Hunter, *To 'Joy My Freedom: Southern Black Women's Lives and Labors after the Civil War* (Cambridge: Harvard University Press, 1997), 14.

27. *ADI*, September 22, 1863; *MA*, September 22, 1863; Cozzens, *This Terrible Sound*, 59; Steven F. Woodworth, *Six Armies in Tennessee: The Chickamauga and Chattanooga Campaigns* (Omaha: University of Nebraska Press, 1998), 102–3, 116–17, 120, 127, 133.

28. Glenna R. Schroeder-Lein, *Confederate Hospitals on the Move: Samuel H. Stout and the Army of Tennessee* (Columbia: University of South Carolina Press, 1994), 125–26.

29. Ibid., 129; J. P. Logan to S. H. Stout, October 24, 1863, Samuel Hollingsworth Stout Papers, EMU. Richmond, Virginia, housed the Confederacy's largest hospital. The Chimborazo pavilion-style hospital had 150 buildings and eight thousand beds; Jane E. Schultz, *Women at the Front: Hospital Workers in Civil War America* (Chapel Hill: University of North Carolina Press, 2004), 31.

30. *ADI*, September 27, October 4 and 14, 1863. There were ninety-nine civilian burials during the final quarter of 1863; Georgia Lin to Charles Lin,

October 3, 1863, Lin Family Papers, AHC; Atlanta City Council minutes, January 1, 1864, AHC.

31. John Davidson to Julia Davidson, September 24, 1863, in "Davidson Letters," 66; A. J. Neal to John Neal, September 21, 1863, Andrew Jackson Neal Papers, EMU.

32. *ADI*, October 11, 1863; James Lee McDonough, *Chattanooga: Death Grip on the Confederacy* (Knoxville: University of Tennessee Press, 1984), 36–37.

33. *SC* quoted in *ADI*, October 31, 1863; *MA*, October 2, 1863; Annie Sehon to Bettie Kimberly, September 28, 1863; see also October 25, 1862, in which Sehon blames Bragg for not recapturing Nashville, John Kimberly Papers, UNC.

34. *ADI*, August 16 ("see the war out"), October 11, 1863 (socks); Julia Davidson to John M. Davidson, October 21, November 1, 1863, February 25, 1864, "Davidson Letters," 68–71, 80.

35. *ADI*, October 30, 1862, July 26, 1863.

36. Ibid., October 11, 22, and 25, 1863; *MA*, October 15, 1863; Cyrena Stone, "Miss Abby's Diary," January 20, 1864, reprinted in Dyer, *Secret Yankees*, 286–87.

37. *ADI*, October 22 and 28, 1863; City Council minutes, January 1, 1864, AHC; Emory M. Thomas, *The Confederate State of Richmond: A Biography of the Capital* (Austin: University of Texas Press, 1971), 128, 146.

38. Benjamin Hunter diary, August 4, September 20 and 21, October 6, 1863, AHC; *MA*, October 15, 1863; David Williams, Teresa Crisp Williams, and David Carlson, *Plain Folk in a Rich Man's War: Class and Dissent in Confederate Georgia* (Gainesville: University of Florida Press, 2002), 45–46.

39. Georgia Lin to Charles Lin, September 29, October 7, 1863, Lin Family Papers, AHC; Richards, *Sam Richards's Civil War Diary*, 192–94 (August 15, 29, 1863); Rable, *The Confederate Republic*, 192–93; Stephanie McCurry, *Confederate Reckoning: Power and Politics in the Civil War South* (Cambridge: Harvard University Press, 2010), 154–55; Levine, *The Fall of the House of Dixie*, 199.

40. Annie Sehon to Bettie Kimberly, September 22 and 28, 1863, John Kimberly Papers, UNC.

41. Sarah Conley Clayton, *Requiem for a Lost City: A Memoir of Civil War Atlanta and the Old South*, ed. Robert Scott Davis (Macon, Ga.: Mercer University Press, 1999), 101–2.

42. Ibid., 101–5.

43. Ibid., 105–8.

44. *ADI*, November 25, 1863.

45. Ibid., November 26 and 27, 1863; *SC*, November 24 and December 3, 1863; *MA*, November 26, 27, 28, 1863; A. J. Neal to Emma Neal, November 25, 1863, Andrew Jackson Neal Papers, EMU; McDonough, *Chattanooga*, 140, 202–13.

46. Annie Sehon to Bettie Kimberly, December 6, 1863, John Kimberly Papers, UNC; *ADI*, November 29, 1863; Richards, *Sam Richards's Civil War Diary*, 204–5 (November 28, 1863).

47. *ADI*, December 3, 4, and 5, 1863; *SC* quoted in *ADI*, December 9, 1863.

48. *ADI*, December 10, 1863; *MA*, December 9, 1863; Rable, *God's Almost Chosen Peoples*, 299–300.

49. Mary S. Mallard to Mary Jones, December 2, 1863, in Myers, *The Children of Pride*, 1118–21; Erskine Clarke, *Dwelling Place: A Plantation Epic* (New Haven: Yale University Press, 2005), 429–32.

50. Mary S. Mallard to Mary Jones, December 2 and 21, 1863, in Myers, *The Children of Pride*, 1118–21, 1128–30.

51. Mary S. Mallard to Mary Jones, December 11, 1863, February 8, March 2, 1864, and Mary Jones to Rev. R. Q. Mallard, January 18, 1864, ibid., 1124–26, 1136, 1140–41, 1143–45. Regarding the separation of slave couples in wartime, see Laura F. Edwards, *Scarlett Doesn't Live Here Anymore: Southern Women in the Civil War Era* (Urbana: University of Illinois Press, 2000), 102–3; Levine, *The Fall of the House of Dixie*, 195.

52. Clarence L. Mohr, *On the Threshold of Freedom: Masters and Slaves in Civil War Georgia* (Athens: University of Georgia Press, 1986), 207–9; Jacqueline Jones, *Saving Savannah: The City and the Civil War* (New York: Knopf, 2008), 175.

53. Thomas G. Dyer, "Half Slave, Half Free: Unionist Robert Webster in Confederate Atlanta," in *Inside the Confederate Nation: Essays in Honor of Emory M. Thomas*, ed. Lesley J. Gordon and John C. Inscoe (Baton Rouge: Louisiana State University Press, 2005), 295–300.

54. Ibid., 298–300.

55. *ADI*, December 6, 1863. In the mayoral contest, Calhoun defeated James E. Williams.

56. Ibid., December 22 and 23, 1863; *MA*, December 24, 1863.

57. *ADI*, December 29, 1863.

58. Annie Sehon to Bettie Kimberly, December 23, 1863, John Kimberly Papers, UNC; diary of Jennie Lines, December 25, 1863, UGA; Beach and Root ad in *ADI*, December 16, 1863. The city sexton noted 94 civilian burials for the last quarter of 1863, compared with 143 for the previous quarter; Atlanta City Council minutes, October 16, 1863, and January 1, 1864, AHC.

59. *ADI*, July 23, 1863; Russell Duncan, *Where Death and Glory Meet: Colonel Robert Gould Shaw and the 54th Massachusetts Infantry* (Athens: University of Georgia Press, 1999), 107–19, citing forty-five casualties in the skirmish on the sixteenth.

60. *ADI*, December 24, 1863.

7. CIVILIAN LOYALTY IN A TIME OF "INTENSE ANXIETY"

1. Mary S. Mallard to Mary Jones, May 27, 1864, in *The Children of Pride: A True Story of Georgia and the Civil War*, ed. Robert Manson Myers (New Haven: Yale University Press, 1972), 1173–75; Thomas G. Dyer, *Secret Yankees: The Unionist Circle in Confederate Atlanta* (Baltimore: Johns Hopkins University Press, 1999), 267.

2. Benjamin Hunter diary, January 1, February 17, 1864, AHC; *ADI*, January 3, 8, and 10, 1864.

3. *ADI*, December 6, 16, and 17, 1863. *MA*, January 12, 1864, advertised "Morgan's Capture" at Richards's bookstore. Mary S. Mallard to Mary Jones, February 8, 1864, in Myers, *The Children of Pride*, 1140–41.

4. *MA*, January 9 (quotation) and 13, 1864; *ADI*, January 13 and 24, 1864; James A. Ramage, *Rebel Raider: The Life of General John Hunt Morgan* (Lexington: University Press of Kentucky, 1986), 204; "Sally Garrison's Account of the Atlanta Campaign," AHC.

5. *MA*, January 20, 1864; Ramage, *Rebel Raider*, 200–201.

6. Atlanta City Council minutes, January 19, April 8, 1864, AHC; *ADI*, January 22, 1864; *SC*, January 31 and February 2, 1864.

7. *MA*, February 6, 1864, and *ADI*, February 7, 1864, reporting Calhoun speech. An ad for Morgan fund-raising appeared in *SC*, January 29, 1864. Samuel P. Richards, *Sam Richards's Civil War Diary: A Chronicle of the Atlanta Home Front*, ed. Wendy Hamand Venet (Athens: University of Georgia Press, 2009), 218 (February 6, 1864). See also Ramage, *Rebel Raider*, 139, 219.

8. Mary S. Mallard to Mary Jones, February 22, 1864, in Myers, *Children of Pride*, 1141–43; *ADI*, March 20, 1864.

9. *ADI*, February 5, 1864; David Goldfield, *America Aflame: How the Civil War Created a Nation* (New York: Bloomsbury, 2011), 339.

10. *SC*, January 31, March 15, 1864; A. J. Neal to Mary Jane Neal, February 3, 1864, and to Emma Neal, March 23, 1864, Andrew Jackson Neal Papers, EMU.

11. *ADI*, February 5, 1864; *MA*, January 1 and 15, March 9 (quotation) and 16, 1864; *SC*, January 29, 1864.

12. *SC*, January 29, 1864; *MA*, January 1, February 9 and 24, 1864; *ADI*, March 6, 1864. Private Smallwood deserted in Chattooga County, Georgia; Lillian Henderson, ed., *Roster of the Confederate Soldiers of Georgia, 1861–1865*, 6 vols. (Hapeville, Ga.: Longino and Porter, 1959), 2: 933.

13. *SC*, March 10, 1864 (Louisiana); *MA*, February 6 (interracial marriage), March 16, 1864 ("fanaticism"); *ADI*, June 23, 1864 (murder).

14. Mark A. Weitz, *A Higher Duty: Desertion among Georgia Troops during the Civil War* (Lincoln: University of Nebraska Press, 2000), 72–79, 171–79.

15. Dyer, *Secret Yankees*, 144–46.

16. Sidney Root, "Memorandum of My Life," 8, AHC; diary of Morris Mayer [after July 26, 1864], David Mayer Papers, Breman. John Wellborn Root became a distinguished architect.

17. *Pioneer Citizens' History of Atlanta, 1833–1902* (Atlanta: Byrd, 1902), 279–80.

18. Dyer, *Secret Yankees*, 148. It is unclear whether Peck was motivated by ideology or opportunism.

19. "Miss Abby's Diary," March 13, May 15 and 24, 1864, reprinted ibid., 293, 303, 310.

20. Dyer, *Secret Yankees*, 160–65, and Stone, "Miss Abby's Diary," April 9, 1864, reprinted ibid., 297–98.

21. Ads for Bohnefeld's coffin shop appeared often. See, for example, *ADI*, January 15, 1864, and *SC*, March 16, 1864; Dyer, *Secret Yankees*, 147.

22. *ADI*, February 11, 1864; Richards, *Sam Richards's Civil War Diary*, 218 (February 6, 1864) and 222–23 (April 22, 1864); Jennie Lines to My dear Sister, February 11, 1864, Akehurst-Lines Family Papers, UGA; Sarah Huff, "My 80 Years in Atlanta," *Atlanta Journal Magazine*, May 24, 1936, one of many newspaper articles that Huff published about her wartime experiences in the 1930s; E. Milby Burton, *The Siege of Charleston, 1861–1865* (Columbia: University of South Carolina Press, 1970), 263–64.

23. *SC*, April 29, 1864; *ADI*, March 20 (hotel prices), April 3 (produce) and 5, 1864; *MA*, April 21, 1864; Cornelius Hanleiter diary, April 14, 1862, AHC.

24. "Miss Abby's Diary," January 20, 1864, reprinted in Dyer, *Secret Yankees*, 286–87; Cora Warren Beck Memoir, ECU; *SC*, January 31, 1864.

25. *ADI*, February 18, 1864; Jacqueline Jones, *Saving Savannah: The City and the Civil War* (New York: Knopf, 2008), 193; Emory M. Thomas, *The Confederate State of Richmond: A Biography of the Capital* (Austin: University of Texas Press, 1971), 168–69; Arthur W. Bergerson, Jr., *Confederate Mobile* (Jackson: University of Mississippi Press, 1991), 100–101.

26. *SC,* April 5, 1864; *ADI,* April 8, 1864; *MA,* April 18, 1864; Mary S. Mallard to Mary Jones, March 31, 1864, in Myers, *The Children of Pride,* 1157–58; Richards, *Sam Richards's Civil War Diary,* 221 (March 22, 1864).

27. *ADI,* January 12 and April 19, 1864; *MA,* April 18, 1864; B. G. Ellis, *The Moving Appeal: Mr. McClanahan, Mrs. Dill, and the Civil War's Greatest Newspaper Run* (Macon, Ga.: Mercer University Press, 2003), 277–78.

28. *MA,* April 1 (Peachtree house) and May 13, 1864 (two stories); *SC,* March 30, 1864 (Herring); "Miss Abby's Diary," January 20, March 12, 1864, reprinted in Dyer, *Secret Yankees,* 287, 291–93; Benjamin Hunter diary, March 8, 1864, AHC.

29. Mary S. Mallard to Mary Jones, March 24, 1864, in Myers, *Children of Pride,* 1151–52; *MA,* June 14 (cabbage) and 16, 1864.

30. *SC,* January 29 (quotation), April 2, 1864 (post office); *MA,* February 12, 1864; *ADI,* March 1, 1864.

31. *MA,* February 16, 1864; *ADI,* January 14, 1864.

32. *MA,* April 1, 1864; Paul D. Lack, "Law and Disorder in Confederate Atlanta," *Georgia Historical Quarterly* 66 (Summer 1982): 187.

33. Lack, "Law and Disorder in Confederate Atlanta," 188.

34. *ADI,* March 16 and 20, 1864; Richards, *Sam Richards's Civil War Diary,* 225 (May 29, 1864).

35. Now called Athenaeum Auction and Commission House, it included an advertisement by Isaac Litton and Company for the auction of a "No. 1 Negro Boy about 20 years old." See *ADI,* March 15, 1864. See also February 19, March 20, 1864.

36. *ADI,* January 13, February 17, 1864. The Frazers now sold slaves in Montgomery, Alabama.

37. *ADI,* January 7 (proposal) and 16, 1864 (hospitals); *MA,* June 28, 1864; Mary S. Mallard to Mary Jones, June 23, 1864, in Myers, *Children of Pride,* 1185–86; Clarke, *Dwelling Place,* 430; "Miss Abby's Diary," [Sabbath, June 1864], reprinted in Dyer, *Secret Yankees,* 317.

38. *ADI,* January 26, 1864.

39. *MA,* April 9, 1864; *ADI,* March 8, 1864. Webster is identified in the *ADI* as Bob Yancey.

40. Atlanta Mayor's Court, February 12, 1864, AHC; *SC,* February 16, 1864, listing his office as No. 3 Marietta Street, located near the intersection with Peachtree Street; Annie Sehon to Bettie Kimberly, May 20, 1863, John Kimberly Papers, UNC. Annie acknowledged Badger as Atlanta's best dentist but chose to patronize a dentist in Augusta rather than use "a negro."

41. *MA*, March 5 (Jesse), May 11, 1864; *ADI*, February 13, June 19, 1864 (Lavonia); *SC*, April 23 and June 25, 1864 (Anthony, etc.). For Richmond's runaways in 1864, see Ernest B. Furgurson, *Ashes of Glory: Richmond at War* (New York: Knopf, 1996), 298–99. For Mobile's runaways, see Sean Michael O'Brien, *Mobile, 1865: Last Stand of the Confederacy* (Westport, Conn.: Praeger, 2001), 21.

42. *SC*, April 23, 1864; *MA*, April 22, 1864. *ADI*, April 5, 1864, printed the names of officers in Gartrell's regiment. *OR*, ser. IV, vol. III, 196. In a telegram on May 16, 1864, Gartrell indicated that he had recruited 550 men. See Richard W. Iobst, *Civil War Macon: The History of a Confederate City* (Macon, Ga.: Mercer University Press, 1999), 296. See also Samuel Joseph Lewis, Jr., "The Life of Lucius Jeremiah Gartrell," M.A. thesis, University of Georgia, 1947, 91–94.

43. *SC*, March 20, 1864; *ADI*, March 18, 1864; Eugenia Goode Morgan reminiscences, *Atlanta Journal*, August 8, 1909.

44. *MA*, May 11, 1864; Lee Kennett, *Marching through Georgia: The Story of Soldiers and Civilians during Sherman's Campaign* (New York: HarperCollins, 1995), 64–65; Albert Castel, *Decision in the West: The Atlanta Campaign of 1864* (Lawrence: University of Kansas Press, 1992), 39–43; Richard M. McMurry, *Atlanta 1864: Last Chance for the Confederacy* (Lincoln: University of Nebraska Press, 2000), 20.

45. *MA*, May 11 (Johnston), 14 and 17 (rumors), June 4, 1864 (cemetery); *ADI*, May 7 and 12, 1864 (rumors); Atlanta City Council minutes, April 15, 1864, AHC.

46. *MA*, April 22, May 3, 1864; *ADI*, May 7, 1864; *SC*, April 30, 1864; Ellis, *The Moving Appeal*, 278–80; Steven Hahn, *The Political World of Slavery and Freedom* (Cambridge: Harvard University Press, 2009), 69.

47. *MA*, May 7 and June 11, 1864; *ADI*, May 13 and 23, 1864; *SC*, June 16, 1864.

48. *ADI*, May 1 and 3, 1864; *MA*, June 17, 1864; Kennett, *Marching through Georgia*, 63; William G. Thomas, *The Iron Way: Railroads, the Civil War, and the Making of Modern America* (New Haven: Yale University Press, 2011), 153–57.

49. *MA*, May 11, 1864; Kennett, *Marching through Georgia*, 63; Mary S. Mallard to Mary Jones, May 14, 1864, citing sixteen-mile retreat, in Myers, *Children of Pride*, 1168–69.

50. *ADI*, May 17 and 18, 1864 (wrongly identifying Calhoun as Captain J. L. Calhoun); Patrick H. Calhoun, "Reminiscences of Patrick H. Calhoun," *Atlanta Historical Bulletin* 1 (April 1931): 43.

51. Mary S. Mallard to Mary Jones, May 14 and 19, 1864, in Myers, *Children of Pride*, 1168–71; Kate Cumming, *The Journal of Kate Cumming: A Confederate Nurse, 1862–1865*, ed. Richard Harwell (Savannah: Beehive, 1975), 181–84 (May 17, 1864); *ADI*, May 18, 1864; James O. Breeden, "A Medical History of the Later Stages of the Atlanta Campaign," *Journal of Southern History* 35 (February 1969): 37–38.

52. Cumming, *The Journal of Kate Cumming*, 181–84 (May 17, 1864); Mary S. Mallard to Mary Jones, May 27, 1864, in Myers, *Children of Pride*, 1173–75; *ADI*, May 27, 1864.

53. R. J. Massey, "Memories of Brown Hospital," *Sunny South*, October 21–26, 1901.

54. *ADI*, May 4 (Wiggins), 6 (prostitutes), 14 (Amateurs), 28, 1864 (Babel); Cumming, *The Journal of Kate Cumming*, 215 (September 7, 1864). Cumming wrote after Atlanta's surrender.

55. Richards, *Sam Richards's Civil War Diary*, 224 (May 15, 1864).

56. *MA*, May 19 and 22, 1864; *ADI*, May 26, 1864; "Miss Abby's Diary," May 24, 1864, reprinted in Dyer, *Secret Yankees*, 309–10.

57. *ADI*, May 26 and 27, 1864.

58. Ibid., May 18, 1864 (inspection); *SC*, May 29, 1864 (Brown); *MA*, May 23, 1864 (Calhoun).

59. Mary S. Mallard to Susan Cumming, May 20, 1864, in Myers, *Children of Pride*, 1171; *ADI*, May 18, 1864; *MA*, May 26 and 27, 1864; Richards, *Sam Richards's Civil War Diary*, 225 (May 29, 1864).

60. *ADI*, June 2 and 8, 1864; Keith Bohannan, "Cadets, Drillmasters, Draft Dodgers, and Soldiers: The Georgia Military Institute during the Civil War," *Georgia Historical Quarterly* 79 (Spring 1995): 5–21.

61. A. J. Neal to John Neal, May 15, 1864, to Mary Jane Neal, May 20, 1864, and to Emma Neal, June 2, 1864, Andrew Jackson Neal Papers, EMU.

62. Atlanta City Council minutes, June 1, 1864, AHC; Richards, *Sam Richards's Civil War Diary*, 225 (June 10, 1864); *SC*, June 18, 1864; *MA*, June 9 and 10, 1864; *ADI*, June 1 (*Mobile Advertiser*, whose report was on May 29, 1864) and 10, 1864.

63. "Miss Abby's Diary" [June 1864], reprinted in Dyer, *Secret Yankees*, 316–17.

8. THE BARBAROUS WAR

1. Samuel P. Richards, *Sam Richards's Civil War Diary: A Chronicle of the Atlanta Home Front*, ed. Wendy Hamand Venet (Athens: University of Georgia Press, 2009), 228 (July 23, 1864).

2. *MA,* June 14, 1864; *ADI,* June 14 (army's location) and 16, 1864 (Polk); Albert Castel, *Decision in the West: The Atlanta Campaign of 1864* (Lawrence: University of Kansas Press, 1992), 45–47, 148, 195, 275–76.

3. Benjamin Hunter diary, June 14, 1864, AHC; *ADI,* June 19, 1864; *MA,* June 14, 1864; Sarah Conley Clayton, *Requiem for a Lost City: A Memoir of Civil War Atlanta and the Old South,* ed. Robert Scott Davis (Macon, Ga.: Mercer University Press, 1999), 114–15.

4. *ADI,* May 12 and June 12, 1864; *MA,* May 26, 1864; Dr. J. P. Logan Special Orders, May 26, 1864, Samuel Hollingsworth Stout Papers, EMU; Glenna R. Schroeder-Lein, *Confederate Hospitals on the Move: Samuel H. Stout and the Army of Tennessee* (Columbia: University of South Carolina Press, 1994), 135.

5. *ADI,* June 19 (Forrest) and 21, 1864 (July 4). Jefferson Davis declined to release Forrest from Mississippi, believing that the state would fall into Yankee hands if he did so. Castel, *Decision in the West,* 345–46.

6. *MA,* June 28, 1864; Samuel G. French, *Two Wars: An Autobiography* (Nashville: Confederate Veteran, 1901), 206–11; Angus L. Waddle, *Three Years with the Armies of the Ohio and Cumberland* (Chillicothe, Ohio: Scioto Gazette and Job Office, 1889), 70; Castel, *Decision in the West,* 309–21.

7. *MA,* June 28, 1864; *ADI,* July 1 and 2, 1864 (ambulances; new life); *SC,* June 29, 1864; Mary S. Mallard to Mary Jones, July 1, 1864, in *The Children of Pride: A True Story of Georgia and the Civil War,* ed. Robert Manson Myers (New Haven: Yale University Press, 1972), 1187–89.

8. Orlando M. Poe diary, July 3, 1864, Papers of Orlando M. Poe, LC.

9. Clayton, *Requiem for a Lost City,* 116; Susan Lin to Bud Lin [Opelika, 1864], Lin Family Papers, AHC; Andrew Jackson Neal Papers, biographical description, EMU; Annie Sehon to Bettie Kimberly, March 28, May 22, June 8, July 4, 1864, John Kimberly Papers, UNC.

10. *ADI,* June 26, 1864.

11. Ibid., June 30, 1864.

12. *SC,* May 1, 1864. The City Council created a Board of Health to meet weekly and address sanitary conditions. See *ADI,* June 30, 1864 (Board); *MA,* July 2 (privies) and 5, 1864 (manure sink).

13. *ADI,* July 2 (tents) and 3, 1864 (destitute circumstances); *MA,* July 1 (618), 2 (City Council), 4, 1864 (arriving wounded); Elizabeth S. Wiggins to "Dear Mother," June 12 [1864], Elizabeth S. Wiggins Papers, Duke. Wiggins lived in DeKalb County.

14. *ADI,* July 6, 1864; *SC,* July 5 and 6, 1864.

15. *MA,* July 2 and 4, 1864.

16. Moses H. Wright to Josiah Gorgas, June 2, 1864, Moses Wright to R. M. Cuyler, July 5, 1864, Moses Wright to W. W. Mackall, July 7, 1864, RG 109, War Department Collection of Confederate Records, ch. IV, vol. 16, NA.

17. *ADI*, August 10 and 12, 1864; Henry C. Lay to wife, July 22, 1864, Henry C. Lay Papers, UNC; Martha Winship Personality File, AHC; R. J. Massey, "Memories of Brown Hospital," *Sunny South*, October 21–26, 1901; Jack D. Welsh, *Two Confederate Hospitals and Their Patients: Atlanta to Opelika* (Macon, Ga.: Mercer University Press, 2005), 37, 80–83; James O. Breeden, "A Medical History of the Later Stages of the Atlanta Campaign," *Journal of Southern History* 35 (February 1969): 37.

18. Joseph Semmes to Jorantha Semmes, July 13, 1864, Benedict Joseph Semmes Papers, UNC; typescript reminiscences of Mary Bellingrath Burnett, McMillan-Bellingrath Collection, AHC; Emma J. Slade Prescott reminiscence, in Emma Prescott Collection, AHC.

19. Mary S. Mallard to Mary Jones, July 1, 1864, and to Laura E. Buttolph, July 18, 1864, in Myers, *The Children of Pride*, 1188, 1191–92.

20. Castel, *Decision in the West*, 336–44, 348.

21. Charles Harding Cox to Dear Frank, July 13, 1864, Charles Harding Cox Papers, EMU; David Douglass to Dear Mother, July 30, 1864, Miscellaneous Manuscript Collection, LC; Andrew J. Boies, *Record of the Thirty-Third Massachusetts Volunteer Infantry* (Fitchburg, Mass.: Sentinel, 1880), 93.

22. Colin Dunlop to dear Sister, August 13, 1864, Colin Dunlop Papers, AHC; A. J. Neal to John Neal, July 20, 1864, Andrew Jackson Neal Papers, EMU; Castel, *Decision in the West*, 347, 360–62.

23. Richards, *Sam Richards's Civil War Diary*, 227 (July 17, 1864).

24. *MA*, July 20, 1864, quoted in B. G. Ellis, *The Moving Appeal: Mr. McClanahan, Mrs. Dill, and the Civil War's Greatest Newspaper Run* (Macon, Ga.: Mercer University Press, 2003), 311; Castel, *Decision in the West*, 365–83; Richard M. McMurry, *Atlanta 1864: Last Chance for the Confederacy* (Lincoln: University of Nebraska Press, 2000), 151–52.

25. Richards, *Sam Richards's Civil War Diary*, 228 (July 22, 1864); Rufus Mead to Folks at Home, July 24, 1864, Rufus Mead Papers, LC; William E. Bevens, *Reminiscences of a Private* (Fayetteville: University of Arkansas Press, 1992), 183–87; Castel, *Decision in the West*, 383–414; McMurry, *Atlanta 1864*, 155. The two armies clashed a third time, at Ezra Church, west of the city center, on July 28.

26. Julia Davidson to John Davidson, July 21, 1864, in Jane Bonner Peacock, "A Wartime Story: The Davidson Letters, 1862–1865," *Atlanta Historical Journal* 19 (1975): 93–95, hereafter cited as "Davidson Letters"; Richards, *Sam Richards's Civil*

War Diary, 228 (July 22, 1864); "Miss Abby's Diary," July 21 and 22, 1864, reprinted in Thomas G. Dyer, *Secret Yankees: The Unionist Circle in Confederate Atlanta* (Baltimore: Johns Hopkins University Press, 1999), 323–26; see also 176–78.

27. Richards, *Sam Richards's Civil War Diary*, 228–29 (July 22 and 24, 1864); Atlanta City Council minutes, July 11 and 18, 1864.

28. Gussie Clayton to Mary Lou Yancey, June 1, 1864, Benjamin C. Yancey Papers, UNC; Clayton, *Requiem for a Lost City*, 118–29, 175–76; typescript reminiscence of Mary Rawson, Rawson-Collier-Harris Family Papers, AHC. Augusta Clayton was later reburied at City Cemetery. On children in war's path, see James Marten, *The Children's Civil War* (Chapel Hill: University of North Carolina Press, 1998), 101–47.

29. Richards, *Sam Richards's Civil War Diary*, 228 (July 23, 1864); *Atlanta Journal*, May 23, 1909 (Augusta King) and July 8, 1934 (Sarah Huff); Sarah Huff, *My 80 Years in Atlanta* (Atlanta: n.p., 1937), 65.

30. A. J. Neal to Ella Neal, August 4, 1864, James Neal to Mary Jane Neal, August 24, 1864, and A. J. Neal obituary, Andrew Jackson Neal Papers, EMU; obituary in *ADI*, August 19, 1864; Henry Ossian Flipper, *The Colored Cadet at West Point: An Autobiography* (New York: H. Lee 1878), 11; Lee Kennett, *Marching through Georgia: The Story of Soldiers and Civilians during Sherman's Campaign* (New York: HarperCollins, 1995), 125.

31. William T. Sherman to Ulysses S. Grant, August 10, 1864, Sherman to George Thomas, August 10, Sherman to Oliver Otis Howard, August 10, 1864, *OR*, ser. 1, vol. 38, pt. 5, 447–48, 452; Charles Harding Cox to Dear Sister, July 23, 1864, Charles Harding Cox Papers, EMU; Walter S. Burns to Parents, August 20, 1864, Walter Burns Correspondence, AHC; Fannie A. Beers, *Memories: A Record of Personal Experience and Adventure during Four Years of War* (Philadelphia: Lippincott, 1889), 165–66.

32. Joseph Semmes to Jorantha Semmes, July 25, 1864, Benedict Joseph Semmes Papers, UNC; Castel, *Decision in the West*, 464.

33. Typescript reminiscences of Madeline Mayer Warner, David Mayer Family Papers, Breman; typescript reminiscences of Cornelia Venable (Mrs. E. H. Venable) and Lucy H. Kicklighter, Atlanta Women's Pioneer Society, AHC; *Atlanta Journal*, August 1, 1909.

34. Julia Davidson to John Davidson, July 26, 1864, in "Davidson Letters," 95–97.

35. O. L. Braumuller reminiscences in *Atlanta Journal*, February 3, 1929; typescript reminiscences of Lucy Asenath Pittman Ivy, Atlanta Women's Pioneer Society, AHC.

36. Carrie Berry diary, August 3, 11, 14, 15, 1864, AHC.

37. Ibid., August 21, 23, 25, 1864.

38. *ADI*, August 3 and 6, 1864.

39. Richards, S*am Richards's Civil War Diary*, 230–33 (August 7, 14, 18, 21, 28, 1864); *ADI*, August 6 and 13, 1864. Stephen Davis discusses casualties and hearsay about casualties in *What the Yankees Did to Us: Sherman's Bombardment and Wrecking of Atlanta* (Macon, Ga.: Mercer University Press, 2012), 138, 165, 209, 215, 243–48.

40. *ADI*, August 16 (no provisions), 19 (Francis Hale), 20 (shelling, byline August 18), 23 (worst shelling, rations), 25 (armistice), 27, 1864 (retreat); Joseph Semmes to Jorantha Semmes, August 25, 1864, Benedict Joseph Semmes Papers, UNC.

41. *ADI*, August 26 and 27, 1864.

42. Carrie Berry diary, August 26, 1864, AHC; Richards, *Sam Richards's Civil War Diary*, 233 (August 29, 1864); typescript reminiscences of Augusta King, Atlanta Women's Pioneer Society, AHC; *Atlanta Journal*, May 23, 1909; Davis, *What the Yankees Did to Us*, 226.

43. A. T. Halliday to Elizabeth Halliday, August 26 and 27, 1864, A. T. and Elizabeth Halliday Papers, AHC. See also William Jewel to Martha, August 10 [1864], Confederate Miscellany, EMU.

44. J. A. Flournoy to Anna Elizabeth Winship Flournoy, August 28, 1864, Winship-Flournoy Family Papers, AHC; Caleb Henry Carlton to Dear Little Wife, August 22, September 3, 1864, Caleb Henry Carlton Papers, LC; Castel, *Decision in the West*, 428–36, 495–503.

45. Richards, *Sam Richards's Civil War Diary*, 233 (September 1, 1864); Rufus Mead diary, September 4, 1864, Rufus Mead Papers, LC; typescript reminiscences of Mary Rawson, Rawson-Collier-Harris Family Papers, AHC; French, *Two Wars*, 222; Kennett, *Marching through Georgia*, 198–201.

46. Richards, *Sam Richards's Civil War Diary*, 233 (September 1, 1864).

47. Affidavit of James M. Calhoun, as to Facts in Regard to Surrender of Atlanta, September 2, 1864, Calhoun Family Collection, AHC; H. W. Slocum to E. M. Stanton and Sherman to H. W. Halleck, September 3, 1864, *OR*, ser. 1, vol. 38, pt. 5, 763, 777; typescript reminiscences of Mary Rawson, Rawson-Collier-Harris Family Papers, AHC; Dyer, *Secret Yankees*, 191; Davis, *What the Yankees Did to Us*, 262–65; Castel, *Decision in the West*, 529.

48. James Neuman to Mr. and Mrs. Hiram Tripp, September 1, 1864, Neuman Trip Collection, AHC; Boies, *Record of the Thirty-Third Massachusetts*, 89; W. L. Nugent to Nellie Nugent, October 14, 1864, in William M. Cash and

Lucy Somerville Howorth, eds., *My Dear Nellie: The Civil War Letters of William L. Nugent and Eleanor Smith Nugent* (Jackson: University Press of Mississippi, 1977), 219.

49. *ADI*, September 15, 1864; Richards, Sam *Richards's Civil War Diary*, 235–36 (September 9, 1864); Carrie Berry diary, September 7, 1864, AHC; Sidney Root, "Memorandum of My Life," 4, 16, AHC; typescript reminiscences of Ann Cozart Harralson, Atlanta Women's Pioneer Society, AHC; *Atlanta Journal*, March 7, 1909.

50. Rufus Mead to Dear Folks at Home, September 8, 1864, Rufus Mead Papers, LC; George Washington Baker to Dear Mother, September 3, 1864, George Washington Baker Papers, UNC; Orlando M. Poe to Dear Wife, September 7, 1864, Orlando M. Poe Papers, LC; John Geary to Mary Geary, October 1, 1864, John W. Geary Papers, AHC.

51. Henry D. Stanley diary, September 5, 1864, and John S. Lockman to Dear Mother, September 9, 1864, Civil War Papers; George Lawson to wife, November 12, 1864, George C. Lawson Papers, AHC; George M. Patton diary, November 1, 1864, UNC.

52. Richards, *Sam Richards's Civil War Diary*, 235–36 (September 4 and 9, 1864); Carrie Berry diary, September 2 and 4, 1864; typescript reminiscences of Mary Rawson, Rawson-Collier-Harris Family Papers, AHC; Franklin M. Garrett, *Atlanta and Environs: A Chronicle of Its People and Events*, 2 vols. (Athens: University of Georgia Press, 1954), 1: 645–47. The concert benefited Mrs. Rebecca Welsh from Columbus, Georgia, currently living in Atlanta.

53. William Tecumseh Sherman, *Memoirs of General W. T. Sherman* (New York: Library of America, 1990), 585; William G. Le Duc, *Recollections of a Civil War Quartermaster: The Autobiography of William G. Le Duc* (St. Paul, Minn.: North Central, 1963), 128–29; John Geary to Mary Geary, July 29, 1864, John W. Geary Papers, AHC. Rufus Mead to Dear Folks at Home, September 13, 1864, Rufus Mead Papers, LC. *ADI* printed Sherman's order on September 15 and Calhoun's protest on September 20, 1864.

54. Garrett, *Atlanta and Environs*, 1: 638–39; Kennett, *Marching through Georgia*, 215–16; Joseph H. Parks, *Joseph E. Brown of Georgia* (Baton Rouge: Louisiana State University Press, 1977), 295–96.

55. *ADI*, September 6 (Sherman, Davis, destruction), 7 (Morgan), 15, 1864 (expulsion order); Richards, *Sam Richards's Civil War Diary*, 236 (September 9, 1864).

56. Root, "Memorandum of My Life," 10, 16–17, AHC; *ADI*, September 15, 1864.

57. Typescript reminiscences of Mary Rawson, Rawson-Collier-Harris Family Papers, AHC; *Pioneer Citizens' Story of Atlanta, 1833–1902* (Atlanta: Byrd, 1902), 253–54.

58. Richards, *Sam Richards's Civil War Diary*, 239–41, 248–49 (October 9, November 8, 1864); Braumuller reminiscences in *Atlanta Journal*, February 3, 1929.

59. Wilbur Kurtz, "What James Bell Told Me about the Siege of Atlanta," AHC; "The Book of Exodus, Containing an account of People Sent South," September 4, 1864, Confederate Papers Relating to Citizens or Business Firms, M346, Reel 114, NA; George Ward Nichols, *The Story of the Great March* (New York: Harper and Brothers, 1865), 18–23; Henry H. Wright, *A History of the Sixth Iowa Infantry* (Iowa City: State Historical Society Iowa, 1923), 335; Davis, *What the Yankees Did to Us*, 309–10.

60. *ADI*, September 17 (poverty), September 28 (home), October 13, 1864 (fund-raisers).

61. Kennett, *Marching through Georgia*, 211 (first quotation). See also Castel, *Decision in the West*, 549; Mark Grimsley, *The Hard Hand of War: Union Military Policy toward Southern Civilians, 1861–1865* (New York: Cambridge University Press, 1995), 188 (second quotation). Davis, *What the Yankees Did to Us*, 310–30, notes both the overall harshness of the exodus to the South and individual stories of leniency.

62. *ADI*, September 24 and 25 (Davis) and 27 (Sherman); Richard W. Iobst, *Civil War Macon: The History of a Confederate City* (Macon, Ga.: Mercer University Press, 1999), 332–33.

63. *ADI*, October 22 and November 15, 1864. Amherst Stone's name was also mentioned as a Unionist, but Stone had left Atlanta the previous year; Le Duc, *Recollections of a Civil War Quartermaster*, 129.

64. *ADI*, September 18, 1864. Sarah Huff described Atlanta's "profound stillness" in *Atlanta Journal Magazine*, July 15, 1934; Mary S. Mallard to Mary Jones, September 5, 1864, in Myers, *The Children of Pride*, 1201; Kennett, *Marching through Georgia*, 213.

65. *ADI*, October 5, 1864; *SC*, December 14, 1864; Davis, *What the Yankees Did to Us*, 370–71, 392–99, 427.

66. *ADI*, November 15, 1864; William R. Buchanan diary, November 11, 1864, UNC; Henry D. Stanley diary, November 14, 1864, Civil War Papers, AHC; Davis, *What the Yankees Did to Us*, 370–71, 392–99, 427.

67. Henry Hitchcock diary, November 15, 1864, Miscellaneous Manuscript Collection, LC.

9. REBUILDING, RECONSTRUCTION, AND THE NEW CITY

1. *ADI*, July 6, 1865. Paul F. Paskoff discusses the rebuilding of southern railroads in "Measures of War: A Quantitative Examination of the Civil War's Destructiveness in the Confederacy," *Civil War History* 54 (March 2008): 27–29.

2. Don H. Doyle, *New Men, New Cities, New South: Atlanta, Nashville, Charleston, Mobile, 1860–1910* (Chapel Hill: University of North Carolina Press, 1990), xv, 22, 88–89; David Goldfield, *Region, Race, and Cities: Interpreting the Urban South* (Baton Rouge: Louisiana State University Press, 1997), 273.

3. Whitelaw Reid, *After the War: A Tour of the Southern States 1865–1866*, ed. C. Vann Woodward (1866; rpt. New York: Harper and Row, 1965), 355; John Erskine to William McNaught, December 9, 1864, William McNaught Papers, AHC.

4. James R. Crew to Dear Wife, December 1, 1864, James R. Crew Collection; John Erskine to William McNaught, December 9, 1864, William McNaught Papers; Oakland Cemetery Collection, AHC; Royce Shingleton, *Richard Peters: Champion of the New South* (Macon, Ga.: Mercer University Press, 1985), 140–41.

5. Cornelius Hanleiter diary, December 30, 1864, AHC; John Richard Dennett, *The South as It Is, 1865–1866* (1866; rpt. New York: Viking, 1965), 264–71; Sidney Andrews, *The South since the War* (1866; rpt. New York: Arno, 1969), 339–40.

6. *Macon Telegraph and Messenger*, June 13, 1882; John Sehon to Bettie Kimberly, October 20, 1864, John Kimberly Papers, UNC; Thomas G. Dyer, *Secret Yankees: The Unionist Circle in Confederate Atlanta* (Baltimore: Johns Hopkins University Press, 1999), 263–64.

7. Diary of Jennie Lines, December 21, 22, 23, 1865, UGA.

8. Samuel P. Richards, *Sam Richards's Civil War Diary: A Chronicle of the Atlanta Home Front*, ed. Wendy Hamand Venet (Athens: University of Georgia Press, 2009), 261 (February 12 and 19, 1865).

9. Typescript reminiscences of Madeleine Mayer Warner, David Mayer Family Papers, Breman; *ADNE*, May 19, 1867.

10. Carrie Berry diary, November 16, 1864, June 17, 1865, AHC.

11. James Ormond to My dear Wife, April 29, 1865, William McNaught Papers, AHC; Richards, *Sam Richards's Civil War Diary*, 268 (April 3, 1865) and 270 (April 10, 1865).

12. Richards, *Sam Richards's Civil War Diary*, 270–71 (April 15, 1865); Mary Louisa Killian Crew diary, April 21, 1865, AHC; *ADI*, April 28, 1865. See also Minerva McClatchey diary, April 1865, McClatchey Family Papers, GDAH.

13. Franklin M. Garrett, *Atlanta and Environs: A Chronicle of Its People and Events,* 2 vols. (Athens: University of Georgia Press, 1954), 1: 669–70.

14. *Augusta Chronicle,* December 21, 1864, by its "Special Correspondent" in Atlanta; Octavia Hammond to Mary Adair, February 10, 1865, Adair Papers, AHC.

15. Octavia Hammond to Mary Adair, February 10, 1865, Adair Papers, AHC.

16. Mary Louisa Killian Crew diary, May 5 [1865], AHC.

17. *ADI,* July 7, 1865.

18. Curkendall speech quoted in Dennett, *The South as It Is,* 168–69. Curkendall served for a few months before being replaced; Paula A. Cimbala, *Under the Guardianship of the Nation: The Freedmen's Bureau and the Reconstruction of Georgia, 1865–1870* (Athens: University of Georgia Press, 1997), 1–8; Tera W. Hunter, *To 'Joy My Freedom: Southern Black Women's Lives and Labors after the Civil War* (Cambridge: Harvard University Press, 1997), 23–24.

19. V. T. Barnwell, *Atlanta City Directory* (Atlanta: Intelligencer Book and Job Office, 1867), 35.

20. *ADI,* October 6 (departure of troops), November 30, December 2 and 5, 1865 (alleged crime); James R. Crew to wife [October 19], 1865, AHC; Hunter, *To 'Joy My Freedom,* 35.

21. Sam Richards diary, September 9, November 17, 1866, AHC; Elizabeth H. Hanna, "Miss Hanna's Reminiscences," *Atlanta Journal Magazine,* June 22, 1930.

22. William A. Link, *Atlanta, Cradle of the New South: Race and Remembering in the Civil War's Aftermath* (Chapel Hill: University of North Carolina Press, 2013), 65–66.

23. *ADI,* October 11, 1865, February 11, 1866; Arthur Reed Taylor, "From the Ashes: Atlanta during Reconstruction, 1865–1876," Ph.D. diss., Emory University, 1974, 128.

24. Taylor, "From the Ashes," 40–41, 79.

25. Ibid., 78; Ralph Benjamin Singer, Jr., "Confederate Atlanta," Ph.D. diss., University of Georgia, 1973, 181; *Pioneer Citizens' History of Atlanta, 1833–1902* (Atlanta: Byrd, 1902), 247–49; Shingleton, *Richard Peters,* 170–72. See ads for McNaught, Ormond Hardware and G. W. Adair, Auctioneer in *ADI,* February 23, 1867. Don L. Klima, "Breaking Out: Streetcars and Suburban Development," *Atlanta Historical Journal* 26 (Summer–Fall, 1982): 67–82. The *Southern Confederacy* newspaper ceased publication at the end of the war.

26. James Michael Russell, "The 'Phoenix City' after the Civil War: Atlanta's 'Economic Miracle'" *Atlanta History* 33 (Winter 1989–90): 19; George Rose, *The Great Country; or, Impressions of America* (London: Tinsley Brothers, 1868), 174–75.

27. Russell, "The 'Phoenix City'" 20; Sven Beckert, "Emancipation and Empire: Reconstructing the Worldwide Web of Cotton Production in the Age of the American Civil War," *American Historical Review* 109 (2004): 1421–27.

28. Reid, *After the War*, 355; Andrews, *The South since the War*, 340–41.

29. *Pioneer Citizens' History of Atlanta*, 364–65; obituary of Alvin Seago in *AC*, July 4, 1910; Sidney Root, "Memorandum of My Life," 10–12, AHC.

30. Grigsby Hart Wooton, Jr., "New City of the South: Atlanta, 1843–1873," Ph.D. diss., Johns Hopkins University, 1973, 368–70.

31. Atlanta City Council minutes, January 5, 1866, AHC.

32. *OR*, series 1, vol. XLIV, 442–46; Samuel Joseph Lewis, Jr., "The Life of Lucius Jeremiah Gartrell," M.A. thesis, University of Georgia, 1947, 94–98. Gartrell advertised his law office in *ADI*, July 2, 1865.

33. Garrett, *Atlanta and Environs*, 1: 684, 705.

34. Ibid., 1: 703, 705, 712, 721; Sam Richards diary, September 15, 1866, AHC.

35. *ADI*, April 4 and 5, 1866; Garrett, *Atlanta and Environs*, 1: 712.

36. *ADI*, April 4, 1866, July 6, 1867; Garrett, *Atlanta and Environs*, 1: 713–14.

37. Sam Richards diary, October 20, 1866, AHC; Garrett, *Atlanta and Environs*, 1: 725.

38. Barnwell, *Atlanta City Directory*, 33–35.

39. *Richard Peters, His Ancestors and Descendants, 1810–1889*, ed. and comp. Nellie Peters Black (Atlanta: Foote and Davies, 1904), 26–30; Shingleton, *Richard Peters*, 144–46.

40. Shingleton, *Richard Peters*, 148–50; Atlanta City Council minutes, October 25, 1867, AHC.

41. *ADNE*, May 19, 1867; Eric Foner, *Reconstruction: America's Unfinished Revolution 1863–1877* (New York: Harper and Row, 1988), 276–77.

42. *ADI*, March 2 and 5, 1867; *ADNE*, March 5, 1867.

43. *ADNE*, March 5, 1867.

44. *ADI*, December 20, 1864, and March 5, 1867; *ADNE*, March 5, 1867. Luther Glenn died in 1886. The wound he received in 1862 coupled with "lingering disease" limited his public career after the war. See obituary in *Atlanta Journal*, June 10, 1886.

45. *ADNE*, March 5, 1867.

46. Ibid., April 21, 1867; Howard N. Rabinowitz, "Continuity and Change: Southern Urban Development, 1860–1900," in *The City in Southern History: The Growth of Urban Civilization in the South* (Port Washington, N.Y.: National University Publications, 1977), 97.

47. *ADI*, March 31, April 2, 12, and 14, 1867; *ANDE*, April 13, 1867; Sam Richards diary, March 24 and April 13, 1867, AHC; Timothy J. Crimmins and Anne H. Farrisee, *Democracy Restored: A History of the Georgia State Capitol* (Athens: University of Georgia Press, 2007), 30–33.

48. *ADI*, September 3, 1867; testimony of David Young, Southern Claims Commission, Approved Claims, 1871–1880, Georgia, Records of the Accounting Officers of the Department of the Treasury, RG 217, NA; Taylor, "From the Ashes," 20; Cimbala, *Under the Guardianship of the Nation*, 44, 281 n. 119; Atlanta City Council minutes, September 20, 1867, AHC.

49. Atlanta City Council minutes, September 2 and 27, 1867, AHC; *ADI*, October 2 and 4, 1867.

50. Elizabeth Studley Nathans, *Losing the Peace: Georgia Republicans and Reconstruction, 1865–1871* (Baton Rouge: Louisiana State University Press, 1968), 18–19, 23, 25–26, 29–33; John M. Matthews, "Negro Republicans in the Reconstruction of Georgia," *Georgia Historical Quarterly* 60 (Summer 1976): 146–47; *ADI*, September 27, 1867.

51. Nathans, *Losing the Peace*, 38–44, 74–76; Taylor, "From the Ashes," 64; Clarence L. Mohr, "Harrison Berry: A Black Pamphleteer in Georgia during Slavery and Freedom," *Georgia Historical Quarterly* 67 (Summer 1983): 202–3. Berry owned a confectionary business in Covington, Ga.

52. Russell Duncan, *Entrepreneur for Equality: Governor Rufus Bullock, Commerce, and Race in Post-War Georgia* (Athens: University of Georgia Press, 1994), 8–11.

53. Ibid., 29; *Journal of the Proceedings of the Constitutional Convention of the People of Georgia, Held in the City of Atlanta in the Month of December, 1867, and January, February and March, 1868* (Augusta: E. H. Pughe, 1868), 8; Cimbala, *Under the Guardianship of the Nation*, 281 n. 119; Matthews, "Negro Republicans," 148–49.

54. Matthews, "Negro Republicans," 149–50; Duncan, *Entrepreneur for Equality*, 34.

55. Atlanta City Council minutes, December 13, 1867, AHC; Sam Richards diary, February 29, 1868, AHC; Garrett, *Atlanta and Environs*, 1: 775; Crimmins and Farrisee, *Democracy Restored*, 33.

56. Nathans, *Losing the Peace*, 44–45; Matthews, "Negro Republicans," 151–52; Duncan, *Entrepreneur for Equality*, 40–49; Garrett, *Atlanta and Environs*, 1: 776–77.

57. James M. Russell and Jerry Thornbery, "William Finch of Atlanta: The Black Politician as Civic Leader," in *Southern Black Leaders of the Reconstruction Era*, ed. Howard N. Rabinowitz (Urbana: University of Illinois Press, 1982), 313–14; Matthews, "Negro Republicans," 151–52; Nathans, *Losing the Peace*, 120–24.

58. Russell and Thornbery, "William Finch of Atlanta," 309–15.

59. Ibid., 314–16, 319; Edmund L. Drago, *Black Politicians and Reconstruction in Georgia: A Splendid Failure* (Baton Rouge: Louisiana State University Press, 1982), 81.

60. Wooten, "New City of the South," 221, 321, and 326, citing 1870 Federal Census and 1874 Fulton County Tax Digest; Taylor, "From the Ashes," 86; *Proceedings of the National Union Republican Convention held at Philadelphia June 5–6, 1872* (Washington, D.C.: Gibson Brothers, 1872). Badger advertised his dental practice in *AC*, January 13, 1871.

61. Taylor, "From the Ashes," 222, 256, citing *ADNE*, May 19, 1867; *Atlanta Daily News*, March 7, 1875; Wooten, "New City of the South," 326, 337–38.

62. Alice E. Reagan, *H. I. Kimball: Entrepreneur* (Atlanta: Cherokee, 1983), 5–6, 9–10, 19–24; *AC*, January 13, 1869.

63. Reagan, *H. I. Kimball*, 38–39; Duncan, *Entrepreneur for Equality*, 149, 162.

64. Reagan, *H. I. Kimball*, 39–43; Robert Somers, *The Southern States since the War, 1870–71* (1871; rpt. Tuscaloosa: University of Alabama Press, 1965), 94–96.

65. *New York Times*, April 17, 1871, rpt. in *ADNE*, April 21, 1871; Taylor, "From the Ashes," 260–61; Garrett, *Atlanta and Environs*, 1: 894. The Kimball House burned in 1883, and H. I. Kimball returned to the state to rebuild it. The second Kimball House opened in 1885; Reagan, *H. I. Kimball*, 40–42, 112–18.

66. Agnes Salm-Salm, *Ten Years of My Life* (New York: R. Worthington, 1977), 113. Salm-Salm's husband Felix served as army commander in Atlanta from July to October 1865. The clothing was donated by "Judge Root," possibly Sidney Root. *New York Times*, April 17, 1871; Adelaide L. Fries, ed., "The Elizabeth Sterchi Letters," *Atlanta Historical Bulletin* 5 (April 1940): 123; Kate Massey, "A Picture of Atlanta in the Late Sixties," *Atlanta Historical Bulletin* 5 (April 1940): 34.

67. *ADNE,* February 20, 1868; *ADI,* March 28, 1867; *Atlanta Journal Magazine,* July 21, 1935; Cimbala, *Under the Guardianship of the Nation,* 90, 100.

68. *ADNE,* February 14, 16, 17, 19, 1871; *AC,* January 2, 1869; Eula Turner Kuchler, "Charitable and Philanthropic Activities in Atlanta during Reconstruction," M.A. thesis, Emory University, 1937, 72–77.

69. *ADNE,* February 26, 1871. Atlanta finally opened a municipal hospital in 1892; Garrett, *Atlanta and Environs,* 2: 257–60.

70. Adelaide L. Fries, ed., "The Elizabeth Sterchi Letters," *Atlanta Historical Bulletin* 5 (July 1940): 107–11, 199, 202, 208.

71. *ADI,* October 1, 1867; Henry Ossian Flipper, *The Colored Cadet at West Point: An Autobiography* (New York: H. Lee 1878), 12–13; Taylor, "From the Ashes," 211–17, 225–28; Wooten, "New City of the South," 284–93. Ronald E. Butchart discusses the American Missionary Association's educational mission in the South in *Schooling the Freed People: Teaching, Learning, and the Struggle for Black Freedom, 1861–1876* (Chapel Hill: University of North Carolina Press, 2010), 97–113.

72. *ANDE,* March 25, 1871; Dorothy Orr, *A History of Education in Georgia* (Chapel Hill: University of North Carolina Press, 1950), 213–14; Hunter, *To 'Joy My Freedom,* 42; Taylor, "From the Ashes," 242–43, 248; Garrett, *Atlanta and Environs,* 1: 877–79.

73. Wooten, "New City of the South," 238–43. Atlanta got a waterworks in 1875 and a sewer system in 1890; Garrett, *Atlanta and Environs,* 1: 914–18, 2: 209–10.

74. Abbie M. Brooks diary, March 8, May 24, 1870, AHC.

75. Ibid., March 29, April 1 and 15, June 11, July 13, September 27, 1870.

76. *AC,* January 17, 1878; Duncan, *Entrepreneur for Equality,* 135–36, 143–44; Reagan, *H. I. Kimball,* 113. Lucius Gartrell attempted to revive his political career when he ran for governor in 1882 but lost to Alexander Stephens. Gartrell died in 1891; Martin, *Atlanta and Its Builders,* 2: 651.

77. *AC,* January 12, 1872; Atlanta City Council minutes, September 5 and 13, 1867, AHC; *Atlanta Journal Magazine,* June 22, 1930; Wooten, "New City of the South," 316–17.

78. *AC,* January 3 and 25, 1873; Caroline Lewis Gordon, "De Gin'ral an' Miss Fanny," typescript reminiscence, Gordon Family Papers, UGA; Ralph Lowell Eckert, *John Brown Gordon: Soldier, Southerner, American* (Baton Rouge: Louisiana State University Press, 1989), 10, 16–17, 36, 154; Nathans, *Losing the Peace,* 135.

79. *AC,* January 21, 1873; *Atlanta Daily Herald,* January 21, 1873; David W. Blight, *Race and Reunion: The Civil War in American Memory* (Cambridge: Harvard University Press, 2001), 258–62.

80. *AC,* January 25, 1876; *Atlanta Daily Herald,* January 25, 1873.

81. *AC,* January 16 and January 25, 1873; Melanie Susan Gustafson, *Women and the Republican Party, 1854–1924* (Urbana: University of Illinois Press, 2001), 47–51, 58–59.

82. *AC,* January 16 and 28, 1873; Heather Cox Richardson, *West from Appomattox: The Reconstruction of America after the Civil War* (New Haven: Yale University Press, 2007), 225.

10. REMEMBERING AND FORGETTING

1. *ADI,* May 11, July 6, 1867; William A. Link, *Atlanta, Cradle of the New South: Race and Remembering in the Civil War's Aftermath* (Chapel Hill: University of North Carolina Press, 2013), 59–62. David W. Blight, *Race and Reunion: The Civil War in American Memory* (Cambridge: Harvard University Press, 2001), 2, wrote of three competing narratives of Civil War memory that "collided and combined over time": reconciliationist, white supremacist, and emancipationist.

2. *ADI,* July 6, 1867; Sam Richards diary, July 4, 1867, AHC; Cecilia Elizabeth O'Leary, *To Die For: The Paradox of American Patriotism* (Princeton: Princeton University Press, 1999), 113; Russell Duncan, *Freedom's Shore: Tunis Campbell and the Georgia Freedmen* (Athens: University of Georgia Press, 1986), 47–50. The Saxon Club was undoubtedly named for General Rufus Saxon, the Freedmen's Bureau administrator in charge of Georgia and South Carolina; Edmund L. Drago, *Black Politicians and Reconstruction in Georgia: A Splendid Failure* (Baton Rouge: Louisiana State University Press, 1982), 113.

3. See, for example, *AC,* July 6, 1871, July 5, 1889, July 5, 1894, July 5, 1897.

4. *AC,* January 2, 1889, January 2, 1890; O'Leary, *To Die For,* 114; Blight, *Race and Reunion,* 305, 368–70; W. Fitzhugh Brundage, *The Southern Past: A Clash of Race and Memory* (Cambridge: Harvard University Press, 2005), 59; Kathleen Ann Clark, *Defining Moments: African American Commemoration and Political Culture in the South, 1863–1913* (Chapel Hill: University of North Carolina Press, 2005), 51, 218.

5. *AC,* January 2, 1897, January 2, 1903; William A. Blair, *Cities of the Dead: Contesting the Memory of the Civil War in the South, 1865–1914* (Chapel Hill: University of North Carolina Press, 2004), 145. In 1876, Wright was

valedictorian of Atlanta University's first graduating class; Link, *Atlanta, Cradle of the New South*, 112.

6. *ADI*, February 18, 1861; *SC*, February 16, 1861; Blight, *Race and Reunion*, 391.

7. *AC*, July 5, 1898, July 5, 1900; Brundage, *The Southern Past*, 61. President William McKinley spoke in Atlanta during December 1898, celebrating the war's successful conclusion; Franklin M. Garrett, *Atlanta and Environs: A Chronicle of Its People and Events*, 2 vols. (Athens: University of Georgia Press, 1954), 2: 357–58.

8. Typescript of Mary Williams's letter to *Columbus Times*, March 12, 1866, Atlanta Ladies Memorial Association Papers, AHC; Caroline E. Janney, *Burying the Dead but Not the Past: Ladies' Memorial Associations and the Lost Cause* (Chapel Hill: University of North Carolina Press, 2008), 39.

9. *ADI*, June 14, 1866; Janney, *Burying the Dead but Not the Past*, 39–40.

10. Maria Jourdan Westmoreland, *Heart-Hungry* (New York: G. W. Carlton, 1872) and *Clifford Troupe: A Georgia Story* (New York: G. W. Carlton, 1873); *AC*, October 8, 1871, April 13 (free love, suffrage), 20 (wages), and 25, May 31, 1873 (education); Drew Gilpin Faust, *Mothers of Invention: Women of the Slaveholding South in the American Civil War* (Chapel Hill: University of North Carolina Press, 1996), 256–57.

11. *AC*, May 18, 1873 (criticism of her novels); September 21, 1873 (moves to New York); December 14, 1873, January 6 and 20, 1874 (special correspondent); November 30, 1873, February 15, 18, 26, March 25, April 24, June 23, 1874 (lectures); December 6, 1882 (wedding); June 28, 1890 (Willis obituary); November 1, 1896 (Maria obituary); Jane Turner Censer, *The Reconstruction of White Southern Womanhood 1865–1895* (Baton Rouge: Louisiana State University Press, 2003), 235–37.

12. "History of the Atlanta Ladies Memorial Association," 22–23, AHC.

13. Ibid., 24, 27; *ADI*, June 15, 1866; Gaines M. Foster, *Ghosts of the Confederacy: Defeat, the Lost Cause, and the Emergence of the New South 1865–1913* (New York: Oxford University Press, 1987), 22–23; Blair, *Cities of the Dead*, 65.

14. "History of the Atlanta Ladies Memorial Association," 26–28, 387, AHC; Ralph Lowell Eckert, *John Brown Gordon* (Baton Rouge: Louisiana State University Press, 1989), 10, 12, 37, 115, 263.

15. Undated newspaper obituary [1931]; "The Bride of the Gray Chevalier," *Holland's Magazine of the South*, February 1938; "Mrs. John Gordon," United Daughters of the Confederacy printed material, 1955; Caroline

Lewis Gordon, "De Gin'ral an' Miss Fanny," Gordon Family Papers, UGA; *ADNE*, May 8, 1868. Winship continued to be celebrated in Macon, Georgia.

16. "History of the Atlanta Ladies Memorial Association," 24–27, AHC; Drew Gilpin Faust, *This Republic of Suffering: Death and the American Civil War* (New York: Vintage, 2008), 236.

17. "History of the Ladies Memorial Association," 27–28, AHC.

18. Ibid., 27–30; *AC*, June 30, 1870, April 26, 1890. On Fanny Gordon's view of women's role, see "Ladies and Politics," ibid., February 28, 1879.

19. *AC*, October 18, 1870.

20. Ibid.

21. Ibid., April 28, 1874; "History of the Atlanta Ladies Memorial Association," 33–34, AHC; Ren Davis and Helen Davis, *Atlanta's Oakland Cemetery: An Illustrated History and Guide* (Athens: University of Georgia Press, 2012), xx.

22. *AC*, April 27, 1892; "History of the Atlanta Ladies Memorial Association," 57–59, AHC.

23. *AC*, April 27, 1894; Henry Clay Fairman, *Chronicles of the Old Guard of the Gate City Guard, Atlanta, Georgia, 1858–1915* (1915; rpt. Easley, S.C.: Southern Historical Press, 1986), 36.

24. *AC*, April 27, 1894; "History of the Ladies Memorial Association," 56–59, AHC; Foster, *Ghosts of the Confederacy*, 96.

25. Faust, *This Republic of Suffering*, 249.

26. Mrs. Neal, a devout Methodist, honored A.J.'s memory by donating his letters to the local Methodist school, Emory College.

27. Davis and Davis, *Atlanta's Oakland Cemetery*, 87.

28. Ibid., 161.

29. Ibid., 120; Janice O. Rothschild, *As But a Day: The First Hundred Years, 1867–1967* (Atlanta: Hebrew Benevolent Congregation, 1967), 2, 25–27. David Mayer died in 1890 and is buried at Westview Cemetery; see undated obituary, Clementine Mayer Pinkussohn Family Papers, Breman.

30. Robert Webster died August 22, 1880. He wrote to the editor of the *AC*, July 18, 1879, to correct a report that identified him as "Bob Yancey." The article announced his decision to "enter the lecture field"; Subject File, Oakland Cemetery, AHC.

31. Carrie and William died within a few weeks of one another. See their respective obituaries in *AC* on May 24, 1921 (Carrie, age sixty-six), and June 5 and 6, 1921 (William, age seventy-four). On Dr. Crumley, see ibid., December 7, 1915, March 2, 1919, August 10, 1924.

Index

Adair, George W., 58, 187–88, 194, 202

African Americans: buried at City Cemetery, 2, 222–23; commemorations organized by, 211–13; education and, 204–6; as exodusters, 210; as free people before and during the war, 9–10, 169; in Georgia cities, 7, 200; as percentage of Atlanta population, 7–8, 185–86; Reconstruction and, 184–87, 194, 197, 199–201, 208, 211; Republican Party and, 197–200, 212; as soldiers, 129, 136, 149, 186; as victims of crime, 142, 146; as wartime tradesmen and professionals, 146. *See also* slave auctions; slaves

African Methodist Episcopal Church, 205

AHA. *See* Atlanta Hospital Association (AHA)

Alexander, John F., 29, 32

Alston, Robert A., 133, 193, 216

American Colonization Society, 16–17

American Missionary Association, 204–5

Andrews raid, 70

Angier, Nedom: grave of, 222; prewar Unionism of, 25, 34; Reconstruction and, 194, 197, 201

Antietam, battle of, 80–81

Athenaeum: closed by smallpox contagion, 97; closed for economic reasons, 144; construction of, 12–13; destroyed, 179; performances at, 41, 73–75, 97, 132, 174; rowdiness at, 117

Athens, Ga., 12, 13, 75

Atlanta: becomes state capital, 198; bombardment of, 166–71; charitable efforts in, 203–4; citizens meetings in, 30, 57–58, 70; crowding in, 108, 125, 152, 160; destruction of, 179; expulsion of civilians from, 174–77; looting in, 102–4, 172–73; population of, 6, 15, 56, 67, 185–86; port of entry for Confederacy, 42; poverty in, 34, 120–22, 130–32, 140–43, 202–4, 206–7; prewar growth of, 5–13; rebuilding of, 180, 184, 187–91; refugees in, 67–68, 117–18, 125, 131, 152, 160–61; sanitary conditions in, 160; surrender of, 172, 183; vigilance committees in, 70, 115–16; weather in, 131–32, 160. *See also* African Americans; churches; commerce; Confederate nationalism; crime; education; family; food; railroads; secessionism; slaves; Unionism

Atlanta, battle of, 164–65, 195–96

Atlanta Amateurs: benefit for Morgan, 132; performances in Atlanta, 39–41, 73

Atlanta and West Point Railroad, 5, 163

Atlanta Arsenal: creation of, 64–65; employees of, 65, 87–90; evacuation of, 161–62; slave labor at, 98

Atlanta campaign: Atlantans' perceptions of, 148, 150–54, 158, 164, 171–72; battles and skirmishes in, 149–50, 158, 163–65;